D1610919

A WILD

ABOUT THE AUTHOR

Darrell Lewis is an historian and archaeologist who, for the past 40 years, has lived among and worked with Aboriginal and white Australians in the Northern Territory. Travelling by four wheel drive, helicopter, boat and on foot, his work has taken him to many remote regions to record historic sites and Aboriginal rock paintings. He has written books on rock art, settler history, cattle station technology and environmental history. Among his publications are *The Rock Paintings of Arnhem Land, Australia* (1988), *Beyond the Big Run* (1995), *Slower than the Eye Can See* (2002) and *The Murranji Track* (2007). He is currently employed at the National Museum of Australia where he is writing a history of the search for the lost explorer, Ludwig Leichhardt.

A WILD HISTORY

LIFE AND DEATH ON THE VICTORIA RIVER FRONTIER

DARRELL LEWIS

MONASH University
Publishing

Monash University Publishing
Building 4, Monash University
Clayton, Victoria 3800, Australia
www.publishing.monash.edu

Monash University Publishing brings to the world publications which advance the best traditions of humane and enlightened thought.

Monash University Publishing titles pass through a rigorous process of independent peer review.

National Library of Australia Cataloguing-in-Publication entry:

Author: Lewis, Darrell

Title: A wild history: life and death on the Victoria River frontier / Darrell Lewis.

Edition: 1st ed.

ISBN: 9781921867262 (pb)
ISBN: 9781921867279 (web)

Notes: Includes index.

Subjects: Frontier and pioneer life--Northern Territory--Victoria River Region; Aboriginal Australians--Northern Territory--Victoria River Region; Cattle industry--Northern Territory--Victoria River Region--History; Ranches--Northern Territory--Victoria River Region--History; Victoria River Region (N.T.)--History.

Dewey Number: 994.295

www.publishing.monash.edu/books/awh.html

Design: Les Thomas
Front cover: photo by Francis Birtles, 1910.

Printed in Australia by Griffin Press an Accredited ISO AS/NZS 14001:2004 Environmental Management System printer.

FSC
www.fsc.org
MIX
Paper from
responsible sources
FSC® C009448

The paper this book is printed on is certified against the Forest Stewardship Council® Standards. Griffin Press holds FSC chain of custody certification SGS-COC-005088. FSC promotes environmentally responsible, socially beneficial and economically viable management of the world's forests

FOREWORD

Many years ago I had an appointment with an eye specialist in Wimpole St in London. As we talked the doctor said that he thought the main problem with Australia was that it had too much geography and not enough history. I was a bit defensive, being very sensitive to the patronising attitudes of the English in those days to Australia and Australians.

But a year later I was reminded of his comments as I travelled into north Australia for the first time. I was flying from Brisbane to Townsville to take up a job at the new University College and in those days it took two and a half hours. I was aghast at the vastness of the landscape and the sparseness of human settlement. The scale of the country was so different from my home state of Tasmania and although I was to remain in the north for thirty years I never really came to terms with the country and with so much geography.

As I was teaching Australian history I had to give some thought to what had happened in the whole of tropical Australia. I quickly realised what little good history had been written about the north. It was the happy hunting ground for exotic adventure and tall stories written to entertain urban readers in both Australia and Britain. There clearly was not enough history in that part of Australia. The problem with mainstream scholarship was that my students could read all the general studies of Australia and yet learn almost nothing about their own part of the country. It was as if nothing of importance had happened north of the Brisbane line and few Australians had actually lived outside the major capitals. Until the 1960s there were no universities north of Brisbane.

Much has changed since then. The new universities in Townsville, Cairns, Rockhampton and Darwin have all encouraged their academics and students to research local history and much good work has been written and published.

A Wild History is a particularly valuable addition to the history of the north. It was originally written as a PhD thesis at the Australian National University so it embodies all the virtues of that genre. It has been deeply researched, it is rigorous in argument and carefully constructed. And it passed through the hands of expert supervisors and experienced examiners. It has the highest academic certification.

But it is more than that because Darrell Lewis is not the typical higher degree student who is normally young, relatively inexperienced and who finds a topic, researches it and writes it up in three years. Darrell depicts a region that he has known, worked in and travelled through for many years, absorbing a multitude of experiences long before he imagined that he would write a thesis on the subject. He came to the historical records with a rich treasury of life experience – and it shows – he really does know what he is talking about. And he has another inestimable advantage. He knows the families of the district, both Aboriginal and European, and they know and trust him. He is one of them and not a blow-in busy-body from down south. So people trusted him with their photos and above all with their memories and reflections on life. Few other people could have gained this access and won this degree of confidence.

As a result what we have here is a valuable history of an important part of the north. It is a story with which every Australian should become familiar. There may still be too much geography in the tropics for some tastes but historians like Darrell Lewis are at last giving us the history of the peoples of the north which the whole of Australia deserves.

— *Professor Henry Reynolds*

CONTENTS

ACKNOWLEDGEMENTS

This book is the end result of a lifetime interest in Australian history and 40 years travelling around the Victoria River District 'learning the country' and researching its history. A great many people have contributed in some way, directly or indirectly, and over such a long time that it's difficult to remember them all. The listings provided here must be considered a minimum, and my thanks go to a great many others who have contributed in some way.

Foremost among them must be Professor Deborah Rose, Professor Tom Griffiths and Professor Peter Read. Deborah assisted, advised and/or shared fieldwork in the Victoria River District for 26 of those years. During the writing of my PhD thesis, upon which this book is based, Tom and Peter in turn argued and cajoled, supported, criticised and sometimes praised my work. My special thanks go to them all.

Among the many white cattlemen and cattlewomen who told me of historic sites, shared their stories or allowed me to copy their collections of photographs and documents are: Charlie Schultz, former owner of Humbert River Station (deceased); Buck Buchester, former drover, stockman and resident of the Victoria River District for over 50 years (deceased); Lloyd Fogarty, former manager of Auvergne Station; Darryl Hill, former stockman, station manager, Conservation Commission Ranger, Victoria River Conservation Association Officer and 'Territorian of the Year'; Doug Struber, manager of Rosewood Station; Ian McBean, former stockman, drover and owner of Bradshaw, Innesvale and Coolibah stations; Cec Watts, former stockman, station manager and general manager for Vesteys; Mick Bower, former drover and ringer on Birrindudu, Leopold, Limbunya, Manbuloo and Nutwood stations; Stan Jones, former manager of Gordon Downs Station (deceased); Tex Moar, former drover, stockman and owner of Dorisvale Station; Alan Andrews, former manager of Auvergne Station; John Graham (deceased), son of Tom Graham, who was manager of Victoria River Downs from 1919 to 1926; Lochie McKinnon, former stockman and self-styled 'last of the bagmen' (deceased); Lexie Simmons (formerly Bates), the 'missus' at Mount Sanford Outstation (VRD) in the 1950s (deceased); Pauline Rayner, daughter of Peter Murray who owned Coolibah Station in the 1950s–60s; Lester Caine, former ringer, station owner and now hotel proprietor in western Queensland; Dick Scobie, former drover and owner of Hidden Valley Station (deceased); Joyce Galvin, daughter of Dick Scobie;

Stan May, former station hand on VRD; Reg Durack, former ringer on Auvergne and Argyle and owner-manager of Bullita, Kildurk and Spirit Hill stations (deceased); Gerry Ash, former ringer on VRD and Wave Hill (deceased); and Marie Mahood, who worked on VRD in the early 1950s (deceased).

Many Aboriginal people shared their stories with me, or guided me to historic sites which would have been difficult or impossible to locate without their assistance. Some who were especially helpful were: Malngin-Bilinara elder Old Jimmy Manngayarri (deceased); Bilinara elders Anzac Munnganyi (deceased) and Old Tim Yilngayarri (deceased); Ngaliwurru elders Big Mick Kangkinang (deceased) and Little Mick Yinyuwinma (deceased); Ngarinman elders Daly Pulkara (deceased), Snowy Kurmilya (deceased), Riley Young Winpilin, Bobby Witipuru (deceased), and Doug Campbell (deceased); Wardaman elder Billy Harney; Gurindji elder Long Johnny Kitinngari (deceased); Karangpurru-Ngarinman elder Alan Young Najukpayi; and finally, Mudbura elders Albert Lalaga Crowson, Nugget Kiriyalangungu and Long Captain Marajala (all deceased).

Other people who assisted in various ways include Vern O'Brien, former director of the Northern Territory Lands Department, who now spends much of his time answering questions and researching history topics for people around Australia; Stuart Duncan, former secretary of the Place Names Committee for the Northern Territory, Department of Infrastructure, Planning and Environment, Land Information, Darwin; Jan Cruickshank, whose grandfather Bob Watson and grand-uncle Jack Watson were managers of VRD in the 1890s; Bob and Sandy Woods, who researched the history of the Canning Stock Route for many years; Kieran Kelly, who in 1999 led a packhorse team along part of the route of Augustus Gregory's expedition; Keith Sarfield, invasive species management officer, Northern Territory Parks and Wildlife Commission; Tony Roberts, historian of the Gulf country and northern Barkly area; Andrew McWilliam, an anthropologist who has worked with Jaminjung people on Bradshaw Station; John Gordon (deceased), former Northern Territory policeman based at times at Timber Creek, and the man who led the last packhorse patrol in the Territory; Patsy Garling (deceased), daughter of cattle duffer Jimmy Wickham; Reg Wilson who shared his family tradition concerning cattle duffer Jim Campbell; and Andrew Barker, President of the Kununurra Historical Society, who generously shared his knowledge of East Kimberley history.

The staff of libraries and archives around the country have been most helpful, either in person or via email. In particular I thank staff at the

ACKNOWLEDGEMENTS

National Library of Australia (Canberra), Mitchell Library (Sydney), Battye Library (Perth), Northern Territory Library (Darwin), James Cook University Library (Townsville), Northern Territory Archives (Darwin), the Australian National Trust (NT), Charles Darwin University Library, Noel Butlin Archives (Canberra), National Archives of Australia (Darwin and Canberra), State Records Office of South Australia (Adelaide); State Records Office of Western Australia (Perth), the Royal Geographical Society of South Australia library (Adelaide), the South Australian Police Historical Society, the Stockman's Hall of Fame (Longreach), the National Museum of Australia (Canberra) and the Edinburgh City Archive (Scotland).

For the use of photographs from personal collections my thanks go to John Bradshaw, Jan Cruickshank, Reg Durack (deceased), Patsy Garling (deceased), Bob Johns (deceased), Gwen Knox, Marie Mahood (deceased), Lesley Millner, Lorna Moffatt (deceased) and Veronica Schwarz. As well as providing photographs the National Museum of Australia paid for production of the maps, and for initial editing of the manuscript.

Finally, for initiating and supporting my interest in Australian history, my thanks go to my parents, Nola and Laurie Lewis, particularly my father (deceased), whose stories of earlier times fascinated me as a small boy and sparked an interest in early Australian and outback history.

INTRODUCTION

> The population of the district consists of station managers, cattle
> duffers, horse thieves, wild and woolly stockmen, and outlaws. A man
> is almost out of the pale of the law when he reaches the Victoria, and
> it may well be called 'No Man's Land'. Unless offence be murder the
> authorities will not trouble to look for him; and he may remain for years
> wandering about the country.

This is how WM Burton, a so-called 'gum tree journalist', described Victoria
River society after he passed through the region in 1909, 26 years after the
first settlers arrived there,[1] and it's a perfectly accurate description – as far
as it goes. The denizens of the district were indeed a wild lot, but Burton
could also have mentioned the 'wild blacks',[2] capitalists, dreamers, battlers,
drunks, fools, madmen and others.

A Wild History looks at them all. It explores the origins of early Victoria
River society, from the explorers in the 1830s and 1850s to the land-seekers
and prospectors in the 1870s and early 1880s, the founders of the big stations
in the 1880s and 1890s, and finally the 'battlers'-cum-cattle duffers of the
early 1900s. It looks at the complex interaction between the environment,
the powerful and warlike Aboriginal tribes and the settlers and their cattle.
Each one impacted on the other, quite often in mutually detrimental ways,
but eventually a society and a way of life evolved which was to persist little
changed for generations.

The Victoria River country is located in the north-west Northern Territory
– east of the Kimberley, south-west of Arnhem Land and north of the Tanami
Desert (Map 1) – and has been occupied by Europeans for over 125 years. In
recent times these surrounding regions have achieved iconic status, visited by
an ever increasing number of 'grey nomads', backpackers and others, but the
Victoria River District has not been so well promoted. While many white

---

1   'An Irresponsible Journalist', *Northern Territory Times*, 30th April 1909, p. 2.
2   'Wild blacks' in historical records and in common usage in the outback today refers to
     Aborigines still living in the bush and potentially hostile to Europeans. By contrast,
     the term 'civilised' or 'part-civilised blacks' refer to Aborigines who had left the bush
     to work for the Europeans and gained a degree of knowledge of European ways
     (*Australian National Dictionary*, Oxford University Press, Melbourne, 1988, pp. 147,
     736; J. Arthur, *Aboriginal English: A cultural study*. Oxford University Press, Melbourne,
     1996, pp. 143–44, 190–91).

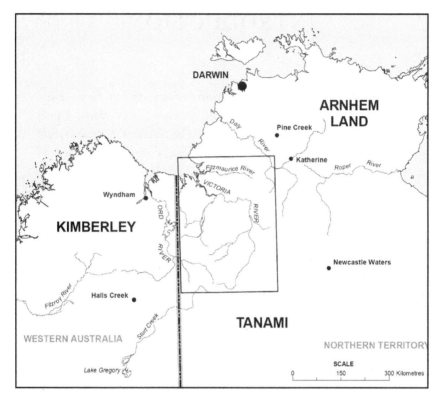

Map 1. The Victoria River District of northern Australia

Australians might have a vague knowledge of the region as the home of great horsemen and famous cattle stations, for most, the land and its history remains a vast and largely silent 'blank'. Most of the stories of the early settlers and events have either been lost, poorly recorded, or remain only vaguely known to outsiders. Few people have done more than travel along the public roads through the area. Partly this is because until recently almost the entire district was effectively 'closed' to outsiders, locked up as big cattle stations. Since the early 1980s several large areas have become national parks which are open to tourists and others, but most of the region still remains inaccessible to the public. Those lucky enough to have lived in the district for extended periods and travelled beyond the public roads know it as an immense and complex tract of country, at times sweeping and majestic, at other times rugged and mysterious. Many of these longer term residents will tell you that eventually the country begins to take hold, to 'get into your blood'.

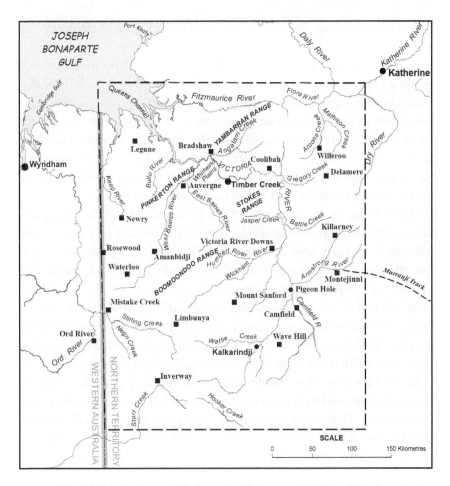

Map 2. Homesteads and outstations in the Victoria River District, c1990

I am one of the fortunate and privileged few who can claim to know the Victoria River country well. My knowledge of the region began in 1971 when I worked there as a field assistant with the Bureau of Mineral Resources (BMR). This job involved driving along the back tracks of stations throughout the district and beyond, and it was during this work that the romantic stories of the pioneering days I'd heard as a child – stories of drovers, stockmen, Aborigines and cattle duffers – gained a degree of substance. I saw Aboriginal and European stockmen still living and working in rough conditions, mustering on horseback, eating beef and damper and using equipment made from greenhide.

As I travelled along the roads and back tracks I saw ruins of old stockyards and an occasional grave, including one with a headstone which declared that the person buried there had been, 'Killed by Blacks'.[3] There were also rock paintings and numerous surface scatters of stone tools. I even found a few broken boomerangs which brought a sense of immediacy, a feeling that what was 100 years gone in the South was present only yesterday in the North. At the time I didn't realise that this was literally true, and applied not only to Aboriginal culture, but to the very frontier itself. There was an aura about the country which fired my imagination, and I was not alone – the 'magic' of the region affected other local whites in much the same way.[4]

While I was in the district in 1971 I perceived a feeling among many local whites that, historically speaking, the region would have been a very wild place. 40 years later this attitude still prevails. To some degree this perception was engendered by the landscape – perhaps due to the vastness of the stations, the rugged and inaccessible ranges, the gorges, the 'devil-devil country'[5], and so on. In some instances their attitude was, and is, derived from stories accessible in print, but in the early 1970s comparatively little of the history of the region had been written, and much of what had, and has since, been written was either inaccurate or generalised, or both.

In other instances the attitude held by local whites was almost certainly the result of limited local knowledge transmitted from person to person since the early days. To give just two examples of this oral history, Charlie Schultz ran Humbert River Station from 1928 to 1971. He told me that when he first arrived in the district he heard from old-timers that, after the spearing

---

3   This phrase is from the headstone for Tudor Shadforth at the old Ord River Station cemetery.
4   This 'aura' has also been noted by Lyn Riddett in her book, *Kin, Kine and Country: The Victoria River District of the Northern Territory 1911–1966* (Australian National University North Australia Research Unit Monograph, Darwin, 1990, pp. 1–7) and by Jock Makin in *The Big Run: The Story of Victoria River Downs Station* (Weldon Publishing, 1992 (1970), p. 9).
5   In the Victoria River District and elsewhere in Australia, 'devil-devil' or 'debil-debil' country is a term used to refer to areas covered with large tussocks 30 centimetres or more in height and much the same in width, separated from each other by gaps of 15 to 30 centimetres. Often there are also holes between the tussocks. Such country is extremely dangerous for horsemen, and terribly difficult and slow to drive over in a motor vehicle. From personal experience I know that in extreme cases it's all but impossible to drive over, even in low gear in four-wheel drive (see the *Australian National Dictionary*, Oxford University Press, Melbourne, 1988, pp. 193–94, 198). For a detailed description of their formation see H Basedow, 'Physical geography and geology of the Victoria River district, Northern Territory of Australia', *Proceedings of the Royal Geographical Society of Australasia, South Australian Branch*, vol. 16, session 1914–15, pp. 147–217.

of a man named 'Brigalow Bill' Ward, the police shot many Aborigines in the Humbert River ranges.[6] Similarly, Lloyd Fogarty, a former manager of Auvergne Station, told me he'd heard that the bones of many Aborigines shot by police were scattered across the Razorback Mountain on Auvergne.[7]

My initial visit in 1971 left me with a lasting impression of the Victoria River District as an immense area of basalt plains and spectacular limestone and sandstone ranges, a region rich in wildlife and Aboriginal cultural remains, but with a 'hidden history'. The lack of a written history intrigued and frustrated me. Surely the region had a rich European history, but what was it? Little did I then realise that one day I'd write the more detailed history of the region I was hungering for.

When the first settlers and cattle arrived in the Victoria River country they were unarguably in a frontier situation. For the next 20 years this frontier was characterised by violent conflict with the Aborigines, extreme isolation, desperately slow communication, and rough living and working conditions. If medical assistance was available at all it was primitive. Supplies often took months to arrive, brought to the stations from the Depot Landing on the lower Victoria River or direct from Wyndham or Katherine on horse and bullock wagons, or by packhorses or pack-camels.

In common with many frontier areas the region attracted its share of adventurers and fortune hunters, and became a last refuge for the brutal, the criminal, the half-mad, the alcoholics and other social misfits who were not tolerated 'inside'.[8] In 1905 a member of a droving team passing through the district declared that, 'This country is more or less full of lunatics; in fact all the loonies of the various states seem to gather in this part'.[9] Some might say little has changed.

---

6   Charlie Schultz, pers. comm.. This comment was originally included in the manuscript of Schultz's biography (C Shultz and D Lewis, *Beyond the Big Run: Station Life in Australia's Last Frontier*, University of Queensland Press, Brisbane, 1995), but at his insistence it was taken out because, as Schultz put it, 'the townies wouldn't understand that it was them or us in those days'.

7   While the historical basis of both stories, and of others, can be found in the documentary record, it's now highly unlikely that any Aboriginal bones from a police shooting are still to be found on Razorback Mountain (Auvergne Station).

8   'Inside' is the term outback bushmen use to describe the long-settled regions of Australia, usually near the coast. The corollary is, of course, 'outside', meaning outside the settled districts (*Australian National Dictionary*, Oxford University Press, Melbourne, pp. 326, 453).

9   H7H (Hely Hutchinson), *The North Queensland Herald*, 21st May 1906, p. 8; other references to misfits and criminals in the district can be found in 'Odd stock and other notes', *The Morning Bulletin*, Rockhampton, 20th January 1906, p. 8, and in 'An irresponsible journalist', *Northern Territory Times*, 30th April 1909, p. 2.

Tudor Shadforth's grave, old Ord River homestead
Lewis collection

Today, one of the interesting social features of the region is the near absence of 'family dynasties' among the white people. In New South Wales and Queensland villages and towns sprang up in the wake of the frontier. Valuable minerals were discovered and stores built, and closer settlement with relatively large and stable populations quickly followed. Third, fourth and fifth generation descendants can still be found in the areas where their pioneer ancestors settled. This never happened in the Victoria River country.

Throughout its history the European population of the Victoria River District has remained comparatively small. For almost 100 years there were no villages or towns in the district; Katherine, Wyndham and Halls Creek were the nearest settlements, all three located well outside the region. There have only ever been one or two mines in the district,[10] too small and too short-lived to attract a large population and lead to a town being established.

---

10   In the 1970s, baryte, a mineral used in heavy-weight parchments and in oil-drilling, was mined on Kirkimbie Station in the south-west of the district (I Sweet, et al, *The Geology of the Southern Victoria River Region, Northern Territory*, report no. 167, Department of Minerals and Energy, Bureau of Mineral Resources, Geology and Geophysics, Australian Government Publishing Service, Canberra, 1974, pp. 120–22).

INTRODUCTION

No descendants of the original pioneers live in the region today and only a few families have roots that extend as far back as the 1950s. Very few of the older locals were born or grew up in the district and there has always been a relatively high turnover of staff on the stations.

A number of factors have contributed to this situation. The climate is one of the harshest in Australia with excessively high temperature and humidity levels for about two thirds of the year.[11] The region is remote and until the 1960s land access was difficult. In some areas it remains so, particularly during the summer wet season. The lack of towns meant that health, educational and other services taken for granted elsewhere were not available.

Whatever their reasons may have been, most white people who came to live in the region eventually returned to places where the amenities of 'civilisation' were more readily available. The practical difficulties of living and working in this environment and the physical isolation of the area have caused the region to remain a backwater for most of its history, a backwater which continually collected rejects from more climatically congenial though less socially tolerant climes.

One result of the general absence of family dynasties and the high turnover of station staff has been a weak transmission of local knowledge from generation to generation among local whites. By contrast, Aborigines don't come from somewhere else, stay for a period and then leave. Instead, their family dynasties extend back to the Dreaming. Older Aborigines know their country intimately from years spent working on the stations and from going on extended wet season walkabouts. Their parents and grandparents told them stories of early contact and showed them the places where 'something happened' – old homestead sites, graves, massacre sites, and so on.

Generally speaking, Victoria River Aborigines know far more than local whites about the history of the stations on their traditional lands. They are in fact the 'keepers' of much 'European' history.[12] Nevertheless, a great deal has been forgotten by the Aborigines or was never known to them. Furthermore, as traditionally non-numerate people they had no interest in, or means of, remembering the year an event happened, so it's often difficult to place the stories and events they do remember into a time frame that makes sense to non-Aborigines.

---

11   DHK Lee, 'Variability in human response to arid environments', in WG McGinnies and BJ Goodman (eds), *Arid Lands in Perspective*, University of Arizona Press, Tuscon, 1969, p. 234.
12   See D Rose and D Lewis, 'A pinch and a bridge', in *Public History Review*, vol. 1, no. 1, 1994.

Since 1971 I've worked in the region for a variety of government and non-government organisations, beginning as a site recorder with the Northern Territory Museum and later on history projects with both regional and national organisations. Among these projects were four surveys of historic sites in the Victoria River country, carried out for the Northern Territory branch of the National Trust of Australia. From this work I produced four major reports – *The Ghost Road of the Drovers*, *In Western Wilds*, *The Boab Belt*, and *The Final Muster*. Local Aboriginal people guided me to many of the historic sites documented in these reports and they shared their knowledge of the sites with me. This work, combined with intensive archival research, significantly increased my understanding of Victoria River District terrain and history.

In 1990 I completed a Masters degree on the Aboriginal rock art of the region. The research for this study involved close liaison with local Aboriginal people, and many long-distance bushwalks into otherwise inaccessible country. More recently I helped elderly Victoria River district identities Charlie Schultz and Lexie Simmons to publish their memoirs of life in the region.[13]

In the course of these projects I was privileged to record the stories of many Aboriginal elders and to have them guide me to historic sites, including many that only they knew about. Some of my teacher-guides grew to adulthood in the bush, including Old Jimmy Manngayarri and Big Mick Kanginang, both of whom were born in about 1910. These men had lived through the greater part of the period of white settlement and had been told about earlier events by their parents and older relations – people who had seen the white settlers come and fought against them. In 1981 I began copying historic documents held in public archives and later discussing these records with my contacts in various Victoria River Aboriginal communities. Now almost all of my original Aboriginal teachers have died, taking their wealth of untapped knowledge with them and breaking the direct living link to the early days of the region.

Through my growing contacts within the 'cattle station network' I heard about former residents of the Victoria River District living in, literally, the four corners of Australia. From 1991 I began visiting these people, recording their stories and copying their photographs or documents, and asking them to comment on photos from other collections. From them and from other sources I've been able to amass and document a collection of over 6000 historical photographs that were taken in the Victoria River country.

---

13   Shultz and Lewis, 1995; D Lewis and L Simmons, *Kajirri, the Bush Missus*, Central Queensland University Press, Rockhampton, 2005.

A boab against a big Victoria River District sky
Lewis collection

While it's impossible to separate the history of black and white in this region,[14] it is possible to focus on one group or the other. Deborah Rose's *Hidden Histories*[15] presents a history of the region from an Aboriginal perspective and covers the period of European settlement up to 1990. I've chosen to tell a white man's history – literally a white *man's* history because, from the beginning of European contact and for much of the settler period, white men have outnumbered white women by as much as 50 or 100 to one. While there were one or two white women in the district as early as 1896 and their numbers increased slowly during the next two decades, there's very little documentation about them and, as far as is known, they were not major players in the stories dealt with here.

In *A Wild History* I have explored two major themes: the various moments and types of early contact between Aborigines and whites, and the formation of a local settler society. This local white society was widely dispersed and

---

14   See D Lewis, *A Shared History: Aborigines and White Australians in the Victoria River District, Northern Territory*. Cooperative Research Centre for Tropical Savannas, Darwin, 2002.

15   D Rose, *Hidden Histories: Black Stories from Victoria River Downs, Humbert River and Wave Hill Stations*, Aboriginal Studies Press, Canberra, 1991.

nomadic.[16] Most of the men who lived in the north were highly mobile, moving from job to job across a seemingly unlimited expanse of country. They often worked at diverse occupations – at one time perhaps a stockman, at another a prospector, and yet another maybe a drover. They knew, or knew of, each other. Their tracks crisscrossed over the years, and together they formed a network of individuals and stories. Their society was primarily oral, their social currency, stories.

They were a coherent group of people, not only because of a primary shared objective – settlement – but equally significantly because the men involved were participants in a relatively closed network of communication. Around many a campfire, in flood-bound homesteads and during the occasional drunken 'gumtree spree', they told their stories or retold those of others, and commented on events that typified the process of settling a frontier.[17] Some of the stories were not for public consumption – accounts of murders, massacres, cattle heists and so on – and so were not written down, or only mentioned in passing and often in euphemisms. Other stories were benign, but nevertheless many were lost. I have attempted to resurrect stories that 'disappeared', to flesh out some stories which are still known, and to correct them where errors have crept in. Within the matrix of these stories are characters whose lives give flesh and blood to many of the key icons of white Australian mythology – the brave explorers, the noble pioneers, the 'wild blacks', the wild bush and 'the battler'.

While the book tells stories of white men it doesn't concentrate on the usual 'big name' explorers, cattle barons and pastoral empires. Instead, it has more to say about the ordinary working men of this long-term frontier region – the stockmen, station managers, bagmen, teamsters, police and others. It tells of brutal frontiersmen like 'The Gulf Hero' Jack Watson who collected Aboriginal ears and skulls; big-time cattle thieves like 'Diamond' Jim Campbell who was caught with over 400 head of Victoria River Downs cattle and forced to flee into the wilds of Arnhem Land; and battlers like 'Brigalow Bill' Ward who, when his small block was taken from him by the government, defiantly remained there, only to be speared by the 'wild blacks'.

---

16 The term 'nomad tribe' was coined by Russel Ward to describe the highly mobile outback workers of the nineteenth and early twentieth centuries (R Ward, *The Australian Legend*, Oxford University Press, Melbourne, 1958).

17 P Woodley, "'Young Bill's happy days": reminiscences of rural Australia, 1910–1915', MA thesis, Australian National University, vol 2, 1986, pp. 230, 302). According to 'Young Bill' (William Lavender) who worked in the Victoria River country during 1914, a 'gumtree spree' was the name given to a drinking session held out in the bush away from any homestead or other European centres.

Unfortunately I haven't been able to cover all major aspects of this history. Among various omissions are sexual relations between blacks and whites, the role of alcohol, and the annual horse races. Sexual relations between white men and black women were common throughout the Australian frontier and, although there's little documentation about this from the first decade or two of Victoria River District history, there's no reason to believe that the region was exceptional. Certainly in the years beyond the period covered here (post-1912) sexual relations with Aboriginal women was a significant part of white male identity.[18] Alcohol appears to have been an important factor in many of the violent conflicts between Aborigines and settlers, and between the settlers themselves, and also in the high frequency of suicide among white men in the district. The local horse races, initially impromptu, though later organised into annual events in various places, were another important component in social cohesion.[19] It was at such gatherings that the oral culture was maintained, friendships and alliances cemented, alcohol was consumed and grudges 'worked out'.

While the stories in *A Wild History* have been rigorously researched, I've written them in a vernacular style, for the ordinary reader rather than for academics. As far as possible I've avoided academic jargon and I have not directly engaged with current (and usually ephemeral) historical controversies and debates. In addition, I've used words such as 'Aborigines', 'wild blacks' or 'myalls' that are still in common use in the Victorian River District among both Aboriginal and white people.

Historically speaking, for most white people the history of the region remains largely unknown and inaccessible, and instead 'wild imaginings' hold sway. For 40 years I've worked in and travelled through the Victoria River District, carried out archival research, and had innumerable conversations with people who have connections to the region. When woven together the field work, oral history and archival research provides a unique picture of the rich and fascinating history of the region. My aim in this book is to repopulate the land with some of the main characters and events of the past, and to replace current wild imaginings with a more soundly based 'wild history'.

---

18   This was made clear by 'Young Bill' (p. 336). For discussion of black/white sexual relations in the Victoria River District more generally see Rose, *Hidden Histories* (p. 179–88) and A McGrath, *'Born in the Cattle': Aborigines in Cattle Country* (Allen & Unwin, Sydney, 1987, pp. 68–94).

19   D Lewis, *A Brief History of Racing in the Victoria River District*, Timber Creek Race Club Incorporated, NT, 1995.

Chapter 1

THE VICTORIA RIVER COUNTRY

Land and People

The Victoria River country of north Australia is almost mythic in its wild beauty, the glamour of horsemen and cattle, the violence and danger of frontier times, and the sheer size and remoteness of stations such as Bluey Buchanan's Wave Hill, Captain Joe's Bradshaw, and Victoria River Downs – VRD or 'The Big Run'. The topography of the region is complex, distinctive and often dramatic, and has shaped much of Aboriginal and settler history. The Victoria River itself rises in the arid plains of the northern Tanami Desert, and winds northward through increasingly well-watered savannah grasslands and range country to the estuarine reaches, where the highest and most rugged mountains predominate (Map 2). Mesas and flat-topped ranges of broken sandstone and limestone border much of the Victoria catchment or cut haphazardly across the valley floor through a mosaic of basalt and limestone plains. In the northern high rainfall areas there are wetlands and pockets of 'jungle'. Further inland open savannah predominates, but there are patches and swathes of country known locally as 'desert' – waterless areas of spinifex, eucalypts and acacia scrub. Cliffs and gorges are common, and extensive Mitchell grass downs have provided the foundation for great cattle empires.

From a European scientific perspective, Victoria River District landforms have their origins in deep time. Over hundreds of millions of years seawater covered the region several times, laying down vast beds of sandstone and limestone. Each time these beds were exposed they were weathered into gorges and valleys, and in some areas folded and faulted, only to be overlain by new sediments when the sea encroached again. One of the great lava flows of geological history occurred here, too, creating the massive Antrim Plateau Volcanics, a basalt formation that covers much of the Victoria River and

East Kimberley districts.[1] For thousands of years this igneous rock provided Aborigines with the raw material for stone axes, and it also produced the wide black soil plains that were to be prized by cattlemen. The end result of these geological events is the complex of ranges, mesas, gorges and plains that give the region its distinctive topography today.

Although fundamentally different from the scientific explanation of how the Victoria River District achieved its present form, at a broad level the traditional belief of Victoria River Aborigines about the creation of the world has some interesting parallels. In the beginning the earth was covered with salt water which rolled back to reveal a land devoid of life, but with some geographical features already in existence. Right across the newly revealed land all the different forms of life, including some entities regarded by Europeans as inanimate (for example, the moon) or imaginary (for example, Rainbow Snakes), emerged from the moist ground. These supernatural beings, which Victoria River Aborigines generally refer to as 'Dreaming' or 'Dreamings', interacted with or avoided other Dreaming beings and performed actions which left indelible imprints on the landscape. Some of the Dreamings travelled great distances across the land while others were 'localised' – active within quite limited areas.

Aborigines today say that the Dreamings, whether animate or inanimate (in European terms), travelling or localised, were at one and the same time human beings. Walking, dancing, digging or fighting, lighting fires, discarding artefacts or foods, leaving on the ground their bodies, parts of their bodies, or bodily secretions, they created many of the natural features still to be seen in the landscape.[2] As well as shaping the land the Dreamings also laid down laws and patterns of behaviour that were followed by generations of Aborigines, and are still followed by many Aborigines today.[3]

Regardless of which explanation is accepted – Aboriginal or European – the fact is that the topography of the district determined the pattern of

1   The origin of Victoria River topography has been traced back to the Proterozoic period, 2.5 billion to 543 million years ago (I Sweet, et al, The Geology of the Southern Victoria River Region, Northern Territory, report no. 167, Department of Minerals and Energy, Bureau of Mineral Resources, Geology and Geophysics, Australian Government Publishing Service, Canberra, 1974; I Sweet, et al, The Geology of the Northern Victoria River Region, Northern Territory, report no. 166, Department of Minerals and Energy, Bureau of Mineral Resources, Geology and Geophysics, Australian Government Publishing Service, Canberra, 1974).

2   D Lewis, 'They Meet Up At Bilinara': Rock Art in the Victoria River Valley, vol. 1, MA thesis, Australian National University, 1990, p. 92; D Lewis and D Rose, The Shape Of The Dreaming: The Cultural Significance Of Victoria River Rock Art, Aboriginal Studies Press, Canberra, 1988, p. 46.

3   D Rose, Dingo Makes us Human, Cambridge University Press, Melbourne, 1992, pp. 54–55.

European land settlement and influenced other aspects of regional history. The Antrim Plateau basalt produced the rich black soil that supports the Mitchell grass plains, most of which were taken up early by wealthy pastoral companies, while areas of rough sandstone and limestone country or 'desert' areas became refuges for Aborigines driven out of the 'cattle country' by the cattlemen. Later 'small men' keen to raid cleanskin (unbranded) cattle on the big stations settled on the edges of, or within, these refuge areas and this brought them into conflict with the last Aboriginal 'holdouts'.

The history of Europeans on the Victoria River frontier is a history of conflict and accommodation with Aboriginal people. Aborigines have been involved with white people in one way or another since the first whites came, and they were key players in almost all significant events in the region. In early frontier times they were a largely unseen and threatening presence in the bush, a presence that sometimes became all too real when they clashed violently with the settlers. Later, when employed by the whites, they were 'boys' and 'lubras' (or 'gins') – stockmen, domestics, assistants, guides, lovers and trackers.[4]

It's beyond the scope of this book to comprehensively describe the various Aboriginal groups who lived in the district. However, there are a number of important aspects of the traditional way of life and social organisation of the tribes that came to be directly relevant to the way social relations developed between Aborigines and the European newcomers, and the way that history unfolded in the region. These were: multiple identities, fire use, information networks and long-distance travel for ceremonies.

In historical times the Victoria River District has been the home of at least 13 different language-groups or tribes. Those whose traditional lands are largely or wholly within the bounds of the Victoria River valley are the Gurindji, Bilinara, Karangpurru, Ngaliwurru, Nungali, the eastern, western and Wolayi or 'sandstone' Ngarinman, the Jaminjung and Kajerong. The Mudbura, divided into eastern, central and western groups, straddle the watershed that divides the south-eastern portion of the region from the Barkly Tableland.[5] Likewise, Wardaman country extends from the Victoria River catchment to the Katherine–Daly catchment,[6] while Malngin territory overlaps the western

---

4   See D Lewis, *A Shared History: Aborigines and White Australians in the Victoria River District, Northern Territory* (Create-A-Card, Darwin, on behalf of the Timber Creek Community Government Council, 1997).

5   P Sutton, L Coltheart and A McGrath, *The Murranji Land Claim*, Northern Land Council, Darwin, 1983, pp. 70–74.

6   F Merlan places the north-eastern boundary of the Wardaman in the vicinity of the Scott Creek – Katherine River junction, about 60 kilometres from Katherine (*A*

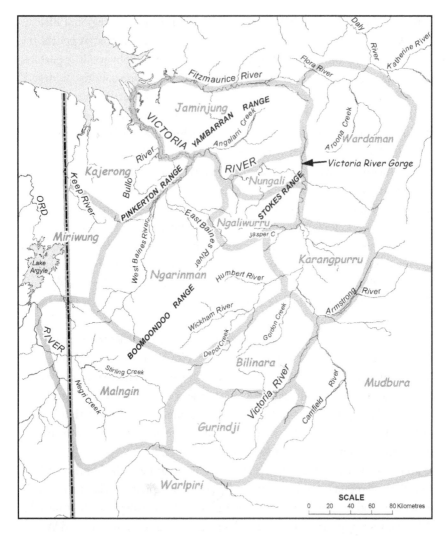

Map 3. Approximate boundaries of Victoria River District Aboriginal 'tribes'

headwaters of the Victoria River, but lies largely within the Ord River valley. Miriwung territory may lie partly within the Victoria River valley, but is primarily within the Ord River and Keep River catchments (Maps 3 and 4).

The members of these tribes were hunter-gatherers, and numerous studies in Australia and overseas suggest that the typical size of self-identifying

Grammar of Wardaman: A Language of the Northern Territory of Australia, Mouton de Gruyter, New York, 1994, p. 7).

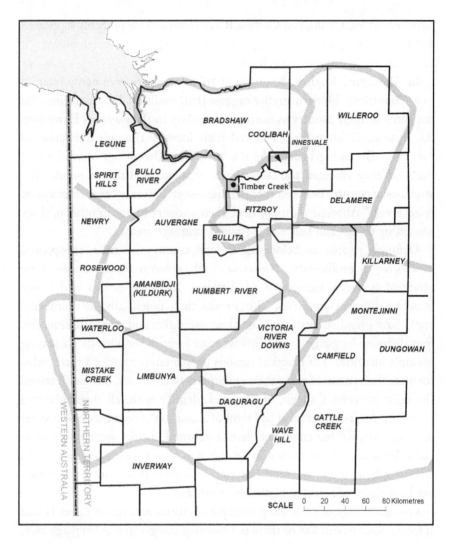

Map 4. Aboriginal boundaries in relation to European boundaries, c1990

hunter-gatherer groups was at least 500 and possibly as high as 1500.[7] At the most conservative estimate of 500 people in each tribe, when the cattlemen came the Aboriginal population of the entire Victoria River District would

---

7   J Birdsell, 'Some environmental and cultural factors influencing the structuring of Australian Aboriginal populations', *American Naturalist*, vol. 87, 1953, pp. 171–207; N Butlin, *Our Original Aggression: Aboriginal Populations of Southeastern Australia 1788– 1850*, George Allen & Unwin, Sydney, 1983, pp. 175; J Peter White and DJ Mulvaney, 'How many people?', in DJ Mulvaney and J Peter White (eds), *Australians to 1788*, Fairfax, Syme & Weldon Associates, Sydney, 1987, 115–17.

have been at least 5500, and Victoria River Downs alone probably supported 1400 people. Chances are the population of the region was much higher – it certainly was to become much lower.[8]

In Aboriginal English, language or tribal areas are commonly referred to as 'countries'.[9] Modern studies suggest that, traditionally, Aborigines did not think of their country as having a boundary in the way that Europeans do. Instead, different areas received their identity through the action of particular Dreaming beings. As the 'travelling Dreamings' moved across the land they changed the language they spoke at different points. The stretches of country between these 'change-over' points became language or tribal areas.[10] Aboriginal groups trace their ancestry to one or other of these Dreaming beings and hence to particular language areas.

Defining people as belonging to one country or tribe as opposed to another is problematic. It was (and is) common for marriages to be arranged between individuals of different language groups and hence between different countries. This means that, potentially, an individual could have grandparents from, and therefore rights and responsibilities for, four different language areas. This was the basis of individuals possessing multiple identities. For practical reasons people rarely exercised their rights for more than two or three of their grandparents' countries, but they retained the right to travel through, live in, and identify with, all their inherited countries. An individual also had right of access to the countries of his or her marriage partner, but could not claim a personal identity with any of these countries unless one or more also belonged to one of their grandparents. In other words, an individual might strongly identify with one or two countries, but have rights of access to a number of others.

One advantage of possessing multiple identities and access rights is that if food resources run low or there is a looming danger in one language area, individuals or groups with appropriate affiliations can move to another. There was, however, a dynamic tension between the various groups and limits beyond which individuals could move only in particular circumstances, or not at all. If people made unauthorised visits to country where they were considered strangers, they risked being killed by local people. Consequently, individuals could not evade punishment by going to a place where they were unknown if they broke the law in their own country.

---

8   Rose, *Dingo*, p. 7.
9   J Arthur, *Aboriginal English: A cultural study*, Oxford University Press, Melbourne, 1996, pp. 119–20.
10   Rose, *Dingo*, pp. 54–55.

Aboriginal Women on walkabout, Delamere region, 1922

Basedow collection, National Muesum of Australia

Aboriginal hunters, Wardaman country, 1921

AIA collection, Charles Darwin University

Possession of multiple identities could be used by people to distance themselves from an individual or group deemed responsible for a particular event, even if they had an identity in common with that individual or group. Anthropologist Deborah Rose cites an example of this in recent times when a Mudbura man killed a Ngarinman woman. Individuals who had both Mudbura and Ngarinman affiliations began to emphasise their Ngarinman identity and play down their connection to the 'murdering Mudbura'.[11] Similar disassociation almost certainly occurred when frontier police questioned Aborigines about the murder of a European, or other crimes. This flexible identity has led to problems in accepting the reliability of historic records where a particular tribal identity was attributed to Aborigines involved in an event at a particular place.

Trade, marriage and ceremonial relationships, referred to by anthropologists as information networks, were the means by which Aborigines could travel hundreds of kilometres into regions far beyond their own country. Details about this long distance travel were gathered by the early ethnologist, RH Mathews, who sent questionnaires to Victoria River District residents in the 1890s seeking information about the Aborigines. From the settlers he learned about:

> Periodic journeys ... made into the territories of adjoining and distant tribes for the purpose of exchanging manufactured or natural products. The routes along which the people travel on these occasions seem to have been used and acknowledged from time out of mind ... the natives of the upper Victoria travel eastward to Newcastle Waters; thence northerly to Daly Waters, Birdum Creek and Katherine River, returning by way of Delamere and Gregory Creek. Residents of the Wickham River go westward to the Negri and Ord Rivers, which they run down a long way, coming back by Auvergne on the Baines, and thence up the Victoria River home. There are several of these bartering or trade routes in different districts, and the journeys, which occupy a long time, are marked by good feeling and festive corroborees throughout.[12]

The Norwegian zoologist and explorer Knut Dahl also mentioned such long distance travel. While visiting the lower Victoria River in 1895 Dahl

---

11   ibid., pp. 153–64.
12   RH Mathews, 'Ethnological notes on the Aboriginal tribes of the Northern Territory', *Queensland Geographical Journal*, vol. 16, 1901, pp. 69–89.

met a 'myall'[13] Aboriginal man who had visited Pine Creek, apparently out of curiosity to see the whites.[14] When people made these long trips they were likely to meet others who had travelled a similar distance from a different direction, so there were 'chains of connection' across most of the continent, and people received goods and information from regions far beyond their maximum range of travel.[15] Pearl shell ornaments that originated on the Kimberley coast were worn in the Victoria River District and are known to have reached South Australia.[16] Boomerangs from the Newcastle Waters area reached the Victoria and many were passed northwards to the Daly River region. In return the Daly River people sent bamboo spears south, some of which were traded on to Newcastle Waters and beyond.[17] As well as material items, songs, dances and stories passed along these networks.[18] This long distance travel and flow of information from great distances has implications for understanding the reaction of Aborigines to the settlers when they eventually arrived in the Victoria River region.

Thousands of years of accumulated experience gave Victoria River people a deep knowledge of the ecology, resources and terrain of their territories. They had developed sophisticated methods to control their environment and to maintain and promote the growth of the foods on which they survived. The territories of most groups contained areas that were more productive than others. Generally speaking there was much more food on the lowland plains, along the river systems and around other water sources – the very areas which would become prime cattle lands – than in the rocky sandstone, limestone and basalt ranges or desert areas. Different foods were abundant at different times of the year in different places, and the Aborigines knew exactly when and where in their country such resources were available. They thus led a relatively structured life, moving to and exploiting different resources in a methodical way.

---

13   'Myall' was the term applied to Aborigines who maintained a traditional and independent life in the bush, and who were ignorant of European ways. It is still in widespread use, particularly among Aborigines (J. Arthur, 1996, pp. 161–2).

14   K Dahl, *In Savage Australia: An Account of a Hunting and Collecting Expedition to Arnhem Land and Dampier Land*, Phillip Allan & Co., Ltd, London, 1926, pp. 183–84.

15   DJ Mulvaney, '"The chain of connection": the material evidence', in N Peterson (ed.), *Tribes And Boundaries In Australia*, Social Anthropology Series no. 10, Australian Institute of Aboriginal Studies, Canberra, 1976, pp. 72–94.

16   DJ Mulvaney and J Kamminga, *Prehistory of Australia*, Allen & Unwin, Sydney, 1999, p. 97.

17   Personal observation.

18   Mulvaney, pp. 72–94.

The most visible, powerful and dramatic of Aboriginal land management techniques was the use of fire. A common understanding of the reason for Aboriginal burning is that it cleared the grass and undergrowth to make walking easier and safer and assisted in hunting and gathering food. While this is true, there was much more to their burning than this. Fire and smoke were (and are to this day) central to virtually every aspect of daily life and to every life passage. Birth, initiations, dispute resolutions and funerals all require fire and smoke. The right to use fire in particular contexts is allocated among kin and defended in the same way that rights to songs, designs and other forms of knowledge are defended.[19]

Scientific, historical and anthropological studies of Aboriginal land use around Australia have shown that burning practices were highly systematic, complex, and based on an intimate knowledge of territory, ecology and local climatic conditions.[20] To give just a few examples, Aborigines in many areas knew that fires lit at particular places would burn into previously burnt or wet areas and go out, and they knew that fires lit at certain times of the day in certain seasons would go out later in the day because of a predictable wind change, or overnight as the dew fell. Some Aborigines burnt firebreaks around valued, resource-rich and fire-sensitive plant communities such as rainforest patches, or around certain sacred sites or burial grounds. They knew that burning at the appropriate time would promote the flowering of certain plant species, and the growth of particular food plants, or would attract desirable animals to the burnt area, and they knew that if they burnt certain food plants in patches over time, the plants would fruit over an extended season. Conversely, if they carried out a single large burn they could ensure the production of a large amount of food for a short period of time which was useful for ceremonial gatherings.

Fire clearly was an essential tool in the maintenance of Aboriginal life and, in some environments at least, the number of fires lit in a year could be enormous. For example, the Gidjingali people of central Arnhem Land live in a high rainfall coastal area never successfully taken over by European pastoralists. They have maintained their traditional burning practices to the present day. A detailed year long study showed that the Gidjingali lit well over 5000 fires and increased the rate of fires caused naturally by lightning

---

19   D Rose, personal communication
20   S Pyne, *Burning Bush: A fire history of Australia*, University of Washington Press, Seattle, 1998, pp. 132–135.

strike by a factor of thousands to one.[21] As elsewhere in Australia, the fires lit by these people kept fuel loads low, producing a mosaic effect of burnt, unburnt and regenerating areas.

It's likely that the knowledgeable and regular use of fire by Victoria River Aborigines over thousands of years facilitated the rich biodiversity of the region, creating and maintaining the particular vegetation patterns that existed in the region when the first Europeans arrived – including the extensive grasslands so prized by European cattlemen.[22] Ironically, it was the burning of country, and more particularly, the burning of the grass required by the pastoralists, that frequently brought Aborigines into conflict with the settlers.

So, what was the country like when the first European settlers arrived? A good picture of the Victoria River environment before the introduction of cattle can be formed by drawing on a range of sources: the reports of explorers Lieutenant John Lort Stokes, Augustus Gregory and Alexander Forrest; the observations of a number of early settlers; early photographs; modern studies; and the memories, stories and Dreamings of Aborigines.[23] Dominant features of the landscape observed by early Europeans were lightly timbered, open grasslands, very dense and complex riverside vegetation and steep banks on the rivers and creeks.

The open nature of the country was briefly remarked upon by Stokes in 1839. His explorations were largely confined to a narrow corridor along the Victoria River, but occasionally he moved away from the riverbank or obtained a more expansive view from a hilltop. For example, after taking the view from Curiosity Peak, Stokes was able to describe the trees on the Whirlwind Plains (present-day Auvergne Station) as 'mostly white gums, thinly scattered over it'.[24] Similarly, in the area around present-day Coolibah and Fitzroy Stations he described 'a fine plain ... lightly and picturesquely timbered with the white gum'.[25] (Maps 2 and 4)

Gregory's expedition of 1855–56 followed the Victoria River to its source and beyond, and in the process passed over a lot of country away from the river. A number of expedition members commented on the open and grassy nature of much of the country. References to 'fine grassy flats' are common

---

21   R Jones, 'The neolithic, palaeolithic and the hunting gardeners: man and land in the antipodes', in R Suggate and M Cresswell (eds), *Quaternary Studies*, The Royal Society of New Zealand, 1975, pp. 21–34.
22   Pyne, *Burning Bush*.
23   D Lewis, *Slower than the Eye Can See: Environmental Change in Northern Australia's Cattle Lands*, Tropical Savannas CRC, Darwin, 2002.
24   Stokes, p. 58.
25   ibid., p. 81.

in Gregory's journal[26] and James Wilson, the geologist on the expedition, estimated that the district contained more than 5,000,000 acres of 'well-watered pasture-land'. He remarked that, 'North-West Australia is in reality a grassy country. In no part of the world have I seen grass grow so luxuriantly, and Mr H Gregory observed to me ... that he had seen more grass land than during all his life before'.[27]

Similar observations of 'splendidly grassed' and 'thinly timbered' country were made by a number of early settlers and visitors to the region, and some of these provide more detail than the accounts of the explorers. In 1884 the Government Resident – the man appointed by the South Australian Government to administer the Northern Territory – reported the observations of Nat 'Bluey' Buchanan, the pioneer of Wave Hill:

> Mr Buchanan describes the country as being chiefly basaltic, well watered ... There is also a large quantity of pigweed ... and wild melons, the last being so plentiful in places that Mr Buchanan states it would be easy to load drays with them ... small mobs of working horses have been known to go without water for weeks at a time, getting sufficient for their wants from the abundant supply of wild melons. These melons grow during the months of June, July and August, and are, therefore, doubly valuable ... the grasses are principally Mitchell, Landsborough, or Flinders, and blue grasses, with some barley grass, salt-bush, cotton bush, pigweed and plenty of saline herbage. There is also a bush like an orange tree which the cattle devour readily, and which is evidently very nutritious. The country is well watered back from the river and its tributaries, which are permanent. The timber is good and in sufficient quantities for building and fencing, but the bulk of the country is open plains with bald hills.[28]

Buchanan also took the first cattle to stock Ord River Station in 1884, and provided further comments on that area. 'Mr Buchanan ... reports the country to be very good, basaltic and limestone plains with bald hills, well watered with creeks and springs, timber rather scarce, and herbage chiefly Mitchell grass'.[29]

---

26 AC Gregory, 'North Australian Expedition', in A Gregory and F Gregory, *Journals of Australian Explorations*, facsimile edition, Hesperian Press, Perth, 1981 (1884), pp. 99–194. For typical observations, see 4th and 5th December 1855, 17th January 1856 and 2nd April 1856.

27 J Wilson, 'Notes on the physical geography of north-west Australia', *Journal of the Geographical Society of London*, vol. 28, 1858, p. 141.

28 JL Parsons, 'Quarterly Report on Northern Territory', 11th November 1884, *South Australian Parliamentary Papers*, vol. 3, no. 53B, 1885, pp. 2–3.

29 ibid.

Lindsay Crawford, first manager of Victoria River Downs
Telecommunications Museum, Adelaide

In the same report the Government Resident also published a letter from Lindsay Crawford, the first manager of Victoria River Downs:

At the junction of the Wickham and Victoria [*the vegetation*] consists of mimosa plains, well grassed with Mitchell and barley grasses, cotton bush, blue grass, blue bush, &c. This extends for some twenty miles, when it runs into high downs, with good grasses, and the only timber being nut tree, similar to the quandong. There are lots of herbs and melons. This sort of country extends right up the river, getting slightly better until, at Camfield Creek, you meet with salt bush. Splendid sheep country.[30]

Steep river and creek banks and dense riverside vegetation were first remarked upon by Stokes. On several occasions he and his men encountered banks so steep that they found it difficult to cross creeks and rivers or to access water, and they often had difficulty forcing their way through dense thickets of 'reeds'. For example, on a section of the river which now forms part of the boundary between Fitzroy and Bradshaw stations, Stokes noted that islands in the bed of the river were 'covered with reeds and acacias'.[31] Moving further upstream he encountered reeds throughout the day:

> We found the banks of the river thickly clothed with tall reeds, through which with some difficulty we forced our way; [*we came*] ... to the head of a steep gully, the banks of which were covered with tall reeds; The banks were so high, and so thickly covered with tall reeds, that it was only by the very green appearance of the trees ... that its course could be made out; We found here considerable difficulty in forcing our way through the tall and thickly growing reeds which lined the bank.[32]

These 'reeds' were found at various other places during the rest of their foot explorations. 15 years later Gregory's expedition also encountered dense riverbank vegetation, including 'reeds', presumably the same species seen by Stokes. James Wilson mentioned 'extensive beds of reeds growing along the rivers'[33], and on 27th April 1856, Gregory himself noted that his party:

> left the camp and steered east to the Victoria River, but as we could not find a fording place, turned north to the Wickham ... The bank of the Victoria being so densely covered with reeds that the water was not accessible ... after three hours' search found a practicable ford ... thick brush and reeds ... filled the bed of the river.[34]

When Alexander Forrest reached the junction of the Wickham and Victoria rivers in 1879 he had great difficulty getting across 'Owing to the depth of water and the prodigious growth of palm trees and bamboo cane down to the

---

30 ibid.
31 Stokes, pp. 64, 75, 77, 87.
32 ibid., pp. 67–69, 87.
33 Wilson, p. 145.
34 Gregory, p. 149.

water edge'.[35] The 'reeds' encountered by the explorers have only recently been identified as Fairy Wren Grass (*Chionacne cyathopoda*), a bamboo or cane-like plant which grows in dense tangles up to five metres high.[36]

The dense riverside vegetation provided good cover for the Aborigines whenever they encountered the explorers, or later the settlers and other Europeans. Stokes' party came across two Aboriginal children who 'scampered down the bank in very natural alarm, and were soon lost among the tall reeds'.[37] Near the Wickham River – Victoria River junction, Gregory's party heard Aborigines calling, but couldn't see them because of the 'thick brush and reeds'.[38] William Henry Willshire, the first policeman stationed in the Victoria River District, was unable to follow the tracks of Aboriginal cattle spearers into one creek because it was 'impassable for reeds & large rocks'.[39] On another occasion he came upon a camp of 'cattle killers', most of whom 'escaped in the tropical growth' while others 'were protected by an impenetrable phalanx of reeds'.[40]

Clearly, this was a land of plenty for thousands of Aborigines whose ancestors had lived in and managed the land for thousands of years. Unfortunately for the Aborigines, their country was (potentially) a paradise for European pastoralists. Inevitably, the settlers and their great herds of cattle would come, and cattle – 'the shock troops of Empire'[41] – would march across the traditional lands in their tens of thousands. With the coming of the cattle, nothing would ever be the same.

35 A Hicks, 'The Kimberleys explored: Forrest expedition of 1879', *Journal and Proceedings of the Western Australian Historical Society*, new series, vol. 1, 1938, pp. 11–19.

36 K Kelly, personal communication Kelly is the author of *Hard Country Hard Men: In the Footsteps of Gregory* (Hale and Iremonger, Sydney, 2000); Darryl Hill, personal communication. Hill is a former field officer with the Victoria River District Conservation Association.

37 Stokes, pp. 72, 87.

38 Gregory, p. 149.

39 Northern Territory Archives (NTA): Timber Creek police journal, 28th July 1894, F 302.

40 WH Willshire, *Land of the Dawning: Being Facts Gleaned from Cannibals in the Australian Stone Age*, WK Thomas and Co., Adelaide, 1896, p. 40.

41 S Milton, 'The Transvaal beef frontier: environments, markets and the ideology of development, 1902–1942', in T Griffiths and L Robin (eds), *Ecology and Empire: Environmental History of Settler Societies*, Keele University Press, Edinburgh, 1997, pp. 199–212.

Chapter 2

FIRST CONTACT

Long before the European settlers and their cattle arrived in the Victoria River District Aborigines living there had been in contact with or had heard about people from other lands. First there was direct or indirect contact with Asian and European seafarers, next came European land based exploring expeditions and finally, a series of prospectors and land-seekers crisscrossed the region.

Earliest of all contact is likely to have been with Asian seafarers. For thousands of years, maritime cultures have sailed the seas of the 'spice islands' to the north of Australia. At various times trading vessels from as far away as the Middle East, India and China visited the region. For these same thousands of years the winds of the summer monsoons have blown from the north-west, and it's virtually certain that on occasion there were ships that took advantage of these winds to sail to Australia's shores, or were carried there unwillingly during violent tropical storms.

Pot shards, tamarind trees and other evidence of Macassan (Indonesian)[1] visitors have been found along the Arnhem Land and Kimberley coasts. Archaeologists have dated these relics to within the last 300 years, and historical records indicate that during this time Macassan sailors were making regular seasonal visits to harvest trepang and other resources. However, evidence for earlier visits is ambiguous or even tenuous.[2] Hard evidence that Macassans visited the coast or rivers of the Victoria River

---

1   The term 'Macassan' is generally used to denote any South-East Asian visitor to Australia, some of whom came from the island of Macassar and some of whom came from elsewhere in the Indonesian archipelago.

2   For a detailed summary of the evidence for alien contacts with northern Australia see DJ Mulvaney and J Kamminga, *Prehistory of Australia*, Allen & Unwin, Sydney, 1999. pp. 407–24. See also C Macknight, *The Voyage to Marege: Macassan Trepangers in Northern Australia*, Melbourne University Press, 1976, and D Lewis, *The Rock Paintings of Arnhem Land, Australia: Social, Ecological and Material Culture Change in the Post-Glacial Period*, British Archaeological Reports International Series 415, Oxford, 1988, pp. 103–04.

District has not yet been found. However, there can be little doubt that Victoria River people were at least indirectly influenced by Macassan contact with Aborigines elsewhere along the north Australian coast and the possibility exists that they had occasional direct experience of the Macassans themselves.

In the early 1900s there were reports of a 'forest' of tamarind trees (*Tamarindus indicus*) in the Port Keats area,[3] with some specimens reaching 14 to 17 metres high and 160 centimetres in diameter,[4] a size that suggests considerable age. Tamarinds are not native to Australia but were brought here by Macassans and are known markers of Macassan campsites.[5] If these trees grew from seeds left by Macassans, rather than from seed traded from the Arnhem Land coast or washed ashore, Victoria River Aborigines who went to the Port Keats region to fulfil ceremonial and other social obligations are likely to have seen the Macassan visitors for themselves. Even if they did not actually see Macassans, they would soon have heard about them from information and possibly goods flowing along their information networks.

There are intriguing hints that Macassans may have occasionally entered the Victoria River. On Newry Station there's a rock painting identified as an Indonesian prahu.[6] The Aborigine who made this painting could have seen a prahu in the Port Keats area or one sailing along the coastline north of Newry, but it's also possible that the boat was seen in the Victoria River. In 1992 Ngarinman elder Bobby Wititpuru[7] spoke of a spring near Curiosity Peak where 'Malay men' obtained fresh water, 'before kardia' (Europeans). Curiosity Peak is a short distance below the junction of the Victoria and Baines Rivers and about 100 kilometres from the coast. At this point the river is still tidal, and navigable by large boats. A short distance upstream is Shoal Reach, a major obstacle to all but very shallow-draught vessels.

3   LCE Gee, 'Journal and detailed description of country Traversed', *Explorations Made by the Government Geologist and Staff during 1905*, Government Printer, Adelaide, 1905, pp. 15, 17.
4   Northern Territory Archives (NTA): Government Resident to the Minister Controlling the Northern Territory, 23rd March 1906, Government Resident of the Northern Territory (South Australia) inwards correspondence, 1870–1912, NTRS 790, item 14959.
5   Mulvaney and Kamminga, p. 414.
6   Howard McNickle, pers. comm. McNickle was a freelance amateur recorder of rock art who carried out extensive rock art surveys in the Victoria River District in the 1980s and 1990s.
7   Mr Wititpuru is now deceased.

The first policeman stationed in the Victoria River District claimed in 1896 that 'The racial peculiarities of the natives about here incline very much to the Malays. Many are copper-coloured and very good looking'.[8] Similar observations were made in 1905 and 1932 with respect to Fitzmaurice River Aborigines.[9] At the very least, this suggests gene flow from neighbouring or distant groups who had contact with Macassans, but it also could indicate occasional direct contact with Macassans themselves.

Another indication of 'Malay' influence is the style of beard worn by Victoria River Aborigines at the time of European contact. In a sketch made by Thomas Baines in 1856, an Aboriginal man from the lower Victoria River is shown wearing a wispy goatee-like beard with the ends fastened together,[10] a style very similar to that worn by some Macassan men.[11] This style of beard could have been adopted after Macassans were seen on the lower Victoria River or near Port Keats, but it could also have been initially adopted further afield and the style then spread to the Victoria River District.

Victoria River people might also have suffered from disease introduced by alien visitors. Several studies suggest the possibility of smallpox epidemics having swept Australia in the 1790s, the 1820s to 1830s and again in the 1860s to 1870s. At least two of these epidemics appear to have arrived somewhere on the Arnhem Land coast and spread inland from there, reducing Aboriginal populations by up to 45 per cent wherever they occurred.[12] If this was the case then the Aboriginal populations encountered by the first European explorers and settlers in the Victoria River District may have been much lower than they were 50 or 100 years earlier.

European knowledge of the Victoria River region began with explorations by ship along the coast. The Dieppe map, compiled by Portuguese seafarers in the early 1500s, shows what some believe is the north Australian coastline, including an opening in the Victoria River–Fitzmaurice River area.[13] However,

8   WH Willshire, *Land of the Dawning: Being Facts Gleaned from Cannibals in the Australian Stone Age*, WK Thomas and Co., Adelaide, 1896, p. 34.
9   'Northern Territory blacks', *The Register* (Adelaide), 23rd December 1905, p4; 'Cannabilistic blacks': *The Advertiser* (Adelaide) 1st July, 1932, p. 20.
10   For example, see the illustration on p. 69 of R Braddon, *Thomas Baines and the North Australian Expedition* (William Collins Pty Ltd, Sydney, 1986).
11   Mulvaney and Kamminga, p. 417.
12   J Campbell, *Invisible Invaders: Smallpox and other Diseases in Aboriginal Australia, 1780–1880*, Melbourne University Press, 2002, pp. 216–17; N Butlin, 'Macassans and Aboriginal smallpox: the "1789" and "1829" epidemics', *Historical Studies*, vol. 21, 1985, pp. 315–35; R Kimber, 'Smallpox in Central Australia: evidence for epidemics and postulations about the impact', *Australian Archaeology*, vol. 27, 1988, pp. 63–68.
13   L Fitzgerald, *Java La Grande: The Portuguese Discovery of Australia*, The Publishers Pty Ltd, Hobart, 1984, pp. 80, 82.

this interpretation is disputed.[14] Abel Tasman sailed the northern coastline in 1644 but doesn't appear to have seen the mouth of the Victoria River.[15]

There is tantalising evidence of an undocumented European landing on the Fitzmaurice River in 1814. Carved on the trunk of a boab at the head of the tidal reach of the Fitzmaurice River on Bradshaw Station is a partly illegible name, and a clear number or date of 1814.[16] From what can be deciphered the name appears to be 'Casabila' or 'Casabilo', possibly Spanish or Portuguese – perhaps from Portuguese Timor. While the authenticity of the inscription can't be proven one way or the other, there's a distinct possibility that these markings document an otherwise unknown visit to the Victoria River District.

In 1819 Phillip Parker King was sent from Sydney to chart the northern coastline. Sailing well down the western side of what was to become the Northern Territory, he saw a large opening, but unfavourable winds and currents, and dangerous shoals and rocks, prevented him from exploring further.[17] The opening King saw was the first clear-cut report of this feature of the coastline – but twenty years were to pass before another European expedition discovered it to be the mouth of a large river – the Victoria.

Unknown visits aside, official European knowledge of the Victoria River and its hinterland began in October 1839 when an expedition led by Captain John Wickham arrived at the river mouth in HMS Beagle (Map 5). The ship entered the river on a rising tide during a dark and cloudy night. When it was well into the river the moon rose above the hills and lit up the landscape. All on board were deeply impressed with the scene suddenly revealed to them. Wickham's first mate, Lieutenant John Lort Stokes, captured the mood:

> 'This is indeed a noble river!' burst from several lips at the same moment; 'And worthy,' continued I, 'of being honoured with the name of her most gracious majesty the Queen:' – which Captain Wickham fully concurred in, by at once bestowing upon it the name of Victoria River.[18]

---

14 See W Richardson, *Was Australia Charted Before 1606?: the Java la Grande inscriptions.* National Library of Australia, Canberra, 2006, where numerous references to this debate are given.

15 A Sharp, *The Voyages of Abel Janzoon Tasman*, Oxford at the Clarendon Press, London, 1968, p. 330.

16 D Lewis, *The Final Muster: A Survey of Previously Undocumented Sites throughout the Victoria River District*, report prepared for the National Trust of Australia (Northern Territory), 2000, pp. 148–52.

17 M Hordern, *King of the Australian Coast: The Work of Phillip Parker King in the Mermaid and Bathurst 1817–1822*, The Miegunyah Press, Melbourne, 1997, p. 196.

18 JL Stokes, *Discoveries in Australia*, facsimile edition, vol. 2, State Library of South Australia, 1969 (1846), p. 40.

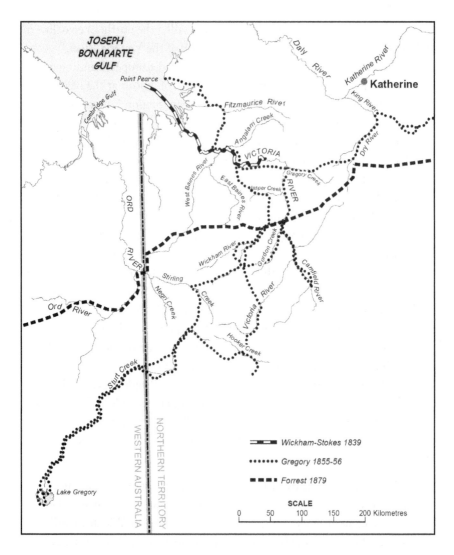

Map 5. Explorers' routes across the Victoria River District

Wickham's expedition explored both the Fitzmaurice River and the Victoria River by boat to the head of the tidal reaches, but Wickham himself became ill before his explorations were complete, so he handed responsibility to Stokes. From then on it was Stokes who led much of the exploration and it was Stokes who later wrote the only first hand published account of the expedition.[19]

---

19   ibid.

Along the tidal reaches of the Victoria, between the river mouth and ten to 15 kilometres above Timber Creek, very few signs of an Aboriginal presence were noted. When Stokes led a foot party along the freshwater reaches however, he quickly found evidence for a large population and became worried about the possibility of attack. Stokes' party walked upstream for six days, to a point close to the location of the present-day Coolibah homestead. Along the way they discovered an abandoned village of 13 huts, old campfires with food remains and burnt-off areas. Then they began to see the Aborigines themselves. First they saw two children who fled into 'tall reeds'. Shortly afterwards they encountered 'three women carrying bundles of bark at their backs ... They were quite naked, with the exception of a slight covering of bark around their waists'. The women called out and were answered by what sounded like a large party nearby, which caused the explorers to hurriedly move on. Later that day they saw a party of natives cross the Victoria and head downstream.[20]

There can be little doubt that the Aborigines quickly discovered the white intruders and kept them under observation until eventually some decided to make contact. When Stokes' party was resting on the riverbank on present-day Coolibah Station they heard 'the shrill voices of an evidently large body of natives'. The explorers prepared themselves for attack, but instead they experienced a peaceful encounter:

> two natives, accompanied by a large cream-coloured dog that howled mournfully, came down suddenly, shouting 'Ho! ho!' upon the opposite bank, as though more clearly to reconnoitre our position. They were fine looking men, with bushy hair and spare limbs, quite naked, and apparently unarmed – a usual indication among the aborigines of Australia that their intentions are peaceful. They amused themselves for a time by making all sorts of gestures, shouting still 'ho! ho!' to those of their body in concealment ... I was of course very glad that no appeal to force was necessary ... against those to whom we appeared in the character of invaders of a peaceful country.[21]

This was the closest contact with Victoria River Aborigines experienced by any of the Europeans on the Stokes–Wickham expedition. The Aborigines eventually withdrew, leaving Stokes to remark that:

---

20   ibid., pp. 5, 69, 72, 74.
21   ibid., pp. 78–79.

the condition and appearance of the two who made themselves visible, indicated their residence in a country fitted to supply abundantly all natural wants ... I could not help comparing the bold, fearless manner in which they came towards us – their fine manly bearing, head erect, no crouching or quailing of eye – with the miserable objects I had seen at Sydney. I now beheld man in his wild state; and reader, rest assured there is nothing can equal such a sight. Before me stood two of the aboriginal inhabitants of Australia who had never, until then, encountered the hitherto blighting look of an European.[22]

When the explorers finally returned to their boats they learned that a large party of Aborigines had been seen 'crawling along the ground with evident caution' towards a watering party. Stokes assumed that the Aborigines were 'intending if possible to surprise them' but it's at least as likely that the Aborigines were merely curious and were sneaking up to get a closer view of the strange white men.[23] The Stokes–Wickham expedition wasn't on the Victoria for long and didn't establish a land based depot, so there was little time or opportunity for the Aborigines to become sufficiently familiar with the Europeans to overcome their fears and make sustained contact. As a result, the expedition learnt very little about local Aboriginal society.

Even though his explorations didn't extend beyond the lower Victoria River, Stokes painted a glowing picture of the region and his report was an encouragement to further exploration. Before leaving the Victoria he expressed the desire that, 'ere the sand of my life-glass has run out ... smoke may rise from Christian hearths where now alone the prowling heathen lights his fire'.[24] Stokes died on 11th June 1885,[25] just two years after the first (at least nominally) Christian hearths appeared on the Victoria. The irony is that today there may well be more Aboriginal Christians in the district than there are European Christians and, over the years, many of the local whites could easily have qualified as 'prowling heathens'.

Sixteen years after Stokes, in 1855, the North Australian Expedition led by Augustus Gregory was sent to explore the upper Victoria River and to determine whether it might in fact be a 'highway' into the interior

22   ibid., p. 80.
23   ibid., pp. 78–80, 89.
24   ibid., p. 46.
25   M Hordern, 'John Lort Stokes', in D Carment, R Maynard and A Powell (eds), *The Northern Territory Dictionary of Biography: Volume 1 to 1945*, Northern Territory University Press, Darwin, 1990, pp. 274–76.

of Australia, perhaps even to the fabled inland sea.[26] Gregory landed the expedition's horses near Port Keats and then led a small party overland through the broken country of the Fitzmaurice River valley, and over the ranges back to the Victoria River. Other expedition members moved up the Victoria in the expedition ship, *Tom Tough*, with orders to set up a base camp from which inland exploration could take place.[27]

Because it was powered by sail the *Tom Tough* was largely captive to the tides. As it moved upstream it grounded on rocks and water entered the hold, destroying a large quantity of stores. Severely damaged and disabled, the ship was carried by the tides from one shoal to another before being stranded for some weeks between the junctions of the Baines River and Angalarri Creek, about 50 kilometres below Timber Creek.[28] The *Tom Tough* was carrying a cargo of over 160 sheep, and while it was incapacitated it had a severe list which caused the sheep to be crowded on top of each other in the hold. Together with heat and lack of water this crowding caused a great many deaths before the sheep could be unloaded near the 'Dome', a distinctive dome-shaped hill on the eastern bank of the river where water and grass had been found.[29]

A depot camp was soon established at a spring about ten kilometres below Timber Creek.[30] From there Gregory made a number of trips into the interior, far beyond the point reached by Stokes, eventually travelling right up to the Victoria River headwaters and beyond, down the inland flowing Sturt Creek to where it ends in a huge salt lake (Map 5). On Gregory's return to the Victoria River depot camp from the Sturt Creek foray, the North Australian Expedition was effectively over and the explorers began to leave. While Gregory started with a group on horseback to travel 3200 kilometres across northern Australia and down to Moreton Bay (Brisbane), the remaining expeditioners boarded the *Tom Tough* and left to obtain provisions at Kopang. From there they were under instructions to sail to the

---

26　JC Wickham, 'Description of the River Victoria on the NW coast of New Holland with directions for approaching it', Mitchell Library, Z A 308; J Cumston, *Augustus Gregory and the Inland Sea*, A Roebuck Book, Canberra, 1972, p. 110.

27　AC Gregory, 'North Australian Expedition', in A Gregory and F Gregory, *Journals of Australian Explorations*, facsimile edition, Hesperian Press, Perth, 1981 (1884), p. 102.

28　JR Elsey, Diary, 27th September 1855, 6 and 29 October 1855, National Library of Australia, MS 25.

29　The Dome is a conical hill on the east bank of the Victoria River at the very end of the Yambarran Range (Millik Monmir 1:100,000 map, sheet 4967, Royal Australian Survey Corps, 1992, co-ords 284 981).

30　Elsey, Diary, 27th September 1855, 6 and 29 October 1855.

Gregory's Depot Camp, Christmas day, 1855

The Leisure Hour, 1868

Gregory's boab on the Victoria River below Timber Creek

Adelaide Observer, 18 April 1925

Albert River in the Gulf of Carpentaria for a rendezvous with the overland party before continuing to Sydney.[31]

From the point of view of his contemporaries the major result of Gregory's explorations was to make known the tremendous extent of prime grazing land in the region. In spite of this knowledge, it took almost 30 years for the tide of settlement to reach the Victoria and cattlemen moved their herds into the region.

A number of expedition members eventually published papers relevant to their own expertise and experience,[32] but the only detailed published accounts of the expedition are the reports by Gregory.[33] These provide relatively short day-by-day descriptions of events. However, expedition members who occupied the depot camp kept an official camp journal, along with personal diaries. They also wrote letters to friends and family in England, some of which have been preserved in archives,[34] though none have been published. These unpublished documents include relatively detailed information on the environment and the Aboriginal inhabitants and describe some amazing encounters between them and the explorers. They reveal a poignant 'what might have been' in view of later race relations in the region,[35] and combined with the published reports of Gregory and others, they provide a kind of 'foundational document' for

---

31 Gregory, 'North Australian Expedition' (1981).
32 T Baines, 'Additional notes on the North Australian Expedition under Mr AC Gregory', *Proceedings of the Royal Geographical Society of London*, vol. 2, session 1857–58, 1858, pp. 3–16; JR Elsey, 'Report on the North Australian Expedition', *Journal of the Geographical Society of London*, vol. 28, 1858, pp. 135–37; J Wilson, 'Extracts from notes on the North Australian Expedition', *Proceedings of the Royal Geographical Society of London*, vol. 1, sessions 1855–56, 1856; J Wilson, 'Notes on the Physical Geography of North-West Australia', *Journal of the Geographical Society of London*, vol. 28, 1858, pp. 137–53.
33 AC Gregory, 'Journal of the North Australian Exploring Expedition, under the command of Augustus C Gregory, Esq. (Gold Medallist RGS); with report by Mr Elsey on the Health of the Party', *Journal of the Royal Geographical Society*, vol. 28, 1858, p. 85; AC Gregory, 'North Australian Expedition', *Journal of the Legislative Council of New South Wales, Session 1856–7*, vol. 1, 1857; Gregory, 'North Australian Expedition' (1981).
34 Elsey, Diary; J Wilson and JR Elsey, 'Journal kept at the Main Camp, Victoria River By JS Wilson – Geologist and JR Elsey Surgeon, to the North Australian Expedition, 1856, entry for 5th January 1856, Mitchell Library, Z C 411–1; JS Wilson, 'Journal by JS Wilson', 31st January – 28th May 1856, entry for 31st January 1856, Mitchell Library, ZC 411–2; see also two letters from Elsey, the first written to his parents over an extended period from Victoria River Depot and one addressed to 'Dear John', 13th April 1856 (National Library of Australia, NLA MS 25).
35 See D Lewis, '"Invaders of a peaceful country": Aborigines and explorers on the lower Victoria River, Northern Territory' (*Aboriginal History*, vol. 29, 2005, pp. 23–45).

the Victoria River District – a baseline from which to measure the social and environmental changes wrought by European settlement.[36]

Gregory's journal indicates that during his inland forays he often saw signs of Aborigines, and occasionally heard them calling, but he had only a few fleeting glimpses of the people themselves.[37] However, at the main depot camp the situation was much different. This camp was permanently manned for nine months, but Gregory spent only half that time there. Understandably, his journal is primarily concerned with what he experienced himself and it provides scant detail about the experiences of the men who manned the depot camp while he was away.

To give one example. On his return from his second excursion inland Gregory recorded that during his absence 'The natives have been frequently at the camp in small parties, and on these occasions were very quiet in their demeanour'. He was also told that Aborigines met by small detached parties of men away from the base camp had made 'hostile demonstrations'. On one occasion they had to be fired on, with one man being slightly wounded.[38] The fact is that Gregory's brief and dry journal entries gloss over these events. Far more occurred between the Aborigines and the men stationed at the depot camp than either Gregory's journal or later books about his expedition would suggest. Furthermore, not all encounters away from the base camp were hostile.

The camp journal, diaries and letters written by men based at the depot camp contain accounts of peaceful 'first contact' between the Aborigines and the Europeans. In combination with some of Gregory's observations they provide an insight into many aspects of Aboriginal society at the time – the people's physical appearance, their material culture, social relations and land use – and their varied reactions to the Europeans. They also hint at a greater awareness of Europeans than might otherwise have been expected.

Initial contacts were either cautious and low key, or unfriendly. The first 'cheek by jowl' encounter occurred on 16th November when Gregory was leading a party on a short reconnaissance to the freshwater reaches of the river. At Palm Island, eight kilometres above the mouth of Timber Creek:

36   See D Lewis, *Slower than the Eye Can See: Environmental Change in Northern Australia's Cattle Lands* (Co-operative Research Centre for the Sustainable Development of Tropical Savannas, Darwin, 2002).
37   Gregory, 'North Australian Expedition' (1981), pp. 126, 132, 134, 140–41, 147, 149–50.
38   ibid., pp. 150–51.

A native approached the bank of the river and came to us, and a parley commenced which was rather unintelligible, and when he found that he could not make himself understood by words, resorted to the language of signs, and expressed his contempt of us in an unmistakable manner.[39]

Undoubtedly the man turned his back to the Europeans and slapped his buttocks, an insult used by Aborigines in many parts of Australia.[40] During the following week Aborigines twice visited a party cutting down trees at Timber Creek. While these visits were later described as 'neither decidedly friendly or hostile,' the first time it happened the timber cutters fled back to the depot in panic.[41] It was probably then that the Aborigines pilfered some items 'imprudently left lying near one of the logs' and later 'set fire to the grass about 200 yards from the camp, and then retired'.[42] In December two men looking for strayed horses about 25 kilometres to the west of the depot thought themselves threatened by a large group of Aborigines; they scattered them by charging them on horseback.[43]

Gregory set out on his second and major excursion inland on 2nd January 1856 and two days later a remarkable incident occurred near the depot camp. On that day two crewmen from the *Tom Tough* went hunting on the opposite side of the river and shot a kangaroo. While one of them was bringing the carcass back across the river four Aborigines appeared. The captain of the *Tom Tough*, David Gourlay, immediately took a boat across to pick up the other crewman, and James Wilson recorded in the camp journal that:

During the time he was ashore the Capt'n had a parley with the Natives and observed that they spoke a few words of English. One asked for tobacco and seemed to understand its use perfectly when a small piece was given him – he said tomorrow in a manner that the Captain understood to mean, that they would come tomorrow. Mosquitos being exceedingly troublesome to him he would strike the place where they stung him with his hand and say, no good, no good.[44]

---

39   ibid., pp. 112.
40   For example, see 'KH Wills diary extracts', John Oxley Library, Henry Brandon Collection, OM 75–75; 'Three north Queensland stations', *Australasian Pastoralists' Review*, 15th June 1899, p. 218; H. Reynolds, *The Other Side of the Frontier*, History Department, James Cook University, Townsville, 1981, p. 84.
41   Elsey, Diary, 18 November 1855.
42   Gregory, 'North Australian Expedition' (1981), p. 113.
43   ibid., p. 118. The men were Thomas Baines and R Bowman. Baines later recreated this encounter in an oil painting, a copy of which is reproduced in Braddon, p. 37.
44   Wilson and Elsey.

In spite of the friendly nature of this meeting Wilson was afraid of problems arising if similar incidents occurred, so he gave orders that no hunting was to be done on the opposite side of the river as long as Aborigines were in the area. The same Aborigines appeared at the same place the next day, but were ignored. They came again the next day, and the next, but were ignored each time. In the meantime work was begun on digging a defensive ditch to enclose the depot camp, to give it a degree of protection against possible attack and to serve as a boundary line inside which Aborigines were not to be allowed.[45]

Wilson was perplexed at the apparent use of English by the man he encountered, and his familiarity with tobacco. He speculated that when the British settlement at Port Essington existed (1838–49)[46] Aborigines living in the area might have learnt 'a considerable number of English words' and transmitted them to the neighbouring tribes. He noted that the man who appeared to use English words was older than his companions and might have learnt the words he used (and gained a knowledge of tobacco) when he was living with Aborigines much further to the north.[47]

Wilson's speculations that English words and knowledge of tobacco may have been passed from tribe to tribe from the old Port Essington settlement were quite possibly correct because of the Aboriginal trade and information networks.[48] George Windsor Earl, the draughtsman and official linguist at Port Essington,[49] noted that information passed rapidly from tribe to tribe so that, 'an event of any importance is known over a large extent of country in the course of a very few months'. He also noted with surprise that Aborigines visiting from further inland spoke of 'white people who dwelt in the country to the south, and who built houses of stone'. He assumed that this must refer to houses in the infant settlement of Adelaide over 3000 kilometres away.[50]

When explorer Ludwig Leichhardt first entered the plains of the South Alligator River in November 1845, he met Aborigines who repeatedly said the words 'perikot' and 'nokot'. Because of their accent Leichhardt didn't

45   ibid., 5th January 1856, 7th January 1856.
46   P Spillett, *Forsaken Settlement: An Illustrated History of the Settlement of Victoria, Port Essington North Australia 1838–1849*, Lansdowne Press, Sydney, 1972.
47   Wilson and Elsey, 4th January 1856.
48   N Peterson (ed.), *Tribes And Boundaries In Australia*, Social Anthropology Series no. 10, Australian Institute of Aboriginal Studies, Canberra, 1976. See particularly the chapters by Peterson, pp. 50–71, and DJ Mulvaney, pp. 72–94.
49   B Reece, 'George Windsor Earl', in Carment, Maynard and Powell, pp. 87–89.
50   George Windsor Earl, cited in Reynolds, 1981, p. 10.

recognise what the Aborigines were saying, but later he understood the words to be 'very good' and 'no good'.[51] This was about 200 kilometres from Port Essington. Apparently these words were used so often by the whites there, and with such emphasis, that they made an impact on the Aborigines who heard them and were passed along from tribe to tribe. It's worth noting that among the Larrakia Aborigines in the Darwin area, 'perikot' is the term they use for 'white man'.[52]

Months after Wilson's encounter with the supposed English-speaking Aborigine, expedition surgeon and zoologist Joseph Elsey had the opportunity to converse with him, and as a result he rejected the claim that any local Aborigines knew words of English, although he admitted that several words sounded like 'tobac' and 'no good'.[53] Given that Leichhardt hadn't recognised the words 'very good' and 'no good' after more than four years experience of listening to Aboriginal English, it's possible that the Victoria River Aborigines really were attempting to say 'tobacco', 'no good' and 'tomorrow', and that Elsey, who had no previous contact with Aborigines, was not experienced enough to understand what he was hearing. The fact remains that upon being understood to ask for 'tobac' and being given a piece, the Aboriginal man 'seemed to understand its use perfectly' – the implication being that he began chewing it. In addition, he apparently also said 'tomorrow' and did indeed come back the next day.

Apart from the discovery of some footprints near the depot camp on 18th January[54] the Aborigines seemed to disappear from the depot area for six weeks, but down river below the Angalarri Creek junction there were several remarkable encounters. On 31st January, Wilson, Gourlay and some sailors set off from the depot camp to look for a suitable place to careen the *Tom Tough* so that repairs could be carried out. As they neared the Yambarran Range darkness fell, and they noticed some Aboriginal campfires. Some of Wilson's men 'cooeed' but got no answer, so Wilson ordered a gun to be fired. Upon hearing the gunshot one might have expected the Aborigines to flee, but instead they began calling to the Europeans and one came towards them with a firestick. The two groups kept calling to one another as the

51 L Leichhardt, *Journal of an Overland Expedition from Moreton Bay to Port Essington*, T & W Boone, London, 1847, p. 495; see J Harris, 'Contact languages at the Northern Territory British military settlements 1824–1849', pt 2, (*Aboriginal History*, vol. 9, 1985, pp. 148–69).
52 Deborah Rose, pers. comm. Rose worked on the Cox Peninsula land claim in which Larrakia people were claimants.
53 Wilson and Elsey, 2nd March 1856.
54 ibid., 18th January 1856.

boat passed, but no contact was made and shortly afterwards the Europeans camped for the night.[55]

The next day saw the most extraordinary encounter of the entire expedition. A few minutes after Wilson and his men resumed their journey downstream they were again hailed by Aborigines. Wilson directed his men to keep going and the Aborigines followed them by running along the riverbank. Eventually Wilson's party pulled up on the opposite bank for breakfast and the Aborigines gathered across the river to watch them.[56]

As the explorers landed they disturbed a flock of cockatoos feeding on wild melons and 'As they rose and were flying overhead one of the men fired up amongst them'. A cockatoo fell from the sky and Aborigines watching from across the river 'simultaneously gave a yell of mixed admiration and astonishment'.[57] Some of Wilson's men went into the nearby bush to try and shoot more game but they soon hurried back, saying they had been hailed by what seemed to be another large group of Aborigines. A conversation ensued between the Aborigines on both sides of the river, and as a result:

> nine of those on the off side marched into the water until out of their depth, then swam to a sandbank in the middle across which they marched in the same regular order and again swam toward the bank carrying their spears above water in the left hand. As they approached the bank (about 200 yards below where our boat was moored, an elderly native swam out to meet them bearing in his hand a green bough. The green bough, the well Known emblem of peace.[58]

Wilson's men feared an attack and loaded their muskets with ball, then 'stood on the high bank and expressed in high terms their admiration of the novel scene … The place added materially to the effect. The broad river, the repulsive red cliffs of Sea Range, the picturesque Dome in the back ground'. The two groups of Aborigines came together some distance away and then came unarmed towards the Europeans. Wilson's party still feared an attack and made signs for them to stop.

All of the Aborigines were young men except for one 'rather elderly man' who had come about 30 yards in advance of the others. This man apparently understood the signs made by the whites and ordered his countrymen to keep back. He 'trampled down the long grass round where he stood to show

55 Wilson, 'Journal by JS Wilson', 31st January 1856
56 ibid., 1st February 1856.
57 ibid.
58 ibid.

that he had no concealed weapon' and then pointed to a running sore on his back. Wilson's men were still fearful and wanted to drive the Aborigines away, but Wilson ordered them to hold their fire, making the rather droll remark that the Aborigines 'came rather to have their wounds healed than to have others added'. He and his men then went up to the injured man.

Elsey, the expedition surgeon, was not with Wilson's party and they had no medicines, so they improvised a treatment. First, one of the men prepared a quid of tobacco. Then, believing he needed to convince the Aborigines that powerful magic was involved, he:

> Muttered a lot of gibberish performed a number of gymnastic movements, which ended (muttering all the time) by taking off his hat looking at the sun, first over his right shoulder then over his left and dashing his hat with violence to the ground proceeded to apply the solaceing weed.[59]

The quid of tobacco was then bound in place with a strip torn from the man's shirt. The puzzle is, what made the injured man think that these strange intruders could help with his wound? It's interesting to speculate that the injured man sought help from Wilson's party because he'd heard that the Europeans at Port Essington were good at healing wounds and curing sickness.

While this 'treatment' was in progress the crewmen approached the other Aborigines and 'an amicable understanding established'. Wilson thought that the friendliness of the Aborigines was probably due to the 'peaceful and distant disposition' the expedition members had maintained since they'd arrived and because the Aborigines 'had evidence of, and felt our superiority'.

According to Wilson, the Aborigines indicated that they knew of the expedition's depot camp and seemed anxious to make a visit. They also invited him to a corroboree at their camp that night, but he declined. Wilson and his men then finished their breakfast, gave the Aborigines a few small gifts, and continued on downstream. The Aborigines followed them along the bank for a distance, but were eventually left behind. Then, as Wilson's party was passing the Dome, a large group of women, children and old men watched them from the hillside and called out to them, but once again the Europeans continued on.[60]

---

59   ibid.
60   ibid.

By analogy with modern ethnographic studies in the Victoria River region it appears that Wilson and his men had arrived in the midst of a ceremonial gathering. This is suggested by the group of young men being led by an old man, the separation of the women and children from these men, the invitation to attend a corroboree, and by another encounter Wilson's party had two days later. On their return upstream Wilson and his men camped near where they had met the large group, and met another, much smaller party of Aborigines. This time there were only six men, four who they had seen before and two others who were very young and who 'stood aloof'. These young men had their two front teeth knocked out and Wilson was 'given to understand by the others that they belonged to another tribe up the River'.[61] Modern studies suggest that the young men were probably undergoing 'young men's' initiation, a prolonged process during which the novices are largely removed from society, placed under the strict control of initiated men, and taken on trips into the territory of neighbouring groups.[62]

The men in this group were fascinated with the physical appearance of the Europeans and, in a manner strangely reminiscent of late-nineteenth-century and early twentieth-century anthropological studies of Aborigines, they examined them 'with extreme minuteness'. They noted that not all of the whites had hair of the same colour and were astonished at their 'superior muscular proportions which they observed with admiration'. One man opened Wilson's shirt and examined his chest 'with the minuteness that a Military Doctor might be supposed to do that of a young recruit'. Then he compared each part of Wilson's arm with the same parts of his own. He noted that Wilson's hand wasn't as large as his own and called to one of his friends to come and look at the difference. While the second man was holding Wilson's hand in his own, Wilson grasped it as hard as he could, causing the man to wince and sing out. According to Wilson all the Aborigines laughed and the butt of his joke 'seemed both pleased and astonished while he rubbed his hand and described his sensations to his brethren'.[63]

The men with Wilson then began to barter with the Aborigines and exchanged a blanket and a red woollen shirt for two spears. They were keen to obtain a stone tomahawk, but Wilson noticed that the Aborigines seemed to value these very highly and admonished his men to only trade something which would be of equal service to the Aborigines. Eventually they parted 'in

---

61   ibid., 3rd February 1856.
62   D Rose, *Dingo Makes Us Human*, Cambridge University Press, Melbourne, 1992, pp. 145–49.
63   Wilson, 'Journal by JS Wilson', 2 February 1856.

the most amicable manner' and the Aborigines followed the boat for some distance before dropping out of sight.[64]

The next encounter occurred at the depot camp over a month later. On 2nd March Elsey was in a gully above the camp when he was alarmed to see three Aborigines approaching. He rushed back to camp to wait for them at the embankment, and described how:

> They came forward boldly, and the eldest of them walked directly up to me & jumping the ditch, stood by my side. I immediately intimated that he must recross the ditch whereon he jumped back laid down his spears & woomera & jumped back again, but it was not till I pushed him over that he seemed to understand that neither he nor his weapons were to cross the ditch. They were very cheerful & communicative, but had no Knowledge of English, though several words sounded very much like 'tobac' 'no good' &c.

Elsey went to his hut to get the Aborigines some old clothes and when he returned he found the oldest of them back inside the ditch again. Somehow he got the man outside the ditch once more and made it clear that he must stay out. Elsey then 'gave him an old merino waistcoat, the second an old pair of drawers & the third a finely made handsome youth, an old silk handkerchief to tie round his head'. After about an hour they left but 'promised to renew their visit'.[65]

While Elsey was dealing with these Aborigines, Wilson and his party were in a boat a short distance below the mouth of Timber Creek and heading downstream. As they floated along they were trying to shoot some cockatoos in the trees when they came upon a large group of Aborigines. Some had climbed high into trees to watch their approach while others were on a high rocky bank that jutted out into the river.[66] They called out and invited the whites to land, but 'not liking appearances about them' Wilson directed the boat to move further towards midstream.

As they passed the Aborigines, the boatmen noticed three of them standing hidden in the shade of a bush with their spears fixed in their woomeras. At the command of an old man one of the three men ran as close as he could and prepared to throw his spear. A shot was fired in his direction at which his arm dropped 'as though it had been shot down' and in fright he ran back to his friends. Then a gun loaded with shot and ball was fired

---

64   ibid., 3rd February 1856.
65   ibid., 2nd March 1856.
66   ibid., 3rd March 1856.

at them. The whites saw the ball hit the rocks and miss the Aborigines, but some of the shot may have hit them 'as several of them jumped as though they had been struck unexpectedly, and they all scampered off across the rocks yelling like so many frightened imps'. Wilson did not believe that any of the Aborigines had been seriously injured, but he thought it would be 'a sufficient warning to them' not to try and throw spears at the white men again.

In a note at the end of this entry Wilson described how on 11th March Elsey made a trip upstream to Reach Hopeless (about 12 kilometres above Timber Creek), and as he began his return journey he found himself cut off when Aborigines appeared on both banks.[67] Luckily they proved friendly and some were the men whom Elsey had seen at the depot camp a few days earlier. Several others were in the group that Wilson's men had fired upon the previous day. According to Wilson these men:

> seemed anxious to explain [*to Elsey*] some affair which he supposed to be their meeting with us, and one of them a young fellow showed him two small fresh scars on his arm from bird shot wounds, [*and*] he patted the gun in a conciliatory manner. Since then he has been met with several times and has been to the camp, but always with expressions of good feeling.[68]

From this time it is clear that relations between the Europeans and the Aborigines improved rapidly. On 28th March, Elsey recorded that 'In the afternoon the natives again appeared on the opposite side of the river & were soon recognised as our acquaintances up the river by their calling out "bit of sugar" & c.'.[69] The Aborigines appeared across the river again on the following two days and on both occasions Elsey and others went over to them. On the first occasion Elsey wrote that the Aborigines:

> were without arms, very friendly & merry & one of them at last understood my endeavours to catch some of their words & gave us a number by which we were enabled to ask for a stone tomahawk, which they promised to bring the next day.[70]

---

67   ibid.
68   ibid.
69   Wilson and Elsey, 28th March 1856. It's not explicit that this and the entries for the following two days were written by Elsey rather than Wilson, but Wilson's attitude toward Aborigines appears to have been much less trusting than that expressed by Elsey.
70   ibid., 29th March 1856.

The Aborigines returned the next day, bringing with them two stone tomahawks, and Elsey added more than 20 words of the local language to his word list, 'most of them signifying parts of the body'.[71] Unfortunately, these word lists are not to be found in any of the surviving records from the expedition. When Aborigines again came to the depot camp two weeks later (13th April) Elsey wrote that:

> At dinner time two of our black friends, Deana & Dearbigen made their appearance, and begged some clothes for their gins. I gave one a cotton waistcoat, the other a pair of drawers. They gave me a few additional words of their vocabulary, and were greatly astonished at the sketches in Stokes' works, especially of their own drawings[72], to most of which they gave names.[73]

In a private letter written in May, Elsey told of a visit to the depot camp by Aborigines, and in spite of the different spellings he gives to the names of the men it's almost certainly the same visit as that which occurred on 13th April:

> I was roused from my solitary dinner of preserved beef & rice ... by the cry 'Doctor, there are natives coming to the camp,' so I was obliged to jump up, take down my rifle, and gird on my revolver and march out to meet them. They proved to be two old friends, Drand & Deartijero, with whom I had become very intimate during a voyage up the river. When I had satisfied their modest desires, frightened them with a looking glass, astounded them with a telescope, ... [I] presented one with an old merino waistcoat & the other with a pair of cotton drawers cut off at the knee, both being singularly suitable garments for bush wear.[74]

The two Aborigines came to the depot again the next day and Elsey:

> had a long chat with them, & obtained a number of words & was surprised to find that they understood the use of the boomerang which they call Karlee. They do not appear to use it themselves, but described with great exactness its course & the peculiar sound it makes in its passage. A still more interesting fact to me was that they recognised at once a drawing of the Australian Porcupine Anteater, or Echidna,

---

71   ibid., 30th March 1856.
72   In Stokes (p. 170), there are illustrations of Aboriginal rock engravings from Depuch Island, Western Australia; presumably these are the pictures that were shown to the Aborigines.
73   Wilson and Elsey, 13th April 1856.
74   Elsey, letter, 13th April 1856.

& pointing to some ants which were attacking a brown snake we had given them, intimated that they constituted its food.[75]

There was another visit by Aborigines to the depot on 27th April, but no details were given.[76] On the morning of 10th April, Wilson was on board the *Tom Tough* where it was careened near the Dome when, 'The tribe of natives whom we had seen on a previous occasion down this way, … came to pay us a visit, and crossed the River for that purpose. They were quite peaceable and sat on the bank watching our movements with Astonishment'.[77] In the afternoon the Aborigines noticed some smoke ascending near Curiosity Peak and moved off in that direction, indicating that they would return later.

Wilson returned to the depot camp on 14th May and recorded that on the way he and the men with him, 'dined in the boat at Sandy Island under the scrutinising gaze of a tribe of Natives'. A week or so later Wilson, Elsey and the expedition botanist, Ferdinand Mueller, made another boat trip down river.[78] On their return they stopped for breakfast at 'Stony Spit' (below Sandy Island) where they were joined by an Aborigine who had previously provided both Elsey and Mueller with words lists.[79] He later went with them in the boat back to the depot. In a paper Wilson published after returning to England he expanded on this meeting:

> we were joined by the old native Deeanna with whom we had already formed a little intimacy. Having given him some bread and tea, he enquired by signs what bread was? In answer I took some seed from a tuft of grass growing by where were sat, and placing it between two stones, rubbed it and showed him the flour; immediately he saw me adopt this operation he expressed satisfaction as though he understood perfectly.[80]

The camp journal kept by Wilson and Elsey was discontinued shortly after Gregory's return on 9th May 1856, and for about a month afterwards only Gregory's published journal documents events. During this time Gregory made few mentions of Aborigines. In one instance he noted that a

---

75   Wilson and Elsey, 14th April 1856.
76   ibid., 27th April 1856.
77   Wilson, Journal by JS Wilson, 10th April 1856.
78   ibid., 21st May 1856.
79   ibid., 28th May 1856.
80   Wilson, 'Notes', pp. 137–53.

Thomas Baines bartering with Aborigines at the Depot Camp, Victoria River, 1856
Rex Nan Kivell Collection, National Library of Australia

few days after he arrived back 'A small party of natives came to the camp in the morning and bartered a few trifles, and then retired'.[81] It was probably on this occasion that Baines, the artist and storekeeper for the expedition, made the sketches of Aborigines at the depot camp that are in his collection.[82]

One of the last encounters nearly ended badly. On 4th June 1856 in the vicinity of Curiosity Peak, four crewmen from the *Tom Tough* went on shore to barter with a group of about 20 Aborigines. One of the Aborigines stole a tomahawk from the boat and the Europeans quickly held another captive to secure its return. This led yet another of the Aborigines to try unsuccessfully to wrestle a gun from one of the crewmen, whereon all the Aborigines decamped. The tomahawk was found later,[83] and based on the accounts of those involved the incident was later recorded in a sketch by Baines.[84] Victoria River Aborigines are only mentioned once more in any document

---

81 Gregory, 'North Australian Expedition' (1981), p. 151.
82 For examples of these sketches, see Braddon (pp. 68, 69); see also Cumston (dust jacket and p. 83).
83 Gregory, 'North Australian Expedition' (1981), pp. 152–53.
84 See Braddon, p. 77.

from the expedition. When the depot camp was abandoned and the *Tom Tough* was moving downstream towards the open sea, some Aborigines at Holdfast Reach called out and one ran for some time along the riverbank.[85]

After the expedition ended James Wilson summarised his view of relations between the Aborigines and the explorers on the lower Victoria: 'Except on one occasion, our intercourse with them was always amicable, and ... there is no impression left on the minds of the native population unfavourable to their English visitors'.[86] Of course, there were actually a number of mildly unfriendly encounters, but overall this appears to be a fair summation. Sadly, relations between Europeans and Victoria River Aborigines were not to be so friendly and mutually fascinating for a long time to come.

---

85 T Baines, 'Journal of the detachment of the North Australian Expedition left by Mr Gregory at the Main Camp Victoria River 1856', Mitchell Library C408, 19th July 1856.
86 Wilson, 'Notes', pp. 137–53.

Chapter 3

THE ADVANCE SCOUTS OF SETTLEMENT

Gregory's expedition revealed the tremendous extent and richness of grazing lands in the Victoria River country, but for almost a quarter of a century the region remained free from what John Lort Stokes called the 'blighting look' of Europeans.[1] The next blighting look came in 1879 when Alexander Forrest's party made a west-to-east traverse of the district. When Forrest reached the western edge of the Victoria River country his party was in dire straits, suffering sickness and hunger. Desperate to reach 'civilisation' on the Overland Telegraph Line the expedition pushed on as fast as possible, in the process adding comparatively little to European knowledge of the district.[2] Nevertheless, it was Forrest's report of limitless grasslands that caused a land rush to both the Victoria River and Kimberley regions. At least, that's the popular belief. The facts are otherwise.

While Forrest's report may have caused or at least accelerated a land rush to the Kimberley, in the Victoria River District the rush had begun years before. Initially the motivation was to secure leases over the country, with the first pastoral applications being lodged at the South Australian Lands Department as early as March 1876.[3] On paper most of the region had been taken up by the time Forrest arrived,[4] and at least two private expeditions had been out to inspect areas of land so held. In fact, between

1   JL Stokes, *Discoveries in Australia*, facsimile edition, vol. 2, State Library of South Australia, 1969 (1846), p. 80.

2   A Forrest, *Journal of Exploration from DeGrey to Port Darwin*, Government Printer, Perth, 1880; see also G Bolton, *Alexander Forrest – His Life and Times* (Melbourne University Press, in association with the University of Western Australia Press, Perth, 1958).

3   Northern Territory Archives (NTA): Government Resident of the Northern Territory (South Australia), – inwards correspondence, 1870–1912, NTRS 829, item A1447.

4   For example, see NTA: NTRS 829, items A1517, A1464, A2636, A2722, A2726, A2956, A3318 and A3475.

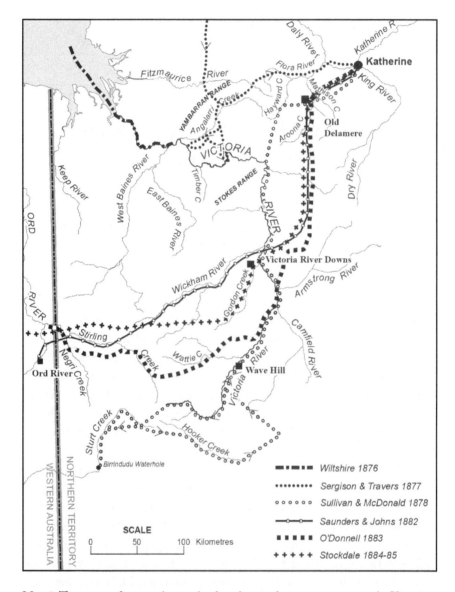

Map 6. The routes of pre-settlement land-seekers and prospectors across the Victoria River District

Gregory's expedition and the arrival of the first settlers in 1883–86, at least 12 parties entered the Victoria River District, and it's highly likely that there were other expeditions the details of which are now lost to history (Map 6).

MR. NATHANIEL BUCHANAN.

Nat 'Bluey' Buchanan, pioneer of Wave Hill Station and the Murranji Track

The Bulletin, 9 July 1881, p. 1

First, in 1878 the great bushman and explorer 'Bluey' Buchanan took up a lease, apparently sight unseen, over an area west of Timber Creek. The following year he relinquished this lease and instead took up leases over vastly superior country further south, leases which formed the nucleus of Wave Hill Station. It's possible, indeed probable, that Buchanan visited the region in 1879 to see for himself where the best land was and later adjusted his leases accordingly.[5]

---

5   According to Bobbie Buchanan (*In the Tracks of Old Bluey*, Central Queensland University Press, Rockhampton, 1997, p. 64), the new leases taken up by Nat Buchanan covered much of the best grazing land in the Victoria River District, and it seems likely that personal observation led Buchanan to identify the location of the best land.

Second, at Murranji waterhole, generally accepted as being discovered by Bluey Buchanan when he opened up the Murranji Track in 1886,[6] there was once a tree marked 'JS 78'.[7] In 1905 drover John 'Jack-Dick' Skuthorpe claimed that he'd marked this tree during a trip he'd made from the telegraph line to the mouth of the Ord River in 1878,[8] but Skuthorpe had a long-standing reputation for wild stories. Twenty-five years earlier he'd claimed he had found the grave of a member of Ludwig Leichhardt's 1848 expedition to Swan River, and retrieved Leichhardt's journals and other items.[9] He demanded a reward of £6000 before he'd hand them over, but never produced the goods. As a result he was accused of fraud, labelled by one critic the 'champion truth-teller of Queensland',[10] and for years afterwards he carried the epithet 'Relics'.[11]

Skuthorpe's claim about the marked tree was dismissed by Hely Hutchinson, a drover-cum-journalist who passed through the Victoria River – Murranji region in 1905 and wrote about his journey under the pen-name 'H7H'. While he was there Hutchinson met Paddy Cahill, the famous buffalo hunter, who at the time was managing Delamere Station.[12] Cahill told Hutchinson the tree at Murranji waterhole had been marked by a man named John Scanlan during a trip he (Scanlan) had made across the Victoria River country to Cambridge Gulf in 1878.[13] Whoever it may have been, someone appears to have been at the waterhole in 1878, but whether he continued westward to the Victoria River country or beyond remains unknown.

---

6   G. Buchanan, *Packhorse and Waterhole*, Angus and Robertson, Sydney, 1933, p. 121. The Murranji Track ran from Newcastle Waters to Top Springs, on the headwaters of the Victoria River tributary, Armstrong Creek. It was a short-cut for people travelling from Central Australia or Queensland to the Victoria River and Kimberley country, and became legendary during the droving era, 1904–1967 (D. Lewis, *The Murranji Track*, Central Queensland University Press, Rockhampton, 2007).

7   H7H (Hely Hutchinson) 'Odd Stock and Other Notes', *The Morning Bulletin* (Rockhampton), 20th January 1906, p. 8.

8   J Skuthorpe, 'Long Droving Trips', *The Morning Bulletin* (Rockhampton), 23rd June 1905; H7H, 'Odd stock and other notes', *The Morning Bulletin* (Rockhampton), 20th January 1906, p. 8.

9   'The Fate of Leichhardt', *Sydney Morning Herald*, 17th January 1881, p, 7.

10 'The Skuthorpe Libel Case', *Sydney Morning Herald*, 8th February 1881, p. 7.

11 'Them relics', *The Bulletin*, 19th March 1881, p. 13; 'Some bush yarns', *The Australasian Pastoralists' Review*, 15th February 1893, p. 1073.

12 For information on Paddy Cahill see the entry on him by M Clinch in the *Northern Territory Dictionary of Biography; Volume 1 to 1945*, p. 49 and D Mulvaney, *Paddy Cahill of Oenpelli*, Aboriginal Studies Press, Canberra, 2004. Paddy Cahill had two brothers, Tom and Matt, who also were active in the Victoria River District (see chapters 4, 5, 8, 9 and 10).

13 H7H 'Odd Stock and Other Notes', *The Morning Bulletin* (Rockhampton), 20th January 1906, p. 8.

Third, there is an intriguing possibility that the explorer Ludwig Leichhardt may have passed across the southern fringe of the region. Leichhardt's aim was to cross from Moreton Bay (Brisbane) to Swan River (Perth), but he didn't intend to travel in a straight line from one place to the other. Instead, in various letters he wrote, including several he composed in the weeks before he set out, he made it clear that he hoped to map the inland extent of the northern rivers and the northward extent of 'Sturt's Desert' (the Simpson). This route would have taken him across the headwaters of the northern rivers and at times further inland, and there's evidence this is exactly what he did.[14] Apart from a series of 'L' trees along the initial section of this route, a partly burnt gun with a brass plate attached and stamped 'Ludwig Leichhardt 1848' was discovered in the early 1900s 'in a bottle tree' near Sturt Creek, south-west of the Victoria River headwaters. Recent scientific studies leave little doubt that it's an authentic Leichhardt relic[15] so it's highly likely that Leichhardt passed across the southern edge of the Victoria River District or the northern part of the Tanami Desert.

The accounts left by known expeditions vary in length and detail, so it's often difficult to discover the background of the people involved or the ramifications of their visits, particularly with respect to the land-seekers. What is clear is that there sometimes were direct links between people in one expedition and those in another, and it's probable that there were similar connections between members of other expeditions for which there is no clear evidence. Also, in some cases newspapers published extensive reports on the activities and discoveries of expeditions, and there can be little doubt that these reports influenced or assisted those who came later.

As well as possibly influencing the way the region was eventually settled, there's reason to suspect that the actions of one or more of these groups of 'advance scouts' influenced the reception the Aborigines gave the first settlers when they arrived. During Gregory's expedition the Aborigines initially avoided the strangers, but in the one place where the Europeans could be secretly scrutinised for a long period – Gregory's main depot camp – Aborigines eventually made sustained friendly contact. Things had changed by the time the settlers arrived almost 30 years later. Instead of attempting friendly contact, the reception the Aborigines gave the settlers was hostile, and the pre-settlement incursions almost certainly had something to do

---

14   D Lewis, 'The fate of Leichhardt', *Historical Records of Australian Science*, vol. 17, no. 1, 2006, pp. 1–30.
15   D Hallam, 'The Leichhardt nameplate – a report on authenticity testing', unpublished report to the National Museum of Australia, 2006.

with this. Brief accounts of these incursions are provided here including, of course, any interactions between the European intruders and Aborigines. Two post-settler incursions are also provided because, for a short time after the first rough homesteads were established, the country was still almost totally terra incognita to Europeans.

No sooner had Gregory left the Victoria River country than Lieutenant William Chimmo arrived. Concerned for the safety of Gregory's expedition, the 'Governor General of Australia'[16] sent Chimmo in the paddle steamer *Torch* to offer Gregory any assistance he could. He arrived at the Victoria River depot camp two months after Gregory had left, so his assistance wasn't required.[17] From directions carved on a boab by Thomas Baines before Gregory's expedition left, Chimmo found a letter Gregory had left hidden in the camp forge. Before leaving he added the name of his ship to another boab that had also been marked by Baines.

When the South Australian Government decided to establish an outpost on the Northern Territory coast in 1864, Boyle Travers Finniss was ordered to examine several locations for their suitability as the site for a settlement.[18] Finniss travelled north the following year. One of the areas he examined was the lower Victoria River, but he deemed it unsuitable for settlement and instead selected Escape Cliffs, near the mouth of the Adelaide River.[19] This site turned out to be ill-chosen and was abandoned at the end of 1866.[20]

After this fiasco the South Australian Government made another attempt to find a site for a settlement. In 1867 the famous captain, Francis Cadell,[21] was sent to make this new examination, including once again the Victoria River. Cadell was on the lower Victoria River from early to mid-November,

---

16   According to J Cumston (*Augustus Gregory and the Inland Sea*, A Roebuck Book, Canberra, 1972, p. 44), at this time, the governor of New South Wales also held the title of 'Governor General of Australia'.

17   W Chimmo, 'Account of the search for the North-Australian Exploring Expedition under Mr AC Gregory', *Proceedings of the Royal Geographical Society of London*, vol. 1, sessions 1855–56 and 1856–57, pp. 255–63.

18   B Reece, 'Boyle Travers Finniss', in D Carment, R Maynard and A Powell (eds), *Northern Territory Dictionary of Biography: Volume 1 to 1945*, Northern Territory University Press, Darwin, 1990, pp. 95–97.

19   BT Finniss, report to the Governor of South Australia, 1st September 1865 in 'Dispatches from Northern Territory', *South Australian Parliamentary Papers*, vol. 2, no. 83, 1866, pp. 9–10.

20   K De La Rue, *Evolution of Darwin, 1869–1911: A History of the Northern Territory's Capital City During the Years of South Australian Administration*, Charles Darwin University Press, 2004, p. 4.

21   Among other exploits, Cadell was the first man to take a steamship up the Darling River.

at the height of the notorious 'build up' to the summer monsoon – a period of extreme heat, great humidity and fierce electrical storms. In these torrid conditions his crew became ill and Cadell couldn't get as far as the Whirlwind Plains. He was less than impressed:

> owing to the numerous dangers of that rapid and shoal-encumbered river, also taking into consideration the 100–mile belt of the most wretched, rocky, barren and waterless country, a perfect Tierra del Fuego, that if the Elysian fields had been beyond it I should have felt it to have been a duty to report against its selection.[22]

Eventually a new settlement was established in 1869, on the shores of Darwin Harbour.[23] Within a few years construction of the Overland Telegraph Line commenced, and in the process gold was discovered in the Pine Creek region.[24] This led to a gold rush in 1872 and prospecting throughout the Top End over the following decade with many parties eager to be 'first on the field'.[25] Several made plans to prospect in the Victoria River District.

In June or July 1876 a group of prospectors subsidised by the government examined the lower Victoria River by boat. They travelled upriver as far as Curiosity Peak near the mouth of the Baines River,[26] but they found no trace of gold or other valuable minerals before returning to Darwin. Later in the year a prospector named Charlie Bridson, not long back from an expedition into east Arnhem Land where an Aboriginal attack had left him with a crippled hand,[27] announced an extraordinarily ambitious (and unrealistic) plan to lead a prospecting party over 3000 kilometres from Darwin to the McDonnell Ranges, via the Victoria River. Bridson said their intention was:

> to start in a west direction from the Howley, running along the Cullen and crossing the Katherine a considerable way down; to run up that river to its source, and then strike west for the Victoria; after crossing that river, to make for the MacDonnell Ranges, and follow them up as far as Alice Springs.[28]

22 F Cadell, 'Exploration Northern Territory', 7th January 1868 in *South Australian Parliamentary Papers*, vol. 2, no. 24, 1869, p. 1.
23 De La Rue, pp. 6–7.
24 PF Donovan, *A Land Full of Possibilities. A History of South Australia's Northern Territory*, University of Queensland Press, Brisbane, 1981, p. 94.
25 ibid., pp. 95–96.
26 'Trip to the Daly River', *Northern Territory Times*, 8th July 1876, pp. 3.
27 'Country news', *Queenslander*, 19th April 1879, p. 486.
28 Untitled news item, *Northern Territory Times*, 13th May 1876, p. 2.

There can be little doubt that the planned expedition failed. In fact, there's no evidence that it ever got beyond the idea stage and it's probable that it was nothing more than a pipedream, or perhaps, a 'pub-dream'.

The following year Albert W Sergison, Roderick Travers and a man named Moore rode horses into the Victoria River country via the headwaters of the Fitzmaurice River, and travelled back and forth across what later became Bradshaw Station. On their return Sergison and Travers formed a company and obtained pastoral leases over a huge extent of country, including a large part of the Victoria River region.[29] They never stocked the land and Sergison later transferred his share of the leases to the wealthy Melbourne businessmen, Charles Brown Fisher and Maurice Lyons, who were eventually to form Glencoe, Daly River and Victoria River Downs (VRD) stations.[30]

In May 1878 Adrian Sullivan, John Mylrea and Arthur McDonald set out from the Katherine Telegraph Station to examine country McDonald held on the Victoria, and to assess the potential of the country in general.[31] They followed the Katherine River downstream for about 60 kilometres and then headed south-west. Eventually they struck a creek which they followed down to its junction with the Victoria.[32] They then headed upstream and entered the Victoria River Gorge. Soon afterwards 'some blacks came running up in a very excited manner'. These men pointed up a creek on the opposite side of the river and repeated, 'Whitefellow Jimmy very good! Whitefellow Jimmy very good!' The creek indicated was Gregory Creek, but the vegetation along the banks was extremely thick and the whites feared an ambush, so did not investigate. This area was later to become notorious for attacks on whites, so their caution may well have been justified.

The three men had a copy of Gregory's map and report,[33] and from this point on they more or less followed the route Gregory had blazed over 20 years earlier. Like Gregory they travelled up to the headwaters of the

---

29   AW Sergison, *The Northern Territory and its Pastoral Capabilities, with Notes, Extracts, and Map*, Sands and McDougall, Printers, Melbourne, 1878.

30   J Makin, *The Big Run; The Story of Victoria River Downs*, Weldon Publishers, Sydney, 1992 (1970), pp. 57.

31   'Trip to the Victoria River', *Northern Territory Times*, 28th September 1878, p. 2; 'Obituary. Passing of a pioneer', *The Graziers' Review*, 16th May 1929, p. 167.

32   Sullivan's name was given to this creek, but the creek of this name on the maps today doesn't appear to be the same creek that they followed. According to their own account, where they met the Victoria River it ran east-west, but Sullivan Creek joins a north-south section of the river. The creek they followed was probably today's Matt Wilson Creek.

33   'Obituary. Passing of a pioneer'.

Victoria and crossed over to Sturt Creek. They followed the Sturt down for at least 100 kilometres, through country they later described as 'well adapted for either sheep or cattle' and 'the best pastoral country we saw during our trip'.[34]

On their return journey they tried to go east to the Powells Creek Telegraph Station, on the Overland Telegraph Line. They rode from Sturt Creek to Hooker Creek and followed it until it petered out in the desert, but after continuing east across level sandy country for over 70 kilometres, lack of water and horse feed forced them to retreat north to the Victoria River. The rest of their return journey was along their outward track and they reached Katherine on 20th August, 13 weeks after setting out.

In summing up their trip, Sullivan said that they saw 'several parties of natives' but had no trouble with them and that, 'on the whole I was disappointed with the character of the country, an immense deal of it being of little value, that is, for pastoral purposes'.[35] While this may have been his sincere belief, one has to wonder whether he really was disappointed in much of the country he saw or if he wanted to deflect rival pastoral interests from the area. Whatever the truth of the matter, there's no evidence that McDonald retained any of the land he held in 1878, and there's no known connection between him, or Sullivan, and subsequent landholders in the region.

A year after Alexander Forrest's exploring expedition crossed the district in 1879 (see Chapter 1) another party visited the region. In July 1880 Alfred Thomas Woods set out from Springvale Station (Katherine) to look for country on behalf of the owner, Dr WJ Browne.[36] One of the men with him was 'Greenhide' Sam Croker who was later to play a significant role in establishing Wave Hill Station.[37] Woods' party travelled at least as far west as the junction of Gregory Creek and the Victoria River,[38] but the best country they found was along Aroona and Price's Creeks and across to the headwaters of Sullivan and Gregory Creeks, on the divide between the Katherine–Daly river system and the Victoria River. Woods named the area

---

34   'Trip to the Victoria River'.
35   ibid.
36   A Giles, *The First Pastoral Settlement in the Northern Territory*. State Library of South Australia, V 1082, nd., p. 153.
37   D Lewis, 'Samuel Croker', in D Carment and H Wilson, (eds), *Northern Territory Dictionary of Biography: Volume 3*, Northern Territory University Press, Darwin, 1996, pp. 58–61.
38   'The explorer. The fate of Leichardt'[sic], *The Adelaide Observer*, 23rd October 1880, p. 721–722.

Delamere Downs.[39] On his return to 'civilisation' leases were taken up and Delamere became the first station to include country within the Victoria River valley.[40]

In September 1880 Croker travelled out to the Delamere country again to look for more good land, this time in the company of Alfred Giles,[41] and subsequently another block of 600 square miles was added to those already held by Dr Browne.[42] On this trip they probably went as far as the headwaters of the Fitzmaurice River because in November Croker advertised in the *Northern Territory Times* for the owner of a horse he had found there.[43] With Tom Pearce and Rodney Claude Spencer, Giles visited the area again in early June 1881.[44] Over 20 years later Pearce, who was 'Mine Host' in Jeannie Gunn's *We of the Never Never*,[45] became the owner of Willeroo, a station which by then incorporated part of the original Delamere.[46] Spencer, on the other hand, was convicted in 1889 of the murder of an Aboriginal man on the Arnhem Land coast and sentenced to life in prison. After a number of petitions he was released in 1900 and returned to Arnhem Land where he was killed by Aborigines in 1905.[47]

The next incursion was that of Will Forgan (or Fogan or Fargoo) and Patrick Ahern (or Ahearne).[48] In the middle of 1881 these men set out from Springvale, intending to prospect for gold right across to the new stations on the lower Fitzroy River in West Kimberley. In between lay 1000 kilometres of country that to Europeans was wild and little known. Before they left, Giles warned them of the roughness of the Kimberley country 'that baffled Forrest', and the dangers from hostile blacks that two men alone would face. In spite of Giles' warnings, the two rode west. They left the furthest-out

39 A Giles, State Library of South Australia, V 1082, nd., p. 154.
40 Vern O'Brien, pers. comm.
41 A Giles, State Library of South Australia, V 1082, nd., pp. 156–59.
42 NTA: NTRS 829, item A4762; A Giles, State Library of South Australia, V 1082, nd., p. 60.
43 'Found', *Northern Territory Times*, 20th November 1880, p.2.
44 A Giles, State Library of South Australia, V 1082, nd., pp. 161–64.
45 W Farmer Whyte, '"Never Never" people. Their strange fate', *Sydney Morning Herald*, 21st February 1942, p. 9.
46 O'Brien.
47 Nicholas Waters, 'Report of the Inspector of Police for 1912', in JA Gilruth 'Report of the Administrator for the Year 1912', *Commonwealth Parliamentary Papers*, vol. 3, no. 45, 1913.
48 'The murder of Fogan and Ahearne', *The North Australian*, 17th December 1886, p. 3: C Clement, 'Pre-settlement intrusion into the East Kimberley'. East Kimberley working paper no. 24, centre for resource and Environmental studies, Australian National University, Canberra, 1988, p. 32.

station, Delamere, on 4th or 5th August.[49] Marked trees showed that they made it as far as the central Kimberley,[50] but they were never seen again. When the gold rush opened up the Kimberley five years later, a party led by Philip Saunders learned from Aborigines that two white men had been surprised in a gorge about 80 miles from Derby, and killed. Saunders believed that these men were Forgan and Ahern and there was talk of an investigation, but nothing seems to have come of it.[51]

In 1882 Adam Johns, Phil Saunders, JW Quinn and a 'Port Darwin' Aborigine named Crawford set out from Roebourne in Western Australia on what must surely rank as one of the greatest private horseback expeditions ever undertaken in Australia.[52] Their destination was Darwin, over 2200 kilometres away, and the object of their trip was to prospect for gold and other minerals in the untried vastness of the north-west and north of Western Australia, and in the Victoria River District.[53] After travelling up the long desert coastline north of Roebourne, they picked up more supplies at the 'Kimberley Pastoral Company's camp' on the Fitzroy River. They then turned to the east and more or less followed the route of Forrest's expedition, prospecting along the way.[54] They entered the Victoria River region south of present-day Mistake Creek homestead and continued east to Stirling Creek, which they followed upstream. After crossing to the head of the Wickham River and following it down to the Victoria, they then headed straight for Katherine.[55]

At the same time Saunders and Johns were crossing from west to east, a land-seeking expedition led by 'Stumpy' Michael Durack was struggling through the Kimberley ranges to the north. This was the first land-seeking expedition to come to the East Kimberley – Victoria River region as a direct result of Forrest's report. After speaking with Forrest, the Duracks took up large areas sight unseen to safeguard against city-based speculators, and then organised an expedition to determine exactly where the best country

49   A Giles, 'Forgan and his mate', *Northern Territory Times*, 17th March 1883, p. 2.
50   'The murder of Fogan and Ahearne'.
51   ibid.
52   'Exploration and prospecting', *Northern Territory Times*, 24th March 1883, p. 3; A Giles, State Library of South Australia, V 1082, p. 174, records that Adam Johns, Phil Saunders and a man named Alex Grant arrived at Springvale from Fitzroy River with no Aboriginal helpers; but I consider the Saunders–Johns account more reliable.
53   C Clement and P Bridge (eds), *Kimberley Scenes: Sagas of Australia's Last Frontier*, Hesperian Press, Perth, 1991, p. 60.
54   'Exploration and prospecting', *Northern Territory Times*, 24th March 1883, p. 3.
55   ibid.

lay.[56] One of the expedition members was Tom Kilfoyle, a relation of the Duracks and later the pioneer of Rosewood Station.[57]

The party landed their gear and horses in Cambridge Gulf and set off to the west side where they (incorrectly) believed the Ord River entered. Over the following weeks they battled through rough ranges and crossed several rivers before finally reaching the Ord near its junction with the Negri River. On the way they were threatened by a large group of Aborigines who set fire to the grass but then retreated without attacking. By the time they had examined the Ord River country downstream for 100 kilometres they'd lost a number of their horses and their rations were running low. As a result they returned to the Negri junction, then travelled west as quickly as possible to a rendezvous with a ship at Beagle Bay on the south-west Kimberley coast. The expedition was considered a success and the Duracks and Kilfoyle later established a number of cattle stations in the region, including Newry and Rosewood on the Northern Territory side of the border.

In April 1883 a party led by Billy O'Donnell set out from Delamere Station for the Ord River to examine country taken up on paper by the Cambridge Downs Pastoral Association.[58] The expedition probably had the benefit of local knowledge about the best route to take in the first stage of their trip, because instead of travelling down Gregory Creek and upstream through the rough Victoria River Gorge as Gregory and later Sullivan and McDonald had done, they went south by south-west through relatively easy going over basalt downs and hills. They reached the Victoria River more or less opposite the Stockyard Creek junction, crossed over and travelled some distance upstream before turning westward across 'immense open plains and downs as far as the eye could reach'. Continuing to 'Gregory's Stirling Creek', they followed it down for about 40 kilometres before turning west across country. A further 70 kilometres brought them to the Negri River which they followed down to the Ord. In all, the expedition spent four months in the Ord River country before returning to Springvale along its outwards track.

---

56 M Durack, *Kings in Grass Castles*, Corgi Books, Sydney, 1986. I am unable to locate any other source for this expedition and the summary presented here is based upon the description of the journey provided in Durack's book.

57 G Byrne, *Tom & Jack: A Frontier Story*, Fremantle Arts Centre Press, Fremantle, 2003, p. 19.

58 An official account of this expedition was published in two parts in *The Argus* under the heading, 'An exploring expedition' (5th January 1884, p. 5 and 17th January 1884, pp. 13–14). Unless otherwise stated my summary of the expedition is based on this source.

Members of the O'Donnell expedition to the Kimberley, 1883

National Library of Australia

Harry Stockdale
Stockdale collection

In October 1884 the *Northern Territory Times* reported that the ship *Ivy* had returned to Darwin with RO and JR O'Grady and party, and seven horses.[59] The men had been on a four-month trip to examine the country between Darwin and Western Australia. They almost certainly were prospecting, and the fact that they had horses indicates that they were examining country away from the immediate coastline or along the river corridors. However, the news report has no detail about exactly where they'd been or what they discovered, and there appears to be no information from other sources.

59   Untitled news item, *Northern Territory Times*, 11th October 1884, p. 2.

The last expedition to cross the region was that led by Harry Stockdale in 1884.[60] Stockdale had been hired by the Victorian Squatting Company, the Cambridge Downs Pastoral Association, Lawrence and Adams, and Boyd and King, to report on land that each group or partnership held in the Kimberley.[61] The expedition landed on the western side of Cambridge Gulf in September – the beginning of the torrid 'build-up' to the wet season – and set out on a great loop though the Kimberley ranges. First they travelled west for 150 kilometres, then south to near the headwaters of the Fitzroy River, and finally east to the Ord River.[62]

Their rations ran low long before they reached the Ord and the entire party began to suffer from dysentery, exhaustion, severe weight loss and physical weakness. Their clothes and boots fell to pieces and they were reduced to living on boiled flour and whatever fish or game they could catch.[63] About 100 kilometres west of Ord River two men, Patrick Mulcahy and George Ashton, announced that they wanted to stop and rest, and requested a share of the available rations and a supply of ammunition.[64] One of these men was an experienced miner and it's possible that he'd discovered traces of gold in the area. Certainly Stockdale and others believed they wanted to stay behind to prospect, rather than to rest.[65] The other members of the party tried hard to convince them to continue but they were insistent, so they were given three weeks rations and ammunition, and left behind.[66]

Further to the east Stockdale and his second in command, Henry Ricketson, rode ahead of the others to try and get rations from the newly established Ord River Station. Several days later they reached the Ord, but didn't recognise it because they were expecting a much larger stream. By the time they realised their mistake they decided they'd gone too far east

---

60   H Stockdale, 'Exploration in the far north west of Australia 1884–5', unpublished manuscript, Mitchell Library, mss A1580; JH Ricketson, 'Journal of an expedition to Cambridge Gulf, the north-west of Western Australia, and a ride through the Northern Territory of South Australia, 1884–1885' unpublished manuscript, Mitchell Library, mss 1783, item 2. Ricketson's manuscript includes extracts from the diaries of two other expedition members, Richard Pitt and John McIllree.

61   Ricketson, pp. 23–24. The team comprised Ricketson (second in command), George Ashton (described as a 'young Englishman'), Carl Bottmer (blacksmith), Richard Pitt (a representative of the Cambridge Downs Pastoral Association), John McIllree (surveyor) and Patrick Mulcahy (assistant surveyor).

62   'Return of Mr. Stockdale's exploring party', *Northern Territory Times*, 7th February 1885, p. 2.

63   Ricketson, pp. 221–25, 228–29.

64   ibid., pp. 229–30; *North Australian*, 8th May 1885, p. 3.

65   'News and Notes', *Northern Territory Times*, 24th January 1885, p 2.

66   Ricketson, pp. 229–30.

to consider returning. From the diaries of the two men it's clear that they continued east across what later became Limbunya Station, north of Stirling Creek, and entered the Victoria River valley south-west of present-day Mt Sanford homestead.

Soon they entered the catchment of Gordon Creek and followed it downstream, eventually stumbling upon Victoria River Downs homestead.[67] They continued on to Springvale which they reached on 6th January. There they paid Wave Hill manager Sam Croker £125 to go and look for Mulcahy and Ashton, but no trace of the men was ever found.[68] Of the three expedition members they'd left behind near Ord River, one died before he reached the Ord. More by good luck than good management, the two survivors found their way to Wave Hill homestead. There one of them went mad and had to be watched closely. Later they were taken on to Springvale where they arrived on 3rd March 1885.[69]

What can be said about the overall impact these pre-settlement incursions may have had on Victoria River Aborigines? A common Aboriginal reaction to encounters with early European explorers was to watch them from a distance, or to run away and then keep out of sight and watch them from hiding. Based on his wide-ranging study of Queensland Aboriginal responses to early European incursions into their lands, Henry Reynolds concluded that, 'As a general rule clans did not react immediately to European trespass ... Indeed the history of inland exploration indicates that local groups tolerated the passage of European expeditions provided they behaved with circumspection'.[70] The available accounts of European incursions into the Victoria River District between 1876 and 1881 suggest that these expeditions experienced a similar reaction from the Aborigines, but eventually this response changed.

In 1882 Saunders and Johns had to 'try conclusions with [*fight off*] a very large mob, after which they gave no trouble'. They later remarked that, 'The natives in this high rangy country are very numerous, and from the reception they gave us on several occasions I should say they are very hostile'.[71] Also in 1882 the Durack party was threatened, but no violence was reported. O'Donnell's account in *The Argus* in 1883 describes various

67   ibid., p. 272.
68   'West Australian Exploration', *Sydney Morning Herald*, 11 March 1885 p. 6.
69   'News and Notes', *Northern Territory Times*, 7th March 1885, p. 2.
70   H Reynolds, *The Other Side of the Frontier*, History Department, James Cook University, Townsville, 1981, p. 52.
71   C Swan, cited in Clement and Bridge, p. 67.

peaceful meetings with, or sightings of, Aborigines and the Melbourne *Age* reported him as saying that he 'had no difficulty with the natives' who were 'of a harmless nature'.[72] However, in a telegram he sent to Darwin when he first arrived at Katherine he said that the expedition encountered hostile Aborigines and were 'compelled to fire on them in self defence'.[73] In other words, O'Donnell 'sanitised' his later accounts. Finally, Stockdale's party had two violent encounters with Aborigines, each of them almost certainly causing the deaths of Aboriginal men,[74] but these occurred after VRD, Wave Hill and Ord River had been stocked with cattle, a circumstance which completely changed the situation for the Aborigines.

Clearly something had changed by 1882. The obvious question is what happened to cause this change? Why didn't the Aborigines treat the Duracks, Saunders and Johns and O'Donnell in the same way that they'd treated the earlier intruders? There are a number of possible explanations. One is that one of the earlier expeditions had experienced violent conflict with Aborigines that it didn't report, and the affected Aborigines exacted a reprisal on the next group of white men who appeared. Trouble could easily have occurred by 'accident', with one side or the other feeling threatened and acting in self defence. For example, a ritualised friendly approach by a group of Aborigines could have been misinterpreted by the whites as a pending attack. Trouble could also have occurred if innocent actions by one side caused an affront to the other. For example, a white party could have inadvertently entered or damaged a sacred area.

Another possible source of trouble was interference with Aboriginal women. According to an 1893 report in the *Adelaide Advertiser*, 'a half-caste youth, aged about 20, has been found among the Osmond tribe' on Ord River Station.[75] It was suggested that he was a 'relic' of the Leichhardt expedition of 1848, but if his age estimate was correct he would have been born around 1873, more than 20 years after Leichhardt's party was likely to have been anywhere near the region. If he'd been fathered by a member of one of the known land-seeking or prospecting expeditions which had passed through the Ord River area, he would have been no more than 14 rather than 'about twenty', so perhaps his age was overestimated, or there was an unknown expedition in the area in early 1870s.

---

72   'Exploration in the Northern Territory', *The Age*, 6th November 1883, p. 6.
73   'Latest telegrams. Return of the Kimberley exploration party', *Northern Territory Times*, 28th March 1885, p. 3.
74   Ricketson, pp. 115–17, 201.
75   'The Leichhardt party', *Adelaide Advertiser*, 28th November 1893, p. 5.

Another reason for the change in Aboriginal response from avoidance to aggression could relate to events well outside the region. Construction of the Overland Telegraph Line began in 1870. After its completion Europeans were permanently based at telegraph stations at Katherine River, Elsey Creek, Daly Waters, Powells Creek and elsewhere,[76] and there was a constant movement of teamsters, prospectors and others up and down the line. Wherever it went the line cut through Aboriginal land, so it was inevitable that Aboriginal people living in those lands would come into contact with Europeans. The countries of two tribes, the Mudbura and the Wardaman, extend from the Victoria River valley to within 50 kilometres of the telegraph line – only a 'spears' throw' away.[77] Members of these tribes undoubtedly were well informed about the activities of the whites and had opportunities to visit the line to see white men for themselves. Such contact could explain how Aborigines in Wardaman country knew the words 'whitefellow Jimmy very good' which they called out to Sullivan and McDonald on Gregory Creek in 1878.[78]

Aborigines from deeper within the Victoria River region also could have had direct experience of Europeans who were based on or travelling along the telegraph line during the 1870s. The long-distance 'periodic journeys' described by RH Mathews would have brought Victoria River people into contact with white people, or at least, direct contact with Aborigines who had done so. Likewise, Aborigines living in areas where whites were active would have made similar journeys deep into unsettled regions and passed on their knowledge of the whites.

The significant role that such networks could play in frontier race relations was first revealed by Reynolds in 1978 in an article which examined how Aborigines responded to the coming of the white man in Queensland.[79] Later, in a major work titled *The Other Side of the Frontier*, he expanded this study to include data from elsewhere in Australia.[80] These ground-breaking studies revealed a wide variety of responses to early contact with Europeans

---

76   I Nesdale (ed.), *The Shackle: A Story of the Far North Australian Bush*, Lynton Publications, Adelaide, 1975.

77   P Sutton, L Coltheart and A McGrath, *The Mudbura Land Claim*, Northern Land Council, Darwin, 1983, pp. 73–75; N Tindale, *Aboriginal Tribes of Australia*, Australian National University Press, Canberra, 1974, p. 232, and boundaries map, N.W. Sheet; F Merlan, *A Grammar of Wardaman: A Language of the Northern Territory of Australia*, Mouton de Gruyter, New York, 1994.

78   'Trip to the Victoria River'.

79   H Reynolds, 'Before the instant of contact: some evidence from nineteenth-century Queensland', *Aboriginal History*, vol. 2, part 1, 1978, pp. 63–69.

80   Reynolds, *Other Side*, chapter 1.

and showed how these responses were modified and evolved as the realities of white settlement became apparent. Many of these responses were repeated as the frontier reached new areas including, as will be seen, the Victoria River District.

Reynolds presented evidence that by means of indigenous networks, items of European manufacture including steel axes, pieces of iron and glass, and tobacco reached Aborigines far beyond the frontier. In addition, Reynolds showed that people received a substantial amount of reliable information about Europeans – their behaviour and possessions, weapons, animals, the ecological impact of their livestock, and even massacres committed by them. He suggested that the information received 'was probably a vital influence on Aboriginal behaviour' towards the Europeans, and that 'White–Aboriginal relations did not begin anew in every district despite the pioneers' widespread perception about entering an untouched wilderness'. Instead, he argued, 'Aborigines responded to the newcomers armed with knowledge and expectations about them'.[81] While there is virtually no direct evidence in the historical record, it is inconceivable that descriptions of Europeans, English words and material goods did not precede actual European settlement in the Victoria River region. There can be little doubt that this was the situation when the first settlers arrived in the Victoria River country.

In the decade before the settlers reached the Victoria River there were occasional conflicts between Aborigines and Europeans along the Overland Telegraph Line. These included several attacks on whites in the Newcastle Waters area in 1872,[82] the killing of August Henning on the Howley north of Pine Creek in 1873,[83] and the killing early in 1878 of a teamster named James Ellis on the headwaters of the Douglas River, north-west of Pine Creek. In the latter case a party of police and volunteers followed tracks leading from the crime scene towards the Daly River. Near the river they came upon a group of Aborigines allegedly involved in Ellis' murder and shot 17 of them.[84] News of this massacre, and probably news of

81 Reynolds, 'Before the instant of contact', pp. 63–69.
82 A Giles, *Exploring in the 'Seventies and the Construction of the Overland Telegraph Line*, Friends of the State Library of South Australia, Adelaide, 1995 p. 144–45, 150–51.
83 'The Murder by natives', *Northern Territory Times*, 21st November 1873, p. 9. The Howley was a mine about 60 kilometres north-west of Pine Creek (see foldout map in T Jones, *Pegging the Territory: A History of Mining in the Northern Territory of Australia, 1873–1946*, Northern Territory Government Printer, Darwin, 1987).
84 'News and Notes', *Northern Territory Times*, 2nd February 1878, p. 2; State Records of South Australia: Northern Territory 'Department' incoming correspondence (outgoing correspondence), 87/1878, telegram from Government Resident Edward Price to the minister of education, 26th January 1878.

the other conflicts, would have been rapidly communicated to the Victoria River tribes.

Whatever the Aborigines learnt, it seems unlikely that much of it would have inspired them to welcome the newcomers. At the very least, the appearance of the prospectors and land-seekers in the district would have contributed to a growing awareness among Victoria River Aborigines of the approach of European settlement. Hearing of violent encounters occurring anywhere in the wider region would have made them very wary of the settlers when they finally did arrive, and more inclined to warfare than a warm welcome.

Chapter 4

THE COMING OF THE CATTLE

When the first cattlemen arrived in the Victoria River country they entered a landscape dominated by thinly timbered grasslands. Today, vegetation in much of the region can still be characterised as thinly timbered grassland, but there's clear evidence that the landscape is no longer as open as it was 100 or more years ago. Between 1995 and 2002 I compiled over 100 repeat photo pairs[1] – a technique that involves rephotographing a scene in an historical photograph by locating as closely as possible the original vantage point. By comparing the second photo with the original, various environmental changes in the intervening time period may be revealed. I also interviewed many elderly Victoria River District residents (or former residents), including cattlemen, cattlewomen and Aborigines. Together, the repeat photos and the oral testimony document a major increase in the number of trees on the riverine plains throughout the district.[2] There is also evidence that some formerly widespread plant and animal species have severely declined in distribution and overall numbers, and that the steep and thickly vegetated banks of the rivers and creeks that once gave so much trouble to the explorers no longer exist.

The obvious question here is, what happened to change the environment from that encountered by the explorers and early settlers to what is seen today? Changed fire regimes, feral animal invasions, long-term climatic cycles and even climate change are likely to have played a part, but there can be little doubt that a major factor has been the impact of cattle.

Bringing cattle to the Victoria River country was part of a much larger process. First, land speculators – identified as such because their names appear and very quickly disappear from the historic record – began taking up options

---

1   My study was the first in Australia to use repeat photography to document environmental change across an entire region and from almost the time of first settlement to the present. It is now recommended by the CRC as a model for similar work elsewhere in the northern savannahs (see *Savanna Links*, no. 29, July–September, 2004, p. 6).

2   D Lewis, *Slower than the Eye Can See: Environmental Change in Northern Australia's Cattle Lands*, Tropical Savannas CRC, Darwin, 2002.

for leases in the district. In the Victoria River District this began early in 1876,[3] and various other options and leases were taken up before the first settlers arrived with herds of cattle in 1883. One of the reasons it took so long for bona fide cattlemen to arrive may have been the cost. Before 1881 pastoral rent was sixpence per square mile for the first seven years of a 25 year lease, rising to ten shillings per square mile thereafter. In 1881 the rent after seven years was reduced to two shillings and sixpence per square mile.[4] Before and after the cattle arrived there was a degree of 'juggling' of the various blocks taken up, and the boundaries of the stations today often bear little relationship to the boundaries that existed when the stations were first established.

Delamere Station was stocked in 1881. It straddled the divide between the Victoria River and the Daly River, though most of it was on the Daly River side. The cream of the country south and west of Delamere was stocked a few years later – Wave Hill and Victoria River Downs (VRD) in 1883,[5] Ord River in 1884,[6] Rosewood in 1885,[7] Auvergne in 1886,[8] and Newry (formerly Keep River) in 1888.[9] These were followed by Bradshaw in January 1894,[10] Waterloo, between 1895 and 1900,[11] and Inverway, in

3   For example, see Government Resident of the Northern Territory (South Australia) – inwards correspondence, 1870–1912, Northern Territory Archives (NTA), NTRS 790, items A1447, A1464, A1517, A2956 and A2957.

4   F Bauer, *Historical Geography of White Settlement in Part of the Northern Territory, Part 2. The Katherine–Darwin Region*, divisional report no. 64/1, CSIRO Division of Land Research & Regional Survey, Canberra, 1964, footnote, p. 112. PF Donovan claims that the regulations were changed in 1874, with the number of head per square mile being reduced from three to two and the time allowed for stocking increased to three years (*A Land Full of Possibilities, A History of South Australia's Northern Territory*, University of Queensland Press, Brisbane, 1981, pp. 121–22).

5   JL Parsons, 'Quarterly Report on Northern Territory', 11th November 1884, *South Australian Parliamentary Papers*, vol. 3, no. 53B, 1884, p. 2; A Giles, 'Early drovers in the Northern Territory – leaves from the diary of Alfred Giles', *The Pastoralists' Review*, 15th March 1906, p. 40.

6   D Swan, cited in C Clement and P Bridge (eds), *Kimberley Scenes: Sagas of Australia's Last Frontier*, Hesperian Press, Perth, 1991, pp. 94–95.

7   M Durack, *Kings in Grass Castles*, Corgi Books, Sydney, 1986, p. 267.

8   'Country notes. Katherine River', *Northern Territory Times*, 28th August 1886, p. 3.

9   'The late Mr Frank Connor, MLC', *The Pastoral Review*, 16th September 1916, p. 827; M Durack, *Sons in the Saddle*, Corgi Books, Sydney, 1985, pp. 25–26.

10   NTA: Log Book of Bradshaw's Run, January 1894, NTRS 2261.

11   The Government Resident's Report in the *South Australian Parliamentary Papers* (vol. 2, no. 45, 1900, p. 28) and the Timber Creek police journal (12 October 1900, NTA: F302) both indicate that Waterloo was stocked in 1900, but Charlie Flinders, an early resident of Wyndham, reckons it was taken up in the mid–1890s (C Flinders, 'Forty-five years in the great nor-west of Western Australia', unpublished typescript, Australian National University library repository, 1933. The memoir is divided into different sections, most of which are called chapters, but page numbering restarts at the beginning of each section. The information about Waterloo is on p. 2 of the section headed

about 1902.[12] Willeroo was formed to the south of Delamere in 1884,[13] but in a remarkable series of lease forfeitures and boundary adjustments, within 20 years their positions were reversed, with Willeroo located north of Delamere.[14] Large areas along the north coast (Legune, Bullo River) were originally held under grazing permits, later converted to pastoral leases.[15]

Obtaining a lease in the Victoria River District was only the first step in what was a huge undertaking. First, cattle had to be obtained to stock the lease. For most of the early leaseholders this wasn't a great problem; they were often already relatively wealthy and the owners of stations in the eastern states. They could send cattle north from their own properties or purchase them closer to the intended destination. Among such men were Dr WJ Browne, the original owner of Springvale, Delamere and Newcastle Waters stations,[16] the wealthy Melbourne businessmen and pastoralists CB Fisher and Maurice Lyons, who owned VRD and other Top End properties[17] and JA Macartney, owner of a pastoral empire in Queensland, who stocked Auvergne Station.[18] Bluey Buchanan, who first took up Wave Hill, was of much more limited means, but he was able to form a partnership with his

'Why give our north away?' While the broad outlines of Flinders' commentary are accurate, many of the details he provides are unreliable).

12   There are several different claims about when Inverway was taken up and when it was stocked (L Biltris, 'The passing of the pioneers', *Walkabout*, 1st May 1951, p. 44; M Hilgendorf, *Northern Territory Days*, Historical Society of the Northern Territory, Darwin, c. 1995, p. 35; R Reynolds, 'Recalling the past. The brothers Farquharson', *The Pastoral Review*, 19th April 1965, p. 363–64). However, the facts appear to be that the station was taken up in the late 1890s and 1900, and was stocked late in 1901 or early in 1902 (JAG Little, 'Notes of annual inspecting journey of overland telegraph line, from Port Darwin to Attack Creek', *Northern Territory Times*, 30th August 1901, p. 2; Timber Creek police journal, 16th October 1901, NTA: F302).

13   'Notes from the Victoria River', *Northern Territory Times*, 29th August 1885 p, 4.

14   Vern O'Brien, pers. comm., summary of Northern Territory Lands Department records on Willeroo, Delamere and related leases, January 2004.

15   An article in *Hoofs & Horns* magazine (August 1959, p. 46) announced the ballot for the Bullo River block and said that it was '... an old Grazing Licence formerly held by Connor, Doherty and Durack'. According to Flo Martin, Legune was first gazetted in about 1905 and initially the land was held under grazing licenses (F Martin, *Three Families Outback in Australia's Tropic North*, privately published, Geralton, 1980, p. 29). Records in the NTA (F199, PP 114, 1914) indicate that an area of 706 square miles was taken up under pastoral permit on 21st April 1903 by IS Emanuel, Sydney Kidman and Alexander Reith Troup.

16   GR McMinn, 'Quarterly Report on the Northern Territory', 7th August 1883, *South Australian Parliamentary Papers*, vol. 4, no. 53A, 1884, pp. 1–2; 'Notes of the Week', *Northern Territory Times*, 14th December 1894, p. 3.

17   J Makin, *The Big Run: The Story of Victoria River Downs*, 2nd edition, Rigby Publishers, Adelaide, 1983, p. 57.

18   H Gibbney, 'JA Macartney (1834–1917)', *Australian Dictionary of Biography*, vol. 5, Melbourne University Press, 1966, pp. 126–27.

brother William, a successful New South Wales pastoralist.[19] The main exception to this cavalcade of the wealthy was the Farquharson brothers who established Inverway. After they obtained their lease they had to spend several years droving and horse dealing in Queensland before they could afford to buy cattle to stock the property.[20]

Sometimes the cattle were bought from stations in north Queensland. This saved on droving costs because the distance to drive the cattle was shorter and the drover could hire a team of stockmen and a cook from the same area. The classic example here is the famous cattle drive of 1881–82 when Bluey Buchanan organised the movement of 20,000 head into the Territory on behalf of Fisher and Lyons.[21] These were obtained from Norley, Wilmot, Currawillingi, Richmond Downs, Dalgonally and Dougall River[22] – all Queensland stations – and were destined for Marrakai, Glencoe and Daly River stations in the Adelaide River and Daly River country. Many were later taken from these stations to stock VRD.[23] Other stock came from much further afield; for instance, Willeroo was stocked with cattle from the owners' property near Lake George, in New South Wales.[24]

There was nowhere to buy supplies between Burketown and Katherine, a distance of about 900 kilometres, so sufficient rations for the men had to be bought and carried with them. There are no records to tell us exactly what these rations were or what quantity was required. No doubt the basics were flour, tea, sugar and salt, and we can gain an idea of the quantity by looking at the amount needed by drover John Skuthorpe's team of 25 men in 1906. Skuthorpe had been hired to take 3000 cattle from Wave Hill to Narrabri in northern New South Wales. Because the Wave Hill store had burnt down before he arrived there he had to arrange for supplies to be sent to him from Katherine. He ordered seven tons.[25]

Once the first herd got past Katherine, or perhaps Delamere, someone had to ride ahead to find the best track. At least one of the early drovers had a copy of Augustus Gregory's journal and followed his route for part of the way. This was Paddy Cahill's brother, Tom, who was taking some of the first cattle

19 B Buchanan, *In the Tracks of Old Bluey: The Life Story of Nat Buchanan*, University of Central Queensland Press, Rockhampton, 1997, p. 106.
20 Biltris, p. 44.
21 B Buchanan, *Tracks*, p. 69.
22 ibid., pp. 71, 78; 'The wide north', *Sydney Morning Herald*, 19th February 1921, p. 14.
23 B Buchanan, *Tracks*, p. 86.
24 'Mr Robert Cowley Cooper', *The Pastoral Review*, 15th April 1914, p. 332.
25 'A big overland trip. Notes by the way.' *The Morning Bulletin* (Rockhampton), 28th April 1906, p. 9.

to Wave Hill.[26] The existence of a copy of Gregory's map in the collection of VRD records at the Noel Butlin Archives in Canberra suggests that the early settlers on VRD may have used it to find their way around the district.[27] Later drovers benefited from the knowledge of those who preceded them. Bob Button, a drover employed by Bluey Buchanan to take the first cattle across to stock Ord River Station, hired stockman Bill Weldon to guide him on the last stage from VRD.[28] Weldon, a young man who claimed to have been an active sympathiser with the Kelly gang,[29] knew the track to the Ord because he'd helped the Duracks take cattle there a few months earlier.[30]

When the settlers reached their destination, or even before they arrived, someone had to explore enough of the station to find a good place to release the cattle and a good site to build a homestead. The Duracks had explored the Ord River country before they brought cattle overland[31] and probably had a fair idea where to take their herds. Even so, when their cattle arrived on the Ord, MJ Durack went ahead 50 kilometres with a packhorse to select a site for a homestead.[32] On Wave Hill Sam Croker erected a rough homestead before the first cattle arrived,[33] and on VRD Croker and Lindsay Crawford were looking for a homestead site shortly before the first cattle arrived there late in 1883.[34]

The cattle were released in the best area for water and grass, but they were kept within a 'cattle boundary'. One reason for this was that until cattle (and horses and mules) become familiar with their new territory they're inclined to stray, or even to return to their old haunts, sometimes hundreds of kilometres away. To prevent this, men had to 'ride the tracks' to turn straying cattle back towards the main herd.[35] A case of cattle probably trying to return 'home' happened soon after Wave Hill was stocked when a number of beasts headed

---

26   *Sydney Morning Herald*, 19th February 1921, p. 14.
27   Noel Butlin Archives (NBA), The Australian National University: Goldsbrough Mort Collection, F246, 2/859/378.
28   Durack, *Kings*, p. 267.
29   W Linklater and L Tapp, *Gather No Moss*, Hesperian Press, Perth, 1997 (1968), p. 22.
30   Durack, *Kings*, p. 264.
31   ibid., pp. 217–30.
32   ibid., p. 267.
33   A Lucanus, cited in Clement and Bridge, p. 24.
34   'Massacres in the Northern Territory ... Paddy Cahill's list', *The Register* (Adelaide), 18th December 1905, p. 5.
35   Lindsay Crawford mentioned that 'It is not the cattle that causes so much wear and tear on horses but keeping the blacks out side the cattle boundaries'. L Crawford to HWH Stevens, 8th November 1886, Goldsbrough Mort and Co. Ltd, Head Office, Melbourne: letters received from HWH Stevens, Port Darwin, re. NT property and butchering business, 1889–1892, NBA: 2/872.

east across a long stretch of desert country south of the Murranji Track. With the benefit of showers of rain, Croker and a couple of Aboriginal stockmen followed the cattle through the desert, a region that probably hasn't been crossed on horseback since and which is still regarded by whites as a fierce and dangerous place which they rarely visit. Croker and his men caught up with the cattle on Tomkinson Creek, over 250 kilometres from Wave Hill.[36]

Another reason to keep the cattle within a particular area was that it was easier to muster them and, as it was soon discovered, easier to protect them from attack by Aborigines.[37] In 1886 the manager of VRD spent £500 on horses without authority from head office because, he remarked, 'It is not the cattle that causes so much wear and tear on horses but keeping the blacks outside the cattle boundaries'. Even in 1894 and 1895 there were still 'cattle boundaries' on VRD.[38]

In the 1880s the law required leaseholders to stock their land within three years with two head of cattle per square mile,[39] but it's doubtful if more than one or two stations ever fulfilled this requirement. For example, allowing for natural increase amongst cattle brought onto the station during the first year, the 12,000 square mile VRD would have needed a founding herd of at least 12,000 head in 1883 to be able to have 24,000 head by 1886.[40] However, in 1889 the Government Resident reported that VRD had only 13,000 to 14,000 cattle on the station.[41] Extensions of time to stock could be applied for, but the reality was that compliance with the law was rarely if ever investigated.[42] Once the first herd or two reached a station the leaseholders would declare the stations stocked with any shortfall in legal requirements eventually corrected as the foundation herds grew.

---

36 G Buchanan, *Packhorse and Waterhole: With the First Overlanders to the Kimberleys*, facsimile edition, Hesperian Press, Perth, 1984 (1933), pp. 120–21; 'Recalling the past: some notes on Nat Buchanan', *The Pastoralists Review and Graziers Record*, 18th August 1961, pp. 899–90; C Hemphill, letter to the editor, *The Adelaide Observer*, 4th April 1891, p. 27.
37 G Buchanan, *Packhorse*, pp. 164–65.
38 For example, see the Timber Creek police journal, 8th July 1894 and 29th November 1895 (NTA: F302).
39 F Bauer, footnote on p. 112; Donovan, 1981, pp. 121–22).
40 On the basis of data I provided to him in 2004, this estimate was made by Ian McBean, a former stockman and drover, former owner of Innesvale, Coolibah and Bradshaw stations, and formerly chairman of the Top End branch of the Northern Territory Cattlemen's Association.
41 HWH Stevens, cited in JL Parsons, 'Report on the Northern Territory for Year 1889', *South Australian Parliamentary Papers*, vol. 2, no. 28, 1890, p. 2.
42 R Duncan, *The Northern Territory Pastoral Industry 1863–1910*, Melbourne University Press, 1967, p. 117.

No matter what the numbers of cattle were when the stations were declared stocked, only a small portion of each run was occupied by the cattle and large areas which were potentially cattle country were still effectively 'blackfella country'. For example, six years after the first cattle arrived on VRD a visitor noted that 'little really is known of any part of the property except that occupied by the cattle, which is scarcely 1/8th of the whole area, & that eighth not more than one third stocked'.[43] As cattle numbers grew, more land was occupied by them, causing a corresponding reduction in the area of land that Aborigines had more or less to themselves. On VRD it was not until about 1920 that cattle numbers reached an estimated 120,000, a level at which they were to remain for decades, if efforts to calculate them were remotely accurate.[44] This was nearly 40 years after the first cattle arrived and it's possible that, even then, numbers were still increasing.

Initially, most 'homesteads' are unlikely to have been more than rough camps, with a canvas fly or two for shade or rain protection. This was certainly the case on Inverway where the Farquharson brothers lived under canvas for four years until their homestead was built.[45] It was probably a similar situation on Rosewood Station where Anne Spring, on the Behn River above Cowardys yard, is identified by local Aborigines as the site of the first homestead.[46] The site doesn't appear to have any of the debris usually associated with other early European sites in the district – fragments of glass and iron, empty cartridge cases, worn-out horseshoes, a stone fireplace and so on.[47] It may be that a more intensive search will reveal such remains, but it's just as likely that it was a temporary canvas 'homestead'.

On Bradshaw, a temporary camp was established in May 1894 on the banks of the Victoria River at the base of the Dome and all the stores and equipment were landed there.[48] However, everything was soon moved back onto a boat to

43   NBA: Goldsbrough Mort & Co: sundry papers re. CB Fisher and the Northern Australia Territory Co., 1886–92, 2/876/7, B Blair to Goldsbrough Mort & Co., 24 October 1889.
44   By 1921, estimates of cattle numbers on VRD ranged from 119,000 ('Central Australia. Cattle and horse breeding', *Sydney Morning Herald*, 21st June 1921, p. 8) to 170,000 ('The Northern Territory. Its pastoral possibilities', *The Age*, 4th October 1921, p. 6), and similar estimates were made for many decades to come (see Lewis, *Slower*, p. 80; Makin, p. 169).
45   Hilgendorf, p. 35.
46   Doug Struber, pers. comm. Struber has been manager of Rosewood since 1998.
47   I have documented many of the early (pre-1910) homestead sites in the Victoria River District for the National Trust of Australia (see references in bibliography), and all have the type of debris described here.
48   NTA: NTRS 2261, 17th May 1894.

prevent theft by Aborigines.[49] In September a homestead was established some distance up Angalarri Creek at 'Youngsford'.[50] A year later this 'homestead' was described as 'an open shed' and the outbuildings as, 'very sketchily built'.[51]

As soon as possible more substantial homesteads were built, mostly from available bush materials. At Ord River, 'a hut was built of bloodwood saplings, with a greenhide roof, as grass was out of the question ... There was plenty of ventilation. When the wind blew it whistled through the cracks in fine style'.[52] All the timber for the first Inverway homestead was cut on the property, but because of the hostility of the Aborigines 'the work of the three men was hampered by the necessity of always keeping guard. One brother stood guard at all times with the guns loaded while the others cut and adzed the timber for their homestead'.[53] Slab huts with bark roofs were built at Wave Hill while at VRD (Stockyard Creek) in 1891, the buildings were described as a 'Hipped roof house 30' x 20' Iron roof, paper [bark] walls 10 ft verandah ... One Building including Beef room, Saddle room, men's room 50' x 12' all paper [bark]'.[54] At the site today there is a large flagstone floor, probably from the house. Other buildings may have had floors of hard-packed earth or antbed.[55]

If homesteads built of timber or clad in bark were not continuously occupied there was a danger that they could be destroyed by fire – either bushfires or fires lit deliberately by Aborigines. This happened at least twice in the early days, first in 1893 at Price's Creek, in the north-east of the district,[56] and again

---

49   HYL Brown, 'Government Geologist's Report on explorations in the Northern Territory', *South Australian Parliamentary Papers*, vol. 3, no. 82, 1895, p. 3.

50   NTA: NTRS 2261, 22nd September 1894. Probably named after Hugh Young, one of Joe Bradshaw's employees.

51   K Dahl, *In Savage Australia: An Account of a Hunting and Collecting Expedition to Arnhem Land and Dampier Land*, Allan, London, 1926, p. 190.

52   Swan, p. 96; normally grass was considered out of the question because of the risk of fire, but at least two of the early settlers roofed their huts with cane grass.

53   Biltris, p. 44.

54   NBA: Goldsbrough Mort and Co. Ltd: sundry papers re. CB Fisher and the Northern Australia Territory Co., 1886–92, 2/872, HWH Stevens to Goldsbrough Mort, 1st June 1891.

55   Personal observation at the site of the Stockyard Creek homestead (see D Lewis, *The Final Muster: A Survey of Previously Undocumented Sites throughout the Victoria River District*, report prepared for the National Trust of Australia (Northern Territory), 2000, pp. 64–70).

56   NTA: Government Resident of the Northern Territory (South Australia) – inwards correspondence, 1870–1912, NTRS 790, item 5889, A Giles to Government Resident Charles Dashwood, 15th December 1893; NTA: NTRS 790, item, 6050, 'The Government Resident's Trip Up Country', diary of Government Resident Charles Dashwood. Dashwood's trip began on 27th October 1893 and finished on 15th November 1893.

at Wave Hill in 1899.[57] In both instances Aborigines were blamed. A number of very early homesteads and outstations had walls of local stone, which had the advantage of being fireproof, termite-proof, spear-proof and cheap.[58] Some stations quickly progressed to construction with manufactured materials. A new homestead built at Delamere in about 1886 had three rooms and a veranda, sawn timber floors, and was constructed of iron and cypress pine,[59] while at Willeroo there was 'a two roomed galvanised iron house' by the early 1890s.[60]

Supplies often took months to arrive and were brought by boat to the Depot Landing on the lower Victoria River, or to Katherine or Wyndham, then on to the various stations. Initially, the stores were shifted by bullock and horse teams, or by packhorses, but the bullocks and horses couldn't take the often extreme heat, and horses also were prone to 'Walkabout disease'.[61] As a result, they were eventually largely replaced by pack-camels and donkey teams. Because of their isolation and the cost of cartage, the stations needed to be as self-contained as possible. On most of the original large holdings there was a blacksmith's shop, men's quarters, kitchen, saddle room and wagon shed. Station supplies came only once or twice a year, so a storeroom was also needed for the large amount of food, horseshoes, tools and other goods that arrived.

Water for domestic use was carried from a nearby waterhole in buckets attached to a yoke, or it was drawn from a well. Furnishings and other goods were often improvised from bush materials. At Ord River the table and bunks were made of bush timber and greenhide, with grass used for mattresses.[62] On one occasion the station had no lamps for a long period, so used 'cow manure instead of [*indecipherable*] fat which gave a good light … a fat lamp

---

57   A Richardson, *The Story of a Remarkable Ride*, The Dunlop Pneumatic Tyre Co. of Australasia Ltd, Perth, 1899, p. 14; 'The story of a remarkable ride', *Northern Territory Times*, 15th June 1900, p. 3.

58   See D Lewis *In Western Wilds: A Survey of Historic Sites in the Western Victoria River District*, report prepared for the National Trust of Australia (Northern Territory), 1993, vols 1 and 2, sites 25, 39, 40, 41, and 45; Lewis, *Final Muster*, site 8.

59   'For sale', *Northern Territory Times*, 11th June 1887, p2; A Giles, cited in 'Government Resident's Report on the Northern Territory for the Year ended June 30th 1891', *South Australian Parliamentary Papers*, vol. 2, no. 28, 1891.

60   NTA: NTRS 790, item 6891, 'Government Resident's Trip to the Victoria River', 10th November 1895 to 25th December 1895 (Government Resident Charles Dashwood).

61   'Walkabout disease' is caused by *Crotalaria crispata*, a small plant common in the Kimberley region of Western Australia. Poisoned horses become unaware of their surroundings and wander blindly (AL Rose et al, 'Field and Experimental Investigation of "Walkabout" disease of horses (Kimberley horse disease) in northern Australia: Crotallaria Poisoning in horses. Part 1', *The Australian Veterinary Journal*, February 1957, pp. 25–33 and Part 2, *Australian Veterinary Journal*, March 1957, pp. 49–62.

62   Swan, p. 96.

An east Kimberley bulllock team, early 1900s.

Western Australian Pastoralist and Grazier, 30 November 1925, p. 32

Camels and packs at the Victoria River Depot, c1912

Johns collection

was then considered an amenity, and an oil lamp was a luxury!'[63] Ord River and probably neighbouring stations obtained salt for salting beef and table use from a natural salt deposit on the Negri River. This was 'scraped off the rocks by the blacks and often had a lot of small stones in it which one found at times when eating salt beef'.[64]

On many stations conditions for employees (other than, perhaps, the manager) remained rough for decades. For example, Myra Hilgendorf visited many of the homesteads and outstations in the district in 1939. She described Birrindudu Outstation as being 'in a most deplorable condition' with the buildings consisting of 'bough shades and iron huts'. There was no stove in the kitchen 'and apparently no utensils'.[65] At Limbunya she found the floor of the main room was stone-flagged and the others made of crushed ant-bed. There was no glass or fly wire on the windows which were instead covered with an iron flap that could be propped open with a pole. The beds were made from 'logs and rawhide' and in cold weather heating was provided by a wood fire in a drum.[66] At Gordon Creek Outstation on VRD the first 'homestead' was built in about 1930 of bush timber and paperbark.

As well as homesteads and outbuildings, yards had to be built. The method of 'cattle management' that prevailed on the stations during the first 80 years or so of settlement was what is now known as the 'open-range system'. As described above, the first cattle were turned loose on the most favourable part of the run but no fences were built, and as their numbers increased the cattle spread onto new areas of the station. In the late-nineteenth century cattle could only be branded in yards, but yards were expensive to construct.[67] On most stations only a few yards were built in convenient centralised locations and cattle were mustered and brought to them. Twelve years after VRD was settled there were only three yards on the station and many cattle had to be driven 70 kilometres to reach the nearest one.[68] Some of the managers complained about the lack of yards and requested permission to construct more. For example, in March 1899 Bob Watson, the manager of VRD, wrote to his employers saying that:

---

63 WD Moore, 'Bush ingenuity: on a Kimberley cattle station in the early days', *North Australian Monthly*, December 1959, p. 50.
64 ibid.
65 Hilgendorf, p. 47.
66 ibid., p. 32.
67 Duncan, pp. 66–69.
68 NBA: Goldsbrough Mort and Co. Ltd, report on VRD, Goldsbrough Mort & Co.: Board papers, 1893–1927, 2/124/1659, Jack Watson to Goldsbrough Mort & Co. Ltd, 5th December 1895.

Insufficient yard accommodation has been a great drawback, necessitating many long drives which wastes much valuable time ... With the present [*yard*] accomoditation it is impossible to get through the whole heard once a year ... The most economical way to rectify this, at the present time, would be ... to erect A branding Yard on Camfield Crk. This being the sentre of a large mob of cattle.[69]

In spite of the obvious need, the owners of the stations – usually companies and absentee landlords – were reluctant to spend the necessary money, especially during the depression of the 1890s.[70]

During the 1890s however, H Compton 'Compie' Trew was developing what became known as the 'open bronco' method of handling cattle for branding, a technique which did away with the need for yards. Trew's system involved holding cattle in a 'yard' formed by a number of mounted horsemen while each beast that needed branding or other treatment was roped from horseback and dragged out of the herd. Before beginning this work a tree was prepared by having one side of a fork or a convenient branch cut off about 30 centimetres from its base to form a 'hook'. The horseman dragging the beast would ride past the 'hook' and place the rope in it, and then keep dragging the animal until it was held tight against the tree and largely immobilised. Men on the ground then leg-roped and threw it, and treated it as required. Apart from some initial experimentation at Glen Helen Station in Central Australia, Trew developed his method at Clifton Hills Station in north-eastern South Australia. The technique quickly spread from there, and reached the Victoria River District some time in the early 1900s.[71]

One drawback to the bronco technique was that it was labour intensive. Because there was continuous conflict between the Aborigines and the settlers during the first 20 or so years of settlement, stockmen were either white people or Aborigines brought in from distant areas. Coming from distant areas meant that these 'foreign' Aboriginal workers had no relationships or allegiances with local Aborigines and didn't speak or understand the local languages.[72] Consequently they were as much the enemy to local Aborigines as the whites were and could be trusted to always side with the whites.

---

69 NBA: Goldsbrough Mort and Co. Ltd: Reports on station properties, 1898–1901, 2/307/1, Watson to Goldsbrough Mort and Co. Ltd, March 1899.

70 'The Victoria River and the meat works', *Northern Territory Times*, 20th June 1902, p. 3.

71 D Lewis, *Roping in the History of Broncoing*, Central Queensland University Press, Rockhampton, 2007, p. 40–41.

72 E Hill, *The Territory*, Angus and Robertson, Sydney, 1951, p. 175.

Whether black or white, stockmen had to be paid, and wages in this remote and dangerous area were high.[73] However, when 'blacks camps' were established near the homesteads in the period 1900–05, local Aborigines provided a ready pool of unpaid labour and the reliance on Aborigines from distant places diminished. The 'blacks camps' thus provided the necessary labour when the open bronco technique was introduced. Many of the so-called 'civilised' local people – Aborigines who ceased opposing the whites and learnt basic English and station skills – quickly became proficient at station work and a particular station economy developed which was to last for more than 50 years. The situation at Wave Hill in 1910 was typical:

> There were only two white men and about thirty blacks. The natives were real wonderful workers. Both the men and the gins are experts, and throwing and branding went along like clockwork. Amongst the women were three black gins, who were doing the best work I have ever seen on the face of a cattle camp. The gins are the best workers on horse back – far before the boys ... The minute you cut a beast out on the edge of the camp there was a gin to take it away from you. One little halfcaste girl about fourteen was a splendid hand at the game. I never saw better work than she was doing ... The blacks only work during the branding and mustering, and when the busy season is over they take off their clothes and return to the bush until again wanted.[74]

The only details that can be added to this description are that Aborigines who were too old, sick or young to work were provided with subsistence rations[75] and that the clothes the Aboriginal workers took off at the end of the 'busy season' were handed in to the station store. These clothes were held there and re-issued to the workers at the beginning of the next work season.[76]

During the first two decades of settlement the stations had difficulty finding markets for their cattle.[77] In the 1880s and 1890s small numbers were sold on the short-lived Kimberley and Pine Creek goldfields, a few herds

---

73   In the Ord River country in 1905 it was reported that wages for station hands were £2 per week whereas, in Queensland, it was £1 per week ('A big cattle trip. From Western Australia to Queensland', *The Morning Bulletin*, 29th August 1905, pp. 5–6).

74   'Station life', *Northern Territory Times*, 10th June 1910, p. 3.

75   R Berndt and C Berndt, *End of an Era: Aboriginal Labour in the Northern Territory*, Australian Institute of Aboriginal Studies, Canberra, 1987, p. 70; D Rose, *Hidden Histories: Black Stories from Victoria River Downs, Humbert River and Wave Hill Stations*, Aboriginal Studies Press, Canberra, 1991, pp. 201–02; A McGrath, *'Born in the Cattle': Aborigines in Cattle Country*, Allen & Unwin, Sydney, 1987, pp. 38–39.

76   Rose, pp. 201–02; McGrath, pp. 38–39.

77   Duncan, p. 46–77.

were taken overland around the West Australian coast to the Murchison goldfields and some were exported live to South-East Asian countries or to Fremantle[78] – but these markets either failed or were too small to absorb more than a fraction of the cattle available. However, events in Queensland finally gave the district an outlet for its stock.

In 1895–96 an epidemic of Redwater Fever, also known as Tick Fever, swept through Queensland and decimated the herds there; stations lost up to 90 per cent of their stock.[79] This calamity was followed by a series of dry years which lead up to another disaster – the great Queensland drought of 1902.[80] When the drought finally broke there was a big demand for cattle to restock the stations and to supply meat to the eastern markets. Prices rose to the point where two Victoria River station owners decided to see if it would be cost-effective to send cattle overland to the Queensland markets. As a result, throughout 1903, drovers began to converge on Wave Hill and VRD and the first herds left the region early in 1904, crossing the infamous Murranji Track and the immense Barkly Tableland, into Queensland. The experiment was successful and was the beginning of a great droving tradition that persisted for the next 60 years.[81]

The growth of the herds quickly outstripped the provision of infrastructure to handle them. In the absence of fencing, and with numerous creeks and frequent stretches of rough or scrubby country, it was impossible to muster every beast. The cattle quickly became wild and very difficult to handle and breeding was totally uncontrolled. On VRD, and probably elsewhere, these problems were noticeable as early as 1895 when the manager, Jack Watson, wrote a report on the station and commented on the state of the herd:

> one thing against them is their wildness it is necessary to gallop and gallop hard [after] Every lot of cattle you see & then almost invariably one or more will get away … of all the cattle branded so far ten per cent were from two years of age upwards … on Camfield creek I got fourteen hundred branders of this number five hundred were over eighteen months of age with calves at foot [and] bulls up to five years old I have shot two hundred and seventeen (217) unbranded bulls that

---

78   B Buchanan, *Tracks*, pp. 125–26, 133–34.
79   G Bolton, *A Thousand Miles Away: A History of North Queensland to 1920*, The Jacaranda Press in association with the Australian National University, Brisbane, 1963, p. 220.
80   ibid., p. 221.
81   D Lewis, *The Murranji Track: Ghost Road of the Drovers*, Central Queensland University Press, Rockhampton, 2007.

it was useless to brand & among them were brindled, brown, yellow spotted & every objectionable sort of beast.[82]

The cattle soon established an annual pattern of movement. When the rains came they spread out across the runs, then as the smaller waters dried up they gradually retreated to other waters until, by the end of the dry season, many were forced onto the river frontages. This wasn't a particular problem while the cattle numbers were small,[83] but by the 1920s on stations like VRD and Wave Hill, anything from 50,000 to 100,000 cattle or more could be concentrated on the river, with obvious and damaging implications for the environment.

The very fact of European livestock entering the region meant that changes to its ecology would occur.[84] Early reports make it clear that European animals found some plant species particularly attractive. Explorer AC Gregory's geologist, James Wilson, noted that the expedition horses were 'exceedingly fond' of the 'reeds'.[85] This fondness of horses for 'reeds' (*Chionacne*) was confirmed by Kieran Kelly who in 1999 led a packhorse expedition retracing part of Gregory's route.[86] Kelly noted that when his horses found relict patches of this grass they would eat compulsively and could hardly be driven away,[87] and similar grazing behaviour has been reported for cattle.[88] I've examined long stretches of the Victoria River, including specific areas where 'reeds' were reported by Stokes and Gregory, and I found that the impenetrable thickets of the early days no longer exist. It appears that intensive grazing by European livestock has wiped out this species in most of its former range.

The same fate has overtaken other plant species. In 1889 a pastoral inspector named B. Blair reported that in the wet season on VRD 'herbage & vines grow very prolific, & of these the stock are very fond'.[89] The vines would have included the species of melons described by Bluey Buchanan

---

82 NBA: 2/124/1659.
83 F Burt, cited in C Herbert, 'Government Resident's Report on the Northern Territory', December 1905, *South Australian Parliamentary Papers*, vol. 2, no. 45, 1906, p. 23.
84 Lewis, *Slower*, 2002.
85 J Wilson, 'Notes on the physical geography of north-west Australia', *Journal of the Geographical Society of London*, vol. 28, 1858, p. 145.
86 See K Kelly, *Hard Country Hard Men: In the Footsteps of Gregory* (Hale and Iremonger, Sydney, 2000, p. 253).
87 Kieran Kelly, pers. comm.
88 Darryl Hill, pers. comm. Hill was an officer with the Victoria River District Conservation Association.
89 NBA: 2/876/7.

in 1884 as being so plentiful in places that it would be easy to load drays with them.[90] The particular species Buchanan saw can't be identified with certainty,[91] but no species of indigenous melon is now common in the region, and when they are found it would be difficult to fill a bucket with them, let alone a dray.

Elderly Aborigines remember harvesting plants such as *kunjalu*, a water plant not yet identified and, *kayalarin*, a 'bush onion',[92] the latter once so prolific in the northern part of VRD that the Aborigines living there were referred to by their neighbours as 'kayalarin people'.[93] Extensive field surveys have failed to locate either of these plants in the region where they once grew.[94]

Early accounts make it clear that wildlife was abundant,[95] but they don't enable the full variety of species and their relative numbers or distribution to be assessed. Modern faunal surveys indicate that some mammal and bird species are uncommon or rare in the district today,[96] but Aboriginal memory and Dreamings show that this was not always so. The oldest Aborigines in the district can identify Dreaming sites for bandicoots, native cats, ringtail possums and gliding possums; species which they once hunted but which are now extremely rare or extinct in the region. A number of bird species have also declined markedly since European settlement. These include emus and flock pigeons. The latter (*Phaps histrionica*) is a species once seen in untold thousands on the inland plains.[97] According to senior Bilinara man, Anzac Munnganyi, Pigeon Hole, a waterhole and outstation on VRD, got its name because these pigeons once came to drink there. They are now seen only occasionally and usually in flocks of less than 100.

---

90   Parsons, 'Quarterly Report', vol. 3, pp. 2–3.
91   It was probably *A. Cucummis*, a species whose favoured habitat is black soil country.
92   Tentatively identified as *Typhonium lilifolium*.
93   P McConvell and A Palmer, *Yingawunarri Mudburra Land Claim*, Northern Land Council, Darwin, 1979, p. 14.
94   In the 1980s, Deborah Rose and I made a number of trips into areas where our Aboriginal guides had once harvested this plant, but none could be found.
95   For example, see JL Stokes, *Discoveries in Australia … During the Voyage of H.M.S. Beagle in the years 1837–43* (facsimile edition, State Library of South Australia, 1969 (1846), vol. 2, pp. 53, 61, 62).
96   W Low, B Strong and L Roeger, *Wave Hill Station Pastoral Lease 911*, report prepared for the Conservation Commission of the Northern Territory, Alice Springs, by WA Low Ecological Services, Alice Springs, 1986; WA Low, WR Dobbie and L Roeger, *Resource Appraisal of Victoria River Downs Station Pastoral Lease 680*, prepared for the Conservation Commission of the Northern Territory, Alice Springs, by WA Low Ecological Services, Alice Springs. 1988.
97   N Caley, *What Bird is That?: A Guide to the Birds of Australia*, Angus and Robertson Publishers, Sydney, 1985 (1931), p. 247.

Eroded country on Limbunya Station
Lewis collection

Team about to cross the Victoria River, 1922
Feast collection, National Museum of Australia

While cattle have grazing capacities and tastes that differ from native animals, they are also much heavier and have hard hooves which cut the surface of the ground, leaving it vulnerable to erosion. In 1889 a visitor to VRD noted that:

owing to the steep banks, it is only in odd places & rocky bars that stock can come to drink, the cattle are however gradually making fresh watering places. The numerous creeks have ... the same difficulty of stock getting at the water ... as in the rivers, steep treacherous banks.[98]

Thus, within six years of the station being stocked degradation of the riverbanks had begun. This was when the VRD herd only numbered something like 15,000. By 1896 the herd had increased to an estimated 30,000 and was already said to be out of hand.[99] By 1905 it had increased to 56,000,[100] by 1912 to between 110,000 and 120,000,[101] and by 1921 estimates ranged from 119,000[102] to 170,000.[103] It's clear that by this time the station had lost count and for decades afterwards estimates of cattle numbers were only 'guesstimates'.

By the 1920s there were several hundred thousand head of cattle in the Victoria River valley. When they congregated at the permanent waters towards the end of each dry season feed became very scarce for many kilometres out from the riverbanks and the ground was churned to dust. If the season had been a particularly bad one and the rains were late arriving, the situation became dire. In 1914 Wave Hill suffered a severe dry season and lost half its herd and a large number of horses.[104] Late in October 1936 VRD manager Alf Martin wrote to headquarters advising that 'we have been shifting cattle from place to place. We must have about 80,000 head of cattle on the River frontages and there is not a blade of grass for them to eat'.[105]

The effect these drought-induced concentrations had on the cattle themselves are revealed in a letter Martin wrote early in 1943:

At the latter end of 1942 we had very heavy losses in stock ... the cattle would go out chasing a storm and by the time they got back to the rivers

---

98 NBA: 2/876/7.
99 NBA: Goldsbrough Mort Papers, 2/176/206, Agreement between Goldsbrough Mort and John Stevenson, agent for John Richard, for sale of VRD, 1896.
100 Herbert, p. 8.
101 'News and Notes', *Northern Territory Times*, 15th March 1912, p. 3.
102 'Central Australia. Cattle and horse breeding', *Sydney Morning Herald*, 21st June 1921, p. 8.
103 'The Northern Territory. Its pastoral possibilities', *The Age*, 4th October 1921, p. 6.
104 'Victoria River Notes', *Northern Territory Times*, 21st January 1915, p. 14.
105 NBA: Bovril Australian Estates Pty Ltd, correspondence between Perth office of Bovril and Alfred Martin, manager/attorney at VRD, 1933–37, 87/8/274, A Martin to E Waugh, 12th October 1936.

they would be done. After a big drink in the river many were too weak to climb the steep banks. Practically every waterhole in the river had dead cattle in it. That is why we wrote ... that 20% should be written off for mortality percentage but am afraid we lost them as the writer had a good ride around the run before forming that estimate'.[106]

For years VRD alone suffered losses of up to 20,000 head every time there was a bad season. Such seasons occurred with monotonous regularity and similar losses are likely to have occurred on other stations in the district.

When the rains finally came there was widespread erosion and severe gullying occurred along the banks. When a major flood followed a prolonged dry period, the effects could be dramatic. This occurred in the wet season of 1934–35 when Martin reported that there had been:

> very big floods in our Rivers and miles of fencing has been washed away but there has been no loss of stock. Am afraid the big waterhole at the Head Station has suffered considerable damage by thousands of tons of the banks and timber falling into the bed. Big land slides caused the banks [*to collapse*] and trees that were 50 to 60 feet high on the banks are now standing upright in the centre of the stream. A few more floods like this one and we shall have to shift the station back from the River.[107]

The collapse of the banks wasn't limited to VRD homestead but extended well up the Wickham River[108] and, judging by the state of the river banks today, probably along much of the Victoria as well. It's unclear if a big flood similar to that of 1935 also occurred in the Ord River country, but after a decade of very dry years on both VRD and the Ord there were terrific floods on both rivers early in 1937. On Rosewood, owner-manager Jack Kilfoyle (son of Rosewood pioneer Tom Kilfoyle), remarked that 'Banks have been washed away, big old trees & great holes swirled out in the creeks. Cowdy [*Cowardy*] Crk is now nearly as big as the Behn [*River*]'.[109]

---

106 NBA: Bovril Australian Estates: correspondence between Australian Mercantile Land & Finance Co. Ltd, (AML&F) Sydney, and BAE Ltd, London, and station manager, 1939–1955, 119/6, A Martin to Lord Luke, 18th May 1943.

107 NBA: 87/8/274, A Martin to L Eichhorn, 25th March 1935.

108 C Schultz and D Lewis, *Beyond the Big Run: Station Life in Australia's Last Frontier*, University of Queensland Press, Brisbane, 1995, p. 156.

109 Rosewood Station rainfall book, held at the station.

Wason Byers (left) counting cattle with Jim Martin, c1940

Walkabout collection

Camels crossing the Wickham River, c1915

Townshend collection

In 1955 much the same sequence of events occurred again on VRD when a series of poor wet seasons and prolonged dry seasons were followed by a severe flood:

> The Wickham River finally rose to a height of 42 feet and the low ground encircling the Station buildings was under water for 12 hours. As the water subsided very large landslides occurred more or less continuously along the Wickham with the result that a large proportion of the splendid stand of timber which lined the banks has been deposited in the centre of the stream. Permanent and extensive damage has been done to the River.[110]

In this instance at least, the collapsing banks appear to have had a major impact on aquatic life. Lexie Simmons (formerly Bates) was living at VRD when the river banks collapsed. She recalled that, 'during the night, every now and then we'd hear a distant roar as parts of the riverbank caved in'.[111] Weeks later when the river had almost stopped running, a large congregation of birds was seen upstream near the crossing on the road to Pigeon Hole. Lexie and some other station people investigated and:

> couldn't get near it for the stench of rotting fish. The place was alive with kite hawks, crows and even a pair of wedge-tailed eagles, all feasting on the carcasses. About a month later we went back again to see what the birds had left, and found the whole crossing was covered with fish bones. Thousands of fish had perished there and from the size of some of the jawbones some of them were monsters. If you put your fingertips together and make a circle with your arms, you'll have some idea of the size of the mouths of these jawbones.[112]

As the herds grew, so did the number of cleanskin cattle. Wild bulls in particular became a serious problem, posing a danger to stockmen and preventing any chance of improving the quality of the herd. In 1929 an 'agricultural adviser' wrote that:

> With no exception the cattle in the outlying parts of all the large runs are wild and neglected.

---

110 NBA: Bovril Australian Estates Ltd, Records, Bovril Australian Estates: correspondence between AML&F Co. Ltd, Sydney, and station manager 1953–55, 119/7, VRD manager to AML&F, 16 March 1955.
111 D Lewis and L Simmons, *Kajirri: The Bush Missus*, Central Queensland University Press, Rockhampton, 2006, p. 113.
112 ibid., pp. 168–69.

There is no chance of segregation – cows and calves, steers and bullocks, bulls, young and old, mingle together and race away to cover at the approach of horsemen.

I spent two weeks with the musterers on Auvergne Station and in a mob of 1000 head gathered after three days (more than that number were too wild to hold and broke away) there were 270 unbranded cattle of all ages ranging from one month to ten years; there were approximately 100 bulls from 2 to 10 years old never before in a yard.[113]

On VRD the wild bull problem became especially severe and the station was renowned for the prodigious number of these animals. In 1934 there were said to be 1260 branded bulls on the books, but during an inspection 'thousands of clean skin bulls were seen of all ages and the most mongrel types imaginable. We have it on reliable authority that 20,000 clean skin bulls would be a conservative estimate'.[114] This situation prevailed for many decades. Although hundreds of bulls were shot every year the problem was only brought under control with fencing programs and the advent of helicopters in the 1970s.

In addition to the actual cattle numbers (both branded and cleanskin), there were also feral horses and donkeys throughout the region. Horses undoubtedly became brumbies at an early period but facts and figures are difficult to locate. Donkeys were being used as draft animals in the East Kimberley from at least 1896,[115] and from about 1917 to 1938, they were being used to haul station supplies from the Victoria River Depot to VRD, Wave Hill and other stations.[116] There are likely to have been occasional escapees from these sources, but during the 1930s motor vehicles began to supplant wagons as a means of transportation and many of the donkeys were turned bush.

Donkeys are remarkably fecund animals whose numbers can increase annually at a rate exceeding 20 per cent.[117] In the freedom of the bush they do exceptionally well. One of the earliest indications that they'd reached significant numbers is a Wave Hill police journal entry from November 1946 which states that a 'Truck load of donkey hides from Ord River ... passed

113 National Archives of Australia (NAA): FJS Wise, agricultural adviser to Sir Charles Nathan, Perth, 15th August 1929, A494/1, Item 902/1/82.
114 NAA: CRS F658, item 12 (Bradshaw), 'Report by the Northern Territory Pastoral Leases Investigation Committee'.
115 M Donaldson and I Elliot, *Do Not Yield to Despair: Frank Hugh Hann's Exploration Diaries in the Arid Interior of Australia 1895–1908*, Hesperian Press, Perth, 1988, p. 25.
116 The first mention of a donkey team in the Victoria River District comes from the Timber Creek police journal of 8th January 1917 (NTA: F302).
117 B Walsh, 'Feral animals', *Northern Grassy Landscapes Conference 29–31 August 2000 Katherine NT: Conference Proceedings*, Tropical Savannas CRC, Darwin, 2000, pp. 73–76.

en route Darwin'.[118] These were being sent by Vesteys for tanning to see if donkey leather was commercially viable, but it proved to be of poor quality.[119] Donkeys eventually reached such numbers that they seriously competed with the cattle for grass. For years station staff and professional shooters killed all they could, but they made little impact on overall numbers. It wasn't until the 1990s when the combined use of helicopters and 'Judas collars' – collars with radio transmitters, fitted on captured donkeys which are then released to rejoin their 'mates' in the bush – that the feral animal problem was largely solved.[120] Brumbies also became a problem, though never to the same degree as the donkeys. They were controlled with the same methods used against the donkeys.

The huge numbers of feral donkeys and brumbies which overran the district added enormously to the damage being inflicted on the land, flora and fauna by the uncontrolled and excessively large cattle herds on the stations. The end result of this 'system' of land management has been the extinction or severe reduction in range and numbers of various native plants and animals, widespread sheet and gully erosion, and the collapse of a large percentage of the original steep banks of the rivers and creeks. Water can now be accessed within a short distance almost anywhere.[121]

Attempts to decrease dependence on natural waters and increase the use of the abundant grasslands away from natural water sources began more than 30 years after the stations were stocked. Bores were first put down on Wave Hill in 1915[122] and on VRD in 1918,[123] but their numbers were limited and they were usually equipped with windmills which sometimes ceased to work at critical times through lack of wind. Gordon Buchanan wrote in 1936 that VRD had:

> only eight bores on thirteen thousand square miles of country all of which are hopelessly useless to water any quantity of stock, because they are neither equipped with storage tanks nor engines and solely depend on the windmill. The neighbouring company [*Wave Hill*] fares a little better on this point. They have a few bores, equipped with storage tanks and engines but far from being adequate for their requirements.

---

118 NTA: Wave Hill police journal, 11th November 1946, F292.
119 C McCool, et al, *Feral Donkeys in the Northern Territory*, Technical Bulletin no. 81/39, Conservation Commission of the Northern Territory, Darwin, 1981, p. 15.
120 D Lewis, *Slower.* p. 84.
121 ibid.
122 'Shipping', *Northern Territory Times*, 14 May 1914; *Northern Territory Times*,' News and Notes', 3 June 1914; 'Victoria River notes', *Northern Territory Times*, 21st January 1915.
123 Makin, pp. 111–12.

It is safe to say that the Bovril Company lose from ten to fifteen thousand head of cattle yearly for the need of bores and the necessary equipment to give them a drink.[124]

Fencing remained extremely limited and the open-range system of running cattle continued for decades. Gerry Ash, a stockman who worked on VRD in the early 1950s, described VRD as then possessing 'the largest uncontrolled herd in the world'[125] and on most other Victoria River District cattle stations the situation was little different.

The shortcomings of the open-range system were probably known from experiences in Queensland, well before the Victoria River country was stocked. Certainly, the advantages of fencing off natural waters were known at least as early as 1913.[126] In 1928 JK Little, who had worked on VRD in 1895–96, highlighted some of the problems in an article he wrote for the *Pastoralist's Review*:

> Victoria River Downs Station (Bovril Estates) is a huge area, including some very fair cattle country. Here, too, not much has been done to make a systematic working proposition of cattle. The long length of frontage does its best, which in any dry year end means loss, while better grassed, badly watered back country lies idle. As a result cattle get a spread on and go brumby ...

> A tremendous lot of the country on and adjacent to the Victoria River is broken by honey-combed limestone out from creek frontages, and a big percentage of the natural grass is not a drought resister. Still droughts, such as the Cooper heads know, do not occur in that part of the world, and the increase of cattle in a run of good seasons is remarkable. The losses sustained over a brief dry period can be likewise so. This, I reckon, is chiefly for want of better distribution to prevent heavy frontage stocking and consequent starvation. One must remember these frontages have had a good many doings during the years since Fisher and Lyons held the Victoria, and Buchanan owned Wave Hill [*1880s early 1890s*]. Also that out there the frontage country is really the least able to stand stocking closely.[127]

---

124 'Undeveloped cattle areas. Resumptions favoured', *Northern Standard*, 24th March 1936, p. 3.
125 Interviewed by the author at Derby, September 2000.
126 'Dr. Woolnough on the N. Territory', *Northern Territory Times*, 27th February 1913, p. 3.
127 S Kyle-Little (Culkah), 'In north Australia', pt 1, *The Pastoral Review*, 15th September 1928, pp. 884–85.

By 1945 there was scientific recognition of the shortcomings of the open-range system,[128] yet little was done to change it until the 1960s and 1970s.[129]

A number of reasons can be suggested as to why the open-range system persisted for so long. Establishing the big stations required considerable capital outlay, beyond the means of most 'small' cattlemen. Capital was also required to sustain the enterprise while the herds grew and markets were developed. As a result, many Victoria River District stations either were originally taken up by large companies or wealthy absentee-owners, or soon fell into their hands. Once the stations were stocked and basic infrastructure was in place, the operation of the open-range system involved relatively small ongoing costs. Vast areas could be leased for very low rents and when hostilities between the Aborigines and the cattlemen subsided the Aborigines provided a large and unpaid workforce. In spite of the recurrent losses of thousands of head of cattle at the end of each dry season, and the obvious damage the uncontrolled herds were inflicting on the land, the owners of most of the stations were content to maximise the profits from their investment while the very basis of these profits, the land itself, was washed and blown away.

There is, however, one change to the Victoria River environment that can't readily be attributed to the impact of European livestock, although these animals may have contributed to this change. In 2002, I published an environmental history of the district, and one of my findings was that tree numbers in riverine areas had increased significantly since European settlement.[130] In many areas of Australia similar increases in the number of trees and amount of scrub has been attributed to the cessation of Aboriginal burning.[131] In the Victoria River country Aboriginal burning practices

---

128 WH Maze, 'Settlement in the East Kimberleys, Western Australia', *The Australian Geographer*, vol. 5, no. 1, June 1945, pp. 1–16. Maze's observations were directly applicable over much of the Victoria River country, but his report had no impact in either the Ord or the Victoria; for years things went along more or less as before. For example, during a drought in 1961 the VRD manager reported that around the Pigeon Hole Outstation the cattle, '… struggled through on surface water. Frontage eaten out. Far too many cattle on river, nowhere to move the cattle to. All river frontage for miles eroded' (Station report by George Lewis, 1960. Hooker Pastoral Company Pty Ltd, Records, Station reports, 1959–1968. NBA, 119/15).

129 D Lewis, *Slower*, pp. 35–6, 42, 87.

130 ibid.

131 For discussion of this issue and for further references see E Rolls, *A Million Wild Acres* (Penguin Books Australia, Melbourne, 1984, p. 248–49); T Griffiths, 'How many trees make a forest?', *Australian Journal of Botany*, vol. 50, 2002, pp. 375–89; S Pyne, *Burning Bush: A fire history of Australia*, University of Washington Press, Seattle, 1998, pp. 132–135.

were disrupted within a few decades of settlement, yet repeat photography suggests that the increase in tree density occurred largely, or solely, in the post-war period. There are a number of factors which might have initiated this change, including a reduction in burning by European pastoralists, increased atmospheric carbon dioxide, global warming, or increased rainfall since the early 1970s. The exact cause remains unknown at this time and requires further scientific study.

The best lands for cattle grazing were also the richest areas for Aboriginal traditional foods. The cattle quickly impacted on these areas, selectively eating some plants and trampling others, disturbing native fauna and degrading the banks of the rivers and springs. The pastoralists used their horses and guns to stop Aborigines burning the country and to force them out of the good cattle lands and into the rough ranges. Even if the settlers had never resorted to violence, the open-range system of cattle management proved a disaster for the environment and would have made it difficult or impossible for the Aborigines to continue living off the land. For the Aborigines, the arrival of the settlers initiated a period of tremendous dislocation and lawlessness, unprecedented in all the thousands of years they had lived in the region. It was the beginning of the end for many age-old patterns of Aboriginal life and indeed for many of the Aborigines themselves but, as will be seen, they didn't go quietly.

Chapter 5

UNQUIET TIMES

When the first settlers entered the Victoria River region they found a cattleman's paradise of wide Mitchell grass plains, abundantly watered with numerous springs and large waterholes in the major rivers and creeks and with generally reliable monsoon rains. A paradise for cattlemen it may have been, but it was also a paradise for the Aboriginal people who had lived there for thousands of years. Each side came to see the other as the serpent in the garden that had to be banished. Ultimately both sides lost – the coming of the cattle began the destruction of the paradise for both.

Within a year of the first cattle reaching the district in 1883, 'intelligence' reached the Government Resident, John Langdon Parsons, that the settlers on the Victoria River and elsewhere on the Northern Territory frontier were having serious problems with the Aborigines. There can be little doubt that at the same time Aborigines in different parts of the Victoria River region were involved in or receiving intelligence of serious problems with the whites, confirming what they'd heard for years about the experiences of Aborigines living along the Overland Telegraph Line.

At the end of 1884 Parsons wrote a report on the situation in the Territory that provided a clear picture of the dilemma faced by Aborigines and settlers alike, and expressed his concerns for the future – concerns that were to prove horrifyingly prophetic:

> I fear unquiet times may be expected in connection with the native tribes. The blacks are beginning to realise that the white man, with his herds, and his fences, and his preservation of water, is interfering with what they properly enough, from their point of view, regard as their natural rights ...

> At the Katherine, Elsey, and Newcastle Waters, difficulties have arisen in connection with the blacks and cattle. Mr Lindsay Crawford states that on the Victoria the blacks are daring and defiant; Mr Creaghe states that at the Limmen River they are spearing his cattle, and that

he must take measures to prevent recurrence; Mr Hay states much the same condition of things as existing on the Roper, where one or two of the natives have firearms.[1]

Parsons included a succinct summary of the reasons for conflict between settlers and Aborigines, pointing out that through the impact of cattle the Aborigines' food supply was damaged and rendered uncertain, and that the settlers prevented them from moving amongst the cattle or burning the country. As a result:

> They can no longer, as they could a few years ago, travel from one lagoon or billabong to another, and be certain that on arrival there would be flocks of wild fowl to be snared. Nor can they, as of old, when they desired a repast of snakes, iguanas, or other reptiles, set fire to the first piece of well-grassed country they encounter. The stockholder uses the billabong for his cattle, and wild fowl are scared away; he wants the grass for his cattle and very vigorously lets the blackfellow understand that it is at their peril that they put the firestick to it. Naturally out of these conditions conflict arises and will continue. The natives will resist the intrusion of the whites and regard themselves as robbed of their inheritance; they will set the grass alight when they are so minded, and, if hungry or by way of reprisal, they will spear cattle when they think they are out of range of the rifle.

If nothing else, Parsons' report shows that at least some of the white authorities were aware of the dilemma that settlement posed. Parsons himself could offer no real solution, and could only state the obvious: 'That settlement and stocking must and will go on is certain – that outrages will be committed by both sides is probable; but', he added, 'even those who do not claim to be philanthropists are not satisfied with the contemplation that the blacks are to be improved off the face of the earth'.[2] This then was the situation that the settlers and Aborigines in the Victoria River valley faced as the first cattle herds moved west of the telegraph line. It didn't take long for the Resident's worst fears to be realised.

While Lindsay Crawford and Sam Croker were riding along the Victoria River looking for a homestead site in 1883 they were met with a shower of

---

1   JL Parsons, 'Quarterly Report on Northern Territory', 1st January 1885, *South Australian Parliamentary Papers*, vol. 3, no. 53, 1885, p. 10.
2   ibid.

spears.[3] The Duracks were attacked by a large group of Aborigines as they arrived on the Ord River with their cattle in August or September 1885.[4] And Battle Creek, on the north-eastern side of VRD, is said to have been named after a fight there between Aborigines and Tom Kilfoyle when he was bringing the first cattle across to stock Rosewood in 1885.[5]

Threatening behaviour by Aborigines and conflict with them is implied in a letter that Crawford sent to the Government Resident about a year after VRD was established. In this letter Crawford commented that, 'Natives are numerous on Victoria and Ord, and are very treacherous; a very fine race, and very independent'.[6] Another report published early in 1885 described Victoria River Aborigines as 'more troublesome and stubborn in those parts than has generally been granted', and went on to say that:

> Croker, whom the natives in most parts are extremely afraid of, has even
> been challenged out on the open plains by the blacks in the neighbourhood
> of the Victoria. Unlike most tribes they do not show cowardice when they
> see a comrade killed, but stand up and fight for a length of time.[7]

At the time ('Greenhide' Sam) Croker was manager of Wave Hill Station where he was said to use 'ruthless and often insensate methods ... to awe the blacks'.[8]

In complete contrast was the experience of Harry Stockdale and Henry Ricketson as they travelled across VRD in December 1884, less than 15 months after VRD and Wave Hill stations had been formed. By chance, the two men rode along Gordon Creek which runs through 'Bilimatjaru', a great 'sandstone sea' and a region which was to become a major refuge area for

---

3   'Massacres in the Northern Territory ... Paddy Cahill's list', *The South Australian Register*, 18th December 1905, p. 5.

4   PM Durack, 'Pioneering the East Kimberleys', *The Western Australian Historical Society Journal and Proceedings*, vol. 2, pt. 14, 1933, p. 27.

5   W. Linklater, untitled, undated article about Raparee Johnson, in Miscellaneous papers of W Linklater, Mitchell Library Mss 198 (microfilm copy CY 3506), p. 5; G Byrne, *Tom & Jack*, Fremantle Arts Centre Press, 2003, pp. 74–75.

6   Parsons, 1st January 1885, p. 2.

7   'Notes from the interior', *North Australian*, 27th March 1885, p. 3; Aborigines continuing to fight while their comrades fell around them was noted in other frontier areas, and it's been suggested that this 'bravery' was due to ignorance of the nature of firearms. Because no spears or other missiles were seen to strike the victims, those still fighting were puzzled when their comrades fell down (for example, see T. Roberts, *Frontier Justice: A history of the Gulf Country to 1900*. University of Queensland Press, Brisbane, 2005, pp. 22; H. Reynolds, *The other side of the frontier*, James Cook University, Townsville, 1981, pp. 44–46, 80–81).

8   G. Buchanan, 'Old Bluey', 1942, p. 175. Unpublished manuscript in possession of Buchanan family.

The Bilimatjaru sandstone, Gordon Creek, Victoria River Downs
Lewis collection

Aborigines for many years. Ricketson observed that 'the blacks are in large tribes about here,' and that they 'seemed very frightened of us'. Twice the two men tried to parley with groups they met, but 'in both cases they were so frightened of us that they ran clean out of sight ... [*and*] ... were tumbling over each other in their haste to get away'.[9]

Initially, at least, Aborigines probably didn't realise that the settlers had come to stay and would gradually take over all their country – they knew the whites had camps at one or two places, but the rest of the country was theirs to use as of old.[10] They probably came into contact and conflict with the settlers by accident in the course of their traditional hunting and gathering, particularly their burning activities, or while travelling to and from or attending ceremonial gatherings. However, once they began spearing cattle and horses they were sought out and confronted by white stockmen.

---

9 James Henry Ricketson, 'Journal of an expedition to Cambridge Gulf, the north-west of Western Australia, and a ride through the Northern Territory of South Australia, 1884–1885', Mitchell Library, mss 1783, item 2, p. 263.
10 H Reynolds, *The Other Side of the Frontier*, History Department, James Cook University, Townsville, 1981, p. 53.

They soon learnt that standing and fighting in open country was a losing proposition and that they had to be able to get into rough country to escape armed horsemen.

Most groups had areas of rough country within their territory to which they could flee; those few who didn't were at a great disadvantage and highly vulnerable.[11] An extreme case was the Karangpurru who inhabited the plains and rolling downs in the north-eastern part of VRD,[12] through whose country passed the early overland track from Katherine to Western Australia. The fight Kilfoyle and his men are said to have had with Aborigines on Battle Creek was in Karangpurru country. During 1886 this track was used by hundreds of miners heading for the Kimberley goldfield.

Many of the overlanding miners were of very bad character – 'the scum of the back blocks' and 'riff-raff semi-outlaws' – and extremely brutal towards Aborigines.[13] Justice Charles Dashwood, the Government Resident between 1892 and 1905,[14] spoke to a number of early Northern Territory pioneers including Jack Watson and Paddy Cahill.[15] The stories they told Dashwood about events along the overland track to the Kimberley led him to claim that the Aborigines along the route had been 'shot like crows'.[16] The first policeman in the Victoria River District, WH Willshire, recorded the names and locations of the various tribes whose country lay within or extended onto VRD.[17] The locations he gave for them conform in broad terms with the boundaries recognised by local Aborigines today. However, he didn't mention the Karangpurru, and neither he nor his successor, Edmund O'Keefe, had

---

11   The key role that topography played in the period of conflict following settlement was noted in the nineteenth century by Edward Curr, cited in Reynolds, p. 50.

12   D Rose and D Lewis, *Kidman Springs – Jasper Gorge Land Claim*, Northern Land Council, Darwin, 1986, figures 7–12, and associated land claim sites map.

13   'W Griffiths' answer to question 2352' in 'Select committee of the Legislative Council on the Aborigines Bill, 1899: minutes of evidence and appendices', *South Australian Parliamentary Papers*, vol. 2, no. 77, 1899; 'Protection from blacks', *Northern Territory Times*, 11th March 1892, p. 2. See also M Costello's *Life of John Costello*, facsimile edition, Hesperian Press, Perth, 2002 (1930), p. 159.

14   P Elder, 'Charles Dashwood' in D Carment, R Maynard, and A Powell (eds.), *Northern Territory Dictionary of Biography: Volume. 1 to 1945*, Northern Territory University Press, Darwin, 1990 pp. 75–78.

15   C Dashwood, 'Justice in the Northern Territory', *South Australian Parliamentary Papers*, vol. 3, no. 60, 1900, p. 2.

16   'C Dashwood's answer to question 516' in 'Select committee of the Legislative Council on the Aborigines Bill, 1899: minutes of evidence and appendices', *South Australian Parliamentary Papers*, vol. 2, no. 77, 1899.

17   WH Willshire, *Land of the Dawning: Being Facts Gleaned from Cannibals in the Australian Stone Age*, WK Thomas & Co., Printers, Adelaide, 1896, pp. 85–86.

cause to patrol in their country. It appears that by the time Willshire arrived in May 1894, this language group had already been decimated.[18]

Whatever may have happened during the first few years of settlement, by 1889 the 'wild blacks' were 'in large numbers among the ranges in the Sandstone Country'.[19] There are many patches of rough terrain scattered across the region, some large and some small, but among the greatest are the Yambarran Range (Fitzmaurice River catchment), the Pinkerton (Ballyangle) Range (Bullo River catchment), the Boomondoo sandstone on the headwaters of the West Baines River, the Stokes Range north of VRD and west of Delamere Station, and the Gordon Creek sandstone. The latter area, located in the central-west part of VRD, was described in 1895 as consisting of:

> enormous columns of sandstone cleft and piled one on the other, gullies, Gorges, tunnels, and caves, comprise hundreds of square miles of sandstone country where it would be impossible for even 20 Trackers to get a passing glimpse of blacks running about in it.[20]

One observer noted that the blacks came out of the ranges to 'kill down on the good flats & take the meat into the sandstone ranges to cook it',[21] while another complained that the blacks were 'most troublesome, particularly in setting fire to the grass, which in the months from June to October burns both night & day'.[22] Walter Rees, a stockman on VRD from 1887 to about 1897,[23] could see that the Aborigines were 'losing more of their game-producing country as the settlers stock the land, and have to be content with the roughest of the country, where they obtain but a poor living'.[24] The Aborigines were anything but content and the blocks and patches of 'roughest country' became natural fortresses from which they planned and

---

18 Rose and Lewis, pp. 9–10; D Rose, *Hidden Histories: Black Stories from Victoria River Downs, Humbert River and Wave Hill Stations*, Aboriginal Studies Press, Canberra, 1991, pp. 75–78.
19 Noel Butlin Archives (NBA), Australian National University: Goldsbrough Mort and Co. Ltd: sundry papers re. CB Fisher and the Northern Australia Territory Co., 1886–1892, 2/876/7, B Blair to Goldsbrough Mort & Co. Ltd, 24th October 1889.
20 Northern Territory Archives (NTA): Timber Creek police journal, 17th April 1895, F 302.
21 ibid., 15th August 1894.
22 NBA: 2/876/7, 24th October 1889.
23 Rees was interviewed in 1950 by Helen West (nee Healy). West wrote various details in a notebook and she gave me this notebook in the 1990s; WA Rees to A Martin, letter, 12th July 1945. In this letter Rees provides details of his time on VRD. An unsigned copy of this letter is in my possession.
24 W Rees, cited in Willshire, *Dawning*, p. 99.

executed attacks against the settlers. They speared livestock, stole the white man's goods and attacked them whenever they could.

The stealing of Europeans' goods by Aborigines began almost as soon as Europeans arrived in the district. As we have seen, Gregory's expedition suffered occasional thefts or attempted thefts, in one instance almost leading to serious violence. The arrival of the settlers greatly increased the amount and variety of goods and the opportunities for Aborigines to steal them. They quickly came to appreciate tobacco, iron axes, wire, billycans, cloth, sugar, flour, tea and other items.[25] In the Aboriginal camps on Gordon Creek in 1884, Ricketson and Stockdale noted billycans made from discarded food tins. A decade later the government geologist passed through the district and remarked that:

> Since the Kimberley rush the iron age has begun amongst them, portions of the springs of drays and other iron or steel fragments, manufactured into tomahawks, &c., replacing diorite and other stone weapons and implements. The tips of spears also are often made of telegraph or fencing wire in place of flint and quartzite, and glass is frequently used by them for the same purpose.[26]

Theft of goods was a major problem for the settlers for many years and in some instances led to violent encounters or other severe consequences. The first Aboriginal man known to have been shot at Wave Hill was one of a group who had raided the homestead camp and stolen a bucket.[27] The Aborigines had a habit of cutting wire from fences to use as prongs on spears, and this led some station owners to leave small coils of wire for them here and there along the fence lines. However, the Aborigines ignored these and continued to cut wire from the fences themselves.[28] This was seen by some as proof of Aboriginal stupidity, but is more likely to be evidence of them deliberately antagonising the whites, or a form of economic warfare.[29]

---

25 An early example of this problem was highlighted in the *South Australian Chronicle* ('The Northern Territory', 13th September 1873, p. 4), which reported that Aborigines in the Pine Creek area 'have tomahawks with them, probably stolen from the overland telegraph camps'.
26 HYL Brown, 'Government Geologist's Report on Explorations in the Northern Territory. Fountain Head to Victoria Downs Station', *South Australian Parliamentary Papers*, vol. 3, no. 82, 1895, p. 13.
27 G Buchanan, *Packhorse and Waterhole: With the First Overlanders to the Kimberleys*, Angus & Robertson Limited, Sydney, 1933, pp. 71–72, 164–65.
28 Untitled news item, *Northern Territory Times*, 6th December 1895, p. 2.
29 Reynolds, p. 87.

After the initial resistance to the settlers when they first appeared in the region, there was a relatively peaceful interlude of several years, a pattern that has been noted elsewhere in the north.[30] However, in 1886 there was a dramatic upsurge in attacks against the settlers. In April 1886 William Jackson, a bullock driver employed to carry stores from the Victoria River Depot to VRD, was struck in the neck with a stone-headed spear. The spear went 'right through the base of the tongue and out at the other side',[31] nearly severing his windpipe,[32] but amazingly he survived the wound. This attack occurred east of Jasper Gorge and led to the naming of a watercourse in the area as Surprise Creek.[33]

At the end of May a white station hand and his Aboriginal assistant were speared and wounded on Willeroo[34] and in June there were several attacks on a team building a road through Jasper Gorge.[35] Early in August, a man known as 'Spanish Charley' (Charles Antonio) was attacked on the Victoria River near the Depot. Charley was employed as a caretaker for goods unloaded at the Depot and had been on friendly terms with local Aborigines. On this occasion he rowed his dinghy across the river to speak with some Aborigines, but before he could land a number of spears were thrown at him. Fortunately for him he was unhurt, although one spear hit his boat.[36]

In September Matt Cahill, a brother of Paddy and Tom Cahill, and a Melbourne man named Fred Williams, were travelling to the Kimberley goldfield. They camped on the upper reaches of Gregory Creek and while fishing in a nearby waterhole were surprised by the blacks. Williams was speared through the neck and died instantly, thereby becoming the first white man killed on the Victoria River frontier. A few months later 'Big Johnny' Durack was murdered on Rosewood Station. When a party led by the police went out to bury the body they found that it had been 'jobbed full of spear holes, quite 80 or 90 holes having been made',[37] a circumstance which suggests extreme fear and/or hatred on the part of the Aborigines.

---

30   Byrne, p. 85.
31   JE Tennyson-Woods, 'A trip to the Victoria River', *Sydney Morning Herald*, 28th May 1887, p 26; 'News and Notes', *Northern Territory Times*, 1st May 1886, p. 2.
32   'Things and Others', *The North Australian*, 9th July 1886, p. 3.
33   Rees, 12th July 1945.
34   'Things and Others', *The North Australian*, 4th June 1886, 2.
35   'The Contributor', 'Troublesome Aborigines', *The Adelaide Observer*, 11th January 1896, pp. 33–34.
36   'Notes and news', *Northern Territory Times*, 14th August 1886, p. 2; 'Things and Others', *The North Australian*, 13th August 1886, p. 2.
37   'Murder of John Durack by Natives at Kimberley', *Northern Territory Times*, 11th December 1886, p. 3.

The events of 1886 beg the question: after nearly three years with virtually no reported attacks, and certainly no severe woundings or killings of whites, why were there were so many attacks across the region in 1886? Was it merely coincidence, or was it part of a deliberate and coordinated campaign against the whites? While this is impossible to answer with certainty, it's clear that Aboriginal groups across the region were not isolated from each other. News travelled from group to group very quickly and there were regular ceremonial gatherings when various issues could be discussed. The appearance of the cattlemen and overlanders and their behaviour towards the Aborigines was undoubtedly the foremost topic at such gatherings. Rather than being mere coincidence it's likely that a collective decision had been made to try and drive the whites away, that the Aborigines were not merely reactive, but took the fight to the whites in an organised way. Examples of such collective decisions are known from other frontier areas, with Henry Reynolds citing an example from Queensland where a gathering of over a dozen tribes discussed the poisoning of 50 or so Aborigines, became very angry, and swore to have vengeance.[38]

The attacks and killings in the Victoria River country and elsewhere in 1886 prompted Parsons to address the issue in his annual report on the Northern Territory:

> In the northern part of the Northern Territory we may be said to be upon the racial frontier, and the question as to which race is to predominate is one full of interest … The river natives particularly are warriors, tall, stalwart, cunning, and with a rooted hatred of the white man. Fear, indeed, is the only protection of the white man's life. The lives of stockmen, boundary riders, and travelling overlanders would not be worth much, and station stores would not be safe from pillage, if the natives were not convinced of the power of the white man to protect his life and goods, and avenge murder and theft.[39]

The settlers did their best to 'convince' the Aborigines. After the spearing of teamster Jackson it was reported that the offenders, 'were followed up with the aid of some blacks from Palmerston, and severely punished'.[40] Following the murder of 'Big Johnny' Durack the Wyndham police and 'a party of sixteen men (most volunteers) had started out for the purpose of settling

---

38   Reynolds, p. 69.
39   JL Parsons, 'Half-yearly Report on Northern Territory to December 31st, 1886', *South Australian Parliamentary Papers*, vol. 3, no. 53, 1888, p. 7.
40   Tennyson-Woods.

accounts with the natives'.[41] No official or other contemporary account of this punitive expedition is known. However, one later source claims there was a fight between the white party and about 100 Aborigines,[42] while another says that the name of Waterloo Station derives from what local bushmen called 'the Aborigine's Waterloo', a reference to the 'unrestrained slaughter' of local Aborigines after this spearing.[43]

After 1886 things seem to have quietened down for a few years. Several different tribes had probably been 'hammered' by punitive expeditions and others are likely to have suffered to some degree at the hands of the miners heading for the Kimberley. If, as seems likely, there were fights where considerable numbers of Aborigines were shot, this would have been something completely outside the Aborigines' experience, and against their ideas of what was justifiable in warfare. Evidence from elsewhere indicates that Aborigines expected an eye for an eye, but when they realised that many Aboriginal eyes were the price for one white eye they were shocked and had to adjust their thinking on such matters.[44] There may have been a lessening or pause in the Aborigines' resistance while they came to terms with what had happened and considered what to do.

There were no reports of attacks or murders by Aborigines during the next two years, although in 1887 when Goldsbrough Mort owned VRD their agent in Darwin, HWH Stevens, reported that, 'The Blacks have been very troublesome both on the River & the Depot road. They are a bad lot and require constant watching on all parts of the run'.[45] However, the killing of whites began again in 1889. Tom Hardy, the overseer on Auvergne, was one settler who tried to make friends with the Aborigines. Nevertheless, near the homestead in September he was speared in the right breast. He barricaded himself in the hut and held off the blacks by shooting through cracks in the walls. Three days later the station musterers returned and broke the siege, and although Hardy believed he would survive his wounds and begged for a boat to be sent to take him to medical help in Darwin, his mates considered it hopeless. A boat was sent but it was unavoidably delayed and Hardy died 'after lingering in terrible agony and without medical assistance

---

41   'Murder of John Durack', *North Australian*, 13th December 1886, p.

42   SA Museum Archives: M Terry, notebook 14, 'No. 1, Port Hedland – Melbourne, 1928'. C62, Tuesday 30th October 1928: D Moore, memoirs, Battye Library, Acc 3829A MN 1237.

43   J Pollard, *The Horse Tamer: The Story of Lance Skuthorpe*, Pollard Publishing Company, Woolstoncraft NSW, 1970, p. 30. Lance Skuthorpe's uncle, Amos, was owner of Waterloo from roughly 1908 to 1916, and was in the Victoria River District for some time earlier.

44   Reynolds, p. 63.

45   NBA: 2/876/7, HWH Stevens to Goldsbrough Mort and Co. Ltd, 11th July 1887.

for thirteen days'.[46] In 1890 a traveller named William Manton was killed on the West Baines River,[47] and an Aboriginal named Bob, 'The best & most valuable native we ever had on the runs',[48] was speared only ten miles from VRD homestead.[49] According to the *Northern Territory Times*:

> The recent murder of Mr. Crawford's blackboy Bob was most cruelly perpetrated. He, in company with two other station natives, were out after horses, and when going through a ravine, with Bob in the lead, a spear was thrown from above which entered behind the shoulder and went through his body, the point coming out in front below the abdomen. Bob pluckily pulled the spear out and walked back to the other boys, and shortly afterwards died.[50]

Once again there were attempts to retaliate. Two troopers were sent from Darwin to try and arrest the Aborigines who speared Hardy, but the offenders had retreated into the mountain wall of the Pinkerton Range and couldn't be followed.[51] Mounted Constables Brooks and Holdaway searched for Manton's killers, but apparently were unsuccessful.[52] The Aborigines who speared Bob were followed 'some 60 miles into some large gorges', but escaped.[53] The *Northern Territory Times* was of the opinion that, 'It is becoming more evident every day that the blacks of the Victoria River require a very severe lesson to keep them in check', and seemed to be advocating retaliation by the settlers by adding that, 'the isolated situation of the locality is dead against any salutary work being done under police superintendence'.[54]

---

46   'The Victoria River outrage', *Northern Territory Times*, 8 November 1889, p. 3; 'News and notes', 4th October 1889, p. 2; 'Outrage by blacks at the Victoria River', *The North Australian*, 5th October 1889, p. 3; NTA: Government Resident of the Northern Territory (South Australia) – inwards correspondence, 1870–1912, NTRS 790, item 1077, HWH Stevens to Government Resident JL Parsons, 1st October 1889.

47   'Another murder by Victoria River blacks', *The North Australian*, 28th February 1890, p. 2.

48   NBA: 2/876/7, HWH Stevens to general manager of Goldsbrough Mort & Co., 3rd March 1890, pp. 7–8.

49   'Murder of a blackfellow', *Northern Territory Times*, 6th March 1891, p. 2.

50   'Victoria River blacks', *Northern Territory Times*, 3rd April 1891. 'Bob' was probably a 'blackboy' listed on a paysheet for May 1891 as 'Bob Herbert' (NBA: 2/876/22). Because it was common for Aborigines to be given or adopt the name of the station or district where they came from, Bob may have come from the Herbert (now Georgina) River District in western Queensland.

51   NTA: NTRS 790, item 1085, Inspector Paul Foelsche to Government Resident JL Parsons, 3rd October 1889; 'The Victoria River outrage', *Northern Territory Times*, 8th November 1889, p. 3.

52   'The Victoria River outrage'.

53   NBA: 2/876/7, 3rd March 1890, pp. 7–8.

54   'The Victoria River Outrage'.

Remains of the 'fort' at old Willeroo homestead

Lewis collection

Throughout the district the danger of attack by Aborigines was such that it required unusual precautions to be taken. At Willeroo a two and a half metre high roofless 'fort' was constructed from basalt rocks 'as a harbour of refuge from the attacks of natives'.[55] Several other early homesteads had walls constructed partly or completely of stone[56] and one was later described as 'a little fortress of stone and ant-bed'.[57] The first VRD homestead didn't have stone walls but instead relied upon guns and a unique 'early warning system' – hordes of dogs. When Ricketson and Stockdale emerged from the Gordon Creek sandstone they eventually came upon VRD homestead, which they hadn't known existed until then.[58] Ricketson provides a graphic description of the scene:

55 NTA: NTRS 790, item 6891, 'Government Resident's Trip to the Victoria River' (Diary of Charles Dashwood, entry for 14th December 1895).

56 D Lewis, *In Western Wilds: A Survey of Historic Sites in the Western Victoria River District*, report prepared for the National Trust of Australia (Northern Territory), vol. 1, 1993, pp. 74–76, 110–18, 130–31; vol. 2, pp. 49–53, 89–98, 106–07; D Lewis, *The Final Muster: A Survey of Previously Undocumented Sites throughout the Victoria River District*, report prepared for the National Trust of Australia (Northern Territory), vol. 1, 2000, pp. 33–35, 42–47.

57 E Hill, *The Territory*, Angus and Robertson, Sydney, 1951, p. 399.

58 Ricketson's account, early maps and other records show that the first homestead was located on Gordon Creek but, within a few years, a new homestead had been

As we neared the place, two chinamen and a lot of blacks came out to look at us ... and a perfect army of dogs announced our arrival ... The blacks employed on the station carry revolvers the same as the whites. They have a large number of dogs who remain quite passive during the heat of the day, but as soon as the nightfall sets in they are as active as Kittens, and bark, howl and fight all night long.[59]

At Ord River it seems even the toilet was built with the possibility of Aboriginal attack in mind. It was set on a small rise and surrounded by four-foot high corrugated iron walls with an unobstructed 360 degree view. A woman visiting the station in the 1930s remarked that it had been 'built to the specifications of the pioneer manager. At the time there was conflict between the blacks and the whites and he obviously didn't want to be speared with his trousers down'.[60]

In 1905 Alfred Searcy, formerly a Customs officer based in Darwin and later author of several books on the Territory,[61] recalled how when VRD was first taken up all the staff were armed and 'no man was allowed to go out alone ... At least two men had to be in company, and the amount of money spent in ammunition was pretty considerable'.[62] If travellers believed there was a possibility of attack during the night they sometimes resorted to setting up their mosquito nets and sneaking away after dark to sleep in a patch of scrub or in long grass.[63] By this subterfuge the net might be speared but the traveller would be safe.

For some whites, having to deal with hostile Aborigines placed a great strain on their nerves. In 1890 or 1891 Auvergne Station was being managed by Barney Flynn.[64] When MP Durack visited the station, Flynn confided in

---

established on Stockyard Creek. The original homestead then became an outstation and was probably later dismantled and moved to another location. In 1890 the Stockyard Creek homestead was superseded by a new homestead on the Wickham River where the current homestead is located today. Stockyard Creek then became an outstation but was soon abandoned.

59   Ricketson, pp. 270–75, map, p. 320.
60   B Beckett, *Lipstick, Swag and Sweatrag. Memoirs of a Patrol Padre's Wife*, Central Queensland University Press, Rockhampton, 1998, pp. 64–65.
61   Searcy's books include *In Northern Seas* (WK Thomas, 1905), *In Australian Tropics* (George Robinson & Co., London, 1909), *By Flood and Field* (Keagan Paul, Trench and Trubner, London, 1912).
62   'Massacres in the Northern Territory ... A treacherous tribe. Interview with Mr Searcy', *The Register* (Adelaide), 18th December 1905, p. 5.
63   For example, see M Mallison, 'Adventures on the Murranji Track: droving and spear-throwing', *Sydney Morning Herald*, 27th June 1942, p. 7.
64   M Durack, *Kings in Grass Castles*, Corgi, Sydney, 1986, p. 333; Flynn's Christian name appears to have been James, but he was also known as Barney. W Linklater and L Tapp,

him "'a number of extraordinary hallucinations ...'" Among these was that the station was nightly surrounded by wild blacks and that he was doomed to die by a spear'. Durack described how, 'About midnight, when all were asleep, he [*Flynn*] leaped from his bunk and yelling like a maniac ran into the yard where he discharged the contents of his revolver. A most nerve-wracking experience'.[65]

Before coming to Auvergne, Flynn had worked at Florida Station in Arnhem Land[66] where the Aborigines were so hostile and in such numbers that a light swivel cannon was kept on the high veranda and the homestead was surrounded by a palisade. Apparently he considered the Auvergne blacks to be even worse. Flynn eventually left because of his nerves and the bad reputation of the place with regard to attacks by blacks.[67] He went buffalo shooting on Melville Island with Joe Cooper. Regardless of the fact that several times he was nearly speared there he apparently found the Melville Island Aborigines tame by comparison with those at Auvergne.[68] In spite of his fear of being murdered by Aborigines, after several near misses, he succumbed eventually to snakebite.[69]

Another who suffered psychological problems was Hugh Young, a stockman and sometime manager on Bradshaw Station for a decade after it was founded.[70] According to old Territory identity Tom Pearce, Young was involved in the massacre and burning of Aborigines on Bradshaw. As the bodies were burning the heat caused one to contract and 'sit up' in the flames. Young was so unnerved that he took to drink and was never the same again.[71]

It's clear that by the beginning of the 1890s the Aborigines had a well developed strategy for dealing with the whites and were wreaking havoc

---

Gather No Moss, Hesperian Press, Perth, 1997 (1968), p. 50.

65   Durack, *Kings*, p. 333.

66   Northern Territory 1891 census, compiled by the Genealogical Society of the Northern Territory from original records held at the National Archives of Australia (Darwin), microfiche, 1986.

67   'The late Jim Randell', *Mackay Daily Mercury*, 16th December 1927, p. 3; biography of Jim Randall, compiled by and in possession of the Randall family.

68   'Notes of the week', *Northern Territory Times*, 7th June 1895, p. 3; 'Spearing of J. Cooper on Melville Island', *Northern Territory Times*, 28th June 1895, p. 3; 'As other see us', *Northern Territory Times*, 20th January 1899, p. 2; see also A Briggs, 'Joe Cooper', in D Carment, R Maynard and A. Powell, *Northern Territory Dictionary of Biography: Volume 1 to 1945*, Northern Territory University Press, Darwin, 1990, pp. 61–62.

69   'Country Items. Death of James Flynn', *Northern Territory Times*, 13th February 1903, p. 3.

70   NTA: Log Book of Bradshaw's Run, NTRS 2261.

71   Tom Pearce, letter to Billy Linklater, 9th October 1948, 'Miscellaneous letters and other documents, 1895–1949', Mitchell Library, A1 10/26.

on cattle and horses. In 1891 the *Northern Territory Times* reported that on Wave Hill Station the Aborigines were killing an average of a beast a day for 'tucker', and in the previous year or so had slaughtered some valuable mares and 'a high-priced stallion which it would be extremely difficult to replace'.[72] The *Times* went on to say that:

> The boldness of the [*Wave Hill*] blacks is extraordinary, and their plans are so well matured that, although the station hands keep careful watch, they find it impossible to surprise the marauders, who, if pressed closely, make into the limestone country, where horses cannot travel.

A similar situation existed on other stations in the region. By 1892 it was reported to be 'a common sight ... to see a contingent of wild blacks tramping along carrying the butchered carcase of a station bullock, slayed by their own hands'. This report went on to say that, 'As a rule, if you are alone and accost them they simply drop the meat, ship a spear into the womera, and face you without fear'.[73] On VRD hostilities were reaching a crisis point. There were fears that the constant Aboriginal attacks and harassment could make the station unworkable. Indeed, within a few years Willeroo Station was abandoned for precisely this reason. Crawford described the situation on VRD in a letter to Stevens:

> As the niggers are fast becoming mixed with half civilized ones from the inside districts, they are more & more cunning & treacherous, & will go on getting worse until it will be impossible to travel on the runs. At the present time no man's life is safe. I have now 4 extra men on, on this account, I cannot even allow the Teamster to take rations about without sending men with him. I have also had to build a hut at the site of the old Gordon Creek Station & am putting two of these men there, to try to stop the wholesale slaughter of our Cattle. They are Killing a great number, and two or three days ago after our chasing them, they came on to the 5 mile plain & Killed a Cow on the main road. In fact the blacks are too many for us. They have lookouts posted on the hill tops & Keep up a system of signalizing from one to the other, & if we try to get near them they are off into the Sandstone.[74]

---

72   'Victoria River blacks', *Northern Territory Times*, 3rd April 1891, p. 2.
73   Untitled news item, *Northern Territory Times*, 24th February 1892, p. 2.
74   NTA: NTRS 790, item 5151, HWH Stevens to Government Resident Charles Dashwood, citing letter from Lindsay Crawford, 30th November 1892.

Desert Aborigines at Wave Hill, 1928

Bleakley collection, National Archives of Australia

These examples mirror the situation that often developed on the frontier in other parts of Australia. Reynolds quotes a Tasmanian settler who remarked in 1831 that the Aborigines there, 'now conduct their attacks with a surprising organisation, and with unexampled cunning, such indeed is their local information and quickness of perception, that all endeavours on the part of the whites to cope with them are unavailing'.[75]

Requests for police protection in the Victoria River District and elsewhere began in the immediate aftermath of the Daly River 'Coppermine massacre' of September 1884 in which four European miners were killed by Aborigines. Representations were made to the South Australian Government for a detachment of native police on a similar footing to the Queensland police to be stationed at three places: on the Macarthur River; at the head of the Roper River at Elsey Creek; and on the Victoria River. As a result, a force of six native police was recruited in northern South Australia and Central Australia, and stationed first at Pine Creek (February 1885), then at Elsey and finally on the Roper River.[76] The troop

---

75 Reynolds, p. 91.
76 'The Daly River murders', *Northern Territory Times*, 13th September 1884, p. 3; 'News and notes', *Northern Territory Times*, 10th January 1885, p. 2; 'News and notes', *Northern Territory Times*, 17th January 1885, p. 2; 'News and notes', *Northern Territory Times*,

The Retribution Camp boab, Auvergne Station

Lewis collection

The inscription on the Retribution Camp boab

Lewis collection

was disbanded in 1886 and one of the Aboriginal men was sent to the newly established Borroloola Police Station,[77] but no police were sent to the Victoria River. The Government Resident commented that 'no number of trackers or of police that could be organised can prevent outrages over the immense area of country which is now being stocked'.[78]

The men who made the 1884 request were not based in or strongly connected with the Victoria River District. By contrast, many of those who were so connected were wary of a police presence being established at all. For instance, after a series of attacks on VRD stockmen in 1891 Stevens wrote to the owners of VRD suggesting the formation of a Queensland-style native police, but only if certain conditions were met:

> The only possible means of getting rid of them would be by inaugurating a party of Black Trackers under the management of the Police ... The Government here have offered to station a Police Trooper on the run, but by himself, he would be a constant source of annoyance & of no use in any way, as the mere fact of his being there, would interfere with the present System of dealing with the blacks, which is the only System of being able to protect the property entrusted to the Charge of the Station hands.[79]

The 'system' of 'dealing with the blacks' certainly included ensuring that all station hands were armed and never went out alone, as Searcy noted. It probably also involved the Aborigines being fired upon whenever they were seen and occasional surprise attacks on them. An Aboriginal story from VRD tells of a large group of men at a ceremonial gathering who were surrounded and attacked at night, with many being shot.[80] A boab tree on the East Baines River provides the only known documentation for an apparent massacre in that area. Carved on the tree are names and dates from the 1890s and the words, 'Retribution Camp'.[81]

18th April 1885, p. 2.

77   T Roberts, *Frontier Justice: A History of the Gulf Country to 1900*, University of Queensland Press, Brisbane, 2005, p. 78.

78   Parsons, 1st January 1885, p. 10.

79   NBA: 2/876/7, HWH Stevens to general manager of Goldsbrough Mort and Co. Ltd, 19th December 1891, pp. 8–9.

80   Big Mick Kangkinang, pers. comm. A similar event is said to have happened on Auvergne Station (Bobby Wititpuru, pers. comm.). See Rose (pp. 95–96).

81   D Lewis, *In western wilds: A survey of historic sites in the western Victoria River District*, report prepared for the National Trust of Australia (Northern Territory), 2000, Site 21, vol 1, pp. 64–67 and vol 2, pp. 36–41.

In the short term nothing came of Steven's idea,[82] but pressure for a police presence was building. In March 1892 the *Northern Territory Times* returned to the theme of police protection for the Victoria River country:

> In the Victoria River District – a district famous for troublesome blacks … there has never been a police camp, the nearest station being the Katherine, several hundred miles away, where one trooper is stationed. In the event of an outrage the consequence is inevitable. We complain that the settlers in isolated parts take the law into their own hands to avenge murders committed by natives. Yet by our very callousness in refusing them the protection they require we support them in their summary method of "getting equal." When the State declines to defend you, the only resource left is to defend yourself.[83]

When Sid Scott, the manager of Willeroo, was killed by Aborigines in October 1892 the *Northern Territory Times* again addressed the problem and voiced the 'general opinion' of the settlers that, 'authority should be given to volunteers to follow the murderers for the purpose of bringing them to justice'.[84] It was probably the spearing of Scott that prompted Stevens to write to Goldsbrough Mort again about the need for a police presence, but with a warning that it would require 'very stringent measures to be taken to do any good at all'. He pointed out that as the situation stood, 'the settler is worse than helpless, as he is entirely without any Kind of protection from the Government & is hardly allowed the Exercise of his discretion even when his own life is in daily jeopardy'. Stevens suggested that an arrangement be sought:

> to place not less than two good Mounted Troopers and six Black Trackers on the Victoria River country for a period of say six months, during which there would be ample time to get hold of some of the worst characters amongst the Blacks, some of whom are Known to the station hands.[85]

Still nothing eventuated. In 1893 the Prices Creek homestead and yards were burnt by Aborigines[86] and reports came in that on 'Buchanan Downs' (Wave Hill) and Argyle the 'natives have been killing cattle with a vengeance.

---

82   'Murder of a blackfellow'.
83   'Protection from Blacks', *Northern Territory Times*, 11th March 1892, p. 2.
84   ibid.
85   NTA: NTRS 790, item 5151, HWH Stevens to Government Resident Charles Dashwood, 30th December 1892.
86   NTA: NTRS 790, item 6050, 'The Government Resident's [*Charles Dashwood*] Trip up Country'. Dashwood's trip began on 27th October 1893.

On one occasion lately some natives were surprised roasting a bullock, and it was seen that each one of them was proprietor of a cow's tail, which was being used to keep the mosquitoes on the wing'. This report went on to say that, 'The blacks are fast creating a decided reign of terror out west, and nothing but a firm hand and plenty of it will do the slightest good'.[87] On the eastern side of Rosewood in September 1893 Constable Collins, a Western Australian trooper, was speared during a raid on an Aboriginal camp. As soon as Collins was hit the men with him opened fire on the Aborigines and shot 23 dead before the battle was over.[88] How many got away and died later or were maimed for life is unknown. Remarkably, the police were not satisfied with the number killed because they organised a follow-up 'punitive expedition' which the *Northern Territory Times* hoped would 'distribute leaden medals among [*the Aborigines*] in token of their bravery'.[89]

The main objection the government had to establishing a police station on the Victoria was expense, but this obstacle was finally overcome in February 1894 when Goldsbrough Mort offered to 'find quarters, meat and paddocking free, Rations at cost price and to make a gift to the department of 15 suitable horses for the work'.[90] This proposal was strongly supported by Inspector Paul Foelsche, the head of the Northern Territory police, and as a result, in May 1894 Mounted Constable Willshire arrived on VRD and moved into a hut on Gordon Creek, 60 kilometres south of VRD homestead.[91]

Willshire is the most notorious policeman in Northern Territory (and possibly Australian) history. He was based in Central Australia in the 1880s, a time of severe conflict there between the Aborigines and settlers. In 1891 he was charged with the murder of a number of Aborigines, but in spite of strong evidence against him he was found not guilty. He was not sent back to Central Australia, but after several short-term postings in South Australia he was sent to another region where severe problems with Aborigines existed – the Victoria River District. [92]

Willshire was at Gordon Creek for only 16 months and spent most of his time patrolling between the Victoria River Depot and Wave Hill, especially

---

87   Untitled news item, *Northern Territory Times*, 3rd February 1893, p. 2.
88   Constable A Lucanus to Sub-Inspector Drewry, 7th October 1893, Occurrence Book (Wyndham Police Station), Battye Library, Acc 741-1; 'News and Notes', *Northern Territory Times*, 20th October 1893, p. 3.
89   'News and Notes', *Northern Territory Times*, 3rd November 1893, p. 3; 'Notes of the week', *Northern Territory Times*, 24th November 1893, p. 3.
90   NTA: NTRS 790, item 6004, Government Resident's [*Charles Dashwood's*] notes of interview with HWH Stevens, 26th February 1894.
91   NTA: Timber Creek police journal, 14th May 1894, F 302
92   R Kimber, 'WH Willshire' in Carment, Maynard and Powell, pp. 317–20.

UNQUIET TIMES

in and around the sandstone country on Gordon Creek, the country of the Bilinara Aborigines. He didn't patrol west of Wave Hill, VRD or Auvergne and consequently the western parts of the district remained effectively without a police presence. In his police journal entries Willshire rarely mentions firing a shot for any reason, and when he came across Aborigines in the bush, in most cases he claimed they were friendly or that they saw him coming and fled.[93]

It would appear that after the traumatic experience of being tried for murder, Willshire was extraordinarily careful to avoid providing evidence that might lead to a similar experience in future. However, while he was on VRD he wrote a book, *Land of the Dawning*, in which he describes five violent encounters with groups of Aborigines.[94] He provides dates for some of these encounters so it is possible to compare them with his official journal entries. In his book he describes a patrol in June 1894 during which he came upon an Aboriginal camp on the upper Wickham River, and the next day another one on Black Gin Creek, at the southern end of VRD. According to Willshire the people in the first camp fled into tropical growth at his approach, but on Black Gin Creek the Aborigines were:

> camped amongst rocks of enormous magnitude and long dry grass ...
> they scattered in all directions, setting fire to the grass on each side of
> us, throwing occasional spears, and yelling at us. It's no use mincing
> matters – the Martini-Henry carbines at this critical moment were
> talking English in the silent majesty of those great eternal rocks.[95]

In the equivalent journal entry there is absolutely no hint of a fight occurring. Willshire states that when he found the camp on the upper Wickham the Aborigines, 'soon cleared out when they espied us'. After destroying a heap of spears he 'went on day after day on the tracks of other cattle Killers on the sandstone ridges', eventually returning to his station, apparently without making further contact.[96]

The question is which version is correct? Was Willshire being honest in his journal and spinning yarns in his book, or vice versa? There are three points to consider. One is that when he arrived on VRD he found himself in a situation of great hostility between the Aborigines and the settlers and his

---

93 NTA: Timber Creek police journal, 26th June 1894, 3rd December 1894, 17th April 1895, 18th July 1895. F 302
94 Willshire, *Dawning*, pp. 6, 40–41, 43, 46, 61.
95 ibid., pp. 40–41.
96 NTA: Timber Creek police journal, 26th June 1894, F 302.

job required that he deliberately follow up and attempt to arrest Aborigines accused of wrongdoing. In such circumstances it would be difficult indeed to avoid violent conflict. The second is that Victoria River Aboriginal oral history speaks of the first policeman shooting people in the same general areas where fights with Aborigines are documented in Willshire's book.[97] The third is that when Willshire was stationed at Gordon Creek there was a sizeable Aboriginal population in Bilinara country, but for decades after he left the Bilinara were numerically one of the weakest tribes in the entire Victoria River District.[98] It thus seems likely that the journal was deliberately incomplete and that the book is a more reliable account of his actions. If the 'admissions' in his book caused questions to be raised he could always have declared that these parts were fiction. Indeed, he may even have written it with the idea in mind that it would upset the same people who had previously caused him to be taken to court.

In 1894 Crawford claimed that during the first ten years of settlement on VRD there had been 'constant attacks and reprisals', and that there'd been 'no communication with the natives at all, except with the rifle. They have never been allowed near this station or the outstations, being too treacherous and warlike'.[99] However, there is other evidence that on VRD and elsewhere in the district there had been some 'friendly' contact by this time. There is even an intriguing possibility that such contact may have begun within a year and a half of settlement. When Ricketson and Stockdale were passing through the Gordon Creek sandstone in December 1885, they captured several Aboriginal women. The two men tried to learn from these women if there were any Europeans in the area, and when their attempts to communicate in English failed Ricketson related how:

> Stockdale got off his horse and walked on all fours, and sticking two of his fingers on top of his head he bellowed like a cow. They seemed to understand this and they all laughed ... We were just getting tired of interrogating them, when one gin called out 'whitefellow' and grinned ... Stockdale said 'Which way whitefellow' She answered 'That way' pointing with a wommerah down the creek the way we were going.[100]

---

97 In the 1980s Aborigines I spoke with named a number of places in the Gordon Creek sandstone (Bilinara country) and on the upper Wickham River (Ngarinman country) where they said the police had shot people.
98 Rose, p. 117.
99 L Crauford [sic], cited by Edward Stirling in 'Victoria River Downs station, Northern Territory, South Australia', Journal of the Royal Anthropological Institute of Great Britain and Ireland, vol. 24, 1895, p. 180.
100 Ricketson, 1st January 1885.

Stockdale himself wasn't so sure that the woman did speak words of English.[101] If Ricketson was correct it is, of course, impossible to know whether the woman had learned the words from the settlers on VRD or if she had learned them via traditional networks. It should be noted, however, that on Australian frontiers it was common for Aborigines to send in women to make first contact with the settlers, just as it was common for young Aboriginal women to be abducted and held against their will by white men, or by the white man's 'tame' blacks.[102]

Stevens' claim in 1892 that some of the worst characters amongst the Aborigines were known to the station hands suggests that, at the very least, they were physically recognisable. However, there is a strong possibility that these 'worst characters' had been identified by local Aborigines who were working for the whites and were known by name. Soon after Willshire arrived on VRD he began to bring Aboriginal women to his Gordon Creek Station and eventually he had 11 women there.[103] He also had sufficient numbers of 'old and infirm' Aborigines at or near his station – possibly elderly husbands or other relations of the women Willshire had brought in – to prompt him to write to the Government Resident (via Inspector Foelsche) asking for '20 blankets and 20 bags of flour' to be sent for them with his next loading. Providing such rations, he said, 'would help me to control them, and their young men cattle Killers'.[104] Willshire began to obtain intelligence from these people and it was probably one or more of them who helped him communicate with a large number of Aboriginal men, women and children who came to the station in June 1895.[105] From this time on local Aboriginal placenames and the names of Aboriginal offenders began to appear in the police journal.[106]

---

101 H Stockdale, 'Exploration in the far north-west of Australia, 1884–85', 31st December 1884, unpublished journal, Mitchell Library, MLA 1580, undated.

102 Reynolds, pp. 57–58, 140–41; see Patrick Sullivan, *All Free Man Now: Culture, Community and Politics in the Kimberley Region, North-Western Australia* (Aboriginal Studies Press, Canberra, 1996).

103 Willshire, *Dawning*, pp. 41, 61–62, 70–71.

104 NTA: NTRS F790, item 7210, WH Willshire to Inspector Paul Foelsche, 2nd October 1894.

105 NTA: Timber Creek police journal, 6th and 25th June 1895, F 302. Of interest here is the story that VRD Aborigines tell of a policeman at Gordon Creek sending out a woman to bring the bush blacks in, and then either giving them poisoned food or chaining them up and shooting them (P Read and J Read, *Long Time, Olden Time*, Institute for Aboriginal Development Publications, Alice Springs, 1991, pp. 57–60; Rose, pp. 37–39)

106 NTA: Timber Creek police journal, 25th and 26th June 1895, F 302.

By 1895 Aborigines in Jasper Gorge knew the name of the teamster John Mulligan.[107] Further east, by 1896 Wardaman people were able to swear very well.[108] Certainly by early 1895 a number of local Aborigines were working for station whites. In March of that year three Aborigines employed on VRD cleared into the bush with firearms, and Willshire wrote that, 'The three of them belong to this country, and will no doubt join the cattle killers and shoot beasts for them'.[109] In April 1895 Knut Dahl visited the Victoria River Depot and tried unsuccessfully to make contact with 'an old woman who had once worked on Victoria River Downs',[110] and in May 1895 the contract teamsters taking stores from the Depot to VRD had three Queensland Aboriginal men working for them, one of whom had an Aboriginal wife from Wave Hill.[111]

Just how these Aborigines came to work for the whites is unknown. Some may have 'come in' from the bush of their own accord, out of curiosity or to escape the constraints of their own society,[112] but in some cases cooperation may have been coerced. The abduction of Aboriginal boys and girls was a widespread practice on the early Queensland and Northern Territory frontiers.[113] Referring to Aboriginal children working for her pioneer ancestors in the East Kimberley region, Mary Durack commented, 'How they got hold of them was nobody's business'.[114] The Wyndham Police Occurrence Book shows that one child was picked up during a police raid on an Aboriginal camp on 'Durack's station' (probably Argyle) in July 1888.[115] The only reference I've found to children being 'picked up' in the Victoria River District comes from Willshire's Land of the Dawning. Willshire described the appearance of a large number of Aboriginal men, women and children at the Gordon Creek Police Station in June 1895 and claimed that,

---

107 Willshire, *Dawning*, p. 77.
108 F. Burdett, 'Aboriginal Marauders', letter to the *Northern Territory Times*, 3rd July 1896, p. 3.
109 NTA: Timber Creek police journal, 18th March 1895, F 302.
110 K Dahl, *In Savage Australia: An Account of a Hunting and Collecting Expedition to Arnhem Land and Dampier Land*, Phillip Allan & Co., Ltd, London, 1926, p. 184.
111 NTA: NTRS 790, item 6539, Inspector Paul Foelsche to FE Benda, secretary to the minister controlling the NT, 14th June 1895.
112 For discussions of the various reasons for Aborigines 'coming in' in different parts of Australia see Reynolds, pp. 93, 105–07; R Baker, 'Coming in? The Yanyuwa as a case study in the geography of contact history', *Aboriginal History*, vol. 14, pt 1, 1990, pp. 25–60; P Read and J Read, pp. 73–93; J Long, 'Leaving the desert: actors and sufferers in the Aboriginal exodus from the Western Desert', *Aboriginal History*, vol. 13, pt 1, 1989, pp. 9–43.
113 Roberts; Reynolds, p. 93, 140–41.
114 Durack, *Kings*, p. 291.
115 25th July 1888, Battye Library, Acc 741-1.

'They gave me three little boys, ages respectively nine, ten, and eleven, also one girl of eleven, who soon got fat at my camp. There are now fourteen children here'.[116] We might accept that Willshire was 'given' the children on this occasion, but how did he come by the other ten already at the station? Some may have belonged to the women Willshire had 'collected' at Gordon Creek, but one can't help wondering if some were survivors of one of the 'encounters' with the bush blacks that he describes elsewhere in his book.

At many different times and places on the frontier young Aboriginal women were enticed or kidnapped to assist in stock or domestic work, and to be sexual partners.[117] Old Tim Yilngayarri, a man from VRD, told how 'that first one policeman' would kill all Aborigines he came across except young women with 'big *ngapalu*' (large breasts) who he would take back to the police station.[118] At the very least, Willshire would entice young women to come with him to the police station, or allow his trackers to do so – but placenames such as 'Kitty's Capture' and 'Rilly's Capture' mentioned in the Gordon Creek police journal apparently allude to the abduction of women and add weight to Yilngayarri's claim.[119]

Coerced or voluntary, once local Aborigines began to work for the whites it was the beginning of the end for what, until then, had been a uniform resistance. Initially at least, those who changed sides were treated by their own people as renegades. Two of the VRD employees who ran away with guns in June 1895 were killed by bush Aborigines because, 'they had in the past taken a prominent part with whitefellows in tracking up their countrymen'.[120] This was learnt by Willshire from one of the women who had come to the station a few weeks earlier. As more Aborigines came in the whites gained more information about the bush blacks – the names of troublemakers, their whereabouts, and the location and timing of ceremonial gatherings. Some of the Aborigines were able to act as guides and trackers to help the whites locate wanted individuals or groups.

In spite of the police presence at VRD, attacks, robberies and killings by Aborigines continued. In 1894 men guarding the stores at the Depot landing were besieged all night,[121] and Captain Joe Bradshaw was ambushed

116 Willshire, *Dawning*, p. 73.
117 Reynolds, pp. 140–41.
118 Pers. comm.; see Rose, pp. 49–54.
119 NTA: Timber Creek police journal, 25th November 1895, 5/6 and 18th January 1896, F 302.
120 ibid, 25th June 1895. According to Reynolds (pp. 107–08) similar revenge was taken against 'turncoats' in other parts of Australia.
121 Dahl, p. 190.

near the Gregory Creek junction. Bradshaw escaped unharmed but a white employee was injured and his 'boy', Nym, was fatally speared.[122] In May the following year teamsters John Mulligan and George Ligar were severely wounded and besieged at their wagons in Jasper Gorge. In November or December 1895 Aborigines decoyed some white men away from a building they were erecting and, while they were gone, other Aborigines stole pieces of thick iron from gates to make into tomahawks.[123]

In June 1895 Joe Bradshaw and two others wrote to Charles Dashwood urgently requesting extra police and trackers for the Victoria River area,[124] and during a South Australian Government inquiry Bradshaw suggested that if additional police protection couldn't be provided, known Aboriginal troublemakers should be outlawed.[125] Inspector Foelsche agreed with the desirability for additional police but stated that none could be sent because of the expense and lack of appropriate personnel.[126]

A traveller, ER Johnson, was attacked at Dead Finish Creek (Delamere Station) in May 1896.[127] This led to a call for a regular police patrol to be established in that area,[128] but nothing was done. In June 1896, while Mounted Constable O'Keefe was on patrol to the Depot, Aborigines raided the Gordon Creek Police Station and took away 'everything they could get even Revolver & cartridges Knives and forks and all my clothing, all my private property'.[129] Two months later Patrick O'Neil, alias 'Paddy the Lasher', was speared on VRD south of Pigeon Hole,[130] and towards the end of the year VRD was almost burnt out by the Aborigines.[131]

122 NTA: NTRS 2261, 29th May 1894.
123 Untitled news item, *Northern Territory Times*, 6th December 1895, p. 2.
124 NTA: NTRS 790, 6539, Joe Bradshaw (per Aeneas Gunn), HWH Stevens and P Allen, to secretary to Government Resident, 10th June 1895.
125 Report of the Northern Territory Commission together with Minutes of Proceedings, Evidence, and Appendices. Government Printer, Adelaide, 1895, J. Bradshaw's answers to questions 3774 and 3356 .
126 NTA: NTRS 790, item 6539, Inspector Paul Foelsche to Government Resident Charles Dashwood, 11th June 1895. Foelsche's letter was written in response to Bradshaw's letter of 10th June 1895 (NTA: NTRS 790, [item number lost]).
127 NTA: Timber Creek police journal, 27th May 1896, F 302.
128 F Burdett, 'Aboriginal marauders', letter to the editor, *Northern Territory Times*, 3rd July 1896, p. 3.
129 NTA: Government Resident of the Northern Territory (South Australia) – inwards correspondence, 1870–1912, NTRS 790, item 6982, Edmond O'Keefe to Inspector Paul Foelsche, 26th June 1896.
130 'Police court, Palmerston', *Northern Territory Times*, 11th December 1896, p. 3.
131 E O'Keefe, 'Report on the Victoria River District', 7th December 1896, in 'Government Resident's Report for the Northern Territory for 1896', *South Australian Parliamentary Papers*, vol. 2, no. 45, 1897, p. 15.

Auvergne homestead was attacked on the night of 10 January 1897 when two stone-headed spears were thrown at Ah Fat, the Chinese cook. One spear 'went through a galvanised iron bugget & also through the iron wall of the Kitchen. This cause a noise & the blacks went into the water & crossed the river & cleared out'. Mounted Constable O'Keefe and his trackers tried to follow the attackers but couldn't cross the flooded West Baines River. O'Keefe remarked that, 'There is a large Mountain [*the Pinkerton Range*] close to west baines & this is a great home for the Natives as it is impassable for man or horse only [*except*] at the north end about twelve miles from the Station'.[132]

In April 1898 the police station at Gordon Creek was closed and a new station opened at Timber Creek.[133] The Timber Creek Station was bounded on two sides by precipitous ranges up to 200 metres in height, and almost from day one it was under surveillance by Aborigines. For the next eight years the police journal has regular reports of 'blacks on the mountain', or similar.

At the end of the 1890s attacks against the settlers intensified. On VRD the blacks were reported as 'excessively troublesome, going in amongst the cattle all over the run, and giving the stockmen a great deal of trouble to keep the herds together'. In late 1898 a 'boy' working for drover Joe Stevenson was speared in the side as he was unhobbling some horses. Around the same time Aborigines at Wave Hill 'made a most determined assault' on the Wave Hill manager Tom Cahill and his mustering team. While the musterers were taking a midday break near the area where O'Neil had been speared two years before, the attackers crept up unobserved and threw a shower of spears amongst them. Cahill and his men 'quickly rose to a fighting attitude, on seeing which the blacks beat a retreat'.[134] Later that year Wave Hill homestead was 'burnt to the ground by the natives. The niggers put a fire-stick to the building to windward while the men were away mustering, and the place was quickly demolished'.[135] On Wave Hill, VRD, Bradshaw and Ord River, Aborigines were said to be killing cattle wholesale.[136]

---

132 NTA: Timber Creek police journal, 18th January 1897, 20th January 1897.
133 ibid, 5th April 1898. F 302.
134 'Attack by blacks at Wave Hill', *Northern Territory Times*, 20th January 1899, p. 3.
135 A Richardson, *The Story of a Remarkable Ride*, The Dunlop Pneumatic Tyre Co. of Australasia Ltd, Perth, 1900, p. 14.
136 E O'Keefe, 'Report on the Victoria River District' 16th December 1899, in 'Government Resident's Report for the Northern Territory, 1899', *South Australian Parliamentary Papers*, vol. 3, no. 45, 1900, p. 26.

In February 1900 a lone traveller named Stanley was believed to have been killed near Campbell Spring on Limbunya.[137] His body was never found, so his murder couldn't be confirmed, but at the time no one had any doubt about the manner of his death. In 1989 Old Jimmy Manngayarri took me to a site near Campbell Spring where he said a white man – undoubtedly Stanley – had been killed and his body hidden in a hollow tree.[138] A man named Tom Walton was speared in the thigh on Bradshaw in March 1900[139] and in October a herd of 500 cattle being taken through Jasper Gorge by drover Stevenson was attacked by a mob of over 100 Aborigines. A number of bullocks were killed or injured in the ensuing rush and provided the Aborigines with a good supply of fresh beef. Soon afterwards they let it be known that they planned further attacks.[140]

Attacks were particularly frequent in the Willeroo–Delamere area. Between December 1899 and May 1900 several drovers were attacked there. Most escaped without injury but the last, drover Mork, was speared in the thigh.[141] After this attack, Foelsche advised the Government Resident that it would be of no use sending police out from Timber Creek or Katherine as it 'takes some days from each station to get to "Willeroo" ... and the Natives would know that the police are coming before they could get there, and clear out into the Ranges, and return as soon as the police leave again'. He suggested that police should be stationed at Willeroo but warned that this would be very expensive as it would need at least two constables with three or four trackers and twelve horses, 'for almost constant patrolling that district is in my opinion the only means of affording more security to the travelling public in that county'.[142]

Nothing was done and problems in the Willeroo/Delamere region continued. Travellers and drovers were attacked, horses speared, and camps robbed of rations and firearms. Towards the end of October 1900 a lone traveller was attacked several times. He was badly wounded and abandoned his packhorses which were then killed. His pack-bags containing all his possessions were looted and destroyed, but he got away with his life.[143]

---

137 NTA: Timber Creek police journal, 25th March 1900, 19th and 20th October 1900, F 302.
138 Old Jimmy Manngayarri, pers. comm., 1989.
139 FD Holland, 'Trouble with the Victoria River natives', letter to the editor, *Northern Territory Times*, 7th December 1900, p. 3.
140 'More trouble with the blacks', *Northern Territory Times*, 23rd November 1900, p. 2.
141 NTA: Timber Creek police journal, 9th June 1900, F 302.
142 NTA: NTRS 790, item, 9722, Inspector Paul Foelsche to Government Resident Charles Dashwood, 20th June 1900.
143 'Another outrage by blacks', *Northern Territory Times*, 9th November 1900, p. 2.

This was the final straw for many Territory people. Within days of news of the attack reaching Darwin, residents there petitioned the Government Resident to outlaw the offending Aborigines and offered to assist the police in arresting them.[144] The government didn't outlaw anyone or take up the offer of assistance, but this latest attack finally prompted the authorities to take action. In mid-October 1900 Inspector Foelsche wrote to the Government Resident advising that he could at last send an extra mounted constable and two trackers to assist Mounted Constable O'Keefe at Timber Creek. His initial suggestion was that the extra constable could be stationed at Willeroo, but this never eventuated. Foelsche also asked the Government Resident for permission to arm the trackers with carbines rather than revolvers as:

> revolvers are not Sufficient for effection [*effecting*] protection to them
> where ... the natives are Known to be as treacherous and it is a well
> Known fact the Natives have no fear of revolvers and the trackers Know
> this but with a Carbine in their hands they are more Couragions and
> the natives Know the affect of them and are not so defiant.[145]

Mounted Constable Thompson joined O'Keefe at Timber Creek in December 1900, and over the next three years he or O'Keefe followed their instructions to carry out patrols:

> between Willeroo and Victoria River and particularly around Sullivan's
> and Gregory's Creek junctions with Victoria River, and at Jasper Gorge.
> Patrol should roam the area in question and also escort any travellers,
> drovers etc through the dangerous places.[146]

On one patrol in August 1901 O'Keefe located a large camp of blacks on Sullivan Creek. He and his trackers:

> rounded some of the lubras up and told them who we were and then
> told them the blackfellows not to growl at whitemen and not to kill
> their horses & cattle and we would not growl at them. The natives knew
> who we were and where we came from and said blackfellow sulky fellow

---

144 NTA: NTRS 790, item 10088, petition presented to Government Resident Charles Dashwood, 13th November 1900.
145 NTA: NTRS 790, item 10033, Inspector Paul Foelsche to Government Resident Charles Dashwood, 13th October 1900.
146 NTA: NTRS 790, item 10033: Inspector Paul Foelsche to Mounted Constable E O'Keefe, 28th November 1900.

also wild fellow. None of the lubras could speak English. Tracker Billy could speak to them.[147]

If the police journals are any guide, apart from this encounter there seems to have been virtually no contact between the police and the Aborigines, and in spite of the increased police presence harassment of white people and attacks against them continued as before. In August 1902 another traveller had a skirmish with Aborigines near Delamere. He got away unharmed, but a few days later a German traveller disappeared in the same area, presumed murdered.[148] At the same time two men who had taken up the old Willeroo run abandoned the lease almost immediately because of harassment by Aborigines.[149]

Then, almost overnight across most of the region, the violent attacks against Europeans slowed to a trickle. This is not to say that all resistance to Europeans ceased; as Reynolds noted, 'Black resistance did not conclude when the last stockman was speared'.[150] Activities such as cattle spearing and theft of European property continued for decades, but across the region Aborigines seem to have made a decision to no longer try to kill Europeans. There were other Europeans killed or attacked over the following 30 years, but these incidents were widely separated in time and most attacks were on lone white men on the fringes of, or within, the last great Aboriginal refuge areas.

So, why did this change occur? There is little to suggest that it happened because of the special patrols alone. There is nothing either to suggest that they had any physical impact on Aborigines, and even if they did it would only have applied to Willeroo, Delamere and the northern part of VRD, because the special patrols didn't extend to other parts of the district. Rather,

---

147 E O'Keefe, 'Report on patrol by MC O'Keefe', 27th July 1901. This meeting took place on 5th August 1901. Notes taken from the Timber Creek police letter book, written by an unidentified policeman and now housed at the Northern Territory Archives (NTA: Timber Creek Police Station, copy book, 1895–1940, NTRS 2224). In part, this set of notes overlaps with a photocopy of the Timber Creek police letter book held at the Berrimah Police Station in Darwin. However, the letter book at Berrimah only covers the period 1894 to 1911, whereas these copies continue to 1925. The copies thus cover a period when there are no surviving original Timber Creek police documents (1919–1923), and a period when there are no surviving Timber Creek police letters (1912–1923). In instances where the copies and the original records co-exist, the copied notes are reliable, but whoever made the copies occasionally made his or her own comments and connections, and in at least one instance was mistaken.
148 'Supposed outrage by blacks', *Northern Territory Times*, 5th September 1902, p. 3; 'Notes and news', *Northern Territory Times*, 24th October 1902, p. 3.
149 'News and notes', *Northern Territory Times*, 21st September 1900, p. 3.
150 Reynolds, p. 96.

it appears to have been the coalescing of a number of factors, one of the most important of which was the establishment of 'blacks camps' at station homesteads and outstations across the region.

The first clear indication that local Aborigines were visiting station homesteads of their own free will appears in 1892 when a group of bush Aborigines camped near Willeroo homestead the night before Scott was killed. Next is O'Keefe's statement in 1895 that he 'heard that there was a tribe of nigars at Wave Hill Station'.[151] While these Aborigines were camping near the homesteads with the tacit approval of the whites, there is no evidence that they stayed there permanently.

At the end of 1898 the *Northern Territory Times* reported that some stations were allowing bush blacks to camp near the homesteads, but the only station mentioned by name was Argyle, in the East Kimberley.[152] However, by the early 1900s most stations in the Victoria River District had adopted a policy of allowing or perhaps forcing the bush blacks to come in to the homesteads and outstations. Bradshaw had a 'myall' camp by June 1900, and possibly a year earlier.[153] VRD had the 'Wickham blacks' in a station camp by October 1900.[154] They were supplied with beef, but the manager, Jim Ronan, complained to the Timber Creek police that he was 'unable to feed all the blacks in the country'. He also reported that Aborigines 'have driven off all the cattle off the lower Victoria on to the Katherine Crossing' and added that if the police couldn't help, 'I will have to take full responsibility of dealing with them myself.'[155] Wave Hill also had a camp by 1901[156] and Ord River by 1905.[157]

The camp at Ord River was established 'with an element of coercion' when the manager and his men rode around the station and mustered the bush people back to the homestead,[158] but in most cases there is no contemporary documentation as to how these camps came into being. However, Aboriginal

---

151 NTA: Timber Creek police journal, 9th December 1895, F 302.
152 'Wyndham', *Northern Territory Times*, 9th December 1898, p. 3.
153 NTA: NTRS 2261, 7th June 1899 and 28th June 1900.
154 'News and notes', *Northern Territory Times*, 11th October 1901, p. 3.
155 DJ Ronan to Mounted Constable O'Keefe, 25th January 1901. Timber Creek police letter book, photocopy held at Berrimah Police Station, Darwin; NTA: Timber Creek police journal, 14th November 1900, F 302.
156 Mounted Constable E O'Keefe to Inspector Paul Foelsche, 9th March 1901. Timber Creek police letter book, copy held at Berrimah Police Station, Darwin.
157 G Bolton, 'A survey of the Kimberley pastoral industry from 1885 to the present', MA thesis, University of Western Australia, 1953, p. 124.
158 ibid; NTA: NTRS 790, item 14787, JA Davis to Copley and Co., Perth, 1905 (probably October).

Aborigines not long in from the bush at Argyle Station, c1900
Durack collection

oral tradition on VRD, Willeroo and Delamere suggests that local people who had previously joined the whites were eventually sent out to tell the rest to 'come in'.[159]

Wherever the first station camp appeared, news of its existence and the experience of those living in it would have circulated among Aborigines throughout the region, and no doubt they would have discussed the 'pros and cons' of 'coming in'. Some of these 'pros and cons', from a European perspective, were outlined in 1905 by an 'old stockman' writing under the pen name of 'Magenta Joe':

> Some managers make it a point to keeping the blacks out all together. But it takes a lot of trouble to watch the niggers, and at the same time to also watch the cattle and keep them out of harms way.

> Other managers try and gather the blacks into a camp, close to the head station, and kill an old lumpy or worthless beast for them now and then; and I think, myself, that this is the best way. I think they do not do so much damage if the niggers are got in. The old niggers and old lubras will very often tell what is going on in the camp; and the station boys

---

159   Rose, pp. 80–81; J Wozitsky, *Born Under The Paperbark Tree: A Man's Life*, ABC Books, Sydney, 1996, pp. 5–6; J Sullivan and B Shaw, *Banggaiyerri: The Story of Jack Sullivan as Told to Bruce Shaw*, Australian Institute of Aboriginal Studies Press, Canberra, 1983, p. 65.

also mingle with them and learn what is going on from some of the others. Blacks are greatly divided amongst themselves, and will very often put one another away. But if they are very numerous, and a small portion of the tribe can only be got in, then I am of the opinion that it is just as well to keep them out altogether, because there is always a secret communication with the outside camps, telling them the whereabouts of the station hands.[160]

Other advantages of establishing a camp included making it safer for white men to travel through or work in the district, and the provision of a ready pool of cheap labour for the station. During a visit to VRD in 1905, only a few years after a station camp was established there, the South Australian Governor, George Le Hunte, 'saw some fine healthy looking aborigines' in a camp near the homestead, and noted that 'Mr Townshend, who employs several of the boys to look after cattle, spoke very well of them'.[161]

On the basis of his Australia-wide study, Reynolds listed the pros and cons for Aborigines of coming in or staying out. He noted that dwindling indigenous food supplies made it increasingly difficult for clans to live in isolation from the Europeans. In some areas people died from starvation, but if anyone continued to attack Europeans, spear their livestock or steal their goods, they could be certain of retaliation.[162] Added to this was the possibility that fighting between settlers and Aborigines may have increased the amount of fighting between rival clans.[163] This certainly appears to have been the case in the Victoria River country where Aboriginal oral traditions speak of inter-group fighting and woman-stealing in the early decades of settlement.[164] Reynolds concluded that 'life in the bush became increasingly hazardous and eventually "staying out" became the greater of the two evils'.[165]

Most of these factors applied in the Victoria River country. Certainly Aborigines were being confined to ever-smaller areas of rough, resource poor country. The sandstone and limestone ranges and 'back country' were never

---

160 Magenta Joe, 'Some pastoral notes and comments from an old stockman's point of view', *Northern Territory Times*, 27th October 1905, p 4. Magenta Joe was John Dunn whose death from fever in the Palmerston hospital in December 1909 was recorded in 'News and notes', *Northern Territory Times*, 13th December 1907, p. 3.
161 'Northern Territory, no. 4 – The governor's report', *The Adelaide Observer*, 4th November 1905, p. 49.
162 Reynolds, pp. 92–93.
163 ibid., p. 60.
164 Rose, pp. 101–112.
165 Reynolds, p. 92.

resource rich and, as more and more people were forced into ever smaller areas, these areas may have been eaten out. At the same time the white men were gaining control of more and more country, so foraging in resource-rich lowlands, spearing cattle and horses and using waterholes where cattle were concentrated, increasingly exposed Aborigines to dangerous encounters with the whites.

Even if Aborigines took the risk of hunting and gathering in the lowlands it's likely that, year by year, traditional foods in these areas were becoming scarcer. By the early 1900s cattle had reached significant numbers, with VRD and Wave Hill both estimated to have 60,000 head by 1906.[166] The environmental impact of such cattle numbers was greatly increased in years when the wet season rains came late, especially if the previous Wet had been poor. The year 1898 was very dry throughout the district;[167] on VRD it was 'the dryest Known ... for 12 years. Eleven months elapsed without a downpour'.[168] On VRD and Wave Hill, 1900 was reported to have been the worst season 'for a number of years',[169] and 1902 was much the same.[170] The wet season of 1904–05 was poor and it was ten months before rain fell again.[171] 1906 was yet another poor year and cattle were reported to be dying 'because of their massing on water frontages beyond their carrying capacity in the matter of feed'.[172] It seems likely that this series of dry years exacerbated the other ecological and social factors that led to the decision of Aborigines to start coming in.

In addition, the dangers of living in the refuge areas suddenly increased in the early 1900s as white men began to apply for annual pastoral permits on small pieces of land around the edges of, and in between, the big stations. These patches of land had been left over when the original big stations rationalised their lease boundaries to include only the best land. Most of

---

166 Timber Creek police letter book, 31st December 1906. Photocopy held at Berrimah Police Station, Darwin.

167 O'Keefe, 7th December 1896, p. 26.

168 NBA: Goldsbrough Mort and Co. Ltd: reports on station properties, 1898–1901, 2/307/1, report by R Watson to Goldsbrough Mort and Co. Ltd, March 1899, entitled 'Victoria River Downs'.

169 E O'Keefe, 'Report on Victoria River District', 30th November 1900, in 'Government Resident's Report on the Northern Territory, 1901', *South Australian Parliamentary Papers*, vol. 2, no. 45, 1901.

170 O'Keefe, 7th December 1902.

171 F Burt, 'Report on Victoria River District', 30th December 1905, in C Herbert, 'Government Resident's Report on the Northern Territory, 1905', *South Australian Parliamentary Papers*, vol. 2, no. 45, 1906.

172 Timber Creek police letter book, 31st December 1906. Photocopy held at the Berrimah Police Station, Darwin.

these blocks were on the edges of, or within, the 'sandstone fortresses' of the Aborigines. The white men who owned them ranged throughout the back country seeking cleanskin cattle, places where they might brand them in secret and routes by which they could move them to other areas. Consequently they were active in the very areas where, until then, the 'wild blacks' had been able to live in relative peace and safety. Once life in a station camp became an option, the possibility of accessing desirable European goods without the risk of violence – iron axes, billycans, cloth, sugar, flour, tea, and particularly tobacco – was another strong incentive to come in.[173]

As Magenta Joe pointed out, the Aborigines were 'greatly divided amongst themselves', so the aggregation of large numbers of Aborigines in station camps made it far easier for both station people and the police to gain information on the identity and whereabouts of law-breakers. Potentially, this was an advantage for the Aborigines – instead of offenders being unknown and large groups being 'punished' for a crime they might have had nothing to do with, they became named individuals whom the police could seek out and bring to European justice.

In spite of many advantages for the settlers, O'Keefe wasn't impressed with the appearance of these camps:

> some of the owners will expect us to be continually hunting the blacks of their stations, yet they allow these so called scoundrels to camp within a few hundred yards of their stations, the blacks get acquainted with the boys, & know all the movements of all hands, & if they are not kept well supplied with food, the consequence is they go & kill a beast on their own account.[174]

While O'Keefe may have been leery of the policy of establishing station camps – his own policy was 'to keep the creatures out bush'[175] – he nevertheless took advantage of the new VRD camp to obtain trackers after his previous trackers cleared out.[176]

---

173 P Read and Engineer Jack Japaljarri, 'The price of tobacco: the journey of the Warlmala to Wave Hill, 1928', *Aboriginal History*, vol. 2, pt 2, 1978, pp. 140–48; WEH Stanner, *White Man Got No Dreaming*, Australian National University Press, Canberra, 1979, pp. 46–47; P Read and J Read, pp. 73–93.

174 Mounted Constable E O'Keefe to Inspector Paul Foelsche, 9th March 1901. Timber Creek police letter book, copy held at Berrimah Police Station, Darwin. Note: because the copy has the bottom line or so of each page missing, it's sometimes impossible to be certain of the date. It may be that the date cited here is inaccurate, but related correspondence indicates that it's very near to correct.

175 NTA: Timber Creek police journal, 29th June 1907, F 302.

176 ibid., 14th November 1900.

The most compelling argument that it was the station camps which led to the decline in violent resistance against the whites comes from Timber Creek. As soon as the Timber Creek Police Station was established in April 1898, Aborigines began to keep the place under surveillance. For years there were regular entries in the journal about Aborigines calling out from or being seen on the nearby mountains, or their fires being noticed there. Sometimes the Aborigines prowled around the station after dark, they occasionally threw spears at the trackers and once or twice they threatened to kill all station personnel. When they saw the white police leave they sometimes would call out to the tracker who remained behind, asking for tobacco or for information, or they would try to get the tracker to join them. At different times they came down to the foot of the mountains and walked around on the creek flats, but if the police went after them they escaped back up the mountains. The best the police could do was to fire shots in their direction to 'disperse' them and order them to leave.

Over the eight years from 1898 to 1905 there are almost 70 references in the police journal to bush Aborigines in the vicinity of Timber Creek[177] with groups of Aborigines 'dispersed' at least ten times.[178] On one memorable occasion a lone Aboriginal came close to the station and O'Keefe 'dispersed him'.[179] An even more memorable incident occurred on 16th February 1903 when Mounted Constable Gordon reported that:

> a large mob of blacks made their appearance on the side of the mountain near the Station, told them to go away they refused saying that this was their country and they were going to camp on the creek. Told them that if they came near here again they would be shot, still refusing to

---

177 ibid., 24th, 27th, 28th, 29th and 30th April 1898, 31st July 1898, 13th and 20th September 1898, 4th, 5th and 26th May 1899, 4th, 5th, 6th, 7th, 12th, 13th and 23rd September 1899, 10th, 14th and 15th October 1899, 12th, 14th and 15th December 1899, 26th January 1900, 2nd February 1900, 9th March 1900, 6th and 16th June 1900, 17th and 18th November 1900, 7th December 1900, 14th and 15th May 1901, 4th, 10th and 20th June 1901, 6th August 1901, 4th January 1902, 12th, 13th, and 26th April 1902, 6th June 1902, 11th August 1902, 30th December 1902, 11th, 16th and 17th February 1903, 5th March 1903, 18th April 1903, 14th May 1903, 19th, 21st and 26th September 1903, 25th October 1903, 8th February 1904, 21st April 1904, 18th July 1904, 28th October 1904, 3rd January 1905, 24th, 26th and 28th January 1905, 4th and 8th March 1905, 5th May 1905 and 18th March 1906.

178 'Dispersals' are mentioned in the Timber Creek police journal (NTA: F 302) on 29th April 1898, 13th and 20th September 1898, 13th September 1899, 14th October 1899, 15th December 1899, 9th March 1900, 15th May 1901, 6th July 1902 and 16th February 1903.

179 NTA: Timber Creek police journal, 9th March 1900, F 302.

go fired shot from carbine in the air. This didn't seem to concern them much as they walked away slowly up the creek.[180]

From the time Mounted Constable O'Keefe established the Timber Creek Police Station he persisted with a very 'hard' attitude towards the bush blacks and maintained a policy of keeping them 'out bush', a policy which was repaid by low level harassment and the occasional spearing of police horses.[181] Within a year or so of O'Keefe's departure in 1905 the new officer in charge allowed a camp to be formed near the station.[182] It's clear that as soon as the bush people had the option of camping alongside the white men at Timber Creek they took it, even though these particular white men were police. From this time journal entries about 'blacks on the mountain' abruptly ceased.

Whatever the reasons may have been, the fact that many Aborigines did come in indicates that, for them, being in the station camps was a better option than staying in the bush – Reynolds' 'lesser of two evils'. Of course, while blacks camps appeared on most stations within a matter of a few years, not all Aborigines came in at once. There were 'bush' Aborigines in some of the old refuge areas for decades after the camps were formed. The killers of Alex McDonald on Auvergne in 1918 came down out of the rugged Pinkerton Range.[183] The Aborigines who speared Brigalow Bill Ward at Humbert River in 1910[184] and Jim Crisp at Bullita in 1919[185] came out of the Stokes Range sandstone country.

Some people stayed out for life,[186] while others moved back and forth between the bush and station camps.[187] In 1927 'about 30 myall natives' came in for the first time to Wave Hill Station[188] and in 1933 another group came in to Timber Creek.[189] In the latter case it wasn't stated exactly

---

180 ibid., 16th February 1903.
181 ibid., 18th October 1898, 10th June 1901, 12th September 1901, 25th January 1905, F 302.
182 ibid., 30th May 1906. On this date the police reported 'A mob of 40 blacks with their King now camped near station'.
183 'Tragedy at Auvergne', *Northern Territory Times*, 20th April 1918, p. 24.
184 NTA: Timber Creek police journal, 26th June 1910, F 302.
185 'Murdered by blacks', *Northern Territory Times*, 17th January 1920, p. 5.
186 C Schultz and D Lewis, *Beyond the Big Run: Station Life on Australia's Last Frontier*, University of Queensland Press, Brisbane, 1995, p. 69.
187 M Richards, 'Aborigines in the Victoria River region: 1883–1928', *Australian Institute of Aboriginal Studies Newsletter*, new series, no. 17, 1980, pp. 26–34.
188 NTA: Wave Hill police journal, 1st August 1927, F292.
189 R Weddell, 'Report of the Chief Protector of Aborigines, Northern Territory', in 'Report of the Administrator of the Northern Territory for the Year ended 30th June 1933', *Commonwealth Parliamentary Papers*, session 1932–33, vol. 3.

Aborigines examining one of the first cars at Victoria River Downs, 1922

Feast collection, National Museum of Australia

how many arrived or where they came from, but both examples show that the movement of people from the bush to white centres was continuing to this time.

Possibly the last region where 'wild blacks' held sway was the Fitzmaurice River basin. Even as late as 1940 the Timber Creek policeman, Tas Fitzer, 'strongly advised' a prospector not to go to the Fitzmaurice 'as the blacks in those parts were not to friendly'.[190] The Fitzmaurice was part of the area where the last Aboriginal 'outlaws', 'Nemarluk' and others, reigned until the early 1930s, and where the last white men killed by bush Aborigines were murdered in 1932,[191] but that's another story.

---

190 NTA: Timber Creek police journal, 18th October 1940, F 302.
191 'Murder of prospectors', *Adelaide Advertiser*, 29th May 1934, p. 9; 'Alleged murder of two prospectors', *Northern Standard*, 16th January 1934, 7.

Chapter 6

JASPER GORGE

For a region that's part of Australian folklore, the Victoria River District has very few places which have become the focus of popular interest and imagination. This is probably due to the paucity of published material on the region's history and the poor transmission of local knowledge among the white inhabitants. Another factor is that most of the places which have the potential to become the focus of popular interest are 'locked up' on cattle stations, where they are either known and accessible to only a few station people, or not known at all. The marked boabs at Gregory's main base camp are reasonably well known, the more so because in 1963 an historic reserve was created around them and since then they've been accessible to the public,[1] but the place with the most intense concentration of European stories and legends, myths and misinformation, is Jasper Gorge, located on the road between Timber Creek and VRD.

Jasper Gorge is a dramatic and beautiful cliff-lined pass that runs for about 15 kilometres through the precipitous, flat-topped Stokes Range. It's a complex place, certainly not a straight-sided gorge with a flat floor and sides of uniform height. It follows broad, sweeping curves back and forth, in some places widening, in others narrowing. Winding through it is Jasper Creek, here running through the middle of wide flats, there cutting into the rocky slopes below the cliffs so that, until the modern road was cut and bridges built, people travelling it had to cross the creek six or seven times. In times of flood it was difficult or impossible to get through.

---

1   NT Portion 554 of five acres was declared a National Park to be known as Gregory's Tree National Park (Reserve No. 1103) on 20 June 1963 (*Commonwealth Gazette*, No. 55). In 1979 it was renamed the Gregory's Tree Historical Reserve (*Northern Territory Government Gazette*, No. G38, dated 21 September 1979, pp 5–8), and in 1995 it was declared a Heritage Place (*Northern Territory Government Gazette*, No. G8, dated 22nd February 1995, p.4). Information courtesy Stuart Duncan, Secretary Place Names Committee for the Northern Territory, Department of Infrastructure, Planning and Environment, Land Information, Darwin, 2004.

View west along Jasper Gorge, 1953

FH Jonhson collection, National Library of Australia

Extending off the main gorge are side pockets and one or two long valleys cut by tributary streams, all cliff-lined. At the western end the gorge is up to two kilometres wide. The slopes forming the sides here are steep, spinifex covered, rocky and high, and capped with low cliffs. Moving eastwards the cliffs become higher and the slopes below them correspondingly lower as the gorge becomes narrower and rougher until, at the eastern end, it's less than 200 metres wide. At its narrowest point most of the width is taken up by a long, deep waterhole, bounded on the north by a cliff that rises straight up from the water which makes it impossible to travel along that side, even in the dry season. On the opposite side there is first a narrow flat, then a steep rocky slope rising to a cliff that looms overhead. Until at least the early 1930s

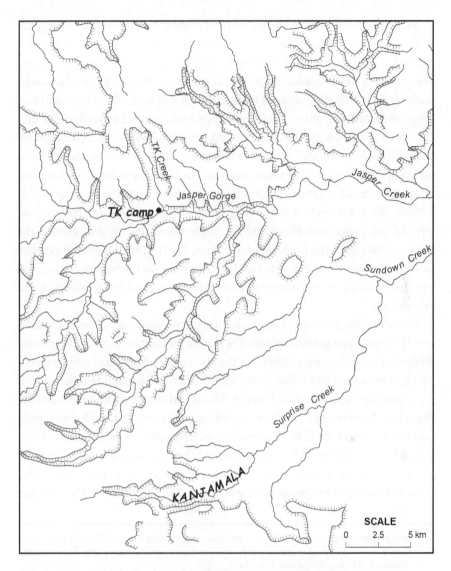

Map 7. Jasper Gorge and its complex of tributary gorges and cliff lines

there was a massive boulder on this flat which left barely enough space for a
wagon to pass around it (Map 7).[2]

---

2   This obstacle was mentioned by Government Resident Charles Dashwood in his report
      on his 1895 trip to the Victoria River ('Government Resident's Trip to the Victoria
      River', entry for 24th November 1895, Government Resident of the Northern Territory
      (South Australia) – inwards correspondence, 1870–1912, Northern Territory Archives
      (NTA), NTRS 829, item 6891) and can be seen in a number of early photographs. It

While Jasper Gorge is a place of hard reality it's also a place of legend and mythology for both blacks and whites. For Aborigines the gorge was created at the beginning of the world when the great travelling Dreaming, *Walujapi*, the black-headed python, slid across the Stokes Range, her body pushing up the curving sides of the gorge as she passed.[3] As she created the gorge she interacted with other Dreamings – *Mulukurr* the 'devil dog', *Kaya* the 'devil', *Wurliyingki* the red ant, and others.[4] Aborigines believe all of these Dreamings are still present in the gorge and some can be seen as rock paintings, or as natural features such as boulders, or hollows and marks on a cliff face. One Dreaming has been destroyed since the coming of the whites. The great boulder that nearly blocked the way through the narrow part of the gorge was *Wanujunki*, a turtle Dreaming; it was eventually blown up to widen the road.[5] And of course, the fish, turtles and crocodiles in the permanent waterholes, and the 'sugarbag' (wild honey), wallabies, echidnas and other resources were, and still are, a great attraction for local Aborigines.

For white people, Jasper Gorge also has many meanings. Most appreciate its wild beauty, and many have heard or read of it as a place of conflict between Aborigines and the early settlers. It's the place where Aborigines attacked and besieged teamsters and killed 'many men',[6] where they rolled boulders down upon passing herds of cattle,[7] where Aboriginal skulls with bullet holes in them have been found and where, according to a patron of the Timber Creek pub in 1971, 'until the 1950s you could demand a police escort when travelling through Jasper Gorge'.[8] One writer claimed that human bones found in rock shelters in the gorge – a common Aboriginal method of 'burial' – were 'the remains of some of the prospectors who came through the lower track on the

was still there when Ted Morey was a policeman in the district in 1932, and he describes how Burt Drew's donkey teams got past without mishap (E Morey, 'The donkey man', *Northern Territory Newsletter*, Feb., 1977, p. 12).

3   See W Arndt, 'The Dreaming of Kunukban', *Oceania* (vol. 35, no. 4, 1965, pp. 241–259), for a description of the movement of snakes and the relationship of that movement to the topography of the Victoria River District and Aboriginal Dreaming stories.

4   D Lewis, 'Report on field work for the Jasper Gorge – Kidman Springs land claim', prepared for the Northern Land Council, Darwin, 1977.

5   This appears to have been done by Burt Drew in stages, beginning in 1931 (Noel Butlin Archives (NBA), Australian National University: Bovril Australian Estates Ltd, Victoria River Downs ledgers, 1909–1944, 42/15/1–4, ledger 4).

6   K Willey, *Eaters of the Lotus*, The Jacaranda Press, Brisbane, 1964, p. 33.

7   For example, see 'Vanguard', 'North Australia: the real backblocks', *Cummins & Campbell Monthly Magazine*, Feb., 1934, pp. 81–83; Morey, p. 12.

8   Conversation between the author and a drinker, name unknown. A similar claim was made by Willey, p. 33.

The Turtle Dreaming rock in Jasper Gorge
Roden collection.

way to Hall's Creek during the gold rush of 1886'.[9] Another was shown a
heap of rusting tin cans under a rock in the gorge and told they were probably
the remains of plunder the Aborigines had taken from wagons after they had
driven the teamsters off.[10] Even the dimensions of the gorge itself have at
times taken on exaggerated proportions, with one account describing the cliffs
as 900 feet high[11] and another saying nearly 1000 feet (330 metres).[12] In reality
they are rarely more than 150 feet (50 metres) and often much less.

Most white people have only limited knowledge of what really occurred in
Jasper Gorge. One particular story has appeared in various accounts over the
years and is fairly well known – the spearing of teamsters John Mulligan and
George Ligar[13] – but few whites know more than the broad outlines of the

---

9   Notes compiled by Flo Martin for a reading at a writer's club in Western Australia
    (Martin family records). Flo was the daughter of Alf Martin, manager of VRD from
    1926 to 1947.
10 D Lewis and L Simmons, *Kajirri: The Bush Missus*, Central Queensland University
    Press, Rockhampton, 2006, p. 28.
11 W Linklater and L Tapp, *Gather No Moss*, Hesperian Press, Carlisle, 1997 (1968), p. 90.
12 D Magoffin, *From Ringer to Radio*, privately published, Brisbane, nd, p. 108. Dave
    Magoffin came to VRD as a young man early in 1938 and left in August 1940. He later
    became a well known radio broadcaster.
13 For example, see A Searcy, *In Australian Tropics* (George Robinson & Co., London,
    1909, pp. 204–05); 'Literary corner. The battle of Jasper Gorge', *The Graziers' Review*,

event or know the exact location where it occurred. There are faint 'echoes' of other stories and yet others that have been long forgotten. So what is the historical reality of the gorge? What is left when the myths are stripped away and the facts reassembled? In other words, what is the 'hidden history' of Jasper Gorge?

The first white men to visit the gorge were members of Augustus Gregory's expedition. On his second trip inland, Gregory ascended the Stokes Range north-west of the entrance of the gorge and then headed east across the stony sandstone plateau. The following day, 7th January 1856, he found a creek trending to the south that he followed to where it plunged over a precipice into a narrow, cliff-lined valley. After a difficult descent Gregory followed the valley four kilometres to where it joined another, much larger cliff-lined valley – Jasper Gorge. Here he struck a wide flooded stream, so he turned east and followed it down. After about seven kilometres his progress was stopped by the cliff-face that rises from the waterhole in the narrow part of the gorge. He went back upstream and managed to get his men and horses to the other side, and this time was able to travel right through the gorge and out onto a large open plain where he camped beside a huge boab tree.[14] Nearby was a range of hills that Gregory had previously named the Jasper Range. Later the settlers applied this name to the gorge and the creek that flows through it. It's a fitting name; at sunrise and sunset the cliffs that line the gorge turn blood red.

After negotiating the gorge Gregory travelled to the headwaters of the Victoria River and beyond, to the termination of Sturt Creek in the salty expanse of Lake Gregory. On his return he chose once again to traverse the great Victoria River Gorge, rather than use the shorter and easier Jasper Gorge. From this it would seem that Gregory didn't realise Jasper Gorge had an opening to the west and formed a natural pass through the Stokes Range.

The first European to travel all the way through Jasper Gorge was the Victoria River Downs manager, Lindsay Crawford. In July 1884 Crawford set out from VRD homestead to meet the first boats bringing stores up the Victoria River, and to find a suitable road for bringing these supplies back to the station. There's a high probability that he had a copy of Gregory's

16th June 1929 (pp. 354–55); G Buchanan, *Packhorse and Waterhole: With the First Overlanders to the Kimberleys* (Angus & Robertson, Sydney, 1933, pp. 114–15); E Hill, *The Territory* (Angus and Robertson, Sydney, 1951, p. 299); J Makin, *The Big Run: The Story of Victoria River Downs Station* (Rigby Limited, Adelaide, 1970, pp. 103–04).

14   AC Gregory, 'North Australian Expedition', in A Gregory and F Gregory, *Journals of Australian Explorations*, facsimile edition, Hesperian Press, Victoria Park, WA, 1981 (1884), pp. 99–194.

map[15] and knew that there were two possible routes to choose from, 'one where the Victoria runs through a gorge 35 miles long and an average of half a mile wide, with very high sandstone cliffs, and the other where Jasper Creek runs through'.[16]

Donald Swan and Bob Button, stockmen who took the first cattle taken to Ord River, passed through the gorge in 1885 on their way to the Victoria River Depot for rations. Years later Swan reported that on the way through, 'All at once we got the fright of our lives, for blacks suddenly appeared along the cliff tops, Hollering. "Good Day! Good Day!"'[17] Swan and Button were surprised at their knowledge of English words and decided they must have learnt them at Daly River where settlement had commenced earlier. However, the extraordinary ability of 'wild' Aborigines to mimic English words spoken to them has often been noted,[18] and it's more likely they'd heard the words 'good day' shouted out by other white men travelling through the gorge.

Four years after Swan and Button's trip, B Blair, a pastoral inspector for Goldsbrough Mort, wrote a report on VRD and provided a more expansive description of the gorge:

> To the north of Jasper Creek right along the boundary of the Coys property, are a series of high sandstone ranges reaching right to the Victoria river in fact this river flows through a gorge among these ranges for a long distance, horses can be ridden only with difficulty along the frontage, and there is only one other known pass through these ranges to the lower Victoria river, & that is by following up Jasper Creek, it is up this creek the road is formed to the depot on the river, where the Boats come with the stores ... [*Jasper Gorge*] is extremely rough for 6 miles by crossing & recrossing the creek there is just sufficient room between precipitous walls of red sandstone for a road to be forced through, since first opened a very considerable amount of work has been done in removing boulders from the creek

---

15   There is an early copy of Gregory's map in the collection of Victoria River Downs records held at the NBA (Goldsbrough Mort and Co. Ltd., F246, 2/859/379).

16   Lindsay Crawford, cited by Government Resident JL Parsons in his 'Quarterly Report on Northern Territory', 31st December 1884, *South Australian Parliamentary Papers*, vol. 3, no. 53, 1885, pp. 1–2.

17   D Swan, cited in C Clement and P Bridge (eds), *Kimberley Scenes*, Hesperian Press, Perth, 1991, pp. 101–02.

18   A good example of this ability is given by Billy Linklater on page 120 of his book, *Gather No Moss* (Linklater and Tapp); see also I White, 'The birth and death of a ceremony', *Aboriginal History*, vol. 4, nos. 1–2, 1980, pp. 32–41.

& other places, both powder & dynamite having been used and as the wild blacks are here very numerous, it was no easy task to get men to work.[19]

Some of the road work referred to had been carried out under contract by Charles Gore in mid-1886. The principal work was done in Jasper Gorge and it was there that Gore and his team endured a series of violent encounters with Aborigines. The experiences of Gore and his men are one of the great 'lost stories' of Jasper Gorge. Except where otherwise stated, the following account is based on an article written by Gore and published in the *Adelaide Observer* in 1896.[20]

With four Chinese and a Frenchman as assistants, Gore arrived at the Victoria River Depot at the end of May and was immediately informed 'that we need not be at all afraid that we should find the road-making contract a dull piece of work, for the natives on the route would make it lively enough'. Some days later Gore met two teamsters who had just arrived from VRD. These men warned him there were large numbers of blacks at the gorge who had 'given [*them*] a taste of their quality by firing a few shots at them'.

Eventually Gore's team reached the gorge and immediately 'noticed several fires spring up on either side, denoting the undoubted presence of a considerable number of blacks'. That night they heard their horses stampeding. In the morning they found two of them wounded with spears and saw the tracks of many Aborigines. Later that day Gore was suddenly surrounded by Aborigines who 'came from all directions, yelling and shaking their spears'. As he fled back to his camp the blacks tried to cut him off, so he fired shots from his rifle to keep them at a distance. He was 'uncomfortably astonished by having his compliment returned in kind'. He later learned that one of the teamsters who had warned him about the blacks had lost two revolvers on the road and evidently these had been found by Aborigines who knew how to use them.[21]

Back in camp Gore and his men constructed a 'spearproof break all round the encampment' and decided to suspend work until the VRD teams arrived from the Depot. When the first wagon arrived the teamsters said it was too dangerous to remain where they were and instead hurried on through

---

19   NBA: Goldsbrough Mort and Co. Ltd: sundry papers re CB Fisher and the Northern Australia Territory Co., 1886–1892, 2/876/7, B Blair to Goldsbrough Mort & Co. Ltd, 24th October 1889.

20   'The contributor', "Troublesome Aborigines", *The Adelaide Observer*, 11th January 1896, pp. 33–34.

21   'Things and others', *The North Australian*, 9th July 1886, p. 3.

the gorge. Gore sent a message with them to Victoria River homestead and remained holed up in camp waiting for reinforcements. For several days they were harassed by the Aborigines night and day:

> From time to time they got bolder and tried to get within spear range, and then a leaden messenger had to be sent in their direction as a warning. They, however, kept dodging from shelter to shelter amongst the tree trunks and rocks and laughing and yelling in defiance.

At about 3am on the third night Aborigines attacked the camp, but Gore and his men were awake and a volley of shots scattered the tribesmen. This was enough for the contractors and the next day they attempted to get through the gorge. They had no trouble until they approached the narrow part of the gorge at the eastern end. It was there that the most dramatic part of their 'adventure' occurred:

> all of a sudden within fifty yards of us fires sprang up amongst the tall grass and undergrowth right across the gully and hundreds of natives presented themselves, yelling and brandishing their woomerahs and spears. I had just time to turn back on our track with the team to escape the fire. The horses and dray were started into a canter over the rough ground strewn with boulders, the dray swaying and falling so that I could hardly keep my hold of the reins, and what with the blacks yelling, 'Frenchy' and the Chinese shooting, and the dog barking, I made sure it was all up with us; but somehow we managed to get back to the open again clear of all trees and rocks, and pulled up on a flat ... where we made another camp.[22]

Although safe enough for the time being, this wasn't the end of Gore's troubles. Soon afterwards another VRD wagon arrived and Gore decided to travel through the gorge with the teamsters the next day. Because of the roughness of the track the party only made it half way before darkness fell. That night they were shot at once more, though no one was hit. The next day they were joined by Lindsay Crawford who was on his way to VRD, and all hands made it through to open country east of the gorge where Gore formed a new base camp. Crawford then went on to his station and a few days later sent back three dogs and two armed and mounted station hands, one white and one black, to patrol the gorge and act as bodyguards for the road builders.

---

22   'The contributor', 11th January 1896.

For some weeks Gore and his men were able to work in peace while the armed horsemen kept the blacks away. Occasionally the crack of a rifle was heard in the distance but Gore remarked that the horsemen were keeping the camp well supplied with game so he never enquired the reason for the shooting. Dynamite was being used to remove large boulders and the regular explosions that echoed for miles through the gorge caused loose rocks to fall, which probably also helped to keep the Aborigines away.

Towards the end of the work the Aborigines struck again, this time attacking the Chinese while Gore and the Frenchman were some distance away. The two men heard an uproar and rushed back in time to see 'the last of the Chinese in full cry disappearing in the timber, and the face of the bluff swarming with blacks'. Some of the Aborigines were already heading towards the dray, but 'As soon, however, as they saw us they bolted back, one or two of them "rather sick" I think'. The Chinese managed to escape unharmed and returned later under escort of the patrol. Soon afterwards the job was finished and Gore and his men returned to Darwin.

In spite of Gore's improvements the road through the gorge remained rough and difficult, and added significantly to the cost of cartage to VRD and other inland stations. In 1891 Crawford gave an example of the high cost of running VRD, explaining that cartage of stores was £20 per ton and that:

> This is due to the difficulties in hauling through the Jasper gorge a distance of 10 miles where the Contractor's plant is annually Knocked to pieces in getting over the big boulders, which only dynamite will ever remove. This year alone I have taken out £200 worth of Timber & iron on a/c of the Contractor, which he will have to repair his wagons with during the wet.[23]

In fact, the road conditions were so severe that some time before 1896 teamster Mulligan had 'three sets of extra-strong wagon wheels sent over from Queensland',[24] and conditions remained severe for years. In 1899 a 'ponderous wagon' capable of carrying ten tons and built 'on special lines' was shipped to Darwin, bound for VRD.[25]

After the attacks on Gore and his team in 1886, Aborigines continued their harassing tactics. In 1887 it was reported that the Aborigines were

---

23   NBA: Goldsbrough Mort and Co. Ltd: Head office, Melbourne: letters received from HWH Stevens, Port Darwin, re NT property and butchering business, 1889–1892, 2/872, report by HWH Stevens to Goldsbrough Mort & Co. Ltd, 9th October 1891, pp. 13–15.
24   NBA: Goldsbrough Mort and Co. Ltd: Board papers, 1893–1927, 2/124/1659, report by Jack Watson to Goldsbrough Mort and Co. Ltd, 5th December 1895.
25   'Notes of the week', Northern Territory Times, 7th April 1899, p. 3.

continually causing trouble and constant vigilance was required.[26] Two years later Alfred Searcy visited the Depot and remarked that 'Messrs. Crawford and Mulligan's teams were camped right on the banks ... It was thought that the blacks would give some trouble this year, especially at Jasper Creek Gorge'.[27] It was even suggested that the passage of the teams through the gorge was what attracted Aborigines there. Searcy noted that Jasper Gorge was 'a favourite place for the blacks to meet and interfere with the teams',[28] and in 1891 HWH Stevens thought that if the stores could be brought in 'overland' – that is, by wagon on the track from Katherine which avoided the gorge – the 'blacks would soon shift their ground'.[29] The fact that the road passed through a narrow gap in one of the 'sandstone fortresses' that the Aborigines had been forced to retreat to certainly gave them opportunity to harass or attack the Europeans, and to escape quickly if necessary. Gore's description of the Aborigines 'laughing and yelling' as they attacked him suggests that they found harassing whites in the gorge highly entertaining.

Crawford reported to Goldsbrough Mort in 1891 that he had 'searched through the ranges on all sides but have failed to find any better way of getting on to the Downs Country'. He added that it wasn't only the rough road that caused the teamsters problems:

> As a further example of the difficulties of teamstering in a new country I would mention that whilst travelling up through this gorge the other day, the blacks during the night drove away one of our saddle horses, (a fine creamy gelding bred on the run,) and all that we found the next day was the head & neck, Some 20 broken spears, & the hobbles. The blacks had literally hacked the horse to pieces & got away with him into the ranges, where it is next to impossible for a white man to follow them up, even on foot: The Contractor on this road therefore runs continual risk.[30]

From the point of view of the settlers the Aborigines' style of attack was puzzling. Searcy commented that:

---

26   NBA: 2/872, report by HWH Stevens to Goldsbrough Mort and Co. Ltd, 11th July 1887.
27   'A trip to the Victoria River', *Northern Territory Times*, 4th May 1889, p. 3.
28   ibid.
29   NBA: 2/124/1093, report by GW Moore to Goldsbrough Mort & Co. Ltd, 27th November 1891.
30   NBA: 2/872, 9th October 1891, pp. 13–15.

The gorge is several miles in length, and from its peculiar formation the blacks, if they had any sense, would be masters of the situation, and could annihilate travellers by rolling rocks down the sides of the steep gorge. Fortunately for travellers the natives have not grasped the strategical strength of the position.[31]

Others since Searcy have made the same observation,[32] or claimed that the Aborigines did roll boulders down,[33] but no first-hand account of such action has yet come to light.

In 1895 there occurred the most famous event in the history of Jasper Gorge, the attack on teamsters Mulligan and Ligar. Over the years this story has been kept alive in the public mind in brief and often inaccurate accounts by various writers.[34] A wonderfully succinct version was written by Jack Watson who was closely involved in events after the attack. Watson had taken over as manager of VRD from Crawford in 1894. He described the attack in his quarterly report to Goldsbrough Mort:

> On 14th of this month [*May 1895*] the Blacks were invited to a picnic in a place called the Gorge, by Mulligan; As they did not think he treated them with sufficient liberality, they speared him and his men and chased them away from the waggons and took what they wanted, which was much.[35]

There was, of course, much more to the story than this, and it involved an amazing cast of North Australian frontier characters – the teamsters themselves, the infamous Mounted Constable William Henry Willshire, Jack 'The Gulf Hero' Watson, and James 'Long Jim' Ledgerwood. In order to more fully understand the way events at Jasper Gorge unfolded some aspects of the personalities and backgrounds of these men should be examined.

***

31   NBA: Goldsbrough Mort and Co. Ltd: 'General letters', papers of head office, Melbourne, 1874–1901, 2/176/130d, copy of Mr John Watson's station reports for May, June, July, 1895.

32   T Ronan, *Deep of the Sky: An Essay in Ancestor Worship*, Cassell & Co. Ltd, Melbourne, 1962, pp. 170, 184.

33   'Vanguard'; 'Attacked by blacks. Shower of spears in a gorge', *The Adelaide Advertiser*, 17th September 1909, p. 8; Willey, p. 33; Morey, p. 12.

34   WH Willshire, *Land of the Dawning: Being Facts Gleaned from Cannibals in the Australian Stone Age*, WK Thomas and Co., Adelaide, 1896, pp. 74–77; Searcy, pp. 204–05; 'Vanguard'; SE Pearson, 'The passing of Mudburra', *Frank Clune's Adventure Magazine*, 1948, p. 34; Hill, p. 235; Makin, pp. 103–04.

35   NBA: 2/176/130d, J Watson to Goldsbrough Mort & Co. Ltd.

John Mulligan had been carting stores from the Depot to VRD since 1886.[36] According to one source he was the first to take wagons across the Murranji Track[37] which was only opened in 1886,[38] so he may have arrived on Victoria River Downs in that year, possibly after coming across from Queensland. As well as carting the annual loading of supplies to VRD it was Mulligan who carried the wool clip from the station to the Depot,[39] and when the sheep were sold in 1894 and shorn at the head of Gregory Creek while en route to Bradshaw, he also transported this wool to the Depot.[40] (See Chapter 9) However, most of the time there was little call for Mulligan's services in the Victoria River area, so to keep him and his 'mate' in the district, VRD employed them as station hands.[41]

George Ligar was a New Zealander who is said to have been, 'a lieutenant in the Hussars and ... a great elocutionist, full of Shakespeare'.[42] He is also said to have fought in the 'New Zealand War', during which he suffered a severe head injury. This injury may have contributed to an ongoing problem, which was 'lifting his little finger', and this sometimes led to eccentric behaviour. On one occasion 'one of his fingers offended him, so he shot the top of it with his revolver'[43] – perhaps it was the little one? Whether Mulligan also was an alcoholic is unknown, but the chances are high that on occasion he, too, enjoyed 'lifting his little finger'.

Ligar's drinking probably also accounts for his colourful career in the Northern Territory. On 19th September 1872 he was sworn in as a Northern Territory trooper, but five days later was dismissed for drunkenness.[44] According to Bluey Buchanan's son Gordon, who came to the district in 1883 and almost certainly knew Ligar, during Ligar's short police career he arrested a Chinese man for theft. On his way back to the police station he stopped at a hotel for a drink and left the prisoner handcuffed and sitting on a horse, but when he came back outside the prisoner had cleared out.

---

36 NBA: 2/872, HWH Stevens to Goldsbrough Mort, 22nd July 1890; 'Murder of Sam Croker by a half-caste', *Northern Territory Times*, 7th October 1892, p. 3; Willshire, p. 77.
37 WA Rees, letter to the editor, *Walkabout*, June, 1950, p. 8.
38 Buchanan, p. 121.
39 NBA: 2/872, report on NT stations, HWH Stevens to Goldsbrough Mort & Co. Ltd, 23rd October 1891.
40 NTA: Log Book of Bradshaws Run, 2 June 1894, NTRS 2261.
41 K Dahl, *In Savage Australia: An Account of a Hunting and Collecting Expedition to Arnhem Land and Dampier Land*, Allan, London, 1926, pp. 188–89.
42 A Lucanus, cited in Clement and Bridge, p. 24.
43 Searcy, p. 205.
44 L Debnam, *Men of the Northern Territory Police 1870–1914: Who They Were and Where They Were*, Elizabeth, South Australia, 1990, p. 38; SA State Records Office, Correspondence files from the police commissioner's office, GRG5/2, 1872/941; Buchanan, p. 153.

Undeterred, Ligar arrested the nearest 'Chinaman' as a substitute and the innocent man was later convicted of the crime.[45]

At various times Ligar was convicted of being drunk and disorderly and charged with petty theft – though acquitted. On one occasion he drank so much he was hospitalised, and when he recovered he was strongly advised by the Government Resident to get out of town.[46] At the end of 1879 he was charged with arson, convicted and jailed for three years with hard labour.[47] His sentence was shortened by 18 months after a petition was presented to the Government Resident requesting his release.[48] As well as policing and teamstering, at other times Ligar worked as a boundary rider,[49] a fencer[50] and a stockman,[51] including a stint at the notoriously dangerous Florida Station in Arnhem Land where he would have worked under Jack Watson.[52]

'Long Jim' Ledgerwood was born in Scotland in 1850.[53] After coming to Australia he worked variously as a drover, prospector, stockman and station manager, including the management of Valley of the Springs Station in the Queensland Gulf country where, in 1893, he was attacked by Aborigines and suffered a minor spear wound in his back.[54] He was head stockman on VRD in 1895 and became closely associated with Mounted Constable Willshire, supporting him in his dealings with the uncooperative VRD manager, Jack Watson. Willshire was clearly very impressed with Ledgerwood. He described him as a 'good all-round bushman ... who stands 6 feet 4 inches, and weighs 14 stone'. He went on to say that Ledgerwood was a great rough rider, boxer, sprinter, horse breaker and drover, and 'a brave man

45   Buchanan, pp. 153–54. An identical series of events is attributed to another Northern Territory trooper, August Lucanus (cited in Clement and Bridge, pp. 9–10).

46   'News and Notes', *Northern Territory Times*, 29th March 1879, p. 2.

47   'Law courts', *Northern Territory Times*, 27th December 1879, p. 3.

48   NTA: NTRS 829, item A4098, telegram from the Minister for Education to the Government Resident, 16th July 1880 and item A4136, telegram from the Minister for Education to the Government Resident, 20 August 1880.

49   NTA: Gordon Creek police journal, 16th January 1895, F302. The Gordon Creek Police Station was the forerunner to the Timber Creek Police Station, and the journals from both are held in the NTA under the listing for Timber Creek.

50   Dahl, pp. 188–89.

51   Willshire, p. 100.

52   CE Gaunt, 'Old time memories. The lepers of Arnhem Land and sketches', *The Northern Standard*, 6th July 1934, p. 4; in the 1891 census he described himself as a stockman, living at Florida Station (Northern Territory 1891 census, compiled from the South Australian 1891 census by the Genealogical Society of the Northern Territory from original records held at the National Archives of Australia (Darwin), microfiche, 1986.

53   Northern Territory 1891 census.

54   'McArthur River notes', *Northern Territory Times*, 10th March 1893, p. 3; M Costello, *Life of John Costello*, Hesperian Press, Perth, 2002 (1930), p. 162.

[*and*] a good-natured, agreeable companion' who had worked on Narrulko, Springfield, Lake Nash, Yanga Lake, Mount Howard, Durham Downs, Hodgson Downs and other places.[55]

Jack Watson was born in Melbourne in March 1852.[56] He grew up there and was educated at Melbourne Grammar.[57] He first appeared in northern Australia in 1883 as manager of Lawn Hill Station,[58] and later was manager of Florida Station in Arnhem Land[59] and Auvergne Station in the Victoria River country.[60] Because of his wild exploits in the Queensland and Northern Territory Gulf country, Watson became known as "The Gulf Hero",[61] a nickname probably applied in sarcasm by those who thought he was either a lunatic or a terrific show-off. On VRD Willshire derided Watson for wearing a football jersey and a pair of Mexican spurs.[62] Yet there were those who thought highly of him. One of his contemporaries described him as 'a wild reckless fellow [*who*] would charge hell with a bucket of water. A splendid athlete and boxer, and a terror on the blacks. He stood six feet one inch, and most men were careful not to cross the "Gulf Hero".[63] Another said that he 'was a thorough "rough diamond" – painfully wild at times, but never wanting in generosity, kindliness of heart, and bravery, three manly attributes … which cover a multitude of sins'".[64]

Watson certainly had a 'multitude of sins' to cover. Many of the stories about him remark on his harsh treatment of the 'wild blacks'. He had shockingly cruel methods of killing or maiming Aboriginal people and collected their ears or skulls as trophies.[65] When a 'boy' of his named Pompey ran away from him and was murdered by bush Aborigines, he asked Willshire to bring in Pompey's skull because he wanted to use it as a spittoon. Willshire

---

55 Willshire, pp. 88–89.
56 Watson family Bible, in possession of Mrs Jan Cruickshank. Cruickshank is Watson's grand-niece.
57 'Obituary', *The Graziers' Review*, 16th January 1926, p. 1296.
58 Tony Roberts, pers. comm. Roberts is the author of *Frontier Justice: A History of the Gulf Country to 1900* (University of Queensland Press, Brisbane, 2005).
59 Gaunt.
60 Jack Watson, letter to Ned Watson, 20th July 1891, Watson family papers; 'The late Mr. John Watson', *Northern Territory Times*, 3rd April 1896, p. 3.
61 Gaunt; alternatively, Watson was known as the 'Gulf King', H7H (Hely Hutchinson), 'The men who blazed the track', *The Pastoralists' Review*, 15th August 1912, p. 594.
62 Willshire, p. 76. A letter held by the Watson family shows that in 1891 Jack Watson asked his brother Ned, who was then living in San Francisco, to get him a pair of the largest Mexican spurs he could find. It's clear from Willshire's description that Jack obtained the spurs he asked for, but their present whereabouts is unknown.
63 Gaunt.
64 'The late Mr. John Watson', *Northern Territory Times*, 3rd April 1896, p. 3.
65 EC Creaghe, diary, 8th February 1883. Mitchell Library, MSS 2982; Hill, p. 232.

Jack 'the Gulf Hero' Watson in bush garb

Cruikshank collection

complied with this request.[66] In his book, *In Australian Tropics*[67] Searcy tells of a man who:

> boasted to me that he never carried a revolver. He said he did all the punishment he wanted with a stock-whip and a wire-cracker.[68] 'When I want to be particularly severe,' he remarked, 'I cut the top off a sapling and sharpen the remaining stump, bend it down, and drive it through the palms of both hands of the nigger'. That seemed awfully brutal

---

66 WH Willshire, letter to Professor E Stirling, 4th December 1896, South Australian Museum, AD43.

67 Searcy, pp. 174–75.

68 The 'cracker' of a whip is a strip of leather at the end which is the fastest moving part when the whip is cracked. The cracker moves faster than the speed of sound (340 metres per second) and the 'crack' of the whip is the sonic 'boom' created when the sound barrier is broken. At the speed of sound, a piece of wire would slice through flesh like a razor.

Jack Watson and his Aboriginal assistant
Cruickshank collection

to me, but that man assured me on his oath that he did it. I wonder whether the cruelty he practiced ever came back to him in his struggle for life in the river – he was drowned in the Katherine.[69]

Searcy doesn't name the storyteller, but various details of the story fit with what is known about Watson from other sources, particularly that he never carried a revolver and that he drowned in the Katherine River.[70] In March 1895 Watson took over management of Victoria River Downs,[71] and it was there that he made the acquaintance of Mounted Constable Willshire.

---

69 Searcy, pp. 174–75.
70 'Drowning at the Katherine', *Northern Territory Times*, 3rd April 1896, p. 3; 'The drowning of Mr J. Watson', *Northern Territory Times*, 10th April 1896, p. 3.
71 NBA: 2/124/1659, 5th December 1895; NTA: Timber Creek police journal, 24th February 1895, F302.

Willshire is infamous as the trooper who was charged with massacring Aborigines in Central Australia in the 1880s. He was acquitted of the charge, but few today believe he was innocent.[72] In 1894 he was sent to VRD where hostile Aborigines were causing many problems for the settlers.[73] Willshire's superiors knew what his record was in Central Australia and they knew what relations between the Aborigines and settlers were like in the Victoria River District. It's difficult to believe that his posting there was anything but deliberate.

There can be little doubt that Willshire was a brave and accomplished bushman, but at least one of his contemporaries, a fellow policeman, thought that he was mentally unstable.[74] He may have been the type of man who would 'crack' when threatened. Early in 1895 four 'civilised' Aboriginal men, including Watson's 'boy' Pompey, took firearms and cleared into the bush on VRD. Local whites, including Willshire, were afraid these renegades would organise the 'wild blacks' and try to drive the whites out, just as the Aboriginal outlaw Pigeon was then trying to do in the Kimberley.[75] In the face of this threat Willshire wrote a journal entry on 21st March which displays a strange mix of bravado and fear:

> this is a rough place with treachery all around you & when blackboys belonging to the country turn out with firearms, matters are getting tropical. I must go out tomorrow & look them up & promise you I will do my duty to the very last out in the open. I am not afraid of any blackfellow with firearms but their treachery lurks beneath so many guises such as long grass, behind rocks, in creeks, and up high in gorges.[76]

The fact that Willshire brought in Pompey's skull for Watson suggests that, initially, they were on friendly terms, but something happened to change their relationship and they grew to hate each other. Among various complaints, Watson accused Willshire of 'cohabiting with a child of the tribe

---

72 R Kimber, 'WH Willshire', in D Carment, R Maynard and A Powell (eds), *Northern Territory Dictionary of Biography: Volume 1 to 1945*, Northern Territory University Press, Darwin, 1990, pp. 317–20; D Mulvaney, *Encounters in Place*, University of Queensland Press, Brisbane, 1989, pp. 123–30.
73 Kimber, p. 319.
74 Mounted Constable W South to Inspector B Besley, cited in R Clyne, *Colonial Blue: A History of the South Australian Police Force*, Wakefield Press, Netley, 1987, pp. 188–89.
75 H Pedersen and B Woorunmarra, *Jandamarra and the Bunuba Resistance*, Magabala Books Aboriginal Corporation, Broome, 1995.
76 NTA: Gordon Creek police journal, 21st March 1895, F 302.

about fourteen years of age or less' and said 'she now has a child by him'.[77] In turn, Willshire accused Watson of bad management, saying that:

> Since Watson came on the run the whole place has been in a state of fermentation, what blackboys and lubras Mr Crawford left behind have all run away since. Watson has such a bad name amongst blacks that they are frightened to remain, nearly every white man has left, and the three that are here now will leave as soon as Watson returns. there will not be a single person left who knows the run.[78]

And if this was not denigrating Watson enough, Willshire claimed that 'even the cattle seemed disgusted with him'![79] This antipathy spilled over into the dramatic events at Jasper Gorge.

***

The story of the attack on Mulligan and Ligar begins on 26th April 1895 when Willshire left VRD for the Depot 'to send mail and to see Mulligan through the Gorge'. Loaded wagons are slow moving and cumbersome at the best of times, all the more so on a rough track in the narrow confines of a place like Jasper Gorge. Clearly Willshire considered the threat of attack sufficient for him to provide a police escort. He'd done this from the time he was stationed in the district the previous year.[80]

Willshire arrived at the Depot on 28th April but found that Mulligan couldn't shift his wagons because two inches (50mm) of rain had recently fallen, so he returned to Gordon Creek. Some time after Willshire left, Mulligan wrote a letter to him reporting that one of his 'boys', Billy, and Billy's 'lubra', went out horse hunting (apparently at or near the Depot) and never returned. He asked Willshire to look for them. Mulligan was afraid that Billy had been murdered by the 'wild blacks' or else had cleared out to his own country on the Barkly Tableland.[81] It's clear that after Mulligan sent the letter Billy returned to the Depot, because he was with the teamsters on the night the attack took place.

With two wagons, each loaded with four and a half tons of rations and other goods bound for VRD, Mulligan and Ligar arrived at TK camp late in the

---

77   NBA: 2/124/1659, 5th December 1895.
78   NTA: Gordon Creek police journal, 18th March 1895, 8th July 1895, F 302.
79   Willshire, p. 38.
80   NTA: Gordon Creek police journal, 26th April 1895, 11th June 1894, 5th May 1895, F 302.
81   ibid., 11th June 1894, 26th April 1895, 5th May 1895, 18th May 1895.

Mounted Constable W.H. Willshire and trackers, c 1888

South Australian Police Historical Society

day of 14th May 1895.[82] TK Camp is a wide flat at the western end of the gorge. It's bounded on the south side by Jasper Creek and on the east side by TK Creek which flows out of the small valley that Gregory had followed down from the plateau top 40 years earlier.[83] The name of the

---

82   Willshire, p. 74.
83   See D Lewis, *The Boab Belt: A Survey of Historic Sites in the North-Central Victoria River District* (report prepared for the National Trust of Australia, (Northern Territory), vol. 2, 1996, site 49, pp. 12–16).

camp referred to Tom Kilfoyle, pioneer of Rosewood Station and one of the Durack clan, who had carved his initials on a boab tree there.[84] At the junction of Jasper and TK Creeks there is a deep, narrow waterhole, and the flat is the last good camp before the gorge narrows down considerably and the numerous creek crossings begin. From TK the slow-moving wagons usually could get right through the gorge in a day, which meant the teamsters could once again camp in open country where they were relatively safe from attack.

Fifty-two years after the event, Jack Kyle-Little, who was on VRD in 1895, said the teams usually had 'an escort of five natives not of those parts … armed with Snider rifles and the teamsters had Winchesters'.[85] In the months leading up to the attack the names of four Aboriginal men who were working for Mulligan are mentioned in the Gordon Creek police journal – Harry, 'Mulligan's Dick', Major and Billy, alias 'Snowball'.[86] One of them, Dick, came from Newcastle Waters and had cleared out well before the attack took place.[87] However, from various sources it's clear that the other three 'Queensland natives' had come to the gorge with Mulligan and Ligar, and were involved in the attack upon them.[88] There were also three Aboriginal women and a 'half caste' child with the teamsters on the fateful trip.[89] In initial reports the women are not named, but later police journal entries record their names as Mabel, Nellie and Rosy.[90] One came from Happy Creek, a short-lived police station near Camooweal on the Queensland border.[91] Another was from Wave Hill

84   Hill, p. 235; see also 'Government Resident's Trip to the Victoria River', 24th November 1895 (NTA, NTRS 829, item 6891).
85   Culkah, 'Early cattle life', *Pastoral Review*, 15th March 1947, p. 273–274. 'Culkah' was a pen name adopted by John Kyle Little, a man who spent a lifetime in the outback as stockman, station manager, mounted policeman and in other occupations ('JK Little', *Pastoral Review*, 16th December 1953, pp. 1205–06).
86   NTA: Gordon Creek police journal, 18th and 19th March 1895, 18th May 1895, F 302; 'Notes of the week', *Northern Territory Times*, 6th September 1895, p. 2.
87   NTA: Gordon Creek police journal, 31st March 1895 F 302.
88   'Outrage by blacks. Two white men speared', *Northern Territory Times*, 14th June 1895, p. 3.
89   NTA: Gordon Creek police journal, 18th May 1895, 22nd July 1895, F 302; Willshire, p. 89; the 'half caste' child may have been the 'half caste little girl known by the name of "Mary Mulligan"', who is mentioned in the Timber Creek police journal, 28th January 1902 (NTA F 302).
90   NTA: Gordon Creek police journal, 16th August 1895, 8th December 1895, F 302.
91   The mention of Happy Creek is in a letter from Inspector Paul Foelsche to someone who is unnamed but who is almost certainly the Government Resident, Charles Dashwood, 14th June 1895 (NTA, NTRS 829, item 6539). Tony Roberts (pers. comm.) was able to identify the location of Happy Creek.

Station and the origin of the third was never clearly stated, but may also have been Wave Hill.[92]

On arrival at TK Camp the teamsters found a large number of Aborigines in the area. It's clear that during the previous nine years when Mulligan had carried the station stores, some sort of peaceful contact between him and the 'wild blacks' had developed. Seventy years after the event Billy Linklater (alias Billy Miller), a contemporary of the teamsters, claimed that the 'wild blacks' used to help Mulligan get his wagon through the gorge by removing rocks along the track, and that he'd reward them with tobacco, flour, tea and sugar.[93] By 1894 some of the Aborigines knew him by name, and would call out 'Mulligan' to travellers in the gorge.[94]

On the night in question, while the teamsters and their 'boys' set up camp 'six or seven myalls … visited the waggons and received some tucker'. They then made a camp across the creek and began a corroboree.[95] Later Harry, Billy and Major took their guns and went across to join them, something they apparently did regularly and with the permission of the teamsters, but their wives remained at the wagons.[96] Linklater claimed that the teamsters enjoyed a nip or two of rum before beginning to cook a meal and that Major, who had acquired a taste for grog, stole a couple of bottles of rum from the wagons and shared it with the bush blacks.[97]

Some time after 8pm the two teamsters were standing near the campfire when they were suddenly showered with spears. A stone-headed spear hit Ligar in the back and he sprang for his rifle. Before he got to it a glass-headed spear hit him on the side of the face, nearly severing his nose and penetrating to the left cheekbone. At the same time Mulligan was hit by a spear tipped with the blade from a sheep shear. The *Northern Territory Times* reported that he was wounded in the thigh,[98] but Aeneas Gunn, who was a cousin of Joe Bradshaw, and for a period was closely associated with

---

92 NTA: NTRS 829, item 6539, Paul Foelsche to FE Benda, secretary to the minister controlling the Northern Territory, 14th June 1895; NTA: Gordon Creek police journal, 13th January 1896, F 302.
93 Linklater and Tapp, p. 90.
94 For example, in 1894 the Government Geologist, HYL Brown, met five or six Aborigines in the gorge. One or two understood a few words of English and one said his name was 'Mulligan'. Brown remarked that 'They seemed rather nervous and doubtful of our intentions, and in a short time retired to their fastnesses in the rocks'. (HYL Brown, 'Fountain Head to Victoria River Downs', in 'Northern Territory Explorations', *South Australian Parliamentary Papers*, vol. 3, no. 82, 1895; Willshire (p. 77).
95 'The late outrage by Victoria River blacks', *Northern Territory Times*, 28th June 1895, p. 3.
96 'Outrage by blacks'.
97 Linklater and Tapp, p. 90.
98 'The late outrage by Victoria River blacks'.

Bradshaw's Run,[99] said that the spear hit Mulligan above the back of his knee and severed the tendons, crippling him for life.[100]

Initially Ligar was so shocked and bleeding so profusely from his face wound that he was temporarily incapacitated. Mulligan reacted first – he pulled the spear out of his leg, drew his revolver and began shooting into the darkness, which probably prevented the Aborigines from rushing the wagons. The spears that hit Ligar either broke off on impact or he managed to remove the shafts. He had soon recovered enough to start using his rifle. It jammed, and before he could free the mechanism the blood flowing from his face clogged it up. When this happened Mulligan handed him a revolver and he fired several shots at random. Thinking that their own Aborigines might be hiding in fear, Ligar called out to them, but got no response. The teamsters then discovered that the women were not in their swags and concluded all were in league with the attacking Aborigines.[101]

To stem the bleeding from his wound, Mulligan got Ligar to fasten a belt tightly around his leg. In spite of his own wounds, Ligar managed to get on top of one of the wagons and drop a tarpaulin down the sides to form a screen behind which they could shelter. At this stage the spearhead in Ligar's back was working loose and Mulligan was able to extract it,[102] but fragments of glass from the other spearhead remained in his face.[103] As Ligar breathed, blood bubbled from his back wound and he realised that his lung had been punctured. Because of his injuries Ligar couldn't crouch under the wagon, so he stood up all night with a rug over his shoulders and his back against a nearby tree. The blacks came back at daylight but mostly kept beyond rifle range.

Mulligan's wound made it extremely difficult for him to move, so throughout the day he kept the Aborigines at bay with rifle fire while Ligar got enough bags of flour and sugar off the wagons to form a barricade against further attack. With the help of two dogs they had with them the teamsters were able to spend the next night in comparative safety and

---

99   T Willing and K Kenneally, *Under a Regent Moon: A Historical Account of Pioneer Pastoralists Joseph Bradshaw and Aeneas Gunn at Marigui Settlement, Prince Regent River, Kimberley, Western Australia*, Department of Conservation and Land Management, Western Australia, 2002, p. 4.

100   Aeneas Gunn, 'The contributor. Pioneering in Northern Australia', *Prahran Telegraph*, 10th June 1899, p. 5.

101   'The late outrage by Victoria River Blacks'.

102   Gunn.

103   'A treacherous tribe. Interview with Mr Searcy', *The Register* (Adelaide), 18th December 1905.

'comfort', but in the morning 'a large band of blacks and gins appeared'. Once again the Aborigines kept well back, sheltering behind rocks and trees, but one got close enough to throw a spear that landed near Ligar, and Harry fired a shot at Mulligan, which fell short. Mulligan tried to talk to the Aborigines, but was cut short by Harry who called out, 'We will kill both you white b——s to night'.[104]

By this time the two men were becoming weak from loss of blood, and probably also from lack of sleep, prolonged stress and inadequate food. They knew the *Ark* was due at the Depot on about 25th May, and that Willshire was planning to meet it there. They expected he would come through the gorge on the 24th or 25th, but that was more than a week away. They could neither wait that long nor take the chance that someone else would arrive in the meantime, so they decided to abandon the wagons and head to the Depot about 100 kilometres away. That evening they took saddles and rifles and went in search of the horses. Of the 40 horses that pulled the wagons the Aborigines had killed one and wounded three, and another three were missing. The other 30–odd were grazing within a mile of the wagons and the teamsters managed to catch two and get away.[105]

The two men rode slowly until about 3am. They then rested until daylight before continuing on to the Depot. They hoped that the *Ark* might have arrived early at the Depot but it wasn't there, so they left a note and continued on to Auvergne Station. After a slow and tortuous trip during which Mulligan suffered severe pain and became delirious for an hour, they reached Auvergne homestead on the evening of 19th May. There they discovered that the *Ark* was stranded on a sandbar some 27 kilometres down the Victoria. They decided to rest for a day before heading down river to the boat.[106]

On 20th May, while Mulligan and Ligar were resting at Auvergne, Willshire was reading the letter Mulligan had written about Billy and his wife going missing. Of course, Willshire wasn't to know that Billy had returned, let alone what had been happening at TK Camp, so on 21st May he and his two trackers left Gordon Creek to begin a search around VRD homestead, as requested by Mulligan. However, the next day he decided to abandon the search and go to meet the teams on the Depot road. On the evening of 22nd May he camped at the eastern entrance of the gorge and at 6am he started through the defile. Twelve kilometres further on:

104   'The late outrage by Victoria River Blacks'.
105   ibid
106   ibid.

we came upon the waggons at TK Camp. I saw at once that they had been looted by the natives. I could see nothing of Mr Mulligan, George Ligar or anyone else belonging to the waggons & goods scattered about, I wrote a note & sent George back to V.H.S. [*Victoria Head Station*] whilst Larry & I remained in charge of the waggons & loading we kept watch all day & all night whilst the range was swarming with natives who waved their spears at us.[107]

At the wagons Willshire found everything covered with blood – 'bloodstains on the felloes and spokes, blood on wearing apparel, blood on flour-bags and rifle cases'. He thought the teamsters might have been killed and their bodies thrown in the nearby waterhole, so he 'fired guns off into it to raise the bodies ... and got [*his*] two blackboys to dive from end to end'.[108] Using rifle fire to try and raise drowned bodies is an old British superstition that the concussion caused by the bullet striking the water 'would break the gall bladder, and cause the corpse to float'.[109]

In response to Willshire's note, at 9am on 24th May, Jack Watson arrived with two Aborigines and two white men, and everyone began collecting the goods that remained scattered on the sides of the gorge. They worked all that day and all the next, and at 6pm eight more white men and four station Aborigines arrived.[110] The whites included a group of overlanders heading for the Kimberley goldfields who had arrived at Victoria River Downs in time to offer assistance.[111] There were now 20 people at the attack site, all mounted and armed.

After the second lot of men arrived a letter written by Ligar was found, 'stating that they were speared through their own boys betraying them, & setting the wild natives upon them & that they had gone on to the Depot to try and find the "Ark" barge'. Someone had brought bandages and medicines to TK, so Willshire left the gorge to try and catch up with the wounded men to offer medical help. At much the same time (the records are mute on exactly when or why) Watson also set out (alone) to find Mulligan and Ligar. Willshire arrived at the Depot at midnight and in the morning found the message left by the teamsters. He immediately

107 NTA: Gordon Creek police journal, 21st May 1895, 22nd May 1895 and 23rd May 1895, F 302.
108 Willshire, pp. 76–77.
109 E and MA Radford, *Encyclopaedia of Superstitions*, Hutchinson & Co., London, 1961, p. 142.
110 NTA: Gordon Creek police journal, 24th and 25th May 1895, F 302.
111 'Outrage by blacks'.

set off for Auvergne, but on the way met Watson who had already been to Auvergne and was returning. Watson told Willshire that the teamsters had gone down river in a boat.[112]

Mulligan and Ligar had set off from Auvergne on 21st May and reached the *Ark* two days later. There they learnt that it was expected to float free on high tides in about five days time, so they remained on board until 27th May, but the tides failed to float the *Ark*. As a result the wounded men had no choice but to wait for the arrival of the schooner *Victoria*, which was due at Blunder Bay on 4th June. In the meantime they were taken by whaleboat up-river to Bradshaw homestead where they arrived 'in a half dead condition'.[113] As soon as they arrived Hugh Young, the manager of Bradshaw, decided to lead an armed party to Jasper Gorge to try and ensure that the wagons and loading were secure. When Young and his men arrived they 'found a large number of whitemen assembled', so they only remained for a short time before returning to Bradshaw.[114] On 5th June Mulligan and Ligar were taken aboard the *Victoria* and arrived at Darwin two days later, three weeks after being speared.[115]

After Willshire and Watson met, the two men started back for the gorge. On the way Willshire decided his horses were too tired to go all the way so he camped again at the Depot, but Watson continued on to TK Camp. Willshire made it back to TK Camp late the next day and found that, 'Watson & a big party of his men & blackboys had gone out after the natives'. He spent the next day at TK, treating the wounded horses and loading the wagons. That evening Watson and his party returned. According to contemporary sources, the only result of their two days in the ranges was the capture of three middle-aged Aboriginal women whom Watson handed over to Willshire.

It's probably no accident that Willshire went to look for Mulligan and Ligar instead of immediately going out after the culprits, or that after he returned to TK Camp he didn't follow Watson and the others into the ranges. After his experiences in Central Australia he would have been extremely reluctant to place himself in a situation where he might be forced to shoot Aborigines – with civilian witnesses present.

Early the next morning (30th May) Watson and his men left for Victoria River Downs, but Willshire and his prisoners were delayed because he wanted to escort the teams through the gorge. A man named Fred May had

---

112   NTA: Gordon Creek police journal, 26th and 27th May 1895, F 302.
113   'The late outrage by Victoria River blacks'; NTA: 27th May 1895, NTRS 2261.
114   NTA: 30th May 1895, NTRS 2261.
115   'The late outrage by Victoria River blacks'; NTA: 27th May 1895, NTRS 2261.

taken charge of the wagons which were loaded with recovered goods, but it took him some hours to get everything ready. They got through the gorge without incident and camped on open ground beyond the eastern end. That night the three prisoners escaped. Willshire was 'of opinion that someone has let them go, either blacks or whites, as they were Secured by neck chain to a small tree, & their ankles handcuffed'.[116]

In private correspondence Watson was later to blast Willshire about the escape of the prisoners and other supposed inaction and incompetence, claiming that Willshire:

> did not recover a single oz of stuff taken off Mulligans waggons beyond what I got my self in fact never tried and when I captured three of the agressors and handed them over to the police they lost them the first night though they were chained together and could not recapture them or said they could not.[117]

Willshire had the last word. In his book *Land of the Dawning* he derided Watson for his 'brilliant capture of three gravy-eyed gins', claiming that one of the women had a broken arm, another was covered in 'wales and stripe-like marks extending round her sides' and the third had her breasts swollen and leaking milk, indicating she had an infant that was unaccounted for.[118] The implication of Willshire's statements is that Watson had flogged or whipped one of these women. Given Watson's extreme cruelty on other occasions this may well be correct.

Willshire returned to Gordon Creek, but there was still unfinished business regarding the events at Jasper Gorge. Billy and Harry were wanted for attempted murder and warrants were issued for their arrest.[119] There are two major sources of information regarding subsequent events, the police journal entries written by Willshire, and his book, *Land of the Dawning*. The manuscript of *Land of the Dawning* was written by August 1895 – while he was still on VRD and some of the events about which he wrote were still unfolding.[120] The journal entries are usually brief, sometimes cryptic, and occasionally appear to contradict what's in the book.

---

116 NTA: Gordon Creek police journal, 27th May 1895, 28th, 29th, 30th and 31st May 1895. F 302.
117 NBA: 2/124/1659, 5th December 1895.
118 Willshire, pp. 75–76.
119 NTA: NTRS 829, item 6539, Paul Foelsche to the Hon. the Minister, Charles Dashwood, 20th June 1895; NTA: Gordon Creek police journal, 29th July 1895, F 302.
120 Thomas Cahill, letter, reproduced in Willshire (p. 101).

Fred May (left) and Joe Cooper, the famous buffalo hunter
Fred May took the wagons through Jasper Gorge after the attack on
Mulligan and Ligar

Pastoral Review, 15 Nov 1941, p.84.

On 3rd July Watson wrote to Willshire advising that 'Mulligans "Harry"
had turned up again & that he secured him, & he eventually broke loose &
made his escape'[121] but he appears to have left out important details in his
letter. In his book Willshire says that Jim Ledgerwood came across Billy,
Harry and Major, and a fight began. The end result was that Major was shot
dead and Billy and Harry were captured.

Ledgerwood took his prisoners to Watson but Watson refused to hand them
over to Willshire because then Ledgerwood (his head stockman)[122] would
have to go to Darwin to give evidence at their trial. Apparently Ledgerwood

---

121 NTA: Gordon Creek police journal, rd July 1895, F 302.
122 Willshire, pp. 88–89.

didn't approve of Watson's refusal to act because he took the Aborigines 'on the road', presumably to deliver them himself to Willshire at Gordon Creek, but they managed to escape. Willshire says that Ledgerwood later made a long statement to him about Major, Harry, Billy and Watson, and castigated Watson for 'not offering any assistance, at such a time'. Strangely, nothing is said in the police journal about the shooting of Major, but after Ledgerwood made his statement, Major's name doesn't appear again.

The search for the 'civilised' Aborigines involved in the attack on Mulligan and Ligar continued for months. Throughout July and August Willshire made several attempts to locate Billy and Harry, without success. In late July Harry's wife and 'the half caste child' were seen near VRD homestead[123] and at one stage Harry himself was believed to be '100 yards from VRD meat house'.[124] On 26th July both Billy and Harry were believed to be 'lurking about the Wickham'[125] (that is, the VRD homestead),[126] but a wide search the next day found no one. During the search Watson again hampered Willshire by taking back a station Aborigine named Tinker who was assisting Willshire, and saying, 'let the bloody police find their own boys if they want any'. Willshire noted that Watson 'blocks me in my work every possible chance, he curses the police all day to every and anyone'. Next came word that Billy and Harry and their women were 'knocking about' in the bush near Wave Hill, so Willshire patrolled there, but again found nothing. In August, Mounted Constable Burt arrived at Victoria River Downs to investigate the circumstances of the escape of Billy and Harry and to assist in the hunt for them. He went with Willshire on at least one patrol,[127] but after that seems to have left the district.

Harry was finally arrested at Powells Creek in late August.[128] On being questioned he was reported as admitting to being involved in everything except the actual spearing of the teamsters. He also said that subsequent to the attack, Billy had been killed by the 'myall blacks' who then 'took possession of the lubras belonging to the Queensland boys'.[129] The news of Harry's capture reached Willshire on 19th September, two days before his

123 NTA: Gordon Creek police journal, 8th, 11th, 12th, 20th, 22nd, 24th and 27th July 1895, 15th and 16th August 1895, F 302.
124 NTA: NTRS 829, item 6716, WH Willshire to J Watson, 24th July 1895.
125 NTA: Gordon Creek police journal, 26th July 1895, F 302.
126 Victoria River Downs homestead has been located on the Wickham River since 1890, and in early times the station and the homestead were often referred to as 'The Wickham'.
127 NTA: Gordon Creek police journal, 27th July 1895, 15th August 1895 – 25th August 1895, F 302; 'Notes of the week', *Northern Territory Times*, 23rd August 1895, p. 2.
128 'Notes of the week', *Northern Territory Times*, 30th August 1895, p. 2.
129 'Notes of the week', *Northern Territory Times*, 6th September 1895, p. 2.

station was taken over by Mounted Constable Edmond O'Keefe. Willshire left Gordon Creek on 26th September, travelling first to Darwin where he was to be a witness at Harry's trial, then on to a new post in South Australia.[130]

After the arrest of Harry the women concerned were wanted as witnesses, so O'Keefe continued to search for them for months, questioning Aborigines on various parts of VRD, at Wave Hill (on three separate occasions) and as far away as Bradshaw, but they were never found.[131] Harry faced court in Darwin in March 1896, but Justice Dashwood threw the charges out for lack of evidence.[132]

This then is the story of the attack on Mulligan and Ligar as revealed in the historical record, but various questions remain. One is, what caused the attack in the first place? There are various clues to the answer. To begin with, it seems likely that there were pre-existing tensions between the teamsters and their Aboriginal assistants which had caused Billy to temporarily disappear a week or so before the attack occurred. At the trial of 'Mulligan's Harry', Justice Dashwood:

> vigorously denounced the conduct of Ligar and Mulligan towards their blacks, expressing the belief that much of the loss of life and limb recorded was brought on by the conduct of white men in supplying liquor to natives and chastising them for every offence they committed. In the opinion of His Honor a person had no more right to take the law into his own hands with a native than one white man had to chastise another.[133]

From this it would appear that on occasion one or the other of the teamsters had beaten Harry and Billy for misdemeanours and on the night of the attack there *was* alcohol in the camp, as Linklater later claimed, and the teamsters had shared it with their Aboriginal 'boys'. Giving alcohol to his Aboriginal employees certainly would have been in keeping with Ligar's past behaviour. He had twice been convicted for supplying Aborigines with alcohol and, in view of his disposition when drunk, it's highly likely that he had at times been violent towards the 'boys'. During Ligar's trial for arson in 1879, storekeeper Frederick Griffiths said in evidence that he was afraid of him and that, 'The only danger was in prisoner's erratic temper ... when he's drunk he's a dangerous lunatic, he

---

130 NTA: Gordon Creek police journal, 26th March 1895, 19th, 21st and 26th September 1895, F 302; 'Notes of the week', *Northern Territory Times*, 4th October 1895, p. 2.
131 NTA: Gordon Creek police journal, 30th September 1895, 21st October 1895, 4th December 1895, 9th December 1895, 11th, 12th, 13th, 15th and 19th January 1896, F 302.
132 *Northern Territory Times*, 6th September 1895, p. 2.
133 ibid,

says so himself'. Mounted Constable W Reed also gave evidence and said of Ligar that, 'he is not quarrelsome when he is drunk but is dangerous'.[134]

Another question is, was the capture of the three women by Watson the only result of his foray into the ranges? The record is clear that for five days, the whites who came from VRD in response to Willshire's letter retrieved goods scattered along and above the gorge. Once this had been done a large party led by Watson 'had gone out after the natives'. They were only out for one night and two days, before returning to VRD. Willshire also returned to VRD and, though the search for Mulligan and Ligar's Aboriginal assistants continued for months, there was no further attempt by Willshire, or anyone else, to find and arrest the other Aborigines involved in the attack.

Two days is a remarkably short time for a 'punitive expedition' to spend in pursuit of Aboriginal offenders – usually such parties were out for at least a week and sometimes for several weeks.[135] Some years earlier Watson himself had spent weeks in pursuit of Aborigines who had attacked some drovers.[136] Billy Linklater, who was in the Territory when the attack occurred and may have heard the 'inside' story from one of those directly involved, wrote an account many years after the event. He claimed that because of 'dissention amongst the party and the roughness of the country they failed to punish the natives'.[137] Gordon Buchanan, who was also in the Territory at the time of the attack and, like Linklater, probably heard about the attack from those involved, told a different story. He said that at first Watson's party could follow a trail of scattered flour and battered tins, finally catching up with the Aborigines 'after a long search and by patient tracking'.[138]

The chances are that Watson sent a couple of his 'station boys' into the ranges ahead of time to locate the Aborigine's camp. Such a move would have made it possible for Watson and his party to move directly to where the alleged offenders were. Did he and his men return on the second day and make no further attempt to find the offenders because they felt that 'justice' had been done? If so, what did this 'justice' amount to? Gordon Buchanan states that 'a large camp of the enemy' was surprised and 'adequate

134 'Law Courts', *Northern Territory Times*, 27th December 1879, p. 3, 18th June 1881, p. 2, 9th July 1881, p 2.
135 For example, the party that went out after the killers of Rudolph Philchowski in 1913 was gone for nearly three weeks (M Durack, *Sons in the Saddle*, Corgi Books, Britain, 1985, p. 398).
136 Gaunt.
137 W. Linklater, 'Mulligan & Liger Tradegy [*sic*]', nd., unpublished manuscript in possession of Buchanan family, South Australia.
138 Buchanan, pp. 114–15.

punishment' was inflicted.[139] His claim finds support in a cutting from the *Northern Territory Times* of 14th June 1895, held by the South Australian State Records Office. This cutting is a report of the attack on Mulligan and Ligar and, at the end, written with a nibbed pen in old-style cursive script, is the comment, 'and 60 were shot'.[140]

Could 60 Aborigines have been shot? After Willshire arrived the Aborigines withdrew to the top of the gorge and, as more whites began to appear in the gorge, they probably kept an eye on proceedings. After a few days with no pursuit they may have felt none was going to happen, so moved to a convenient place in the ranges and settled down to feast upon the large quantity of flour and other foods that they'd managed to get away with. Up to seventeen men rode out with Watson that day, most of them probably armed with modern-style repeating rifles and revolvers. If they knew where the Aborigines were camped, or came upon them by chance and caught them unawares, they could have organised themselves to attack at the most opportune time (daybreak), and easily have shot 60 people.

Victoria River Aborigines speak of many places where they say massacres took place and one of these could relate to the attack on Mulligan and Ligar. According to Big Mick Kanginang, who was born about 1910 and grew up in the Stokes Range country, before he was born a lot of Aborigines were 'singing corroboree' at a place called Kanjamala, roughly 20 kilometres south of Jasper Gorge. During the night they were surrounded and at daybreak many were shot. He said the surviving Aborigines left the bodies unburied and avoided the place for years afterwards, which suggests that a very large number were killed. Big Mick named one of the white men involved as Tommy Wakelin, who was in the Kimberley–VRD region as early as 1887.[141] Another named was Charlie Sweeney, who was on VRD in 1900 and possibly earlier.[142]

And what of Mulligan and Ligar? Both men survived their wounds and the terrible ordeal they endured getting to medical help in Darwin. Some months later Mulligan left for Rockhampton for additional treatment.[143]

---

139 ibid.
140 This cutting is part of a news item published in the *Northern Territory Times*, 14th June 1895, p. 3. It was brought to my attention by Peter Read and Jay Arthur who obtained the original copy from the State Records Office in South Australia many years ago. I've contacted the staff at the State Records Office but they have been unable to relocate the annotated version.
141 State Records Office of Western Australia: Occurrence Book [*Wyndham Police Station*], 1886–1888, entry for 9th August 1887. Acc 741-1; 'Notes of the week', *Northern Territory Times*, 28th February 1896, p. 3.
142 NTA: Timber Creek police journal, 28th September 1900 F 302.
143 'Notes of the week', *Northern Territory Times*, 22nd November 1895, p. 2.

enough, not touching any of the liquor. Trooper Willshire, with one of the trackers, kept watch over the wagons, the other being despatched to Victoria River Downs Station for assistance. On receiving message Mr. Watson, the station manager, immediately started for the scene with a relief party of eighteen Europeans, consisting of station hands and a party of Europeans en route for the Kimberley, who fortunately happened to be at the station. Search made by this strong party resulted in the greater portion of the stolen goods being recovered, some of the articles being found on the ranges, 800 to 1000 feet high, and at a distance of from 16 to 20 miles from the wagons —showing that a large number of blacks must have been engaged in the work of plunder. Some old lubras were captured, and through them it was ascertained that Mulligan's blackboys and their lubras had leagued with the local natives, and were plentifully supplied with ammunition for their revolvers and rifles, stolen from the wagons. The boys had also taken six to eight horses, with saddles and outfits. *& 60 were shot*

The newspaper cutting about the attack on Mulligan and Ligar with the annotation '& 60 were shot'

South Australian State Records Office

When he recovered sufficiently he returned to VRD, probably to retrieve his property, but the blacks seemed to have had it in for him. Some days after he arrived back Aborigines raided his camp and stole, among other things, his Winchester rifle and a lot of cartridges.[144] It's unclear where Mulligan's camp was, but the 'gorge blacks' were suspects. Mounted Constable O'Keefe went to Jasper Gorge and spent a week riding over and around the Stokes Range looking for the offenders, but without success.[145]

---

144 NTA: Gordon Creek police journal, 20th April 1896; 'Notes of the week', *Northern Territory Times*, 15th May 1896, p. 3.
145 NTA: Gordon Creek police journal, 20th April – 1st May 1896, F 302.

Mulligan returned to teamstering, but appears to have shifted his operations to the Katherine region.[146] On 25th April 1900 he arrived in his camp on the Ferguson River looking worried and ill. The next day he looked much worse and was seen to write several letters and to burn some documents. Later he 'vomited much blood' and that night he died peacefully after saying to the Aborigines with him that 'he was tired and sad and going away to his own country'. His death was put down to natural causes, but the wound he received in Jasper Gorge had caused him ongoing pain and he'd become a regular user of morphine.[147] From the circumstances of his death there can be little doubt that Mulligan had suicided by taking an overdose.

Ligar recovered quickly, but for months after the attack fragments of glass were still working their way out of his nose.[148] According to Ernestine Hill, 'for the rest of his life [he] delighted to frighten the girls ... by pushing a peg or hat-pin through the cartilage of his nose, [through] the hole made by the spear'.[149] He returned to Victoria River Downs in August 1895 to assist in retrieving Mulligan's team horses, then left for Katherine a month later.[150] On 1st April 1896 Ligar was at Katherine helping Jack Watson cross some packs over the river in a boat. After several trips Watson decided to swim back to the township side, but he disappeared in mid-stream and wasn't seen again.[151] His body was never found.

After Watson's death Ligar went back out to VRD but in late May he set out for Katherine once again. On the way he found ER Johnson and his 'boy' under siege by Aborigines at Dead Finish Creek, on Delamere Station. Ligar's arrival broke the siege and, after assisting Johnson, he continued on to Katherine.[152] Eventually he drifted over to the Ord River country where he died on the 'Bend of the Ord' in December 1901, from the combined effects of excessive drinking and dysentery.[153] In his will he bequeathed his estate to a sister living in Texas.[154]

---

146 An advertisement which appeared on page 2 of the *Northern Territory Times* of 31st January 1896 advised that Mulligan was removing his teams from VRD to Maude Creek, north of Katherine.

147 'The late J Mulligan', *Northern Territory Times*, 4th May 1900, p. 3.

148 'A treacherous tribe. Interview with Mr. Searcy', *The Register* (Adelaide), 18th December 1905, p5.

149 Hill, pp. 235–36.

150 NTA: Timber Creek police journal, 3rd August 1895, 6th August 1895, 6th September 1895, F 302.

151 'The drowning of Mr J Watson'.

152 NTA: Timber Creek police journal, 27th May 1896, F 302.

153 State Records Office of Western Australia, Occurrence Book [*Wyndham Police Station*], 1899–1902, entry for 29th December 1901, Acc 741-5.

154 Letter dated 29th December 1901, headed 'East Kimberley District Wyndham Station', about the death of Ligar. State Records Office of Western Australia. Letter

The attack on Mulligan and Ligar was the most serious that occurred in Jasper Gorge, but attacks, robberies and other problems continued for years. On his way through the gorge in January 1897 O'Keefe came across a large gathering of Aborigines and dispersed them.[155] In 1899 two cyclists riding through the gorge on a round Australia trip had spears thrown at them, and saw 'a number of natives on Mountain singing out & displaying their spears'.[156]

When drover 'Dead Sweet' Joe Stevenson was taking a mob of about 500 bullocks through the gorge in October 1900, a crowd of over 100 armed Aborigines 'sprang up from behind rocks, trees, etc., and commenced yelling and screaming like so many demons'. As was intended, the entire herd took fright and rushed through the gorge. A number of beasts were killed and others so badly injured they had to be left behind. As soon as the drovers had gone a safe distance 'the blacks swooped down upon the dead cattle, built fires, and then held the corroboree of their lives'. Later the 'black fiends' sent word to the 'station boys' that they intended to do the same to every mob passing through the gorge and that they also intended to attack the station supply wagons, loot them and kill the teamsters. The *Northern Territory Times* expressed the fear that if nothing was done local residents would be tempted to take the law into their own hands. It reported that many were of the opinion that the number of police in the district should be 'very largely increased', but that one old drover suggested withdrawing the police altogether and giving the locals a 'free hand' to deal with the problem.[157]

After Stevenson's experience the authorities finally acted. The practice of providing a police escort for the teams travelling through the gorge was extended to drovers with mobs of cattle[158] and an extra trooper and two trackers were sent to Timber Creek to begin special patrols of troublesome areas, including Jasper Gorge. Between January 1902 and November 1903 the police escorted drovers and travellers through the gorge on seven occasions.[159] Within a few years of the special patrol being introduced, attacks on or harassment of white travellers in the gorge almost ceased. One writer has credited donkey teamster Burt Drew with demonstrating

---

book [*Wyndham Police Station*], 1901–1902. Acc 741-13.
155 NTA: Timber Creek police journal, 16th January 1897, F 302.
156 ibid., 17th November 1899.
157 'More trouble with the blacks', *Northern Territory Times*, 23rd November 1900, p. 3.
158 For example, see Timber Creek police journal, 8th July 1901 (part of patrol report dated 14th July 1901), 13th August 1902, 27th September 1903 (NTA: F 302).
159 ibid., 4th January 1902, 1st and 2nd May 1902, 13th July 1902, 4th, 6th, 7th and 8th August 1902, 13th September 1902, 31st October 1902, 6th November 1903.

'how the cunning could be overcome, and the gorge could be made safe for democracy'. Exactly how Drew was supposed to have done this is not stated.[160] Furthermore, Drew first appeared in the district in 1917[161] but Aborigines had ceased to be a real problem in the gorge more than a decade earlier.

Only two incidents are known to have occurred in, or close to, the gorge after 1901. These are the spearing of VRD manager Jim Ronan and the attempted spearing of Tom Wakelin in 1909. According to Ronan's son Tom, while his father was riding through the gorge he encountered over 100 Aborigines, the largest group he'd ever seen. With Ronan was 'Dutchy' Benning who'd been attacked in 1900 near the Gregory Creek–Victoria River junction. Ronan, Benning and their 'boys' got through the gorge safely and camped in open country a few miles away, but at daylight the next morning their camp was attacked and Ronan was speared in the leg.[162] The incident is said to have been reported to the Timber Creek police, but there's no mention of it in the Timber Creek police journal, or elsewhere.

Wakelin, a blacksmith 'recently employed at Wave Hill' and possibly one of the men involved in the massacre south of Jasper Gorge, had spears thrown at him while he was riding through the gorge in 1909.[163] Wakelin was on the Kimberley goldfields in 1887[164] and in the Victoria River district by 1895.[165] He worked as a carpenter on the Elsey homestead when Jeannie Gunn was there in 1902, appearing as 'Little Johnny' in Gunn's *We of the Never Never*.[166] The Aborigines who threw the spears at him remained hidden behind rocks, but called out in English that they would 'kill all white ———'. Wakelin 'immediately set spurs to his horse and galloped for his life, spears following him until he outdistanced his pursuers'.[167] After a prolonged police investigation Aborigines named Bamboo, Wooroola, and Wanbinola were arrested, charged with common assault, convicted, and each sentenced to a year's gaol with hard labour.[168]

160 'Vanguard'.
161 NTA: Timber Creek police journal, 8th September 1917, F 302.
162 Ronan, pp. 184–86.
163 NTA: Timber Creek police journal, 22nd August 1909, F 302.
164 State Records Office of Western Australia, Occurrence Book [*Wyndham Police Station*], 1886–1888, entry for 9th August 1887. Acc 741-1.
165 'Notes of the week', *Northern Territory Times*, 28th February 1896, p. 3.
166 W Farmer Whyte, '"Never Never" people. Their strange fate,' *Sydney Morning Herald*, 21st February 1942, p. 9.
167 'Attacked by blacks'.
168 'Felonious assault', *Northern Territory Times*, 16th September 1910, p. 3.

Burt Drew's wagon, bogged
Knox collection

Burt Drew's teams at Timber Creek, 1933
Durack collection

The attack on Wakelin was the last known violent incident between blacks and whites in Jasper Gorge, but long after the possibility of violent conflict had become a thing of the past the gorge remained a rough place for travellers. As late as 1937 a donkey wagon loaded with stores for VRD became bogged in the gorge. The teamster was Burt Drew, who had been carrying the VRD loadings since 1917[169] and was known as the 'Donkey King of the North'.[170] Apparently Drew took advantage of being stuck in the mud in time-honoured fashion – he got stuck into the rum. A month later he was brought in to the VRD hospital where for days he 'had the horrors properly'.[171]

For years it appears there was a relic in the gorge which provided tangible proof of its violent history – an Aboriginal skull with a bullet hole in it. From time to time stories are told about Aboriginal skulls with bullet holes, but rarely does the storyteller claim to have actually seen one. For my own part, I've seen numerous Aboriginal skulls in rock shelters throughout the Victoria River country and elsewhere in the north, but never one with a bullet hole. I began to suspect that such stories were white myths – until I finally met a first hand witness. In 1948 Lexie Simmons[172] went to stay with her sister at VRD and soon afterwards some of the station hands took them on a picnic to Jasper Gorge. While there the hands took Lexie to a rock shelter at the eastern end of the gorge and showed her a skull with a bullet hole.[173]

As she was telling me her story a few years ago, in my mind I was planning to go and search for it myself, but when I mentioned this to Lexie she told me that the skull was no longer in the gorge but had been taken back to VRD homestead. However, there may be another one. In the 1980s I was told that a cook with a road working team based in the gorge had wandered around the cliffs and found a similar skull. It's possible that the skull seen by this cook was the same skull that Simmons saw, but it's just as possible it was a different one. Is there still such a skull somewhere in Jasper Gorge? Until every inch of the cliff lines are searched – a massive job – we will never know. Some of the myths of the gorge may have been stripped away and some wild imaginings transformed to a more sober 'wild history', but the aura of mystery in the gorge will remain for a long time to come.

---

169   NTA: Timber Creek police journal, 8th September 1917, F 302.
170   Morey, pp. 12–13; Hill, p. 239.
171   NTA: NTRS 853, Joyce Falconbridge, diary, entry for 28th November 1937.
172   Lexie Simmons was born Alexandra Gurr and in 1949 became Mrs George Bates, George then being head stockman at Mount Sanford, on VRD. In later years she divorced George and remarried to a man named Simmons.
173   Simmons, pers. comm.

Chapter 7

CAPTAIN JOE'S BRADSHAW

It would be no exaggeration to call 'Captain' Joe Bradshaw a 'Colossus of the North'. He was one of the great entrepreneurs of early north Australia, standing with one business 'foot' in the Kimberley and the other in Arnhem Land, with Bradshaw Station strategically placed below. An unenviable metaphorical position, perhaps, but 'Bradshaw's Run' was to become one of the legendary Northern Territory stations, and would long outlast Bradshaw's other pastoral interests.

Captain Joe was born in Victoria on 10th June 1854.[1] He was born into money, the son of Joseph Bradshaw, a wealthy squatter who owned several sheep properties, including one named Bolwarra. As an adult, Joe (junior) was always keen to add to the family fortune. During his life he had interests in mining, railways and shipping, as well as in pastoralism.[2] In fact, his business interests were such that he spent comparatively little time living on any of his stations.

Captain Joe's first love appears to have been sailing. He owned a series of yachts and launches, including a schooner named *The Twins*, a 'steamerette' called the *Red Gauntlet*, a kerosene launch, the *Wunwulla* and another launch, the *Bolwarra*.[3] These vessels were the main means for transport of goods and people to and from his various stations. At Bradshaw the remains of two landings where these boats moored can still be seen adjacent to the pre-1905 and post-1905 homestead sites.[4] Joe's title of 'Captain' may have been

---

1   T Willing and D Kenneally, *Under a Regent Moon: A Historical Account of Pioneer Pastoralists Joseph Bradshaw and Aeneas Gunn at Marigui Settlement, Prince Regent River, Kimberley, Western Australia, 1891–1892*, Department of Conservation and Land Management, Perth, 2002, p. 14.

2   R Maynard, 'Joseph Bradshaw' in D Carment, R Maynard and A Powell (eds.), *Northern Territory Dictionary of Biography: Volume 1 to 1945*, Northern Territory University Press, Darwin, 1990, p. 32.

3   Northern Territory Archives (NTA): Log Look of Bradshaw's Run, April 1894, January 1894, June 1897, NTRS 2261.

4   See D Lewis, *The Boab Belt: A Survey of Historic Sites in the North-Central Victoria River District* (report prepared for the National Trust of Australia (Northern Territory),

honorary, possibly bestowed by a Sydney yachting club.[5] He certainly was not a qualified ship's engineer because twice in 1894 he had to ask permission to sail the *Red Gauntlet* without a qualified engineer on board.[6]

In his schooner *The Twins* (aka *Gemini*) Captain Joe explored a long stretch of the northern coastline. Later he published several papers on the north[7] for which he was elected a Fellow of the Royal Geographical Society (London).[8] For services to trade between Australia and the 'Netherlands Islands' (modern Indonesia) he was made a Life Fellow of the Imperial Institute in the Netherlands.[9] He was also active in public affairs, writing letters on various topics to government officials or to newspapers. He once advocated the adoption of a uniform phonetic system for the recording of Aboriginal words, but unfortunately the idea wasn't adopted.[10]

Joe was a Justice of the Peace in several states and a Special Justice in the Northern Territory.[11] In this capacity he had the power to hear court cases, hold inquests, sign warrants and perform other duties. When Mounted Constable O'Keefe was ordered to close the Gordon Creek Police Station and establish a new station at Timber Creek, it was Captain Joe who 'held a court at the Depot under a box tree'[12] and 'approved of site for new Station'.[13]

---

vol. 1, 1996, sites 21, pp. 110–12); D Lewis, *The Final Muster: A Survey of Previously Undocumented Historic Sites Throughout the Victoria River District* (report prepared for the National Trust of Australia (Northern Territory), 2000, site 32, pp. 129–41).

5   Response to 'Dear Old Hand' by 'Hardup', published in the *Northern Territory Times*, 26th May 1925, p. 3.

6   NTA: Government Resident of the Northern Territory (South Australia) – inwards correspondence, 1870–1912, NTRS 790, item 5948, Under treasurer T Stevens to Government Resident Charles Dashwood; NTA: NTRS 790, item 6256, J Bradshaw to Government Resident, 15th February 1894 and 2 October 1894; NTA: NTRS 790, item 6256, Harbor master H Marsh to Government Resident Charles Dashwood, 2nd October 1894.

7   J Bradshaw, 'The future of northern Australia', *Transactions of the Royal Geographical Society of Australasia, Victorian Branch*, vol. 9, 1891, pp. 107–16; J Bradshaw, 'Notes on a recent trip to the Prince Regent's River', *Transactions of the Royal Geographical Society of Australasia, Victorian Branch*, vol. 9, pt. 2, 1892, pp. 90–103. Bradshaw also published a paper in 1907, 'The Northern Territory' (*Victorian Geographical Journal*, vol. 25, pp. 20–28).

8   C Kelly, archivist at the Royal Geographical Society, letter to NB Nairn, general editor of the Australian Dictionary of Biography, 28th January 1982. File on Joseph Bradshaw at the Australian Dictionary of Biography Centre, Australian National University, Canberra.

9   'The late Mr Joseph Bradshaw', *The Pastoral Review*, 16th August 1916, p. 725; 'Mr Joseph Bradshaw', 'Mr. Joseph Bradshaw', *Northern Territory Times*, 19th March 1914, p. 5.

10 J Bradshaw, letter to the President of the Royal Geographical Society, South Australian Branch, 20th April 1900, Royal Geographical Society of South Australia, MS 14c.

11 'The late Mr Joseph Bradshaw'; 'Mr Joseph Bradshaw'.

12 NTA: 11th May 1898, NTRS 2261.

13 NTA: Timber Creek police journal, 1st May 1898, F302.

Captain Joe Bradshaw
Pastoral Review, 16 August 1916, p. 725

Joe laid down the law at the Depot several times over the next four years, but he wasn't above bending the law a little himself. After one hearing O'Keefe sent a memo to headquarters alleging that Joe and another man attempted to avoid paying the dog licence fee by making out that their dogs belonged to Aborigines.[14]

Exactly when Joe first went to northern Australia is unclear, but he soon gained an extensive knowledge of the north Australian coast and the pastoral potential of areas further inland. In 1890 he obtained a lease for over 400,000 hectares in the north-west Kimberley.[15] In the following year he led a party overland from Wyndham to examine the leased area more closely. Included in this party were Joe's brother Fred, Hugh Young, WF Allen and two Aborigines from Darwin.[16] Deep in the Kimberley they discovered some finely drafted red ochre rock paintings of human

---

14   ibid., 3rd November 1902, 19th April 1903, 29th August 1903.
15   Willing and Kenneally, p. 1.
16   J Bradshaw, 'Journal, 31st Jan – 6th June 1891, on an expedition from Wyndham, WA to the Prince Regent River district, WA', Mitchell Library, B967.

figures. Joe believed these paintings were so different from Aboriginal rock art elsewhere, and so finely executed, that they must have been done by visitors from some ancient civilisation, a theory now long discredited.[17] He published a paper on these paintings in 1892 and they subsequently became known as 'Bradshaw figures'.[18]

In later years he was one of the directors of the Eastern and African Cold Storage Company, which established the massive 51,800 square kilometre Arafura Station in Arnhem Land in 1903. This station was stocked with 20,000 head of cattle and a homestead and yards were built, but in the end it failed, a victim of floods, fever, crocodiles, dense and unpalatable spear grass, and attacks by Aborigines on the cattle and station employees.[19]

Joe soon reduced his Kimberley holdings to only 60,000 hectares between the Prince Regent and Roe Rivers.[20] He named the new station Marigui and began to stock it with sheep in 1892,[21] but a number of factors eventually led him to throw up this lease and shift his attention to the Northern Territory. No doubt these factors included the isolation, severe climate and Aboriginal resistance, but primarily it was the fact that before he could fully stock the lease with a large flock of sheep he'd bought from Victoria River Downs, in 1893 the Western Australian Government imposed a tax of two shillings and sixpence per head on all sheep entering the colony.[22] Rather than pay the tax Joe looked for land in the Territory.

In the early 1890s Captain Joe had visited the Victoria River and discovered that a large piece of country across the river from the Depot was still Crown Land. It was still 'blackfella country' too, the home of the Jaminjung people. On 27th July 1893 Joe applied to the Minister for the Northern Territory to lease '6000 sq miles on the north bank of the Victoria River NT at 6d per mile for 42 years'.[23] The minister wasn't impressed – the official rental was

17 I Crawford, *The Art of the Wandjina*, Oxford University Press, Melbourne, 1968, p. 81; D Lewis, *The Rock Paintings of Arnhem Land, Australia: Social, Ecological and Material Culture Change in the Post-Glacial Period*, British Archaeological Reports International Series 415, Oxford, 1988, pp. 84–85, 94–93, 110–12.
18 Bradshaw, 'Notes'.
19 R Duncan, *The Northern Territory Pastoral Industry 1863–1910*, Melbourne University Press, 1967, pp.134–35.
20 Willing and Kenneally, pp. 4, 6, 7.
21 'Notes of the week', *Northern Territory Times*, 27th May 1892, p. 3; Aeneas Gunn, 'The contributor. Pioneering in northern Australia', *Prahran Telegraph*, 14th October 1899, p. 5.
22 The tax was 30 shillings per head on cattle and 20 shillings per head on horses (*Western Australian Parliamentary Debates*, sessions 1893, vol. 2, p. 257).
23 National Archives of Australia (NAA): J Bradshaw to the Minister for Lands (NT), 27th July 1893, CRS A1640, item 93/302.

one shilling per square mile, so Joe's application was rejected. On 16th August he wrote again, still offering to pay only sixpence per square mile because, he said, 'From reports at my disposal I estimated that nearly one half of the country I applied for is occupied by sterile sandstone ranges, and that I would be paying fully one shilling per mile for such country as I could use'.[24]

Joe's reports were completely accurate. Roughly half the land he applied for was within the Fitzmaurice River basin, almost all of which is wild, rough, stony country. The basin is bounded on the south side by the towering, cliff-lined Yambarran Range,[25] a range that has been a dominating presence throughout Bradshaw history. Joe also told the minister that considering how much unoccupied country there was in the Northern Territory the rent was too high. He appears to have tried some subtle pressure to have the rent reduced:

> I would feel obliged for your early decision on this matter as I am about despatching a cargo of sheep to my country in Kimberley WA but on receiving a favourable reply from you I would probably alter their destination to the Northern Territory.[26]

It's clear Joe didn't receive a favourable reply but nevertheless went ahead with obtaining the lease because when he gave evidence to the 1895 Royal Commission into the Northern Territory he stated, 'I am paying for a lot of useless land, so that my rental is really 2s. a mile for that which is any good'.[27]

Bradshaw's Run came into existence on 1st January 1894 when Joe took up a lease for 6800 square miles.[28] The size of the run was considerably expanded in January 1898 when his brother Fred obtained a lease for 2000 square miles immediately north of Joe's lease. The two leases were run as one station, making Bradshaw's Run a massive 8800 square miles, or 23,000 square kilometres (Map 8).[29] Fred became the manager of the station and appears to have lived there permanently from this time.

24 NAA: J Bradshaw to the Minister for the Northern Territory, 16th August 1893, CRS A1640, item 93/302.
25 JL Stokes, *Discoveries In Australia … During the Voyage of HMS* Beagle *in the Years 1837–43*, vol. 2, T and W Boone, London, 1846, p. 52.
26 NAA: 16th August 1893, CRS A1640, item 93/302.
27 Joe Bradshaw, answer to question 3237, in 'Report of the Northern Territory Commission together with minutes of proceedings, evidence, and appendices', *South Australian Parliamentary Papers*, vol. 2, no. 19, 1895.
28 NTA: January 1894, NTRS 2261.
29 ibid., January 1898.

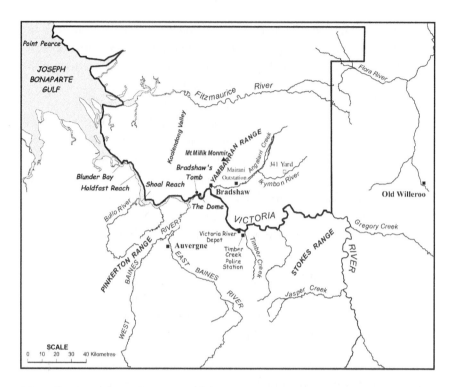

Map 8. Bradshaw station and related settlements and topographic features

Some time after the original lease was taken up a station diary was begun, the *Log Book of Bradshaw's Run*.[30] Initially it was a record of some of the more significant events that took place on the station, quite likely written retrospectively, but from 19th June 1899 it became a day-by-day account of station activities. The surviving part of the diary ends on 13th July 1901. It's a unique document in the early history of the Victoria River region, providing a fascinating insight into the process of exploration and early development of the station, and the complex state of relations between the European newcomers and the 'bush' and 'station' Aborigines.

The log book records that the first boat load of stores and equipment needed to set up a station were landed at the base of the Dome in May 1894, but later was moved back onboard to prevent theft by Aborigines.[31]

---

30   ibid.
31   NTA: 22nd September 1894, NTRS 2261; HYL Brown, 'Port Darwin to Victoria River by sea', in 'Northern Territory Explorations', *South Australian Parliamentary Papers*, vol. 3, no. 82, 1895.

Fred Bradshaw
John Bradshaw collection

In September *The Twins* moved all the stores and other goods up Angalarri Creek to a place called Kumallalay, or 'Youngsford', and a homestead was established there.[32] This homestead was visited by Knut Dahl in April 1895. His description of the buildings and station staff is the earliest on record:

> Having rowed for several hours we heard bells and very soon saw the 'station,' an open shed surrounded by some other buildings of still simpler architecture.

---

32   NTA: 22nd September 1894, NTRS 2261. The exact location of this homestead site has not been determined.

Three Englishmen, a Brazilian and a Swede, besides a couple of Port Darwin blacks with their women, occupied themselves in shepherding a few thousand sheep, and appeared on the whole to lead a precarious existence. The Swede [*Jan Larsen*] got very excited at meeting a Scandinavian. The station itself, as a going concern, looked pretty miserable. The houses were, to put it mildly, very sketchily built, all sorts of implements, as it were, floating around anyhow.[33]

The supply of freshwater at Kumallalay proved unsatisfactory, so in January 1896 the homestead was shifted to a high bank on the north side of Angalarri Creek, close to 'Duetpun spring' which flows from under the cliffs of the Yambarran Range.[34] In 1905 the homestead was shifted once again to a more elevated site about a kilometre away,[35] and this site was occupied until the 1950s.[36]

Bradshaw Station was set up with the help of 'foreign' Aborigines, one from south of Halls Creek[37] and others from Darwin.[38] Although most local Aborigines were still quite hostile to the white settlers at the time Bradshaw Station was established, the use of the placenames Kumallalay and Duetpun indicates that within a year at least one local Aborigine was assisting the settlers. In this circumstance, Bradshaw Station was different from and more fortunate than other stations in the region. Elsewhere the settlers didn't have local Aboriginal guides for many years and had to find various water sources and access routes for themselves.

As might be expected, when a station was established one of the first actions was to begin exploring or examining the lease. The term 'examining' is more appropriate because the country was 'new' or 'undiscovered' to the Europeans, but intimately known to and named by Aborigines. The Bradshaw whites had access to this local knowledge. Some trips were made specifically to quickly gain an overview of where the best pasture land and waters were, while knowledge was also gained incidental to other activities.

---

33 K Dahl, *In Savage Australia: An Account of a Hunting and Collecting Expedition to Arnhem Land and Dampier Land*, Allan, London, 1926, p. 190.

34 NTA: January 1896, NTRS 2261.

35 G Le Hunte, 'Northern Territory (Report by his Excellency the Governor of South Australia)', *South Australian Parliamentary Papers*, vol. 2, no. 49, 1905, p. 6.

36 Lewis, *Boab Belt*, vol. 1, site 17, pp. 96–103.

37 Gunn, 'The contributor', *Prahran Telegraph*, 5th August 1899, p. 5; NTA: Log Book, 8th August 1899, NTRS 2261.

38 'Notes of the week', *Northern Territory Times*, 6th July 1894, p. 2.

For Europeans, 'learning the country' was a process that continued for years. In August 1894, 'Communication was opened between the sheep party now on the Fitzmaurice River and the station at the Dome'.[39] This line of communication was through the Angalarri Valley and if the valley hadn't already been examined, doing so would have revealed the extent of useful land – almost all the good land on Bradshaw. Shortly afterwards Joe examined the Fitzmaurice River by boat.[40] Chances are his observations of the generally rocky country there, similar to that along the lower Victoria, deterred him from further exploration for a period. It wasn't until June 1897 that the log book again referred to exploration of the station:

> Messrs Bradshaw [*indecipherable words*] & party made an exploration
> of the country between the Victoria & Fitzmaurice rivers, discovering
> good country along the course of the Lalxin creek with many fine
> pools of water such as Kĭbura, Dhimon Dhiriji, Laberi, Kokin jĕrima,
> Kulindu, Lābangūla, Dărgatchi etc.[41]

This passage is the first documentation of whites entering the Koolendong Valley, a major Aboriginal access route through the rough ranges between the Victoria and Fitzmaurice rivers.[42] The location can be identified because some of the placenames are still recognisable today: 'Dhimon Dhiriji' is Jiminjerry waterhole, Kulindu is Koolendong waterhole.[43] Once again, the recording of Aboriginal placenames shows that the Bradshaw whites had a local Aboriginal guide or guides and were not making discoveries for themselves.[44]

During the time that the lease was being explored, Captain Joe was also stocking it and establishing basic infrastructure. Initially he brought in over 4500 sheep purchased from Victoria River Downs. Suffice to say the

---

39   NTA: Log Book, August 1894, NTRS 2261.
40   ibid., 4th September 1894.
41   ibid., June 1897.
42   Andrew McWilliam, pers. comm. McWilliam carried out a survey of Aboriginal sites on Bradshaw in the late 1990s.
43   These sites were documented in Lewis, *The Boab Belt* (vol. 1, sites 4 and 5).
44   Further 'discoveries' were yet to be made; the following year Fred Bradshaw found or was shown, 'a fine spring called Wujemon' about 40 miles from the station' (NTA: Log Book, 22nd July 1898, NTRS 2261). Other placenames in the Log Book that are recognisable today are Kullajunga Creek (Kurrajungle), Wūjemon (Widgeman Spring), Eucumbon (Ikymbon Creek), Angalarri (Angalarri Creek) and Mairanyi (Marani paddock). These placenames are mentioned in entries for September 1897, 22nd July 1898, 4th July 1899, 22nd September 1899, and 22nd October 1899, respectively (NTA: Log Book, NTRS 2261).

project was a disaster. Less than two years after the station was established moves were made to replace the sheep with cattle. Within ten years only three or four sheep were left.

The cattle that stocked Bradshaw came from Willeroo Station which had been abandoned after Aborigines killed the manager in 1892. Joe hired Jock McPhee ('Tam-o-Shanter' of *We of the Never Never* fame)[45] to muster the cattle and bring them to Bradshaw. Over the next five years the log book documents the arrival of a total of 1512 head from Willeroo.[46] While there were sheep on Bradshaw, one or two yards and paddocks had been built to hold them, but generally they'd been looked after by shepherds.[47] Shepherds are neither necessary nor practical for cattle, but yards are virtually indispensable so, soon after the Willeroo cattle were bought, work on cattle yards began. At the time the Willeroo brand was 'J41'[48] and during the time that the Willeroo cattle were being transferred to Bradshaw 'J41 yard' was built. [49] It still marked on modern maps.[50] By 1901 a further eight yards had been erected, various areas fenced and several outstation huts built.[51]

In May 1896 a small dam was built at Duetpun Spring and pipes were laid from there to the homestead. The log book has many references to these pipes being cleared of blockages, but when it was flowing the supply to the house was up to '1500 gallons per 24 hours'.[52] For decades Bradshaw was probably the only station in the district to have water on tap. Spring water is still being piped to the homestead building today.

---

45   '"Never-Never" people'.
46   NTA: Log Book, 27th September 1895, 25th October 1895, 30th July 1896 and 15th July 1899, NTRS 2261.
47   ibid., January 1896, April 1896, 22nd July 1896 and 20th September 1900.
48   ibid., 23rd May 1900.
49   ibid., 5th July 1899.
50   J41 Yard is located on the Ikymbon 1:100,000 map, sheet 5067, (edition 1), co-ordinates 949 327. Royal Australian Survey Corps, 1973. Though the yard is still marked on this map it was burnt down many years ago.
51   The Log Book mentions construction of a stub yard near Mount Panton in November 1895, a stockyard 'beyond Anglepoint' in April 1896, one at the homestead in September 1899, Dusty Camp stockyard in September 1900, construction of a 'draughting yard' between October 1900 and January 1901, of a tailing yard at Larrikin Billabong (Larrung Pool) in May 1901, and tailing yards at Wilsons Creek (Ballan-Gootchee) and Snake Billabong in April–May 1901. Fences also were built; a horse paddock in January 1896, Wogura paddock in December 1898, Junction paddock in July 1899, a 'division fence' through the horse paddock in June 1899, a division fence 'from Spring to River' and the 'Dome fence' in January 1900, and a 'Drop fence' at 'Myranna' in December 1900 (NTA: Log Book, NTRS 2261). Old photos show that huts were built at Myranna and Larung in the early 1900s, and there were huts at Wombungie and J41 yard at an early date.
52   NTA: Log Book, May 1896, 19th June 1899.

In 1900 work began on what is probably the most amazing early engineering work ever carried out on any station in the Victoria River District. The log book reported that, on 23rd May, 'JB [*Joe Bradshaw*], FMB [*Frederick Maxwell Bradshaw*], Ivan [*Egoriffe*] and 3 boys' were 'blasting out a horse track to the top of the cliffs at Tyalutyi Spring'. The next day 'All hands except the cook' were 'making a zig-zag road up the cliffs at Tyuluchi'.[53] The result of their work can still be seen. In the 'slot' where a huge section of the cliff was blown out, picks and crowbars must have been used to form a steep one-horse-wide track with two hairpin turns. On part of the downhill side of this track there is a drop of more than five metres, so if a horse or person slipped they would suffer severe injury or death. Immediately below the cliff the slope is steep, so a long sweeping zig-zag track was dug out until a gentler grade was reached.[54]

Given how relatively few cattle the Fitzmaurice River basin could support, it's surprising that construction of this packhorse track was considered worthwhile. However, the top of the Yambarran Range is flat and open from one to ten kilometres back from the edge of the cliff line, and then drops away into a network of rocky gullies, the headwaters of streams flowing to the Fitzmaurice River. Once stockmen reached the summit they could ride along the range for over 45 kilometres, and begin a muster down any creek they chose. How often the track was used is unclear. In the historical record there are only a few references to its use, including by the Liddy brothers who were stockmen on Bradshaw in the 1930s, and by a police patrol during the manhunt for the Aboriginal outlaw Nemarluk in 1932.[55]

By the time Captain Joe arrived to establish his station in 1894 it's clear that hostilities between the Aborigines and whites in the local region were already well established. Just as had happened on other stations in the region, conflict with Aborigines quickly became a dominant aspect of life on Bradshaw. Not long after the sheep arrived the Aborigines began to spear them and consequently the Bradshaw stockmen fired on Aborigines whenever they saw them.[56] After one instance of sheep spearing, a number of Aborigines are said to have been shot dead and their bodies burned by McPhee and Young.[57] The original flock of 4500 sheep had diminished to

53   ibid., 23rd and 24th May 1900.
54   This site is documented in Lewis, *Boab Belt* (vol. 1, site 16, pp. 87–95).
55   E Morey, 'Timber Creek patrols', pt 1, *Northern Territory Newsletter*, July, 1977, p. 18.
56   ibid., p. 190.
57   Tom Pearce, letter to Billy Linklater, 9th October 1948, 'Miscellaneous letters and other documents, 1895–1949', Mitchell Library, A1 10/26 (microfilm copy CY3480).

less than 114 by early 1899 (see Chapter 9), so the shooting and burning of these Aborigines is likely to have occurred some time between the years 1894 and 1898.

When the cattle arrived on Bradshaw in September 1895, the Aborigines soon turned their attention to them. In April 1896 'The Myalls made themselves obnoxious by spearing horses and cows, so had to be dispersed near the stockyard beyond Anglepoint'.[58] Possibly the same 'dispersal' was reported by a 'correspondent' to the *Northern Territory Times*:

> The niggers have speared a few more horses, and were kind enough to send in word (the messenger standing on top of a cliff and sheltered by a big rock) that they would spear all the horses and then come along and spear all hands. They also tackled me and another man while [*we were*] poking about in the ranges, but they only hurt themselves.[59]

Shortly after Fred Bradshaw arrived on the station in 1898 he was rudely awakened to the dangers of living in the north when, for reasons unknown, an Aborigine named Imgbora tried to kill him.[60] In spite of this, Fred later was said to have been very kind to the Aborigines[61] and there's evidence that, in his case, the statement may have been true.

There may have been a camp for bush blacks at Bradshaw homestead by 1899 as the log book entry for 7th June mentions that 'Ivan and five myalls went in the launch to Blunder Bay to meet the Sch [*Schooner*] Midge'.[62] There certainly was a camp a year later because the log book records that, 'During the night the two boys Larraba & Jacky, ran away … Three other myalls vis George, Jacky & Dyrter, were procured from the camp, to fill places of the runaways and were supplied with clothes and blankets'.[63] There can be little doubt that, as on other stations in the region, for many years there was a flow of Aborigines back and forth between the bush, the 'myall' camp at the homestead and station employment.[64]

---

58   NTA: Log Book, 27th September 1895, April 1896, NTRS 2261.

59   'Notes of the week', *Northern Territory Times*, 17th April 1896, p. 3.

60   NTA: Timber Creek police journal, 7th November 1900, F 302; 'Attacked by blacks at the Fitzmaurice River', *Northern Territory Times*, 2nd December 1898, p. 3.

61   For example, see 'Massacres in the Northern Territory', *The Register* (Adelaide), 18th December 1905, p. 5; 'An alleged terrible tragedy', *Northern Territory Times*, 22nd December 1905, p. 3.

62   NTA: Log Book, 7th June 1899, NTRS 2261.

63   ibid., 28th June 1900.

64   M Richards, 'Aborigines in the Victoria River region: 1883–1928', *Australian Institute of Aboriginal Studies Newsletter*, new series 17, 1980, pp. 26–34.

The whites on Bradshaw didn't experience trouble solely with the 'myall' or bush blacks. There were occasional clashes with Aborigines working on the station as well. During the first decade on Bradshaw most of the problems seem to have been instigated by a white employee named Ivan Egoriffe, and fuelled by grog. Egoriffe worked for Joe Bradshaw as engineer and general hand from at least 1894[65] until his death in 1905. He was 'a native of Russia or Finland', a powerfully built man with 'a reputation for surliness and harsh treatment of the natives under him'.[66] It's likely that he was an alcoholic. He certainly was a man who became 'Ivan the Terrible' when drunk. The log book entry for 21st October 1899 mentions that 'Larsen and Ivan have been stealing grog out of the store, hence sundry rows'. Another entry records that 'Towards evening Ivan was intoxicated and behaved like a madman'.[67]

Egoriffe's behaviour 'on the grog' probably accounts for much of his harshness towards Aborigines and sometimes towards whites. In October 1899 he went to the Depot and on his return was seen to be showing the effects of heavy drinking. The next day he was due to go out to 'Myranna', an outstation about 14 kilometres east of the homestead, but before he left he couldn't find his revolver. Egoriffe left without the gun and when he arrived at Myranna, still showing the effects of alcohol, he accused an Aboriginal named Bingey of stealing it. At the homestead the following day Fred Bradshaw questioned Bingey who 'denied having taken Ivan's revolver, and accused Ivan of having fired at him with that weapon'. The revolver was eventually found in a box in Egoriffe's room. Fred Bradshaw, Bingey and George went back to Myranna the next day, taking the revolver with them, and 'On arriving at Myranna found all going on well, but on seeing Bingey Ivan commenced to beat him. FMB interfered, when Ivan became unbearable and abusive, & insulting but subsequently apologised'.[68]

In September or October 1899 Kolumboi, an Aborigine who came from south of Halls Creek and had been part of the team at Marigui,[69] ran away from the homestead with a 'lubra' named Yanimbella.[70] The reason why they absconded is unknown, but on 5th October they were captured and chained up for the night. The next day, 'Ivan gave Kolumboi the father of a bumping and sent him and the lubra to glory'.[71] Being 'sent to glory' would normally

---

65   NTA: Log Book, April 1894, NTRS 2261.
66   'An alleged terrible tragedy'.
67   NTA: Log Book, 23rd December 1900, NTRS 2261.
68   ibid., 9th, 10th, 11th and 12th November 1900.
69   Gunn, 'The contributor', *Prahran Telegraph*, 5th August 1899, p. 5.
70   NTA: Log Book, 6th November 1899, NTRS 2261.
71   ibid.

be taken to mean that they had been murdered, but it's possible it just meant that they had been told to clear out for good. Either way neither Kolumboi's nor Yanimbella's name appears in the log book again.

***

After a trip to Darwin in July 1900 the Bradshaw launch *Wunwulla* anchored at the mouth of the Daly River, waiting for the tide to rise before travelling upstream.[72] On board were Ivan Egoriffe, the skipper Jack Larsen,[73] and a crew of three Victoria River Aborigines, George (aka 'Josey'), Jimmy and a young boy named Georgie.[74] Before the launch moved up the river two Daly River Aborigines were brought on board to act as pilots.[75] At about midnight as preparations were being made to start upstream, someone hit Egoriffe on the back of the head and stunned him, then threw him overboard. The water revived him and he managed to clamber into the boat's dinghy which was tied behind, but it was immediately cut loose. Egoriffe tried to paddle back but a shot was fired at him, so he let the current take him. As he drifted away he heard Larsen cry out, and then a shot.[76] It was later learned that Larsen had been shot in the forehead while being held by the neck and his body thrown overboard'.[77]

Egoriffe was rescued the next day by Captain Mugg on the lugger *Minniehaha*. Eventually Egoriffe and Mugg got word to the authorities in Darwin who dispatched Mounted Constables Stott and Stone from Brocks Creek to investigate.[78] In an Aboriginal camp south of the Daly River mouth they arrested two Daly River men – 'Cammerfor' and 'Monkgum'[79] – who were said to have admitted to others in the camp that they had killed Larsen and the three Victoria River men.[80]

72 'Mutiny of natives. The Daly River murder', *Adelaide Advertiser*, 24th July 1900, p. 5.
73 Larsen appears to have been at Marigui in the capacity of cook (Gunn, 'The contributor', *Prahran Telegraph*, 10th June 1899, p. 5). On Bradshaw in 1894 he was described as 'mate' on the schooner *Twins* (NTA: Log Book, April 1894, NTRS 2261), and was the 'Swede' who became very excited by the visit of the Norwegian, Knut Dahl).
74 NTA: Log Book, 24th August 1900, NTRS 2261; 'Daly River outrage. Arrest of two of the principals at Victoria River', *Northern Territory Times*, 7th September 1900, p. 3.
75 'Mutiny of natives'.
76 NTA: NTRS 790, item 9877, telegram from WJ Byrne to Government Resident Justice Charles Dashwood, 19th July 1900. The telegram cites a letter from J Nieman.
77 'Daly River outrage. Arrest of two of the principals at Victoria River'.
78 'Reported outrage by blacks on the Daly River', *Northern Territory Times*, 20th July 1900, p. 3.
79 'The Daly River outrage', *The Register* (Adelaide), 4th August 1900, p. 6.
80 'The Daly River outrage', *Northern Territory Times*, 3rd August 1900, p. 3.

The police arrived back in Darwin with their prisoners and three witnesses on 1st August. They appeared in court the next day. The Aborigines told their stories through an interpreter and it was reported that 'By their own confession the two prisoners appear to have committed a deed unique in the annals of outrages perpetrated by natives for the cool boldness exhibited in its accomplishment'. The police were 'congratulated on the clever and prompt manner in which they have succeeded in bringing the offenders to book'.[81] But the police were too clever by half and the congratulations a trifle premature. The court was about to find out how cool and bold these Aborigines really were!

While the police were out looking for the murderers, Egoriffe had been with Captain Joe looking for the *Wunwulla*. They found the boat partly looted but undamaged[82] and brought it back to Darwin the day after Cammerfor and Monkgum were in court confessing their guilt.[83] The next day Egoriffe went to identify the prisoners and declared emphatically that he had never seen them before! He repeated his belief that he had been attacked by the Victoria River crewmen.[84] This was confirmed the next day when the *Minniehaha* arrived with Chatpa and Kadeel, the two Daly River Aborigines who really had been on the *Wunwulla*.[85] These men, identified by Egoriffe, maintained that the crew of Victoria River boys first attacked Egoriffe and Larsen and then attacked them, forcing them to jump overboard.[86]

One of the *Minniehaha* party reported that 'the natives all along the [*Daly*] river seemed to be aware of the fact that the two men first captured by the police were entirely innocent of any complicity in the affair, and the mistake was the subject of much amusement among them'.[87] Years later Ernestine Hill was told that the two men arrested by Stott and Stone had lied to the police about their involvement in the murder and unwittingly placed their necks in a noose, because 'that fella too much gammon he savvy eberyting allabout'.[88] In other words, they thought the policemen were real know-alls.

---

81 ibid.
82 'The Daly River outrage', *Northern Territory Times*, 10th August 1900, p. 3.
83 'The Daly River outrage', *The Register* (Adelaide), 4th August 1900, p. 6.
84 'The Daly River outrage', *The Register* (Adelaide), 9th August 1900, p. 6.
85 'The Daly River outrage. Contradictory evidence', *The Register* (Adelaide), 7th August 1900, p 4; 'The Daly River outrage', *The Register* (Adelaide), 9th August 1900, p. 4. Chatpa was also known as Fennem or Datpull, and Kadeel was known as Cockatoo ('News and notes', *Northern Territory Times*, 24th August 1900, p. 3 ; NTA: H Christie to Inspector Paul Foelsche, 29th August 1900, NTRS 790, item 9973).
86 'The Daly River outrage', *The Register* (Adelaide), 9th August 1900, p. 4.
87 'The Daly River outrage', *Northern Territory Times*, 10th August 1900, p. 3.
88 E Hill, *The Territory*, Angus and Robertson, Sydney, 1951, p. 250.

As a result of this debacle Stott had to go out again, this time travelling to Bradshaw on the *Wunwulla* to search for the missing Victoria River boys.[89] He captured Jimmy and Georgie in camps near Bradshaw homestead and, a few days later, George, the supposed ringleader, was found in a group of 50 or 60 Aborigines about 100 kilometres northeast of the station.[90] Some of the Aborigines threw spears at Stott and his Aboriginal assistants as they galloped after George, but none took effect. The police party caught up with George as he was escaping down a cliff. After he threw spears at them and refused to stop he was shot dead. Five days afterwards it was reported that a number of 'myalls' were coming to Bradshaw to avenge the shooting.[91] Nothing came of it, but five weeks later two horses were speared on Bradshaw and the whites thought it looked 'very much like an act of retaliation on the part of his [*George's*] tribe'.[92]

When Jimmy was arrested he protested his innocence and claimed that Larsen had objected to Egoriffe beating Georgie and that Egoriffe then 'been killem Jack'.[93] At the trial it appears evidence was given that Egoriffe had hit George on the neck, and may have used a rope to hit him or tie him up, but this wasn't considered sufficient provocation to reduce the charge to manslaughter.[94] Later a story came out which might have shown such provocation. As it was going past the Point Charles Lighthouse on its way to the Daly River, the lighthouse keeper, Hugh Christie and another man 'noticed the *Wunwulla* stop & come back a considerable distance'. Christie later heard from an Aborigine camped at the Lighthouse that 'Ivan had thrown one of the Victoria River boys overboard off the Lthouse'. Christie heard this story from Datpull, also known as Fennem, one of the Daly River Aborigines who had been on the *Wunwulla* when the attack took place.[95] Datpull and the other witness, Cockatoo, were on the Daly River when the *Wunwulla* arrived there, so the question is, how did they know that the event at Point Charles took place? The most likely explanation is that they were told about it by the man who was thrown overboard, or by the other Aboriginal crewmen on the *Wunwulla*.

89   'News and notes', *Northern Territory Times*, 17th August 1900, p. 2.
90   'Daly River outrage. Arrest of two of the principals at Victoria River'.
91   NTA: Log Book, 29th August 1900, NTRS 2261.
92   'News and notes', *Northern Territory Times*, 5th October 1900, p. 3.
93   'Daly River outrage. Arrest of two of the principals at Victoria River'.
94   'Circuit court', *Northern Territory Times*, 28th September 1900, p. 3.
95   NTA: NTRS 790, item 9850, Lighthouse Keeper Hugh Christie to Government Resident Charles Dashwood, 12 August 1900; NTA: NTRS 790, item 9973, Lighthouse Keeper Hugh Christie to Inspector Paul Foelsche, 29th August 1900.

Georgie laid the blame squarely on Jimmy and George.[96] His evidence was accepted by the court and the charges against him were dismissed, but Jimmy was convicted and condemned to death,[97] the sentence to be carried out at Bradshaw Station, 'as a warning to the natives of that locality'.[98] Mounted Constable Thompson at Timber Creek was ordered to go to Bradshaw 'well armed' and to cooperate with Fred Bradshaw 'to collect and secure as large an assemblage of natives as possible' to witness the hanging.[99] On 8th April 1901 all available Aborigines, including one from Daly River,[100] were 'mustered' to see the execution.[101] Jimmy was duly hanged at 6.40am. Sergeant Waters then ordered Thompson and Tracker Gerald 'to remain guard over body' and also 'to keep [the] Myall Natives around the Gallows' while the officials had breakfast.[102] Jimmy's body was then cut down and buried behind the scaffold and tobacco distributed among the Aboriginal onlookers.[103] Later Deputy Sheriff Little remarked that, 'These natives will no doubt cause the particulars of the execution to be conveyed to other tribes in surrounding districts'.[104]

Four months after the hanging of Jimmy there were two 'singular occurrences' at Bradshaw. First, on 11th August 1901 a tremendous explosion shook the area. According to Joe Bradshaw, 'It commenced with a terrific deafening boom, like the simultaneous explosion of a park of heavy ordinance'. This was followed by 'loud rumbling and violent earthquaking'. A sick man who was convalescing at the homestead was thrown out of his hammock and a number of Aborigines rushed up, declaring, 'Alambul was angry and would destroy them unless they got within the protection of the Whitefellow'. FW Palmer, a stockman who was with a mob of cattle a few miles from the Dome, heard a severe explosion to the north which made his horse stagger under him and his packhorses and bullocks rush. One of Palmer's black stockmen fell off his horse in fright. A few miles away another black stockman and his wife caught their horses and galloped in terror towards the homestead. Egoriffe was in his dinner camp about 40 kilometres north-east of the homestead and felt nothing, though his 'boys' said they heard a distant noise. Apparently it

---

96   ibid.
97   'Circuit court', *Northern Territory Times*, 28th September 1900, p. 3.
98   NTA: Log Book, 5th April 1901, NTRS 2261.
99   NTA: Timber Creek police journal, 4th April 1901 F 302.
100   NTA: NTRS 790, item number not marked on original, Deputy Sheriff J Little to Dashwood, 11th April 1901.
101   NTA: Log Book, 8th April 1901, NTRS 2261.
102   NTA: Timber Creek police journal, 8th April 1901 F302; NTA: Log Book, 8th April 1901, NTRS 2261.
103   NTA: Log Book, 8th April 1901, NTRS 2261.
104   NTA: NTRS 790, item number not marked on original, 11th April 1901.

was a highly localised earthquake centred, as best could be determined, near a 'twin coned mountain called by the natives Mǐlik Měnmïr'.[105]

A little over two weeks later came the second 'singular occurrence'. On 29th August 'a remarkable meteorite' was seen to the west-south-west of the homestead. When first seen at about 7.30pm it was close to the planet Venus and had 'Two bright, sharply defined tails' diverging from it. As it moved these tails 'extended in parallel lines over about 15 degrees nearly horizontal'. It travelled in a southerly direction 'at the rate of one degree in forty seconds' and slowly faded over a period of ten minutes.[106] From this description the object could hardly have been a meteorite as they burn up and disappear within seconds, but whether it was a comet or something else remains a mystery.[107]

In Aboriginal thinking unusual events are connected to other events – it's a case of cause and effect – and it usually takes some time for a consensus to be reached as to what caused a particular event, or what it signified.[108] The initial response of the Aborigines at Bradshaw was that 'Alumbul' was angry, but why 'Alumbul' was angry would only be determined later. What the Aborigines really thought of the earthquake and of the 'meteorite' is unknown. There is nothing in the regional ethnographic literature about Aboriginal responses to or interpretations of earthquakes, and a few years ago when local Aboriginal people were asked who or what 'Alambul' was they appeared quite mystified. However, in current Victoria River Aboriginal thinking, when a meteorite is seen streaking across the sky it is said to be 'traffic', a highly dangerous Dreaming snake travelling to deliver retribution to a human murderer.[109] It's likely that Aborigines would have related both phenomena to recent events. Though we can only speculate as to which events might have been implicated, the killing of Larsen on the Daly River, the shooting of George and the hanging of Jimmy loomed large in recent history.

---

105 'Singular occurrences at Victoria River', *Northern Territory Times*, 27th September 1901, p 2; 'Mǐlik Měnmïr' is a mountain now known as 'Millik Monmir', located at co-ords 471 189 on the Millik Monmir 1:100,000 topographic map (Sheet 4965, Edition 1). Royal Australian Survey Corps, 1973.
106 'Singular occurrences at Victoria River'.
107 The same 'meteorite' was seen from VRD homestead where it resembled a large comet and remained visible for 'three or four minutes' before fading away ('News and notes', *Northern Territory Times*, 1st November 1901, p. 3).
108 D Rose, *Dingo Makes Us Human*, Cambridge University Press, Melbourne, 1992, p. 228.
109 This 'traffic' goes to kill a murderer after some of the victim's belongings are burnt at a site where that Dreaming snake resides – it's a form of sorcery. Rose, p. 153.

The packhorse track up through the cliff behind the homestead was the next scene of conflict. Some time after it was built, Egoriffe and a Bradshaw stockman named Ernest Dannock were driving some horses up the track. When they were nearing the top:

> they heard a yell and spears and stones began to fly everywhere. They hid for a while; but the Aborigines had the best of it, being higher, and keeping back from the edge of a cliff so that they could throw without showing themselves. Ivan Eggeroffe got hit on the shoulder by a stone and his horse was speared in the leg. The attackers were not the local Aborigines but the Wargite tribe, from the mouth of the Daly river.[110]

Soon after this attack the Governor of South Australia, Sir George Le Hunte, visited Bradshaw on his way to the Depot. While at Bradshaw he gave blankets, flour, tobacco and pipes to 'some fine-looking aborigines', and in return the Aborigines 'gave' a corroboree to him.[111] Le Hunte heard from 'Mr Bradshaw' that there were possibly 500 Aborigines between Bradshaw Station and the coast and was told that they 'give no trouble; but those on the high lands above the cliffs, which lie immediately behind the station, are unfriendly, and, to use his [*Bradshaw's*] words, "chivied" his men away when they went up there after cattle'.[112]

On 24th November 1905 the most infamous event in the history of Bradshaw occurred, the so-called 'Bradshaw Massacre', an incident that seems to have had reverberations around the Yambarran Range for years. In fact, the actual massacre occurred on the coast well to the north of the station, but the story begins on 'Captain Joe's Bradshaw', and ends there. The event was called the Bradshaw Massacre because one of the murdered men was Fred Bradshaw, he and two others – Egoriffe and Dannock – came from Bradshaw Station, and the boat involved was the *Bolwarra*, which belonged to Bradshaw. The other murdered man was Jerry Skeahan, brother of Jack Skeahan, the manager of Auvergne Station. The death of Skeahan was doubly tragic. He'd broken his arm in the stockyard at Auvergne and had set out to ride 200 kilometres to Wyndham for medical help. Shortly after he left a message reached Auvergne advising that the *Bolwarra* was about to

---

110   L Moffatt, *Luck and Tragedy in the New Country*, privately published, Melbourne, 1990, p. 51.
111   'Visit of HE the Governor. The Victoria River trip', *Northern Territory Times*, 2nd June 1905, p 2–3.
112   'Northern Territory (Report by his Excellency the Governor of South Australia)', *South Australian Parliamentary Papers*, vol. 2, 1905, no. 49, p. 6.

The 'notorious' Bobby (rear) on board the Wunwulla, 1906

Pastoralist's Review, February 1906

leave for Darwin, so to save Jerry a long and painful ride Jack Skeahan sent a messenger posthaste to bring him back,[113] a decision that was to cause him much grief in the coming months.[114]

News of the massacre broke upon the world on 8th December 1905 when Bobby, one of the Victoria River Aboriginal crewmen, turned up at Bradshaw Station.[115] Bobby told an amazing tale. After continuing engine trouble the *Bolwarra* had called in at a government coal-boring camp near Port Keats and discovered that two white men working at a well there had been murdered by the blacks. The other white men had captured and chained up seven or eight Aborigines and asked Fred Bradshaw to take them to Darwin. The *Bolwarra* took the Aborigines on board and continued up the coast. The next night Fred, against the protests of the other whites, decided to release the prisoners from their chains. No guard was kept and that night the prisoners killed the four whites and the other three Aboriginal crew. Bobby only escaped the same fate by leaping (or being pushed) overboard.[116] He described in detail the

---

113 'News and notes', *Northern Territory Times*, 12th January 1906, p. 3.
114 M Durack, *Sons in the Saddle*, Corgi Books, Sydney, 1985, p. 200.
115 'Massacres in the Northern Territory'.
116 'An alleged terrible tragedy'.

position of each man as he was killed and later said that as Fred Bradshaw was attacked he cried out, 'Bobby, get up. Wild blackfellow been killem along you and me'.[117] After jumping overboard Bobby said he swam to shore and from a hiding place watched as the *Bolwarra* was looted. Then he set out on the 300 kilometre walk to Bradshaw, arriving there 12 days later.[118]

Of course, Bobby's story was rapidly communicated to the Timber Creek police,[119] the Brocks Creek police[120] and the Darwin authorities.[121] His story caused a sensation there and around the country – 'Massacres in the Northern Territory ... Six whites and three blackboys killed'. Later investigations showed that the facts were not quite as Bobby painted them. The *Bolwarra* had left Bradshaw on 12th November and as it moved down the Victoria and up the west coast it experienced a lot of engine trouble, just as Bobby described.[122] There was a government drilling rig boring for coal near Port Keats, so when the *Bolwarra* arrived opposite it Fred Bradshaw, Egoriffe and Jerry Skeahan took a dinghy ashore to borrow some extra fuel and materials for repairs. When they arrived they noticed about 100 armed and excited Aboriginal men near the camp of the drillers, but no women or children. Egoriffe remarked that he recognised several of the Aborigines because he'd seen them at Bradshaw and Jerry Skeahan told one of the bore party they should be on their guard as it looked like there was trouble brewing.[123]

There were no Aboriginal prisoners in the camp and no white men had been killed, but there had been some trouble with the local blacks. When the bore party first arrived at the site the Aborigines had been helpful and friendly and formed a camp nearby. However, they became 'cheeky', began stealing items from the camp and were now said to be 'rapidly becoming dangerously insolent'.[124] The crew of the *Bolwarra* were four Bradshaw Aborigines – Bobby, Calico, Myabilla and Mud-Blanket (aka My-Blanket).[125] They also came ashore, ostensibly to get water, but instead, at the first opportunity, at least three, though probably all of them, cleared out.[126] Perhaps they, too, had read signs of impending trouble.

---

117 'The Port Keats massacre. Bobby's story in court', *The Advertiser* (Adelaide), 9th February 1906, p. 5.
118 'Massacres in the Northern Territory'.
119 NTA: Timber Creek police journal, 9th December 1905, F 302.
120 'Massacres in the Northern Territory'.
121 'An alleged terrible tragedy'.
122 'Massacres in the Northern Territory'.
123 'An alleged terrible tragedy'.
124 ibid.
125 NTA: Timber Creek police journal, 28th December 1905, 30th June 1906, F 302.
126 'An alleged terrible tragedy'.

When the Bradshaw boys were missed, Fred Bradshaw had to find replacement crew. Among the Aborigines in the vicinity of the drilling camp he recognised two, Cumbit and Mallie, who had previously been on his boat in the Victoria River.[127] At least one of them, Cumbit, agreed to go on board the launch, but later one of the bore party alleged that several others – Donah,[128] Wunpulunga,[129] Minemar[130] and possibly Mallie[131] – were frightened into going and were 'practically kidnapped'.[132] With its new crew, the *Bolwarra* left Port Keats about midday.[133] Shortly afterwards Aborigines threatened the coal-boring camp and attacked the foreman while he was working on a well nearby. Fortunately he was not seriously hurt. Meanwhile the *Bolwarra* moved slowly up the coast, first by engine power and then by sail.[134] It anchored for a night and continued on the next day, anchoring in the evening about 80 kilometres up the coast, near Cape Ford.[135]

In the morning, before the boat reached Cape Ford, Donah and Cumbit somehow fell foul of Egoriffe and he commenced to beat them with a stick. Cumbit ended up with a 'sore head', a 'sore hand' and a cut on his face. Donah was sore on the top of his head.[136] Why Egoriffe beat them is not clear – one account says they wanted to go ashore[137] while another says they didn't do their work to Egoriffe's satisfaction.[138] Either way after beating them it appears that he tied up Cumbit, and possibly Donah and the other Aborigines as well. He may have had the help of one or more of the other whites to do this.[139] If Donah and Cumbit were tied up, they were either

127 'Northern Territory massacre. All the bodies recovered', *Adelaide Advertiser*, 3rd January 1906, p. 6. Whether 'Mallie' is the same person as 'Donah' is unclear, but certainly possible.
128 In other documents his name is rendered as 'Donghol' (eg, 'An interesting expedition', *Northern Territory Times*, 27th April 1906, p. 2), but Donah soon became the 'standardised' English version of his name.
129 Alternatively 'Won-pa-lunga' ('An interesting expedition').
130 ibid. Alternatively 'Mi-ma'.
131 'Northern Territory massacre', *Adelaide Advertiser*, 20th December 1905, p. 7.
132 ibid.
133 'An alleged terrible tragedy'.
134 NAA: statement by Wunpulunga at trial of Donah and Cumbit, 25th March 1907, CRS A3 NT 1918/2640.
135 NTA: NTRS 790, item 15086, map of Cape Ford area.
136 NAA: statements by Doc Doc and Ned at trial of Donah and Cumbit, 25th March 1907, CRS A3 NT 1918/2640.
137 NAA, petition on behalf of Cumbit and Donah asking for remission of sentence, 23rd September 1910, CRS A3 NT 1918/2640.
138 NAA: statement by Wunpulunga, 25th March 1907, CRS A3 NT 1918/2640.
139 ibid.

released later (possibly by Fred Bradshaw), or somehow got free after dark. In any event, they killed all four men and threw their bodies into the sea.[140] In the morning they each took tobacco, a pipe and a blanket from the boat and went ashore, eventually coming to a large camp of Aborigines where they told people what they had done, saying, 'white fellow all day kill em me, allright me kill em behind [*afterwards*]'.[141]

News of the tragedy reached Darwin on Saturday 16th December. The next day a party of police and 'special constables' (authorised civilians) were dispatched on the steamer *Wai Hoi*, bound for Port Keats. There they learned that no members of the bore party had been killed though there had been the serious assault described above. The police party remained at Port Keats with the intention of searching for evidence of the murder of Fred Bradshaw and his men, and the *Wai Hoi* returned to Darwin. The steamer reached Darwin on Tuesday and almost immediately it was arranged for two launches to be sent out to search the coast from Darwin to the Victoria River.[142] The departure of the launches was unaccountably delayed for several days and eventually it was decided a sailing lugger would be sent instead, to be towed from Darwin to Port Keats by the *Wai Hoi*.[143] The steamer left Darwin on 23rd December.[144]

Meanwhile, throughout the night of 20th December the coal-boring camp at Port Keats was lashed by a violent storm and the bore workers and police party stationed there were attacked three times by a large number of Aborigines. Flashes of lightning revealed the attackers as close as 15 metres away, but gunfire kept them at bay. During the night the police devised a plan to capture some of the Aborigines. Before daylight they moved to a native well about three kilometres away and hid themselves. Later the trackers moved along the beach and forced eight Aborigines to go inland to the well where they were arrested by the police. Taken back to the drilling camp, two of the prisoners were recognised as being among the four who had gone on board the *Bolwarra*, but when the police brought out handcuffs and chains all eight made a break for the bush. Cumbit and Donah were overpowered and two others were shot dead. The remaining four made their

140 'Northern Territory Massacre'.
141 NAA: statement by Ned at trial of Donah and Cumbit, 25th March 1907. CRS A3 NT 1918/2640. Roughly translated this means 'the white man beat me all day, so I attacked him later'.
142 'An alleged terrible tragedy'.
143 'Northern Territory massacre. No trace of the Bolwarra,' *The Advertiser* (Adelaide), 22nd December 1905, p. 6.
144 'Butchered by blacks', *The Australasian*, 6th January 1906, p. 3.

escape, although one entered the sea and wasn't seen again.[145] The two prisoners were subsequently taken to Darwin and charged with murder.[146]

A party led by Mounted Constable Kelly arrived at Port Keats on the lugger *Turquoise* on 26th December. They found the *Bolwarra* stranded about eight kilometres south of Clump Point, looted, stripped, the engine damaged and with dried blood everywhere. A body identified as that of Fred Bradshaw was found nearby[147] and the bodies of the other men were found a week or so later.[148] All were buried on the beach, with poles set up to mark each gravesite.[149] Nine months later Joe Bradshaw bought some coffins and went out to exhume the remains of the murdered men, intending to rebury them at Bradshaw.[150] He found the remains of his brother Fred, Ernest Dannock and Ivan Egoriffe, but the marker over Jerry Skeahan's grave had disappeared, so his bones couldn't be recovered and presumably are buried on the beach to this day.

At Bradshaw a vault was prepared about two kilometres from the homestead and when the coffins were carried there, 'A large number of friendly natives followed the remains to the grave, and the native women covered their heads with ashes, in token of grief'.[151] Two years later relays of Aborigines carried the coffin containing Fred Bradshaw's bones to the top of an isolated, flat-topped mountain on the banks of the Victoria River, below the mouth of Angalarri Creek.[152] Known ever since as 'Bradshaw's Tomb',[153] this hill has a top of solid rock, so the coffin couldn't be buried. Old photographs show that some flat rocks were placed on the coffin lid and it was then left to the elements. Modern maps

---

145   Telegram from Government Resident Herbert to the Minister Controlling to Northern Territory, January 1906. Minister Controlling the Northern Territory, Inwards Correspondence, GRS 1 581/1905; 'Butchered by Blacks'.
146   'Northern Territory massacre', *The Adelaide Advertiser*, 4th January 1906, p. 7.
147   'Butchered by blacks'.
148   'Northern Territory massacre'.
149   'Butchered by blacks'.
150   'News and Notes', *Northern Territory Times*, 28th September 1906, p. 3.
151   'The Port Keats massacre. Burying the remains', *Sydney Morning Herald*, 22nd October 1906, p. 7.
152   Notes taken from the Timber Creek police letter book by an unknown policeman (14th September 1908). This event is mentioned in the copy of Timber Creek police letter book held at Berrimah police station, Darwin (1st August 1908), but the last line of the entry is missing from the copy (the original letter book is in private hands and its whereabouts is unknown to current police personnel). Several accounts state that the remains of two of the other victims were also placed in this coffin, but this appears unlikely to be correct (NTA: Timber Creek Police Station, copy book, 1895–1940, NTRS 2224).
153   Hill, p. 253; on the current 1:100,000 topographic map (Millik Monmir, Sheet 4965, Edition 1, 1973) the name 'The Tombs' appears at the end of the Yambarran Range (co-ords 300 993). However, early records and photographs show that the correct 'Bradshaw's Tomb' is the hill at co-ords 236 969, since confirmed by the discovery of the coffin handles there.

Fred Bradshaw's grave near Cape Ford, 1906

John Bradshaw collection

Bradshaw's Tomb in the distance
Fred Bradshaw's coffin was placed on top at the right-hand end

Lewis collection

Fred Bradshaw's coffin on Bradshaw's Tomb, c1914

National Archives of Australia

have the label 'The Tombs' near the western end of the Yambarran Range,[154] but by using one of the photos of the coffin and armed with some local folklore, I relocated the correct 'burial' site in 1984. Only the coffin handles, screws and nails remained and these were later removed to the Timber Creek museum.[155]

As soon as news of the murders reached Timber Creek, Mounted Constable Burt went to Bradshaw to interview Bobby. He then asked Bobby to go with him to Brocks Creek and Bobby agreed, but the first night out he ran away into the bush. Because of his apparently detailed knowledge of events, Bobby was already under suspicion of possible involvement in the murders. By absconding he increased suspicions against him.[156] Early in January 1906 he was arrested at Bradshaw and taken to Darwin as a witness in the trial of Cumbit and Donah.[157] As a result of police investigations it was determined that of the four Aboriginal crewmen on the *Bolwarra*, only Donah and Cumbit had committed the crime. They faced court in early

---

154 Millik Monmir 1:100,000, sheet 4967 (edition 1), co-ords 300 994. 1973.
155 See Lewis, *Boab Belt* (vol. 1, site 10, pp. 55–62).
156 *Northern Territory Times*, 22nd December 1905, p. 3.
157 NTA: Timber Creek police journal, 1st, 10th and 18th January 1906, F 302.

February and were remanded to appear at 'the next Circuit Court'.[158] Burt went to Bradshaw in March to try and get statements from Mud-Blanket, Myabilla and Calico,[159] but it appears he was unsuccessful, as in June the Timber Creek police were advised that 'My Blanket, Calico and Myabilla' were required in Darwin as witnesses in July.[160]

Cumbit and Donah appeared in court again in August but the hearing was held over until the next circuit court so that competent interpreters could be found.[161] Bobby was held at Fannie Bay jail as a witness, but on 1st March 1907, less than three weeks before the trial began,[162] he escaped and made his way back to Bradshaw.[163] A fortnight later Mounted Constable Artaud left for Bradshaw to search for Bobby, Calico and others who were wanted as witnesses in the case, with instructions that no effort was to be spared to catch Bobby and bring him to Port Darwin on the *Wai Hoi*.[164] Artaud couldn't find Bobby or Calico, but he did find Mud-Blanket and took him to Darwin.[165] They arrived there on 5th April, too late for the trial which had concluded in March, with Cumbit and Donah being convicted and sentenced to death.[166] After the trial Captain Joe suggested that if Aborigines were involved in cases of murder or attempted murder and the police were unable to capture them, they should be outlawed.[167] Nothing came of his suggestion.

The sentencing of Cumbit and Donah wasn't the end of the sad tale. Artaud left Darwin on 8th April to return Mud-Blanket to Bradshaw. He had instructions that if 'Mybilla' and 'Kalico' could be found he should obtain statements from them about their desertion of the *Bolwarra* at Port Keats and send their statements to headquarters.[168] From events that transpired I can only presume that the statements of all three witnesses were required because an appeal was planned against the death sentences. Such an appeal was made and evidence that Egoriffe had treated Cumbit and Donah cruelly

---

158 'The Port Keats massacre', *The Advertiser* (Adelaide), 9th February 1906, p. 5.
159 NTA: Timber Creek police journal, 10th March 1906, F 302.
160 ibid., 14th March 1906.
161 'Murder', *Northern Territory Times*, 27th July 1906, p. 3.
162 NTA: Timber Creek police journal, 14th March 1907, F 302.
163 ibid., 30th June 1907; NTA: Police Station, Katherine, NTRS 2732, Register of reported felonies, 1887–1930, entry dated 1st March 1907.
164 NTA: Timber Creek police journal, 16th March 1907, F 302.
165 ibid., 27th March 1907.
166 'The Port Keats murder', *Northern Territory Times*, 29th March 1907, p. 3.
167 NTA: NTRS 790, item 151381, J Bradshaw to the Government Resident, Charles Herbert, 25th April 1906.
168 NTA: Timber Creek police journal, 12th April 1907, F 302.

was taken into consideration. In June 1907 their sentences were commuted to life in Fannie Bay Gaol.[169]

The hunt for Bobby continued. He was still at large in August 1907,[170] but was eventually arrested late in September and taken to Darwin.[171] What grounds there were for his arrest and how long he was held in Darwin is unclear, but he must have escaped again within a year because he was back on Bradshaw by then when he, and the other witnesses, were once again being sought by the police.[172] Mounted Constable Holland went to Bradshaw in June 1908 but couldn't find any of the wanted men and later reported that the chances of getting Calico, Myabilla or Mud-Blanket were 'very remote indeed'. He remarked that, 'The Policeman has never appeared as their friend and neither Mud-Blanket or Bobby are likely to forget that the police took them away last Year'.[173] With respect to Calico, Holland's pessimism was more than justified. At the time that he was looking for him, Calico had probably been dead for two months, shot near Bradshaw homestead by the manager, Walter Wye, or one of his Aboriginal assistants.[174]

In November 1909 Mounted Constable Dempsey raided a 'huge blacks camp' in a gorge running off Angalarri Creek. The approach was very difficult and most of the Aborigines escaped, but eight women were caught. They told the police that the 'notorious Bobby' was one of those who got away.[175] Why Bobby was now regarded as 'notorious' is unknown and this is the last mention of him in the historical record.

In 1910 Cumbit and Donah sought a remission of sentence in a petition prepared on their behalf in which they restated their original claim that they'd been tied up and beaten and were not allowed to go ashore.[176] Their appeal was rejected.[177] In September 1911 they escaped, but were

---

169   'The Bradshaw massacre', *The Register* (Adelaide), 20th June 1907, p. 4.
170   NTA: Timber Creek police journal, 24th August 1907, F 302.
171   ibid., 5th October 1907.
172   Memo from Sub Inspector Waters to MC Dempsey, 4th June 1908, Timber Creek police letter book, photocopy held at the Berrimah Police Station, Darwin.
173   Memo from MC Holland to Sub Inspector Waters, 1st August 1908, Timber Creek police letter book, photocopy held at Berrimah Police Station, Darwin.
174   Memo from Sub Inspector Waters to MC Dempsey, 9th June 1908, Timber Creek police letter book, photocopy held at Berrimah Police Station, Darwin.
175   NTA: Timber Creek police journal, 5th November 1909, F 302.
176   NAA: petition to the governor of South Australia on behalf of Donah and Cumbit, CRS A3 N.T. 1918/2640.
177   NAA: memorandum, signed by H Pollard, 10th February 1911, CRS A3 N.T. 1918/2640.

recaptured the following day.[178] They appealed again in 1915 and although their appeal was rejected once more, it was recommended that they try again in two years' time. Donah never got the chance – he died in jail in 1916.[179] Cumbit didn't wait. In May 1916 he and a prisoner named Katerinyan escaped and made their way through the intervening hostile country to the Fitzmaurice River.

First Mounted Constable Richardson, then Mounted Constables O'Connor and Cameron, made separate patrols to try and recapture them. After many weeks in the bush O'Connor and Cameron succeeded in apprehending Katerinyan.[180] There's no direct evidence that Cumbit was recaptured, though presumably he was because in November 1918 Atlee Hunt, the Permanent Head of the Department for Home and Territories,[181] granted him a remission of sentence.[182] As far as is known he was released and returned to his country, bringing to a final end the saga of the 'Bradshaw Massacre'.

On 15th January 1906 something happened to cause all the Aborigines at Bradshaw, 'both civilized & bush', to clear out.[183] Going bush enabled the Aborigines to avoid the whites, but it also meant that they couldn't get any rations, so some of them decided to sneak back to the homestead at night to help themselves. Two days after the Aborigines had left the lock of the store was picked with a nail. Two bags of flour were taken before the door was locked up again. The Bradshaw manager, Charles Webster, sent a message reporting the thefts to the Timber Creek police on 10th February, but floods prevented Mounted Constable Burt from leaving to investigate for another month.[184]

Before Burt arrived the store was raided another four times with a total of nine bags of flour, one bag of rice, six dozen boxes of matches, 15 tins of jam and honey, five towels, four shirts, about ten metres of 'turkey red' cloth and a small amount of sugar and tea being taken. It was only after the third

---

178 'News and notes', *Northern Territory Times*, 15th September 1911, p 3.
179 NAA: memorandum for the minister for home and territories, signed by the Northern Territory Administrator (signature illegible), 11th July 1916, CRS A3 N.T. 1918/2640.
180 NTA: Timber Creek police journal, 7th and 21st June 1916, 15th and 16th July 1916, 21st August 1916, F 302. Photocopy held at Berrimah Police Station, Darwin,
181 H Davies, 'Hunt, Atlee Arthur (1864–1935)', *Australian Dictionary of Biography*, vol. 9, Melbourne University Press, 1983, pp. 403–04.
182 NAA: Atlee Hunt's secretary, to the Northern Territory Administrator, 10th November 1918, CRS A3 N.T. 1918/2640.
183 Mounted Constable FJ Burt to headquarters, 3rd March 1906. Timber Creek police letter book, photocopy held at the Berrimah Police Station, Darwin.
184 NTA: Timber Creek police journal, 10th February 1906, F 302.

raid, with most of the stores gone, that the station hands decided to remove what was left to the homestead. However, because the Aborigines hadn't previously taken much tea or sugar, these items were left in the store. On 16th March when the fourth raid was made and some more sugar and tea was taken, what little remained was removed to the homestead.[185]

When Burt finally arrived at Bradshaw and learnt details of the robberies he was staggered at the stupidity of the station hands. 'It seems almost incredible that 3 white men, were living on this station, & that only after repeated raids, [and] the greater portion of the stores taken, that they should conceive the idea of removing the remainder to where they were living & safety'. The offenders were said to be the 'Cadjerong' (Kajerong) tribe, and because the deserters from the *Bolwarra* were Kajerong people they were believed to be implicated in the robberies.[186] Burt spent ten days searching for the offenders in the ranges and gorges on Bradshaw, without success.[187]

While justice in respect to the Bradshaw Massacre may have been served in the white man's courts, it seems that some Aborigines were not satisfied. In mid 1907 Mounted Constable Kelly was told that a 'Beringan' [*Brinken*] man named Lungmier had been killed by the 'Jumonjoos' [*Jaminjung*]. The story was that Lungmier had swum out to the *Bolwarra* shortly before the massacre occurred and the 'Jumonjoos' believed he had helped kill their 'good friend' Fred Bradshaw. As a result, when Lungmier appeared in a 'Jumonjoo camp' on the Fitzmaurice River he was promptly speared and clubbed to death.[188]

The reign of 'Ivan the Terrible' may have ended, and Donah and Cumbit may have been jailed, but if anything violence against Aborigines on Bradshaw appears to have worsened, and there were sometimes tensions between the whites themselves. In July 1908 Dempsey received several memos from headquarters about 'alleged atrocities on aborigines at Bradshaw's Run'.[189] The information in the memos is scant, but in combination with police journal entries a complicated picture emerges of a series of murders and brutal assaults, at times verging on mayhem.

---

185 Mounted Constable FJ Burt to headquarters, 28th March 1906. Timber Creek police letter book, photocopy held at the Berrimah Police Station, Darwin.
186 ibid.
187 His lack of success isn't particularly surprising as 'Cadgerong' (Kajerong) country is on the west side of the Victoria River, on present-day Bullo River Station and Legune Station.
188 'Aboriginal justice', *Northern Territory Times*, 26th July 1907, P. 3.
189 NTA: Timber Creek police journal, 1st July 1908, F 302. These memos were dated 1st, 4th and 9th June, 1908.

First, it was alleged that the Bradshaw cook had shot an Aborigine in broad daylight so as to take possession of his wife, and in the presence of the manager, Charles Webster,[190] had carried the body to Angalarri Creek and thrown it in. As a result of the murder, all the Aborigines cleared out from the station. It was further alleged that when Joe Bradshaw heard about the murder, all he did was dismiss the cook.[191] Another memo alleged that Bradshaw later said to some friends that, 'if ever a man deserved to be hanged it was a cook of mine as he deliberately shot a man for his lubra'.[192] A third memo revealed that the alleged killing happened some time before 1st August 1906, that the murdered man was Old Fred, and the cook Chas Williams.[193]

Second, it was alleged that in about October 1907 Joe Bradshaw, his manager Walter Wye,[194] and a man named Mullins were involved in a 'big drunk' at the station. Mullins and Wye had a row and when Captain Joe intervened Mullins turned on him. Joe immediately gave a loaded rifle to one of his 'boys' and said to him, 'If that —— comes onto the veranda shoot him'. Third, in about January 1908 Wye was supposed to have severely assaulted an Aborigine named 'Jack Pur' because he wouldn't let Wye have his wife. Fourth, it was alleged that in about April 1908 some cattle had been speared near the homestead and that Wye and Aborigines named Larriba and Billy Wheelah had gone out to investigate. As a result Calico, one of the Aborigines who had deserted the *Bolwarra*, was shot dead near the spring that supplied Bradshaw with water and a man named Tommy and his wife were both wounded. Later Bobby, the survivor of the Bradshaw Massacre, threatened to tell Joe Bradshaw (who was absent) all about these shootings. Wye heard of Bobby's threat and a day or so later Possum, one of Wye's 'boys', had a row with Bobby in the Bradshaw blacks' camp. Bobby was 'badly knocked about' and cleared into the bush that night.

---

190 Webster was manager of Bradshaw from November 1905 until he committed suicide by shooting himself in December 1907 (Northern Territory Library Manuscript Collection, Bradshaw Family 1840–1940, 'Bradshaw Letters – 1/5a-c, Letter to John from F.M. Bradshaw, 2nd June 1905'; *Northern Territory Times*, 10th January 1908. p. 2; NTA: Timber Creek police journal, 15th December 1907, F302).

191 Memo from Sub Inspector Waters to MC Dempsey, 9th June 1908. Timber Creek police letter book, photocopy held at the Berrimah Police Station, Darwin.

192 NTA: Timber Creek police journal, 12th July 1908, F 302.

193 Memo from MC Holland to Sub Inspector Waters, 1st August 1908. Timber Creek police letter book, photocopy held at the Berrimah Police Station, Darwin.

194 In October 1907 Wye was head stockman on Bradshaw. He took over the role of manager after Charles Webster committed suicide in December 1907 (Timber Creek police journal, 15th February 1908, NTA: F 302). He remained in this position until 1910 (Timber Creek police journal, 28th January 1910, NTA: F 302).

Finally, it was alleged that blacks' tobacco steeped in cyanide had been kept in a jar in the station store. Not knowing that it had been poisoned, the current Bradshaw cook had given some to an Aborigine who became so ill after smoking it that he fell down four times before reaching his camp. Fortunately he survived, and later Wye was said to have had the remaining tobacco destroyed. Dempsey was ordered to make 'full and exhaustive inquiries' into these allegations.[195]

At Timber Creek on 12th July 1908, Dempsey was able to question Wye and the Aboriginal stockman, Billy Wheelah. Wye denied the existence of any poisoned tobacco and declined to answer any other questions until he had consulted Captain Joe, but Wheelah made a statement in which he apparently claimed to have seen Old Fred shot for stealing flour, rather than for refusing to give up his wife, and he named other witnesses to the murder.[196]

On 24th July Dempsey went to Bradshaw again to question Aborigines there, but the police horse bells had warned them the police were coming and they'd all cleared out into the Yambarran Range. Supposedly they believed they were going to be arrested for stealing from the station garden. However, one can't help but wonder if Wye had told them the police were coming to arrest them so that they'd clear out and not be available for interview. Dempsey did manage to obtain a statement relating to the murder of Old Fred, but again the reason given for the murder was the theft of flour, rather than wife-stealing. At the time of his visit the alleged murderer, Williams, was long gone from Bradshaw. Dempsey also searched around the spring where Calico was said to have been shot, but found nothing.

In the following months Dempsey questioned an Aboriginal man named Yama about the alleged shooting of Old Fred, but Yama said he only knew of it as hearsay. In November Dempsey received a memo from headquarters ordering that Billy Wheelah and all other witnesses to the alleged murder be found and brought to Palmerston, but there's no evidence this ever occurred. Dempsey interviewed Wheelah shortly afterwards to try and learn the names of the Aborigines present when Old Fred was shot, but Wheelah 'alleged he forgot the names'. In December Dempsey promised Yama and another man a reward if they were successful in bringing in witnesses to the alleged shooting, but nothing came of it.

On 27th December 1908 Dempsey finally caught up with the Aborigines in the Bradshaw camp and interviewed 22 of them about the alleged murder

---

195 Memo from Sub Inspector Waters to MC Dempsey, 9th June 1908. Timber Creek police letter book, photocopy held at the Berrimah Police Station, Darwin.
196 NTA: Timber Creek police journal, 12th July 1908 and 3rd January1909, F 302.

Witnesses in the trial of Aborigines accused of the Bradshaw Massacre, 1907
Moffat collection

of Old Fred. None of them could (or would) give any information so he sent two old men out to bring in Tommy or any other witnesses. On New Years Day they returned alone. For reasons which are not stated, Billy Wheelah and his 'lubra' then asked Dempsey to take them to Timber Creek. They set out on 2nd January 1909 but Wheelah and his wife ran away that night. Headquarters remained completely dissatisfied with the results of the investigation, and late in January sent a memo to Timber Creek ordering that 'nothing is to be left undone to get at the truth re murder of "Old Fred"'.[197] During a patrol in March to investigate horse spearing on Bradshaw, Mounted Constable Holland tried to get information on the murder, but like Dempsey before him he learnt nothing. From this time on there are no further police journal entries or other documents relating to the alleged murder of Old Fred or other Aborigines on Bradshaw, so the entire issue seems to have been dropped.

---

197 ibid., 12th and 24th July 1908, 9th October 1908, 4th and 10th November 1908, 2nd and 19th December 1908, 27th January 1909.

The allegations of poison being used against Aborigines and the recurrent theft of flour and other food from the Bradshaw store may give some credence to an Aboriginal tradition of a mass killing of Aborigines on Bradshaw Station. Peter Murray, who owned the station between 1958 and 1968, was told by an old man named Johnson that in the early days, Bradshaw Station had continual trouble with bush blacks breaking into the store and stealing bags of flour, tobacco and other goods. Johnson said that eventually the station whites left a bag of flour laced with poison in the store. The bag was stolen and a 'big mob' of Aborigines was poisoned.[198]

Although investigations into the allegations of murder and assault came to nothing, trouble between blacks and whites on Bradshaw continued. In April 1909 Wye reported that he had 'found a horse dead in a paddock 4 miles from Station with three spear wounds inflicted and supposed to be done by Jumminju Tribe'. The Timber Creek police investigated and were told by Bradshaw Aborigines that 'the spearing was done by the Cadgeronge Tribe whose country is across the Victoria River from Bradshaw'. The 'Cadgeronge' may have been the culprits, but it's also possible that the Bradshaw Aborigines blamed them for their own actions, or those of guilty relations.

In October the same year, Wye reported to the police that some 70 kilometres from the homestead about 30 natives had thrown spears and rocks at himself, an employee named Raymond, and a 'blackboy'. According to Wye, all three fired all their ammunition at the natives – 14 rounds – and missed! They then rode off and camped four miles away but were followed by the Aborigines who set fire to the grass, forcing them to make yet another camp. It was while trying to locate the Aborigines who had attacked Wye and Raymond that Mounted Constable Dempsey found the big blacks camp that all except eight women escaped from, including the 'notorious Bobby'. Dempsey questioned the captured women, but learnt nothing of the identity of the Aborigines who had made the attack on Wye's party.[199]

According to Surveyor C Boulter, who was at the Depot in 1913, cattle spearing was still rife on Bradshaw and a stockman there had recently been wounded by Aborigines.[200] With one probable exception, this appears to

---

198 Pauline Rayner, pers. comm. Rayner (nee Murray) was the daughter of Peter Murray.
199 NTA: Timber Creek police journal, 11th March 1909, 17th April 1909, 15th October 1909, 5th November 1909, F 302.
200 CC Boulter, diary, 1914, p. 130. Boulter was assistant surveyor to Surveyor Scandrett who passed through Timber Creek in 1913. This diary was given to the Historical Society of the Northern Territory by Boulter's daughter in 1970, and apparently lost in Cyclone Tracy. I have a photocopy of the Victoria River section of the diary.

Joe Bradshaw and Aboriginal assistants crossing the Daly River, c1912
Roberts collection, Australian National Trust (NT)

have been the last time that a white man was attacked by Aborigines on Bradshaw until the murder of two prospectors on the Fitzmaurice River in 1932.

The probable exception was David Byers, who replaced Walter Wye as manager in 1910 or 1911.[201] Byers was married and had his wife with him on Bradshaw. They almost certainly were the 'victims' of the famous 'frogs in the pipes' story told by Ernestine Hill. When Byers first arrived on the station the homestead was the one that had been built in 1905. In November 1913 a storm with hurricane force winds hit the station and unroofed all the station buildings, including the homestead, and drenched the place with two inches (50 mm) of rain.[202] It may have been this storm, and possibly problems with termites, that led to the homestead being rebuilt with a frame of iron water pipes.[203] According to Hill, when the first wet season came after the pipe-framed building had been erected, hundreds of frogs took

---

201 'News and notes', *Northern Territory Times*, 1st September 1911, p. 3; NTA: Timber Creek police journal, 26th August 1913, F 302. Wye was still on Bradshaw in March 1910 (Timber Creek police journal, 26th March 1910, NTA: F 302).
202 'News and notes', *Northern Territory Times*, 4th December 1913, p. 8.
203 NAA: report on Bradshaw Station, 'Northern Territory Pastoral Leases Investigation Committee', CRS F658 Item 25. This report states that the on Bradshaw Station in 1934 was built in 1913, but other evidence suggests that it was rebuilt at that time.

Bradshaw goats and homestead, c1913
The identity of the man is unknown

Donnison collection

up residence in the pipes, and their amplified croaking was so loud that the occupants had to shift into the nearby store.[204]

In 1921 David Byers and a man named Ford set out to ride from Brocks Creek to Bradshaw. About 70 kilometres from the homestead Byers, who was suffering from fever, stopped to rest but sent Ford on ahead, saying he would catch up later. Ford went on some distance and then waited for Byers, but he didn't come.[205] He went back and looked for Byers but couldn't find him, so he continued on to the homestead and raised the alarm. During an intensive search by police and station hands, tracks and other signs were found, but lost again in scrub or on recently burnt areas.[206] No trace of Byers or his horse was ever found.[207] Mrs Byers took the disappearance and undoubted death of her husband very hard indeed. The investigating constable reported that, 'It was impossible to obtain particulars of Byers Age etc. from Mrs Byers when I was at Bradshaw as she used to scream & break down'.[208]

---

204 Hill, p. 254.
205 NTA: Mounted Constable Tom Turner to Superintendent, Darwin, 25th August 1921, NTRS 2224.
206 ibid.
207 'Tragedy of the bush', *Northern Territory Times*, 16th August 1921, p. 3.
208 NTA: NTRS 2224, 25th August 1921.

Byers' disappearance was always treated as something of a mystery, but because he was known to have been suffering from fever it was thought he probably had suffered an attack of delirium, become lost, and died. According to a local Aboriginal story, however, an early white manager of Bradshaw had been speared because he was 'too cheeky' – too rough on the Aborigines – and no one ever found out.[209] Byers was the only Bradshaw manager ever to go missing on Bradshaw.

Bradshaw Station remained in Joe's hands until his death in 1916. In June of that year he travelled overland to his station in the company of the Millar brothers.[210] The brothers took over after Joe died and may have been going out to inspect the station with a view to purchase, although one source suggests that they were already partners at the time.[211] Somewhere on this trip, or at the station, an old injury on Joe's foot turned gangrenous. He returned to Darwin by lugger but the trip was slow because of low tides in the river. After five days, the lugger arrived in Darwin on 19th July and Joe had his foot amputated the following day. Initially the operation appeared to be a success, but he took a turn for the worse and died a few days later. Joe's dying wish was for his remains to be placed with those of his brother Fred on 'The Tomb' at Bradshaw Station, but this never happened. His funeral was held at the '2 ½ Mile Cemetery' (Parap, Darwin),[212] and the fragmentary remains of his headstone can still be seen there.

Thus ended the era of 'Captain Joe's Bradshaw'. In his time Bradshaw's Run had gone from a raw bush block, the home of so-called wild Aborigines, to a working station with a homestead, many yards, huts and a workforce of 'civilised blacks'. This change was achieved in spite of various setbacks and a toll of brutality and murder. If Bradshaw Station was born through the vision, hard work and enterprise of Joe Bradshaw, his brother Fred and their various employees, it was baptised in blood. It had seen more than its share of tragedy and violence, but by the time Captain Joe died both he and his station had become legends.

---

209 Rayner.
210 Untitled news item, *Northern Territory Times*, 27th July 1916, p. 8.
211 NAA: CRS F658 Item 25.
212 'Obituary', *Northern Territory Times*, 27th July 1916, p. 15.

Chapter 8

THE WILD WARDAMAN WARRIORS

In the early days it was said by some that 'the blacks were bad on the Victoria', but of all the tribal groups in the Victoria River District it was the Wardaman – the 'Delamere', 'Willeroo' and 'Gregory' blacks – who put up the fiercest resistance to the white newcomers. For a quarter of a century they remained independent warriors, frequently attacking the white men who dared to travel through their territory or those who took up their land for cattle stations. Indeed, for a while they won the war and drove the settlers from their land, the only Victoria River group to do so, and gained such a bad reputation among the whites that, like some of the famous bushrangers, they were often blamed for attacks that were probably done by others.

After the murder of Tom Hardy at Auvergne in 1889, for instance, it was 'believed by those who know the district that the perpetrators of this crime are half-civilised blacks from the Delamere Downs neighbourhood, who have already gained considerable notoriety for their murderous attacks'.[1] However, Auvergne is well away from Wardaman country and Wardaman people are unlikely to have been the instigators of the crime. Wardaman warriors were also blamed for the attack on Mulligan and Ligar in Jasper Gorge in 1895.[2] At least one early report says that Jasper Gorge belonged to the Wardaman,[3] but more recent studies indicate that the gorge is in the country of their immediate neighbours, the Ngaliwurru.[4] While it's quite possible that Wardaman people were involved, it's also possible that they were blamed by Aborigines from other groups to divert attention from the

---

1   'The Victoria River outrage', *The North Australian*, 8th November 1889, p 3.
2   Northern Territory Archives (NTA): Gordon Creek police journal, 25th June 1895, NTRS F302.
3   W Willshire, *Land of the Dawning: Being Facts Gleaned from Cannibals in the Australian Stone Age*, WK Thomas and Co., Adelaide, 1896, p. 85.
4   D Rose, *Hidden Histories: Black Stories from Victoria River Downs, Humbert River and Wave Hill Stations*, Aboriginal Studies Press, Canberra, 1991, p. 82; T Bauman and J Stead, *Fitzroy (Nungali/Ngaliwurru) Land Claim*, Northern Land Council, Darwin, 1992, map, p. 21.

A Wardaman warrior with spearthrower

Basedow collection, National Muesum of Australia

real culprits. The Wardaman were even accused of 'coercing into evil actions' the Aborigines on Elsey Station, east of Wardaman country.[5]

---

5   NTA: Government Resident of the Northern Territory (South Australia) – inwards correspondence, 1870–1912, NTRS 790, item 11226, Aeneas Gunn (per Jeannie Gunn) to Government Resident, 28th February 1902.

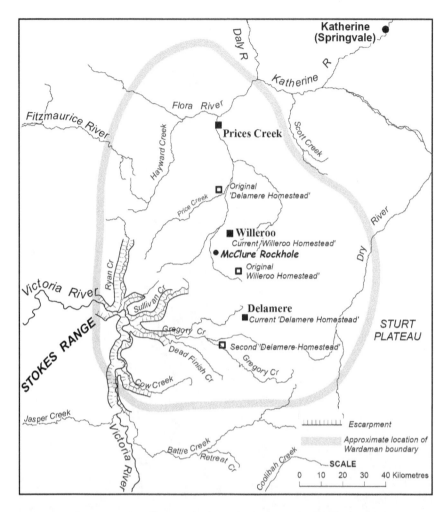

Map 9. Approximate boundary of Wardaman country, and early European settlements

What was it that made the Wardaman so formidable in defence of their country? The fierceness of Wardaman resistance was due, at least in part, to the natural advantages of their country. Their land straddles the divide between the Victoria and Katherine–Daly Rivers and in rough terms can be divided into three sections (Map 9). On the south-eastern side about one third of their land lies on the Sturt Plateau, a flat, almost featureless area, largely waterless in the dry season and boggy in the wet, with numerous patches of almost impenetrable bulwaddy scrub. Another third lies to the north within the Katherine–Daly catchment, a well-watered area with many creeks and scattered patches of sandstone, an area where people on foot stood a reasonable chance of escaping from horsemen. The final third lies to the south-west in the catchment of the Victoria River, well-watered country with many springs and large creeks, including Dead Finish, Little Gregory, (Big) Gregory and Sullivan. These streams rise in rough, hilly, basalt country but soon enter the eastern end of the Stokes Range, a complex area of precipitous flat-topped and spinifex covered sandstone ranges, often capped with cliffs and dissected by gorges. Except for a few major valleys this region is virtually inaccessible for horsemen and was therefore a vast natural fortress for the Aborigines.

Another possible factor in the strength of Wardaman resistance was their location in relation to several Aboriginal culture areas. In Aboriginal Australia, culture areas – regions within which there are strong social and cultural links – tend to be defined by major catchment areas.[6] The Wardaman are located on the divide between three culture areas – Victoria River, Daly River and Katherine River (Arnhem Land). The Katherine and Daly are part of the same catchment but nevertheless form separate culture areas. As might be expected, Wardaman people display influences from all three regions, influences first noted by DS Davidson, an American archaeologist who excavated sites in Wardaman country in the early 1930s:

> Like all tribes to their south, their initiation ceremonies are marked by both circumcision and subincision. The tribes to their north, however, practice only the former. The northern boundary of the Wardaman also forms the approximate northern limit of the use of the boomerang. Their southern boundary, where they meet the Ngainman tribe, represents the most northern limit of the shield and the southernmost appearance of ... the arm-band.[7]

There appear to be relatively few links in mythology between the Wardaman and groups to their west and Wardaman language is not related to other Victoria River languages. It is in fact the most southerly member of the Gunwinyguan family, other languages of which are located in Arnhem Land.[8]

The influence of the three culture areas can be seen in Wardaman rock art. Stylistically this rock art belongs to the Victoria River rock art province,

6   N Peterson, 'The natural and cultural areas of Aboriginal Australia', in N Peterson (ed.), *Tribes and Boundaries in Australia*, Social Anthropology Series no. 10, Australian Institute Of Aboriginal Studies, Canberra, 1976.

7   DS Davidson, 'Archaeological problems of northern Australia', *Journal of the Royal Anthropological Institute*, vol. 65, 1935, pp. 145–83.

8   M Walsh, 'Northern Australia', in S Wurm and S Hattori (eds), *Language Atlas. Pacific Area*, The Australian Academy of the Humanities, Canberra, 1983, map 23.

but a few figures have Arnhem Land style X-ray features and there are examples of 'rayed faces' more characteristic of Daly River rock art.[9] Overall, Wardaman rock art is more elaborate than the rock art of other groups in the Victoria River country, so it may be that their position between three major culture areas has enriched them culturally. It may also have forced them to adopt a more assertive identity and to more aggressively defend their territory. Their rock paintings sometimes depict white men, horses and cattle, which provide us with the only glimpse we have of how Wardaman people perceived the early settlers.

Early accounts only occasionally mention the name 'Wardaman' or a similar derivative. Other names which were used include the 'Gregory blacks', the 'Willeroo blacks' (or natives) and the 'Delamere blacks'. While it's likely that the majority of the Aborigines living within what is now considered to be Wardaman territory were Wardaman-speaking people with primary rights to that area, it's probable that some were from neighbouring language-identified groups. For the purposes of this book, if an event occurred within what is now considered to be Wardaman territory, the Aborigines involved are identified as Wardaman people.

The first Europeans known to have traversed Wardaman territory were members of Gregory's North Australian Expedition. The great Victoria River Gorge marks the western side of Wardaman country, through which, in 1855–56, Gregory rode three times. When the expedition broke up in June 1856 he led a party into the northern end of the gorge and soon turned eastward up Gregory Creek, passing through the middle of Wardaman country as he crossed the tableland to the headwaters of the Roper. As they rode east they saw few signs of Aborigines and had little contact with them,[10] but it's likely that for some of the time the Aborigines were keeping out of sight and watching them.

Between Gregory's departure and the arrival of the first settlers, several of the land-seeking or prospecting expeditions described in Chapter 3 passed through Wardaman country. Of these, only Adrian Sullivan and Arthur McDonald in 1878 and Alfred Woods in 1880 met Aborigines. When Sullivan and McDonald reported that Aborigines near the junction of Gregory Creek and the Victoria had called out, 'White fellow Jimmy, very

9   D Lewis, '"They meet up at Bilinara": rock art in the Victoria River valley', MA, Australian National University, 1990, pp. 148–49.
10 AC Gregory, 'North Australian Expedition', in A Gregory and F Gregory, *Journals of Australian Explorations*, facsimile edition, Hesperian Press, Victoria Park, WA, 1981 (1884), pp. 155–56.

good', speculation arose that 'Jimmy' might have been a survivor of Ludwig Leichhardt's 1848 expedition.[11] Two years later Woods visited the same area with Aboriginal interpreters and was able to question the 'Gregory blacks' about the supposed 'wild white man'. From the answers he received he concluded there was no 'White fellow Jimmy' and consequently, no Leichhardt survivor.[12] Of interest here is the fact that in both instances the Aborigines were (apparently) friendly, although Woods' use of interpreters may have influenced their reaction.

In the first wave of settlement three stations were established within Wardaman territory – Delamere, Price's Creek and Willeroo. The leases that became Delamere and Price's Creek were in the north-west part of Wardaman country,[13] both taken up on behalf of Dr WJ Brown in 1880[14] and stocked in 1881.[15] Although the two blocks were contiguous (Price's Creek was north of Delamere) they were run as separate stations, each with its own homestead.[16] By 1887 Brown was in severe financial difficulties and he placed the stations on the market.[17]

Alfred Giles, Brown's manager at Springvale, bought the three stations, but because of the depression that began in 1890 he couldn't afford to pay the rents on all three. He shifted all the stock off Price's Creek and Delamere and relinquished the leases on Springvale and Price's Creek,[18] but in the

11   'Trip to the Victoria River', *Northern Territory Times*, 28th September 1878, p 2.
12   'The Explorer. The Fate of Leichardt', *The Adelaide Observer*, 23rd October 1880, pp. 721–2.
13   On today's maps, Price's Creek doesn't have a junction with the Flora River but it did so in the past, and what is now referred to as Mathison Creek was originally Price's Creek right to the Flora junction. Today's Price's Creek joins Aroona Creek about 37 kilometres from the Flora River, and Aroona Creek eventually joins Mathison Creek. In 1999 I relocated the remains of the original Delamere homestead site near the Price's Creek/Aroona Creek junction, and in 2000 I found the remains of the Price's Creek homestead site on Mathison Creek a few kilometres above its junction with the Flora River.
14   GR McMinn, 'Quarterly Report on the Northern Territory', 7th August 1883, *South Australian Parliamentary Papers*, vol. 4, no. 53A, 1884, pp. 1–2; A Giles, *The First Pastoral Settlement in the Northern Territory*, pp. 153–54. GRG154/3 Overland Telegraph survey Expedition – Diaries kept by Alfred Giles.
15   Giles, pp. 161–64; 'Early drovers in the Northern Territory: leaves from the diary of Alfred Giles', *The Pastoralists' Review*, 15th March 1906, p. 40.
16   Giles, pp. 181–82; HYL Brown, 'Northern Territory explorations. Fountain Head to Victoria River Downs', in 'Government Resident's Report on Explorations in the Northern Territory', *South Australian Parliamentary Papers*, vol. 3, no. 82, 1895, p. 10.
17   'For sale. The following properties, viz. Delamere Downs', *Northern Territory Times*, 11th June 1887, p. 2.
18   'A visitor's impressions of the Katherine', *Northern Territory Times*, 19th June 1891, p. 3; A. Giles, cited in JG Knight, 'Government Resident's Report on Northern Territory for the Year ended June 30th, 1891', *South Australian Parliamentary Papers*, vol. 2, no. 28, 1891, p. 6.

hope that economic conditions might improve he paid the rent on Delamere up to the end of 1892. He employed a man to caretake the homestead for eight months, but eventually abandoned the lease. Price's Creek homestead lay empty for a period and although 'every possible care was taken to protect the homestead buildings ... from fire the natives have recently burnt the buildings yards & everything'.[19] The homestead was never rebuilt and from about this time the name Price's Creek Station was no longer used.

Willeroo was taken up in about 1881 by a wealthy southern pastoralist, Robert Cooper, and a man named Stuckey, and stocked by them in 1885.[20] Cooper was born on a property near Lake George, New South Wales, which had been granted by the Crown to his father. That property was called Willeroo, the name of the curlew in the local Aboriginal language, and Cooper gave the same name to the land taken up in the Northern Territory.[21]

The first hint of the problems to come occurred late in 1881. Two stockmen, James Walden and W Arboin, were camped on Delamere with a wagon-load of goods and a herd of cattle, waiting on the arrival of the manager, Henry Gosse. In the days before Gosse was due to arrive the stockmen were severely frightened by Aborigines who visited their camp several times. Although the Aborigines didn't threaten them the two men panicked and decided to hide whatever equipment they could before abandoning the camp. They buried all the harness and a lot of other equipment, hid tools and other goods in a spring and threw other items into a waterhole, including a fresh bullock hide, some books wrapped in a new tarpaulin and a tent containing perishable goods.

Gosse arrived an hour after Walden and Arboin had left but rain had washed out their tracks, so he couldn't tell where they had gone. He spent the next three days riding around the cattle looking for them, then decided to ride in to Springvale. While he was out rounding up his horses Aborigines raided his camp, stealing his hammock, a fly, a mosquito net and some cartridges.

When the debacle was sorted out and a party of men returned to where the equipment had been buried, they found 'all the waggon harness dug up and strewn about by the savages' and the leading reins, an axe, a tomahawk, tin plates, pannicans, knives and billycans stolen. In addition, some of the

19   NTA: NTRS 790, item 5889, A Giles to Government Resident Charles Dashwood, 15th December 1893.
20   'Notes From Victoria River', *Northern Territory Times*, 29th August 1885, p. 3; JL Parsons, 'Quarterly Report on Northern Territory, June 30th, 1885', *South Australian Parliamentary Papers*, vol. 3, no. 55, 1885, p. 2; Vern O'Brien, notes. According to O'Brien, only Cooper's name appears on the lease documents.
21   'Mr Robert Cowley Cooper', *The Pastoral Review*, 15th April 1914, p. 332.

goods secreted in the spring had been washed away or ruined by rust, bags of flour had gone rock hard and bags of sugar had dissolved into the ground.[22]

For the next four years things seem to have remained quiet. Then, at the end of May 1886 a more serious incident occurred. While camping on Willeroo about 18 miles from the homestead, a stockman named Harry Keane and a 'blackboy' were attacked by Aborigines at three in the morning. Keane was speared in the stomach and received many cuts on the head from stones, while his Aboriginal companion was speared in the back. Fortunately both recovered.[23] No reason was offered for the attack and it's unknown if any retaliation took place.

Mat Cahill and Fred Williams were attacked while fishing in Gregory Creek in September 1886. Williams was killed instantly and a spear hit Cahill 'in the upper part of the back, and passed downwards and out on the opposite side of the body, cutting a very ugly flesh wound all along'. He was fortunate to escape with his life. A newspaper report at the time said that:

> The part of the country in which this outrage occurred is said to be infested by savage tribes of natives, and travellers who have been there state that extreme caution should be exercised when passing through. The track generally used is lined with pinnacle hills, which shelter the natives and admit them committing outrages unseen by the victims.[24]

Years later Mat Cahill's brother Paddy, who was always inclined to deny or excuse acts of violence by whites against Aborigines, claimed that 'A few of the black scoundrels were shot in this case, but the police brought none of them to justice'.[25]

During the early 1890s the Wardaman were said to have been 'so aggressive as to occasionally spear horses and cattle alongside the [Willeroo] stockyard, and on one occasion they had the Chinese cook besieged for days while the other station employees were away'.[26] In April 1892 it was reported that 'One station owner, at least, has of late been seriously contemplating the withdrawal of all his cattle from his extensive runs in consequence of the incessant and

22   A. Giles, *The First Pastoral Settlement in the Northern Territory*, pp. 178–79. GRG154/3 Overland Telegraph survey Expedition – Diaries kept by Alfred Giles.

23   'Things and others', *The North Australian*, 4th June 1886, p. 2; NTA: NTRS 790, item A9093, telegram from Alfred Giles to Government Resident, 29th May 1886.

24   'Country notes. Katherine River', *Northern Territory Times*, 28th August 1886, p. 3; 'Victoria River', *Northern Territory Times*, 2nd October 1886, p. 3; 'Another outrage by blacks', *The North Australian*, 17th September 1886, p. 2.

25   Paddy Cahill, 'The Aboriginals', letter to the editor, *South Australian Register*, 4th September 1900, p. 6.

26   'The story of a remarkable ride', *Northern Territory Times*, 15th June 1900, p. 3.

increasing troublesomences of the wild blacks'.[27] The station in question was almost certainly Willeroo, still owned at that time by Cooper and Stuckey, and the 'troublesomences' included the wounding of George E Scott, the brother of the manager.[28] Being merely wounded, George got off lightly.

On 10th October 1892 a band of Aborigines appeared at the homestead. Sid Scott was planning to begin a cattle muster the following morning, so he spoke to the Aborigines and told them to go in the opposite direction to that in which the muster was to be held.[29] He gave them some tobacco and other items and they made camp nearby. Later Scott discovered that a little Aboriginal boy named Crawford who had been living with him at Willeroo had gone to the Aborigine's camp, so he sent his black stockman, Rollo, to bring him back. Rollo went to the camp, but stopped there all night and only brought Crawford back at daylight.[30]

Scott's mustering team consisted of Rollo, who came from the Katherine area, Rollo's wife, Alpha, who came from Blue Mud Bay (Arnhem Land) and Crawford. Normally, Sid Scott's brother George would have gone with them, but he'd left for a holiday in Darwin a few days earlier. In the morning the team started out and headed in the direction of McLure Rockhole. While having dinner there at midday a mob of blacks appeared. Scott asked them what they were doing walking about among the cattle and sent Rollo off to bring in the horses, but the Aborigines began acting aggressively, scattering the horses and making them gallop. Scott called Rollo back for fear he might be killed and fired a shot from his rifle to frighten the blacks away. When they'd gone he sent Rollo out once more to bring in the horses, but when Rollo returned he found Scott dead, with several spears in his back and his head split down the centre of the forehead. The blacks had taken Scott's Martini-Henry rifle, cartridges and other gear and cleared out. They'd also taken Crawford and Alpha with them – they were never seen again. Rollo packed up what gear was left and rode back to the homestead. There he told the Chinese cook what had happened and they decided to ride in to Katherine to alert the police, leaving the homestead unguarded.[31]

---

27 ibid.
28 'Murders in the Northern Territory', *South Australian Register*, 17th October 1892, p. 5.
29 Scott almost certainly communicated with these Aborigines through his stockman Rollo, who was a native of the Katherine district and who therefore probably would have spoken the language of the Wardaman, his immediate neighbours.
30 'Another murder in the Victoria River district', *Northern Territory Times*, 21st October 1892, p. 3.
31 ibid.

Manager of Willeroo, Sid Scott, speared in 1892

Katherine Museum

It's clear that the Aborigines hadn't gone far. It's possible they'd followed Rollo back to the homestead and seen both him and the cook leave. In any case, they soon realised there was no one at the house so they broke in and ransacked the place, 'smashed the crockery ... killed all the fowls and threw them in heaps and made a regular mess of things'. They took away most of the wet season loading which had only recently arrived. This included 'about 20 bags flour, 3 bags of rice, all the clothes blankets &c 2 doz pair new boots 60 lb tobacco all matches knives'.[32] Other looted goods included four

---

32   NTA: NTRS 790, item 5861, A Giles to Government Resident, citing information given to him by FW Palmer, 2nd November 1892.

rifles and about 300 rounds of ammunition, two dozen dungaree suits, pipes, rugs, a saddle and bridle, and 'sundries'.[33]

It seems likely that as they rode in to Katherine Rollo and the cook met Lindsay Crawford and one of his men who were on their way to Victoria River Downs because a party which set out from Katherine as soon as the alarm was raised arrived at Willeroo on 20th November, two days after Crawford had been there. The Katherine party included Mounted Constable HP Browne, Arthur Giles (Alfred's brother) and FW Palmer who later provided a detailed account of his observations and the party's actions at Willeroo. According to Palmer a note from Crawford was found pinned to the door advising that he and his man had gathered up various goods found scattered in the vicinity and cleaned up a lot of mess. While doing this they discovered 30 or 40 Aborigines in the horse paddock and 'charged their camp, and found in it Scott's saddle and bridle, and other articles'.[34]

Palmer reported that before he arrived at Willeroo, Crawford and party had left for Victoria River, but he said nothing about what Crawford did to the Aborigines in the horse paddock or anywhere else. Other contemporary documents are similarly mute on this matter, but two later sources suggest that severe retribution was delivered to the Aborigines. First, writing in 1896, Mounted Constable Willshire stated that, 'They were tracked up by an avenging party, and *sic transit gloria mundi!* [*Thus passes the glory of the world!*]'.[35] A decade later Hely Hutchinson, who passed through Willeroo with drover Rose in 1905 and who met many of the early residents, wrote that Crawford had 'found the myalls gloriously drunk and capering about the house like a mob of black devils'.[36] Crawford then avenged Scott's death:

> in a terrible manner, and the 'gruelling' he gave the myalls on that occasion is still spoken of by the niggers in those parts as the Israelites of old oft told to their children the horror of the wrath of the Lord, when he sent plague, pestilence and famine into their land as a correction for their misdeeds ... He and his half-caste dealt out white man's justice with their Winchesters, and when the police arrived from Pine Creek, a couple of days later, they found plenty of employment burying the sons of darkness.[37]

---

33   ibid; 'The Willeroo tragedy', *Northern Territory Times*, 4th November 1892, p. 3.
34   'The Willeroo Tragedy'.
35   Willshire, 1896, p. 19.
36   H7H (Hely Hutchinson), 'The Sketcher. Graves of the Outer Edge,' *North Queensland Herald*, 20th May 1911, p. 25.
37   ibid. Hutchinson may be incorrect on one point: FW Palmer states that the Aborigines hadn't taken or consumed any of the alcohol in the homestead.

The day after they arrived at Willeroo, Palmer and Browne went in search of Scott's body. When they found it, the remains were putrefied, leaving only bare bones. Tracks, bloodstains and other marks told the story. Aborigines had crept along a creek bed to get close to where Scott was sitting or dozing under a tree and attacked him. Scott was hit by at least one spear, but managed to run about 100 metres to another tree where he was surrounded by a large number of blacks. There he was attacked again and killed. The tree where Scott fell was '"bruised with stones" and the ground round about strewn with broken spears'.[38] Palmer noted that Scott's body had been 'terribly mutilated the arms certainly if not the feet, being chopped off with a tomahawk and the front and top of skull smashed in' and that, 'One spear had been thrown or thrust with such force as to cause it to pass right through the thigh joint and was with considerable difficulty driven back from its lodgement in these bones with a stone'. Scott's remains were brought to the homestead and buried there.[39]

On 24th October Mounted Constables Dooley and Freeman, Scott's brother George and several other men arrived. Two parties were formed to go out after the Aborigines. According to reports at the time, they saw traces left by the wanted Aborigines in all directions – spilt flour, bullet holes in trees, or bullocks which had been shot.[40] They found evidence of several large camps near the homestead,[41] but their search for the culprits (other than those who may have been killed by Crawford and his offsider) was unsuccessful.[42] Perhaps the fact that the Aborigines were armed with five rifles and plenty of ammunition was sufficient to discourage serious pursuit.

Scott's murder appears to have made up the mind of the owners to abandon the station, because in June 1895 Cooper and Stuckey sold the Willeroo cattle to Joe Bradshaw for what was said to have been a very low price.[43] These cattle were destined to be the nucleus of the Bradshaw Station herd. By August 1895 Cooper and Stuckey had relinquished the leas. At the time it was recorded that:

---

38 'The Willeroo tragedy'.
39 NTA: NTRS 790, item 5861.
40 'Siftings, local and otherwise', *Northern Territory Times*, 25th November 1892, p. 3.
41 NTA: NTRS 790, item 5861.
42 'Siftings, local and otherwise'.
43 'Notes of the week', *Northern Territory Times*, 23rd August 1895, p. 2; NTA: Log Book of Bradshaw's Run, 25th June 1895, NTRS 2261.

One cause of the failure of the station is said to be that the hostility of the blacks has prevented the herd from being systematically worked, and from what we know of the records of that district it does appear as though the natives had particular designs on Willeroo, for their depredations were most frequent. It is possible that Mr Cooper took very little interest in the station after the brutal murder of WS Scott, the then manager, about three years ago, for as far as we can discover operations have since been carried on in a very easy-going fashion.[44]

The abandonment of Willeroo is one of only two instances in Victoria River District history of a station being abandoned because of Aboriginal resistance. The other instance also involved Willeroo, which was abandoned soon after it was taken up by new owners in 1900.

After Bradshaw bought the Willeroo cattle, Jock McPhee carried out musters in the area for six or seven years, beginning as soon as the sale was finalised.[45] A report in 1898 says he had taken up the Willeroo lease,[46] possibly to safeguard rights to the cattle. While working on Willeroo, McPhee wasn't immune from the attentions of the Wardaman who on one occasion attacked him and his boy[47] and on another 'went through [*his*] camp & took away rations & firearms Etc.'.[48] However, if the report of Billy Linklater can be believed, McPhee displayed a remarkable sangfroid in the face of the danger the Aborigines presented. Linklater, who arrived in the territory in 1887 and worked as a stockman there and in the Kimberley for over 50 years, claimed that, 'One day when it was raining spears, McPhee walked out, picked some up, handed them back and told the blacks to go away like good boys or he would have to send the troopers after them. They went'.[49]

On 26th May 1894, Joe Bradshaw, Jack Larsen and a 'blackboy', Nym,[50] set out to ride up the Victoria River and Gregory Creek to visit the 'sheep camp'

44   'Notes of the week', *Northern Territory Times*, 23rd August 1895, p. 2.
45   NTA: 25th October 1895, 30th July 1896, 8th July 1899 and 7th May 1900, NTRS 2261.
46   Mounted Constable MJ Kingston, 1st February 1899, cited in C Dashwood, 'Government Resident's Report for the Northern Territory, 1898', *South Australian Parliamentary Papers*, vol. 2, no. 45, 1899, p. 23.
47   'Notes of the week', *Northern Territory Times*, 17th April 1896, p. 3.
48   NTA: Timber Creek police journal, 30th November 1900, NTRS F302.
49   W Linklater and L Tapp, *Gather No Moss*, Hesperian Press, Perth, 1997 (1968), pp. 17, 50.
50   The name 'Nym' was common in the early years of 'Top End' settlement. According to W Wildey in *Australia and the Oceanic Region* (George Robinson, Sydney, 1876, pp. 108–09), Nym was a short version of the Larrakia word *nymgorla* meaning 'young man'. The Larrakia people are the traditional owners of the Darwin area.

on Delamere. In a 'narrow defile' on Gregory Creek just above its junction with the Victoria they were attacked by a large number of Aborigines 'securely ambushed in rank dense grass which at this place is fully 10ft high'. Joe escaped unharmed but Larsen and Nym were severely injured, and Nym died a couple of hours later.[51] Joe buried Nym, but apparently the grave was too shallow because in July Mounted Constable Willshire, on patrol from the newly formed Gordon Creek police station, found Nym's bones scattered about by dingoes.[52] He reburied them, but in October they were once again found scattered about on the surface.[53]

An Aboriginal man named Mahdi was also murdered by blacks at Willeroo, in November 1894. Reports at the time said that:

> Mahdi was a boy Constable Wurmbrandt brought to these parts from Alice Springs some years since. Of late he had been employed as a stockman and tracker at Willeroo station. He was noted for his cruelty to the local blacks, and the general impression here is that he played for what he got.[54]

Three Aborigines were arrested for this crime. After they were brought to Katherine a 'rather aged black who is believed to be father of one of the suspected murderers' came up to the police station. Constable Burt went out to meet him, 'but when … [he] had got within fifteen paces of the blackfellow the old villain deliberately hurled a barbed spear at Burt, who, by promptly ducking, caused the spear to do nothing more than graze his face'. After throwing the spear the old man got away. [55]

In November 1895 Paddy Cahill took a mob of horses from Katherine to the Victoria River Depot where he'd agreed to meet the Government Resident, Charles Dashwood. As he was crossing Little Gregory Creek about 14 miles from its junction with the Victoria River, he was attacked. In his words:

---

51 NTA: 29th May 1894, NTRS 2261; 'Notes of the week', *Northern Territory Times*, 6th July 1894, p. 2; Joe Bradshaw, answer to question 3284, in 'Report of the Northern Territory Commission together with Minutes of Proceedings, Evidence, and Appendices', *South Australian Parliamentary Papers*, vol. 2, no. 19, 1895; NTA: 29th May 1894, NTRS 2261; 'Notes of the week', *Northern Territory Times*, 6th July 1894, p. 2; Joe Bradshaw, answer to question 3284, 1895; 'The Northern Territory. Interview with Mr J Bradshaw', *The Adelaide Observer*, 7th December 1895, p. 16.

52 NTA: Timber Creek police journal, 18th June 1894, 22nd July 1894. F 302.

53 HYL Brown, 'Northern Territory explorations. Fountain Head to Victoria River Downs', 'Government Resident's Report on Explorations in the Northern Territory', *South Australian Parliamentary Papers*, vol. 3, no. 82, 1895.

54 'Black murderers arrested', *Northern Territory Times*, 14th December 1894, p. 3.

55 ibid.

We had just started from the luncheon camp, and had hardly gone 300 yards when I noticed some very fresh black's tracks. Knowing that the blacks were very bad in that part of the country I took my rifle from under my saddle flap and filled it with cartridges. I rode on a few yards when one of my boys cried out, 'Look out Paddy!' I knew the blacks must be behind me, so I dodged down alongside my horse's shoulder, and only just in time. A spear struck my hat, going through it, and giving me hard knock on the head. Luckily I am Irish, and a bit thickheaded, so it did very little harm! Before I could say a word I had niggers all around. I could do nothing but shoot as quickly as possible, and I can shoot fairly quickly. I don't know how many niggers I shot — I didn't stop to count them.[56]

Cahill continued on and was followed by the blacks for several days and nights, but wasn't attacked again.[57]

ER Johnson was attacked on Dead Finish Creek in July 1896. Aborigines surrounded his camp before daylight and drove his horses away, but before they launched their attack Johnson and his 'boy' were alerted by their dog. At daylight Johnson tried to make friends with the Aborigines, 'but they showed fight & rushed around the Camp until dispersed by Johnson and his boy'.[58] Johnson knew that George Ligar was due to arrive later that day (the same Ligar speared the year before in Jasper Gorge) so he stayed where he was. Skirmishing continued until about midday when Ligar arrived to break the siege. Johnson and Ligar then tracked the horses for 12 miles over some very rough country to where they found, 'The natives Killed a mare & had the heart taken out to cook'. The other horses had been 'grazed about the front & hind quarters',[59] and 'One of the most valuable of the animals had been speared in the jugular, apparently from sheer wanton wickedness and cruelty'.[60]

Although few details about Johnson's fight survive, F. Burdett, who passed the spot some time later, recorded that 'judging by the heap of broken spears I saw laying on the road ... the attack [*must*] have been most determined'.[61] Burdett noted that 'the blacks there seem to have some half-civilised ones amongst their tribe who can talk, and certainly swear, as fluently as any white

---

56   'Paddy Cahill's list', *The Register* (Adelaide), 18th December 1905, p. 6.
57   NTA: NTRS 790, item 6891, 'Government Resident's Trip to Victoria River [*1895*]'.
58   NTA: Timber Creek police journal, 27th May 1896, F 302.
59   ibid.
60   F Burdett, 'Aboriginal marauders', letter to editor, *Northern Territory Times*, 3rd July 1896, p. 3.
61   ibid.

man', and that in the same area there had been 'two other attempts within the last three months to waylay travellers'. He suggested the establishment of police patrols in the area but, at least in the short term, nothing was done.

In 1899 drovers J McLeod and J Andison each suffered attacks in Wardaman country. No details are known about the attack on McLeod, but Andison had two horses speared while passing Delamere, and the Aborigines drove another of his horses 30 kilometres before killing and cooking it. When their tracks were followed and their camp found, only the horse's head remained.[62]

In May 1900 drover Fred Mork was taking a mob of Hodgson Downs cattle across Willeroo and on to Wyndham for export to Fremantle.[63] On about 10th May one of Mork's black stockmen was driving a lame bullock toward the main herd, which was several miles ahead, when some Aborigines came out of the bush and took the beast off him. A week later one of Mork's white stockmen, Walter Rees, was attacked by Aborigines who showed 'great determination' and called out 'Come on, you white beggars', but he managed to get away.[64] On the evening of 19th May the cattle were camped on McLure Creek. In the morning Mork rode ahead, probably checking the route he would be taking that day, and about ten miles away he unwittingly rode into a camp of 'fifty or sixty' Aborigines:

> He was no sooner observed by its occupants than a shower of spears was sent flying in his direction. One of these, a three pronged wire-headed spear, struck Mork in the fleshy part of the thigh, going right through to the saddle-flap; another spear struck the horse Mork was riding in the stifle, only just missing the joint by about two inches.[65]

The spear that hit the horse was tipped with an old sheep shear blade. If this had hit the joint it could have crippled the horse, with disastrous consequences. Mork 'wheeled round and galloped away, followed by another flight of spears, which fortunately flew wide. He and his horse arrived back in camp, both weak from loss of blood.'[66]

---

62   'Katherine River', *Northern Territory Times*, 19th January 1900, p. 2.

63   NTA: Timber Creek police journal, 9th June 1900, F 302; 'Victoria River', *Northern Territory Times*, 1st June 1900, p. 3; 'Another white man speared by blacks', *Northern Territory Times*, 22nd June 1900, p. 3; NTA: NTRS 790, item 9686, HWH Stevens to Government Resident, 30th March 1900.

64   'Troublesome natives. A drover attacked', *Adelaide Advertiser*, 18th June 1900, p. 5.

65   'Another white man speared by blacks'.

66   ibid; NTA: NTRS 790, item 9722, HWH Stevens to Government Resident Charles Dashwood, nd.

Fred Mork (mounted), 1934
Australian National Trust (NT)

The Timber Creek police reported in June 1900 that, 'Messrs Littleton and Madden arrived from Wyndham en route for Katherine [*they have*] taken up Old Willeroo Run, and going to settle there'.[67] They soon met the Wardaman warriors and a news report in September 1900 suggests that they abandoned their lease almost immediately:

> Mr Madden, who, in conjunction with his partner, Mr Littleton, has lately taken up some country in the Victoria River district, complains bitterly of the ferocious and mischievous character of the blacks in that neighbourhood. He states that his partner and himself took up this

---

67   NTA: Timber Creek police journal, 22nd June 1900, F 302.

country with the intention of stocking, but after his recent experience of the character of the blacks, he feels rather doubtful as to whether they will proceed with their enterprise.[68]

Harry 'Dutchy' Benning, Billy Madden and others thwarted an intended ambush by about 20 Aborigines near the Gregory Creek–Victoria River junction in August 1900. That night, ten miles further on, Aborigines killed two of their horses and badly wounded another. When Benning's party arrived at the Timber Creek police station they found that 'an old man', a French traveller named Clede Pennaman, had been 'stuck up' on Sullivan Creek and robbed of all his possessions, including a sporting rifle.[69] Why he wasn't killed is a mystery.

Towards the end of October 1900 a traveller named James Osbourne was attacked and wounded near the junction of Sullivan Creek and the Victoria River. As reported by the *Northern Territory Times*:

> whilst quietly riding along about midday, he was suddenly struck by a wire spear in the muscle of the right arm, the weapon being thrown with such force and murderous intent as to pass right through the arm and enter his side between the ribs, thus pinning his arm to his side. Frightened by the yells of the blacks his horses bolted. After galloping some distance Osbourne managed to extract the spear, and then feeling sick and faint from loss of blood, he got off and lay down ...[70]

After resting for several hours his horse alerted him that something was wrong, but before he could mount he was again attacked and:

> another shower of spears was thrown, one of which struck him in the head, but fortunately glanced off without inflicting more than a flesh wound. With the blood from this fresh wound running down his face and almost blinding him, and the terrific yells of the black fiends sounding all around him, he succeeded in mounting his frightened horse and again making his escape.

Osbourne rode some distance before camping for the night. In the morning he retraced his tracks to try and retrieve his six packhorses. The heat and his wounds led him to take another rest and the Aborigines attacked him again,

---

68   'News and notes', *Northern Territory Times*, 21st September 1900, p. 3.
69   NTA: Timber Creek police journal, 15th and 28th August 1900, F 302; W Benning, 'Further outrages by Victoria River natives. Three horses speared', *Northern Territory Times*, 28th September 1900. p. 3.
70   'Another outrage by blacks', *Northern Territory Times*, 9th November 1900, p. 2.

but this time he drove them off with his revolver. He eventually found his six packhorses, all dead and the pack bags looted. He then rode 65 miles to 'McPhee's camp on Willeroo' where his wounds were treated. Eventually he returned to Darwin.[71] Mounted Constable O'Keefe visited McPhee's camp some time after Osbourne had left. McPhee told him that the blacks who speared Osbourne were the same ones who had speared Mork and Cahill, and that they'd also raided his camp and stolen rations and firearms.[72]

The attack on Osbourne finally prompted the government to act. At the end of 1900 Mounted Constable Thompson and two trackers were sent to assist O'Keefe at Timber Creek, with instructions to carry out special patrols through Jasper Gorge and around through Willeroo and Delamere. Over the next three years Thompson or O'Keefe regularly made these special patrols. They apparently experienced no serious conflicts with Aborigines, but attacks on other white people in Wardaman country continued for several years.

By 1901 Delamere was owned by WF Buchanan and stocked with cattle from Wave Hill.[73] Europeans were also active on Willeroo in 1901, probably assisting McPhee to muster cattle for Bradshaw.[74] The men on both stations enjoyed the attentions of the Wardaman. A 'Katherine correspondent' to the *Northern Territory Times* reported, 'I have just received a letter from Willeroo Station that one of the mares has been killed and eaten by the blacks quite close to the camp'.[75]

In August 1902 a man named Smith had 'an encounter' with Aborigines 'between the two Delameres', meaning between the original Delamere homestead on Aroona Creek and the 'new' one about 50 kilometres to the south. Smith got away unharmed, but a few days later a German traveller, name unknown, disappeared in the same area. This man's horses were found a few days later but there was no trace of the man himself. The police at Katherine were notified and Mounted Constable Kingston spent about a month investigating, but he, too, found nothing. Eventually it was reported that, 'Bush blacks state that the man was killed and his body, and

---

71   ibid; NTA: Timber Creek police journal, 29th November 1900, F302.
72   NTA: Timber Creek police journal, 31st November 1900, F 302.
73   NTA: Timber Creek police journal, 30th May 1902, F 302; 'News and notes', *Northern Territory Times*, 19th June 1903, p. 3.
74   NTA: Notes on the entry of 7th May 1901 in the Timber Creek police journal, copied by an unknown policeman. Copy book, 1895–1940, NTRS 2224; 'Katherine', *Northern Territory Times*, 5th April 1901, p. 3; 'News and notes', *Northern Territory Times* 4th October 1901, p. 3.
75   *Northern Territory Times*, 4th October 1901, p. 3.

saddles, etc., burnt', but this was never confirmed.[76] Late the following year Aborigines entered the camp of CJ Walker six miles north of the Gregory Creek junction, where they demanded tobacco. Later they followed him, but no other incidents occurred.[77]

In 1905 Wardaman people were involved in a bloody incident with a 'foreign' Aborigine on Willeroo. In August while the manager and all hands were out mustering a dispute arose between Nipper, who came from 'Red Lily' (Elsey Station) and someone at the homestead. There's a suggestion that Lee Gunn, the Chinese cook, had taken Nipper's wife, which may have been the cause of the dispute. In any case, Nipper went bush for several days before returning and demanding tucker from the cook. The cook refused, so Nipper stole his rifle and cartridges and shot him dead. For some reason he also killed an old Aboriginal woman who looked after the Willeroo goats. He then took a horse, the rifle, a blanket and other gear, slung an ammunition belt across his shoulder, and headed in towards Katherine, probably with the intention of returning to Elsey.[78]

By the time Nipper got close to Katherine the alarm had been raised and by chance he was seen. A police party led by Mounted Constable Johnstone quickly got onto his tracks. After a week-long chase in the Katherine area Nipper doubled back towards Willeroo. Eventually the police party came upon him near Flora Falls, but Nipper saw them coming, dismounted, and hid in a patch of thick, long grass and jungle laced with small creeks. The police surrounded the area as best they could and began a search. Suddenly Nipper appeared and 'raised his rifle, and was on the point of firing at tracker Jack when the latter anticipated him by a snap shot … from his revolver'. Jack missed, and Nipper retreated into the thick vegetation. Johnstone called on him to surrender but received no response, so 'The long grass was then set on fire, and being dry soon burnt itself out. But there was no trace of Nipper, who had apparently disappeared like a snake by crawling away through the surrounding grass whilst the conflagration was raging'.[79]

---

76 'Supposed outrage by blacks', *Northern Territory Times*, 5th September 1902, p. 3; 'News and notes', *Northern Territory Times*, 24th October 1902, p. 3.

77 NTRS 2224, 9th August 1903. Note: the Timber Creek police journal entry of 21st October 1903 says this incident occurred on the head of the Little Gregory Creek (NTA: F302).

78 'Alleged outrage by an Aboriginal. A Chinaman shot dead', *Northern Territory Times*, 11th August 1905, p. 3; 'The Willeroo murder', *Northern Territory Times*, 18th August 1905, p. 2; 'Hunting a murderer', *Northern Territory Times*, 25th August 1905, p. 2.

79 'Pursuit of a murderer', *Northern Territory Times*, 1st September 1905, p. 2.

Nipper's horse was almost burnt to death before it was rescued and was found to be carrying 'about 40 lbs of fresh beef', which it was thought Nipper was taking to a 'bush natives camp'. On this occasion Nipper got clear away, but he didn't survive for long. After the fire Johnstone tried unsuccessfully to find Nipper's tracks, but had to return to Katherine for fresh horses and more rations. Before Johnstone left he met three bush Aborigines and asked them to keep a 'bright look out' for Nipper while he was gone.

There are two quite similar versions of subsequent events. In one, the three Aborigines soon found Nipper, but he was suspicious of them, accusing them of being in league with the police and telling them to keep away from him or he would shoot them. He afterwards joined a camp of Wardaman blacks in the area, and 'very foolishly boasted to them that he'd not only shot the Chinese cook, but he'd also shot an old lubra employed as a goat shepherd at Willeroo. This revelation was suicidal on his part, as the old lady belonged to the Willeroo tribe'.[80]

The Wardaman men took revenge by tricking Nipper into leaving his rifle in camp and going on a kangaroo hunt with spears. Not far from camp one of the Aborigines suddenly stopped and called to Nipper, 'There is a kangaroo. Quick! Give me your spears until I spear him!' Nipper did so and was then 'speared to death where he stood'. He was later found by Johnston with, 'two spear wounds in the back, and also a hole in the back from whence the deceased's "kidney fat" had been extracted by his slayers'.[81]

In the other version Nipper had already joined the Wardaman camp before his fight with the police where he escaped from the fire lit to drive him into the open. The three Aborigines met by Johnstone found Nipper in this camp, but Nipper must have seen them talking with Johnstone because he became 'furiously angry, accusing them of being in league with the police' and 'would have shot them had he not been prevented by the other natives'. While he was in this angry state Nipper revealed that he'd shot the old woman at Willeroo. It was this that led to him being killed by the Wardaman warriors in the manner described above.[82]

The German traveller who was said to have been murdered in 1902 appears to have been the last European killed by bush blacks in Wardaman country. There can be little doubt that soon afterwards the Wardaman made the decision to stop attacking and killing whites. Within a few years there's evidence that a station blacks' camp had been established at

---

80 'End of a murderer', *Northern Territory Times*, 8th September 1905, p. 2.
81 ibid.
82 ibid.

Willeroo homestead and possibly at Delamere,[83] and that some Wardaman were living near homesteads elsewhere in the district. For instance, in 1905, four years after an Aboriginal camp had been established at VRD, the Governor of South Australia saw a man there wearing 'a large brass plate inscribed "Naaluk, King of the Wattamon"'.[84] Some diehards kept out of harm's way in the bush,[85] but most eventually came in to the homesteads and accommodated themselves to European settlement.

As discussed earlier, decisions about fighting or ceasing to fight appear to have been made universally across the region. Along with the decision of many Aborigines to accept the 'offer' of life in station camps, there appears to have been a parallel decision to stop attacking white men. From the time that the station camps appeared, or shortly afterwards, the rate of attacks against white men dropped markedly, especially in the territory of the Wardaman. Occasional attacks on or killings of whites still occurred elsewhere in the district, but most of these involved Aborigines who had remained in the bush or who had experienced minimal contact with whites. Eventually only the largest areas of rough country remained dangerous for white men. In 1922 for example, a prospecting expedition went into the Stokes Range and later reported that 'West and north of the Humbert River there were tribes not too friendly disposed towards the whites'.[86] Long after other parts of the district had been more or less subdued, Europeans avoided these areas, or took strict precautions while travelling through them.

Warriors the Wardaman were and warriors they no doubt remained. 'Soft' resistance such as cattle killing continued for many years,[87] but by the early 1900s, after more than two decades of being a force to be reckoned with, and of making their name one of dread to both settlers and travellers, they lay down their spears and accepted the reality of white settlement.

---

83 NTA: Timber Creek police journal, 10th October 1907, 24th September 1907, F 302.
84 'Northern Territory, no. 4 – the governor's report', *The Adelaide Observer*, 4th November 1905, p. 49.
85 J Wozitsky, *Born Under The Paperbark Tree: A Man's Life*, ABC Books, Sydney, 1996, pp. 20–22.
86 'The search for oil', *Adelaide Advertiser*, 27th September 1922, p. 10.
87 For example, in the Timber Creek police journal, 31st July 1917, the manager of Delamere reported cattle killing on Gregory Creek (NTA: F 302).

Chapter 9

THE VICTORIA RIVER SHEEP SAGA

Victoria River Downs, 'the biggest sheep station in the world'? Many cattlemen would probably be horrified to learn that some of the early settlers dreamt of vast sheep empires on the Victoria. These settlers overcame many obstacles and invested a lot of money to successfully bring sheep onto the land, but the only legacy of their experiment is a great tale of dreams that failed.

Sheep first arrived in the Victoria River District with Gregory's expedition in October 1855, intended as meat supplies for the explorers. The expedition ship, *Tom Tough*, had 161 sheep on board when it entered the Victoria,[1] but only 44 made it to the depot camp.[2] Surprisingly, at least one sheep survived long enough to be loaded aboard the *Tom Tough* when the expedition left the district in July 1856. The mouths of the crew watered when they saw this sheep – they must not have had mutton for some time – but instead of chops they were offered steaks from a large saltwater crocodile that had been killed that morning.[3] Thomas Baines reported that the men were at first upset about this, but once they had cooked and tasted the crocodile meat they were keen for more.[4]

The first sheep intended to stock a Top End station were delivered to Springvale by Alfred Giles in 1879. Giles set out from South Australia for Dr WJ Browne's Springvale[5] and Newcastle Waters leases with 2000 cattle and 12,000 sheep in December 1877.[6] Near the Devil's Marbles nearly 600

---

1   AC Gregory, 'Report of the progress of the North Australian expedition', *Proceedings of the Royal Geographical Society of London*, vol. 1, sessions 1855–56, 1857, p. 185.
2   Gregory, pp. 185–91.
3   T Baines, 'Journal of the detachment of the North Australian Expedition left by Mr Gregory at the main camp Victoria River 1856,' 21st July 1856, Mitchell Library, C408.
4   Surprisingly, the last sheep, named 'Tom Tough', was still alive two months later (R Braddon, *Thomas Baines and the North Australian Expedition*, Collins, Sydney, in association with the Royal Geographical Society, London, 1986, p. 113).
5   Springvale is located a few kilometres out of Katherine.
6   A Giles, *Exploring in the 'Seventies and the Construction of the Overland Telegraph Line*, facsimile ed., Friends of the State Library of South Australia, Adelaide, 1995 (1926), p. 167.

sheep died after eating 'poison bush'.[7] This happened on the same spot where Ralph Millner lost nearly 2000 of the 7000 sheep he was taking to the Roper River telegraph camp in 1870–72.[8] No doubt these disasters contributed to the ongoing but largely unfounded fears of Top End pastoralists of sheep losses from 'poison bush'. Giles' trek took almost two years to accomplish, with 1800 cattle and 8000 sheep arriving at Katherine in June 1879.[9] What happened to the other 3000–odd sheep, including all the rams,[10] is unknown. They may have been left at Newcastle Waters or perhaps sold to various telegraph stations and butchers en route.

It was quickly realised that the spear grass at Springvale was unsuitable for sheep because of its 'coarse and rank nature at its maturity in the green state, and the total absence of any nourishing properties when dry, it being exactly like crisp and brittle straw'. The sheep had arrived in June when the grass was very dry. Of the 8000 that arrived at the station nearly 800 died over the next three months.[11] By the end of 1880 there were said to be only 4000 sheep left and sheep-raising on Springvale was considered a failure.[12] The need to find better pasture for the sheep was the driving force behind the establishment of Delamere Station.

Giles stayed on to become the first manager of Springvale and, when the Delamere leases were taken up for Browne, he arranged for them to be stocked with 1100 cattle and 3000 sheep. These arrived in July 1881.[13] While the cattle did well the sheep did not. A traveller passing through the district a decade later remarked, 'They tried sheep here in big numbers for which the country from a practical point of view was utterly unsuitable [because of] sour bladey rank grass with no herbage whatever'.[14]

---

7   A Giles, 'The first pastoral settlement in the Northern Territory', nd., State Library of South Australia, V 1082, p. 32. Giles states that Von Mueller later identified this plant as *Gastrolobium grandiflorium*.

8   ibid., p. 32; H Favelle, 'Ralph Millner', in D Carment, R Maynard and A Powell (eds.), *Northern Territory Dictionary of Biography: Volume 1 to 1945*, Northern Territory University Press, Darwin, 1990, p. 208.

9   A Giles, nd., State Library of South Australia, V 1082, p. 138; 'Early drovers in the Northern Territory – leaves from the diary of Alfred Giles', *The Pastoralists' Review*, 15th March 1906, p. 40; 'Notes of the week', *Northern Territory Times*, 14th December 1894, p. 3; GR McMinn, 'Quarterly report on the Northern Territory', 7th August 1883, *South Australian Parliamentary Papers*, vol. 4, no. 53A, 1884, pp. 1–2.

10 'Notes of the week', *Northern Territory Times*, 14th December 1894, p. 3.

11 McMinn, pp. 1–2.

12 'Northern Territory', *The Adelaide Observer*, 20th November 1880, p. 879.

13 A Giles, State Library of South Australia, nd. V 1082, pp. 161–64; *The Pastoralists' Review*, 15th March 1906, p. 40.

14 Noel Butlin Archives (NBA), Australian National University: Goldsbrough Mort & Co.: sundry papers re. CB Fisher and the Northern Australia Territory Co., 1886–92,

Apparently Giles realised the shortcomings of Delamere very quickly because when he provided notes on his stations to the Government Resident in 1886 he made no mention of sheep on Delamere.[15] When the station was advertised for sale in 1887 the numbers of bullocks, cows and horses were given, but there was no mention of sheep, sheep yards or anything else associated with them.[16] Years later Tom Cahill, who helped bring the first cattle to stock Wave Hill and stayed in the district for more than 20 years, claimed that Browne abandoned the Delamere lease because cattle numbers there were decreasing. He added that the remaining stock was moved to Newcastle Waters.[17] Cattle certainly were shifted from Delamere to Newcastle Waters – 1500 head in 1887 – but the real reason for Browne relinquishing Delamere was his dire financial situation.

Giles bought Browne's Delamere and Springvale leases in 1887 and continued to run sheep at Springvale.[18] At times the sheep were shepherded by Chinese and at other times by Aborigines. In 1891 there were still 200 sheep there, shepherded by 'southern blacks from Alice Springs', but by then Giles knew that, as on Delamere, sheep would never do well. He remarked that, 'In its primitive state it is not a sheep country, as proved by Dr WB Browne, but it can be made capable of supporting small herds'.[19] Exactly when the last sheep disappeared from Springvale is unknown, but eventually the Alice Springs Aborigines were sent home – armed with a revolver and ammunition for self defence during the 1200 kilometre trip.[20]

One positive outcome of the Springvale and Delamere sheep experiments was the discovery that the quality of the wool remained good. Some pastoralists had predicted that in the extreme heat of the north the quality would decline, but the Government Resident reported that 'scarcely if any deterioration in the wool was noticeable. The third clip to be taken off in the Territory was found to be genuine, clean, and good stapled wool – not hair, as many people insisted upon asserting would be the case if sheep were brought to the tropics'.[21]

2/876/6, report on Victoria River Downs, Robert Everett to Gibbs, Bright & Co., January 1888.

15 A Giles, cited in JL Parson, 'Half-yearly Report on Northern Territory to June 30th 1886', *South Australian Parliamentary Papers*, vol. 3, no. 54, 1886, p.2.

16 'For sale', *Northern Territory Times*, 11th June 1887, p. 2.

17 T Cahill, letter to JW Durack, 25th April 1926, copy in possession of author.

18 'A visitor's impressions of the Katherine', *Northern Territory Times*, 19th June 1891, p. 3

19 JC Lewis, 'Veterinary and stock report', *NT Bulletin no. 8*, South Australian Government Printer, 1913, p. 7.

20 A Giles, nd., State Library of South Australia, V 1082, pp. 133, 155.

21 McMinn, p. 1.

Almost as soon as Victoria River Downs was established, plans were afoot to make it a sheep station. Perhaps encouraged by Lindsay Crawford's opinion that the Camfield Creek area was 'Splendid sheep Country',[22] by late 1884 VRD owners Charles Fisher and Maurice Lyons were arranging for a mob of 5000 ewes to be overlanded from Queensland.[23] However, before they could be started the country became so drought-stricken that they couldn't be moved. This drought had eased by the end of 1885,[24] but by then the financial problems being experienced by Fisher and Lyons had become so acute that the sheep project was abandoned.

In 1887 VRD was taken over by the English-owned Northern Australian Territory Company, but two years later it came under the control of the Australian firm Goldsbrough Mort & Co. Ltd.[25] Before Goldsbrough Mort acquired the station there was a prolonged and at times acrimonious series of legal and financial manoeuvres during which two reports on Victoria River Downs were commissioned. The first was produced in 1888 by Robert Everett who was sent to inspect VRD by the Northern Australian Territory Company. Among other things, Everett remarked that 'I cannot write too highly of this country which I believe is adapted for either sheep or cattle'.[26] When Goldsbrough Mort took over they sent B Blair to inspect the station and write a new report. On his return to Darwin he sent the following telegram to the company:

> Finished inspecting Victoria river property mostly Good Stony Country parts worthless permanent waters Good but not sufficient for Sheep on best Country Cattle doing well sheep would also over Considerable area think Valuable property management Good.[27]

Blair later produced a very detailed assessment of the potentials and limitations of the station for both cattle and sheep. Specifically for sheep he recommended the improvement of natural water supplies, the provision of paddocks and the building of a woolshed at the Victoria River Depot (the

---

22 L Crawford, cited in JL Parson, 'Quarterly report on Northern Territory', 1 January 1885, *South Australian Parliamentary Papers*, vol. 3, no. 53, 1885, p. 2.

23 JL Parson, 'Quarterly Report on Northern Territory, March 31st, 1885', *South Australian Parliamentary Papers*, vol. 3, no. 54, 1885, p. 1.

24 J Parson, 'Half-yearly Report on the Northern Territory to December 31st, 1885', *South Australian Parliamentary Papers*, vol. 3, no. 53, 1886, p. 1.

25 J Makin, *The Big Run: The Story of Victoria River Downs*, Weldon Publishing, Sydney, 1992, pp. 67, 69.

26 NBA: 2/876/6.

27 NBA: 2/876/22 (65), telegram from B Blair to Goldsbrough Mort, Melbourne, Sept 1889.

landing on the Victoria River near Timber Creek). Encouraged by Blair's report, Goldsbrough Mort decided to trial sheep on VRD so, in November 1890, 1005 'picked maiden ewes' were shipped to Darwin from James Booth's station in New South Wales.[28]

The decision to try sheep was regarded as one of great importance to the future of the Northern Territory. Goldsbrough Mort's general manager in Darwin, HWH Stevens, thought it 'without doubt the most important pastoral experiment that has yet been undertaken' and 'it will be superfluous to enlarge upon the prospects which the successful depasturing of sheep will have upon the enormous area of the Territory suitable for sheep runs'.[29]

Apparently through fear of poisonous plants in the Darwin/Adelaide River area, and to try and shorten the route, Stevens suggested that the sheep could be landed at Point Pearce (south of Port Keats) from where the drover could 'explore the track'.[30] Clearly he hadn't read Augustus Gregory's account or considered other problems. For the first few hundred kilometres this route would have entailed crossing some of the roughest terrain in the Northern Territory, an area which was then densely populated with uncontacted and potentially hostile Aborigines. It would also have required crossing both the Fitzmaurice and Victoria rivers and, for all anyone knew, the area could have been full of poisonous plants. Fortunately for both sheep and sheepman, the idea was abandoned.

After discussing the matter with Giles, who was the man most experienced with overlanding sheep in the Northern Territory, Stevens decided to land the sheep up the Adelaide River 'and thus have the advantage of travelling them through the most settled and best Known part of the country'. Still concerned about poisonous plants, Stevens obtained 18 head of the local butcher's sheep. He grazed them on the Adelaide River while he 'watched for any symptoms of poisoning'.[31] No poisoning occurred, but when the first consignment of sheep arrived at Darwin on 5th December 1890 it was too late for them to be taken up the Adelaide River, presumably because of flooding

---

28 HWH Stevens, cited in JG Knight, 'Government Resident's Report on Northern Territory for the Year ended June 30th, 1891', *South Australian Parliamentary Papers*, vol. 2, no. 28, 1891, p. 6.

29 Ibid.

30 NBA: Head office, Melbourne: letters received from HWH Stevens, Port Darwin, re. NT property and butchering business, 1889–92, 2/872, report on VRD, HWH Stevens to Goldsbrough Mort & Co. Ltd, 24th July 1890.

31 NBA: 2/872, report on VRD, HWH Stevens to Goldsbrough Mort & Co. Ltd, 19th September 1890.

or boggy conditions. Instead they were unloaded at Darwin and immediately sent by train to the end of the line at Fountain Head siding.[32] From there they were overlanded on the hoof by drover Fred Mork.[33] Luckily the wet season rains were late so none of the rivers was in high flood. Mork swam the sheep over the 'lowest crossing' of the Katherine River and was then joined by Mick Fleming who knew the road.[34] The sheep reached Delamere early in 1891 where they were described as being in good condition, with the loss of only 47 head.[35] Where, or why, the 47 died is unknown, but the surviving 955 ewes finally arrived at VRD on 11th February.[36]

Meanwhile, arrangements were being made for a consignment of 56 rams to be sent to VRD. Stevens wanted them to arrive about mid-April 'for transhipment [*to the*] Victoria depot'.[37] At this stage his intention was to transfer the rams from the ship to 'the local hulk', so that there was no risk of them eating any poisonous plants. From there they'd be sent on the next boat going to the Depot where they'd land only a few rams at first to see if there were poisonous plants in the area. If so, the other rams would be carried to VRD by express wagon. Otherwise they could be walked to VRD, but warned that 'The Blacks, being troublesome on the Depôt Road, increase our difficulties, & I shall have to provide for all such emergencies'.[38]

The rams arrived at Darwin in June and were sent the same way as the ewes. The dreaded poisonous weeds were finally met with near the Douglas River where 12 rams died. Three more died later, but 41 made it to VRD in good condition early in September 1891.[39] When they arrived it was noticed that their wool was full of Bathurst Burr, so they were shorn and

---

32 NBA: 2/872, report on NT Stations, HWH Stevens to Goldsbrough Mort & Co. Ltd, 8th January 1891; NBA: 2/872, telegram from HWH Stevens to general manager, 8 January 1891.
33 NBA: 2/872, 8th January 1891.
34 NBA: 2/872, report on NT Stations, HWH Stevens to Goldsbrough Mort & Co. Ltd, 8th January 1891.
35 'The Victoria River sheep', *Northern Territory Times*, 16 January 1891, p. 2.
36 NBA: 2/872, report by HWH Stevens to general manager Goldsbrough Mort, 9th February 1891; C Dashwood, 'Government Resident's Report on the Northern Territory', 24th July 1894, *South Australian Parliamentary Papers*, vol. 2, no. 53, 1894, p. 3.
37 NBA: 2/872, telegram from HWH Stevens to general manager Goldsbrough Mort and Co. Ltd, 30th January 1891.
38 NBA: 2/872, HWH Stevens to general manager, Goldsbrough Mort & Co. Ltd, 6th February 1891.
39 NBA: 2/872, HWH Stevens to general manager, Goldsbrough Mort and Co. Ltd., August 1891; NBA: 2/872, telegram from HWH Stevens to general manager Goldsbrough Mort and Co. Ltd., 4th September 1891.

the wool burnt. They were then sent to 'the main branch of the Victoria River', presumably Camfield Creek, where they were soon reported to be 'doing famously'.[40]

Another problem was to find someone who knew how to look after sheep. Although Stevens knew that 'several of the station hands are well accustomed to the ordinary work of a sheep Run,'[41] he was concerned to find someone with greater experience. On the recommendation of 'the local butcher' and 'Mulligan, the Victoria River Contractor', Stevens hired an old and experienced sheep man named James Mavor in Darwin in March 1891. He was sent to VRD to look after the sheep and to teach the other station hands about sheep husbandry.[42] A hut which existed on Camfield Creek in 1891 was probably built for Mavor.[43]

Mavor was impressed with the country's suitability for sheep. In October he wrote to Crawford:

> Since I came up it has been very dry & was a long time before I came. On all the stations I been on, on the Barcoo, & Flinders River, the sheep here done fully as well as on the best of them and fewer deaths in comparison to most others. The country is free from boggy water holes, and has good clean water. The country is better than it looks Every way but it is bad for timber for making sheep yards. There has been a good shower of rain & the next will make the green grass spring. The Rams are doing very well in the Ewes: I was out yesterday shepherding them & Everything is all right.[44]

Mavor was only hired for a year and apparently he decided not to stay longer because by February 1892 Stevens was again talking about the need for an experienced sheep man. He wrote to Goldsbrough Mort saying that because:

> the Manager of Victoria River Downs has only limited Knowledge of sheep management, I would suggest for your consideration, that a thoroughly practical working man should be engaged to accompany

40   NBA: 2/871, report on NT stations, HWH Stevens to Goldsbrough Mort & Co. Ltd., 23rd October 1891.
41   NBA: 2/872, HWH Stevens to general manager, Goldsbrough Mort & Co. Ltd, 24th July 1890.
42   NBA: 2/872, 23 October 1891; NBA: 2/872, report on VRD by HWH Stevens to general manager, Goldsbrough Mort & Co. Ltd, 17th March 1891.
43   NBA: 2/872, 23rd October 1891.
44   NBA: 2/872, James Mavor, cited in HWH Stevens to general manager Goldsbrough Mort & Co. Ltd, 19th December 1891.

the Rams & to remain on the station, at any rate, until after the first lambing.

By that time Mr. Crawford would be fully capable of working without any special assistance.

This man could also do the shearing in July, and I would ask you to send the necessary gear with him, the same being unobtainable here.[45]

In October 1891 another 1495 sheep arrived at Darwin and were immediately started on the road to VRD.[46] Of these, 315 died soon after starting out, most from over-eating on board ship and suffering bloat soon after landing. The remainder reached VRD in January 1892,[47] making a total of 2172 sheep on the station.[48] All the sheep were pastured on the open downs country south of Pigeon Hole and along Camfield Creek. Sheep yards were built near Red Rock on Camfield Creek, at Longreach Waterhole and possibly near Ra Ra Spring east of Pigeon Hole (Map 10).[49]

The first shearing was done by 'station amateurs' and took 12 days. The wool was taken by wagon to the Depot and shipped from there to Melbourne. According to Stevens, the 'general opinion is that the wool is good & clean for travelled and shepherded sheep. Unfortunately we could not get sufficient packs out in time so that a large portion had to be compressed into a wagon, and thus brought to the Depot'.[50]

The sheep did well on VRD. The Government Resident reported that by December 1893 there were 3260 sheep on the station, an increase of 50 per cent.[51] By January 1894 the flock had grown to 3858.[52] The Resident said that the wool looked good and clean and he was optimistic about the future of sheep on VRD. However, by the time his report was published, and in spite of the good increase in sheep numbers, Goldsbrough Mort had decided to do away with sheep on Victoria River Downs.

---

45 NBA: 2/872, 6th February 1891.
46 NBA: 2/872, report by HWH Stevens to general manager Goldsbrough Mort & Co. Ltd, October 1891.
47 NBA: 2/872, 19th December 1891.
48 Dashwood, 24th July 1894.
49 Anzac Munnganyi, pers. comm. Munnganyi was shown the sites of these yards by his elderly relations when he was a young man in the 1930s.
50 NBA: 2/872, 23rd October 1891.
51 C Dashwood, 'Government Resident's Report on the Northern Territory', 13th December 1893, *South Australian Parliamentary Papers*, vol. 3, no. 158, 1893, pp. 1–2.
52 Dashwood, 24th July 1894.

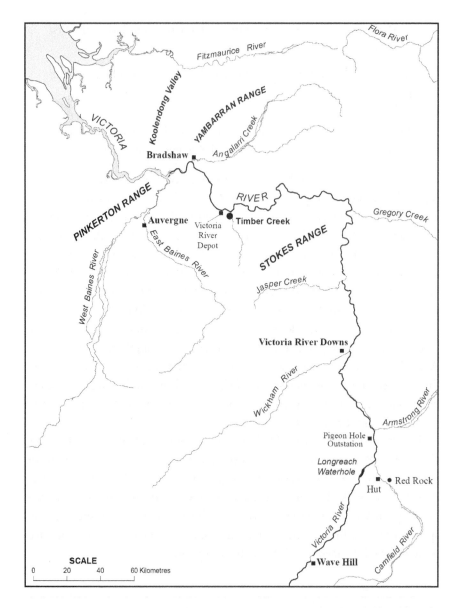

Map 10. Victoria River 'sheep country', Victoria River Downs and Bradshaw Station

Before the sheep had even arrived in Darwin in 1890 Stevens knew what difficulties the project faced, because the sheep would be going into what was effectively a war zone. From the time that the station was first settled there'd been little contact between the Aborigines and the whites and a regime of constant attacks and reprisals prevailed.[53] In March 1890 Stevens reported that only ten miles from the homestead one of the 'foreign' Aborigines employed on VRD was murdered by the bush blacks. He expressed concern about what would happen to the sheep when they came:

> It is with much regret that I have to report the murder of our blackboy Bob Some ten miles from the Victoria homestead. The wild blacks had speared a beast, & the boys were Sent out to drive them away & try to discover the culprit. Our boy Bob got separated from the others who only rejoined him in time to see a spear enter at the shoulder & pass right through to his groin. He pulled the spear out, but died almost at once.
>
> The best & most valuable native we ever had on the runs.
>
> Mr Crawford followed the blacks for some 60 miles into some large gorges, but with a good start, they got away.
>
> I only trust we shall be able to Keep them from ascertaining what sheep are.[54]

Concerns about attacks by Aborigines continued, with the *Northern Territory Times* reporting in April 1891 that 'the worst danger now to be feared will be the blacks, who, when once they get the taste of mutton, are bound to become exceedingly troublesome'.[55] The blacks had long since developed a great fondness for beef and horse flesh, but strangely, they don't appear to have ever 'ascertained what sheep are'. If they didn't discover what sheep were, it wasn't for want of trying. In December 1892 Stevens wrote that 'the Aborigines of the Victoria River district are becoming so hostile, that it is a most difficult matter for the settlers to carry on their ordinary avocations'.[56] He went on to cite a letter that he'd received from Lindsay Crawford stating that the Aborigines were killing large numbers of cattle and were so highly organised that the stockmen couldn't stop them. Crawford feared that the

---

53 L Crauford (Crawford), cited in Dr EC Stirling's article, 'Victoria River Downs station, Northern Territory, South Australia', *Journal of the Royal Anthropological Institute of Great Britain and Ireland*, vol. 24, 1895, pp. 180–82.

54 NBA: 2/872, HWH Stevens to general manager of Goldsbrough Mort & Co. Ltd, 3rd March 1890, pp. 7–8.

55 'Another consignment of sheep', *Northern Territory Times*, 3rd April 1891, p. 2.

56 Northern Territory Archives (NTA): Government Resident of the Northern Territory (South Australia) inwards correspondence – 1870–1912, NTRS 790, item 5151, HWH Stevens to Government Resident Charles Dashwood, 30th December 1892.

station might have to be abandoned and told Stevens that, 'I am always in a funk about the Sheep Camp. They have been within a mile, but so far have not commenced hostilities'.[57]

When the *Northern Territory Times* heard about Goldsbrough Mort's decision to do away with the sheep it expressed surprise and disappointment, remarking that:

> the bulletins which came in from time to time were of so cheerful a nature that we were fully justified in expecting nothing but the very best results. The sheep kept in splendid order, the fleeces showed no sign of deterioration, the grass seeds gave no trouble, and the lambing could not be better.[58]

The paper posed the question, 'What causes the abandonment?' and gave the answer, gathered from 'authoritative sources', which stated that:

> the blacks of the Victoria River district are so troublesome and treacherous that sheep-breeding could not under existing circumstances be made a profitable enterprise. It would be impossible, we are told, to shepherd large flocks and keep them free from native depredations except by a very expensive force of shepherds.

The same article went on to remark that there had never been any reports of shepherds being attacked, or of sheep being taken by the Aborigines, so it now came as a surprise to hear this reason given for the sheep being removed from Victoria River Downs.

Years later Tom Pearce claimed that the sheep were sold because 'the manager [*Crawford*] was a telegraph operator, managing a cattle station, and did not want the sheep there'.[59] A more recent study stated that the sheep were sold 'for reasons unknown today'.[60] However, there can be no question that Aborigines posed a continual and costly threat, and while the manager may have had an ambivalent attitude towards the sheep the main reason for abandoning the attempt to make VRD a sheep run was financial.

The threat posed by the Aborigines required the sheep to be guarded by armed shepherds at all times. This was a major expense over and above the cost

---

57 NTA: NTRS 790, item 5151, L Crawford, cited in HWH Stevens to the Government Resident Charles Dashwood, 30th December 1892.
58 Untitled news item, *Northern Territory Times*, 27th October 1893, p. 2.
59 Tom Pearce, 'The Northern Territory', *The Pastoral Review*, 16th September 1914, p. 868.
60 Makin, p. 71

of running sheep in Queensland or other colonies where the blacks had been 'pacified', and there were other high expenses involved. An audit carried out by B Blair for Goldsbrough Mort in 1893 concluded that 'From a perusal of the accounts of the above Coy. it is apparent that sheep breeding on the Victoria Downs is proving a costly experiment'.[61] He found that the cost of establishing sheep on VRD had amounted to more than £5000, and since then 460 of the old sheep had died, including 18 high-priced rams. Strangely, he claimed that these losses were offset to some degree by an increase in numbers, over two years, of 698, whereas other sources indicated a much larger increase.

Blair noted that the working expenses were extremely high with wages for 1893 estimated at £550 and shearing and wool carriage at £250. However, the 1892 clip had netted less than £250, leaving a loss of £550 for wages alone. He discussed various possible changes in the way the sheep were managed which might reduce costs, but concluded all were financially risky. Even if the wool clip could be greatly improved by running the sheep in paddocks, Blair believed that the cost of shearing and transport of wool to the Depot would absorb all the gains. Even if transport costs could be reduced by taking the sheep to the Depot and shearing them there, the expense of fencing paddocks was too great. He recommended that the sheep be disposed of as soon as possible, but added:

> What to do with the present stock of sheep is a puzzle, it certainly is folly Keeping on shepherding, and if they are turned at large on the country they are now being fed over, the chances are, that what with wild blacks and dingoes rushing them about, and not being able to find water, few, if any will be left in a few months.

Blair thought that the only other possibility was to sell the sheep to sheep stations in the Kimberley – if these stations were still in existence.

The Kimberley sheep stations *were* still in existence, but before they could be approached the problem was solved by an extraordinary stroke of luck. Captain Joe Bradshaw was planning to put sheep on the country that he'd taken up in the north-west Kimberley,[62] so on 8th November 1893 he signed an agreement to purchase the VRD flock. One of the conditions of sale was that Bradshaw would own all lambs born after 8th August 1893, which suggests that a verbal deal had been struck at this time. Other terms were:

---

61   NBA: Reports on station properties, 1890–97, 2/306/146, B Blair to general manager, Goldsbrough Mort & Co. Ltd, 20th June 1893.

62   National Archives of Australia (NAA): J Bradshaw to the minister for the Northern Territory, Adelaide, 16th August 1893, CRS A1640, item 93/302.

that the purchase would include the wool at the station; that he could leave the sheep on VRD for up to six months and; that VRD would pay the wages and keep of the men looking after the sheep before delivery.[63] Clearly Victoria River Downs was keen to dispose of the flock.

Shortly after the deal was done the Western Australian Government introduced a tax of two shillings and sixpence per head on sheep entering the state.[64] Because of this, Bradshaw was inclined to get out of the agreement to buy the sheep, but this wasn't possible.[65] Instead of taking the sheep to his Kimberley property, Marigui, Captain Joe decided to throw up that lease and take the sheep to Bradshaw Station, the property that he'd recently taken up on the lower Victoria River.[66] Bradshaw employees Aeneas Gunn ('The Boss' in *We of the Never Never*) and Hugh Young inspected and took delivery of the sheep on VRD on 20th January 1894. Gunn then returned to Darwin while Young stayed on to take the sheep overland to Bradshaw.[67] Five white men took charge of them and by February or March 1894 the last had left Victoria River Downs. Today one of the few visible signs that there ever were sheep on VRD is a set of rock paintings of sheep in the Stokes Range, on the northern boundary of the station.

The sheep were first taken to Delamere where about a dozen died from poisoning on the headwaters of Gregory Creek.[68] The sheep had been shorn some time before they arrived on the Gregory (probably while they were still on VRD where men to shear the sheep were available) and the wool was carted to the Depot by teamster John Mulligan. From there it was taken by boat to the Dome where it was loaded on Bradshaw's 'steamerette', the *Red Gauntlet*, for shipment to Darwin.[69]

Either because of the poisonings that had occurred, or because of the recent attack on Joe Bradshaw by the Wardaman, it was decided that the route to Bradshaw Station via Gregory Creek was impassable. The sheep were instead taken the long way around via Delamere, the Flora River and

---

63 NBA: Goldsbrough Mort & Co. Board papers, 1893–1927, 2/124/1092, AMD Cooper to GW Moore, Goldsbrough Mort & Co. Ltd, 6th December 1893.
64 *Western Australian Parliamentary Debates*, sessions 1893, vol. 4, 1894, p. 257.
65 NBA: 2/124/1092, 6th December 1893.
66 Untitled news item, *Northern Territory Times*, 10th November 1893, p. 2.
67 J Bradshaw, answer to question 3254, in 'Report of the Northern Territory commission together with minutes of proceedings, evidence, and appendices', *South Australian Parliamentary Papers*, vol. 2, no. 19, 1895; NTA: introductory paragraph for 1894, NTRS 2261.
68 'Notes of the week', *Northern Territory Times*, 6th July 1894, p. 2; J Bradshaw, answer to question 3279, vol. 2, no. 19, 1895.
69 NTA: 2nd June 1894, NTRS 2261.

Stokes Range rock paintings, showing what are arguably sheep, with a shepherd's footprint alongside them

Lewis collection

John Mulligan's wagon with bales of VRD wool, at the Depot landing, Victoria River, 1891

Foesche collection, National Library of Australia

across to the headwaters of the Fitzmaurice River.[70] By August 1894 Young
had formed a sheep station on the 'open tableland' of the Upper Fitzmaurice,
but had 'considerable trouble with the blacks'[71] who on at least one occasion
attacked the camp. No one was injured, but one man received a spear through
his shirt and was pinned to the ground.[72] From the upper Fitzmaurice the
sheep were soon shifted to an area near the homestead.[73] 700 lambs had been
born since the sheep left VRD, so by the time the flock arrived at Bradshaw
it numbered 4558.[74] There's anecdotal evidence suggesting that for a time
the sheep may have been located lower down the Fitzmaurice River at the
Koolendong Valley. In the 1960s Northern Territory cattleman Tex Moar
was mustering in the Fitzmaurice River country. When he arrived at the
Koolendong his Aboriginal stockmen told him that they were at the 'ship
camp'. Moar was puzzled and asked what they meant by 'ship camp'. They
replied, 'Ship! Alla same nanny goat!'[75]

The Government Resident expressed his regret at the demise of sheep
breeding on VRD and the removal of the sheep to Bradshaw Station. He
commented that Bradshaw was, 'a different class of country to that on which
the sheep have been running. It remains to be seen whether the undertaking
will prove a success, which I am sure I hope may be the case'.[76]

The Resident's caution was not misplaced. On Bradshaw the sheep faced
more dangers than they had on VRD. To try to protect them, for at least the
first few years the sheep were shepherded. Shepherding on Bradshaw seems
to have been a lethal occupation. One of the shepherds, Antonis Bolan, died
in January 1896 and was buried at the back of the horse paddock,[77] the first
white man to die on the station.[78] In July another shepherd, James Edkins,
became the second white man to die on Bradshaw.[79] He was buried next to
Bolan.[80]

---

70   ibid.
71   J Bradshaw, 'The Northern Territory', *Victorian Geographical Journal*, vol. 25, 1907, pp.
      20–28; NTA: general summary at the beginning of the document, NTRS 2261.
72   J Bradshaw, answer to question 3284, 1895.
73   NTA: 22nd September 1894, NTRS 2261.
74   Dashwood, 24th July 1894.
75   Tex Moar, pers. comm., Pine Creek. In the 1960s Moar was the owner of Dorisvale
      Station, near the headwaters of the Fitzmaurice River.
76   Dashwood, 24th July 1894.
77   NTA: April 1896, NTRS 2261.
78   'Summary of deaths in the Timber Creek/Bradshaw police district', Compiled by the
      Genealogical Society of the Northern Territory, Darwin. Covers the period 1856–1975
79   'Summary of deaths in the Timber Creek/Bradshaw police district'.
80   NTA: 22nd July 1896, NTRS 2261.

In spite of being shepherded, running sheep on Bradshaw turned out to be a disaster. In December 1895 it was reported that 'extraordinary mortality has taken place amongst the sheep at Mr Bradshaw's station ... About 90 per cent of the last lambing is reported to have been lost through one cause and another'. Deaths among the adult sheep were attributed to poisonous plants.[81] The Bradshaw log book contains regular accounts of Aborigines being sent out to look for sheep. Sometimes they found a good number, but more often they couldn't find any, or only a few. On one occasion sheep tracks led to a waterhole and station Aborigines read the signs showing where an 'alligator' grabbed one.[82] On another occasion sheep were attacked and killed by dingoes, so the carcasses were laced with strychnine and baits were laid. Whether any dingos were poisoned is unknown, but at least one station dog was killed.[83]

Bush Aborigines were an ongoing problem. Unlike at VRD, on Bradshaw they appear to have quickly developed a taste for mutton. After causing 'considerable trouble' on the upper Fitzmaurice, Aborigines continued to 'make themselves obnoxious' near the homestead, spearing cattle and horses – and sheep.[84] When Knut Dahl visited the station in May 1895 he remarked that, 'The local blacks were very aggressive and had taken a fancy to spearing sheep, and for this reason the shepherds fired at them whenever they saw them'.[85]

In at least one instance Aborigines who had killed sheep were apparently tracked down and shot by Bradshaw stockmen. In a letter to Billy Linklater in 1948, Tom Pearce inquired as to Hugh Young's fate:

> let me know how Young died — he was a heavy drinker — and carrying a load on his mind — after Shooting, he & McPhee[86] — many of the Blacks out on the Run for Killing Sheep & burnt them. McPhee informed me — when one of them was partly Burnt — Rose up & scared Young — the eat of the fire Caused this to take place.[87]

---

81   Untitled news item, *Northern Territory Times*, 6th December 1895, p. 3.

82   ibid.

83   NTA: 28th September 1899, 11th July 1899, 13th July 1899, 4th November 1899, 7th July 1900, 21st July 1900, 5th February 1901, 19th December 1901, NTRS 2261.

84   ibid., April 1896.

85   K Dahl, *In Savage Australia: An Account of a Hunting and Collecting Expedition to Arnhem Land and Dampier Land*, Alan, London, 1926, p. 190.

86   This was Jock McPhee, 'Tam-o-Shanter' in Jeannie Gunn's, *'We of the Never-Never'* (Hutchinson, London, 1908); '"Never Never" people. Their strange fate', *Sydney Morning Herald*, 21st February 1942, p. 9.

87   Tom Pearce, letter to Billy Linklater, 9th October 1948, 'Miscellaneous letters and other documents, 1895–1949', Mitchell Library, Al 10/26.

The Government Geologist visited Bradshaw Station shortly before the sheep arrived and remarked that 'Mr Bradshaw ... has a cutter in which stores are kept as a precaution against the thieving propensities of the natives'.[88] After the sheep arrived the Aborigines stole shears and fashioned them into spear blades.

According to the log book, the first shearing on Bradshaw Station was carried out in September 1894 on a billabong some distance east of the homestead. The wool was brought in boats to Joe Bradshaw's schooner *Twins*, and taken to Darwin by Gunn.[89] Unless this account is wrong there was a second shearing early in 1895 which ended in disaster. Like VRD before him, Joe Bradshaw was unable to obtain woolpacks in time for the shearing, so:

> the newly-shorn wool was stacked into huge heaps, handy to the landing place for shipping purposes. One night the creek came down a banker from its head, and swept the lot into the Victoria. There was wool hanging on the mangroves for 40 miles down the river. The niggers along the lower reaches must have thought there had been a snow-storm.[90]

Of the 4558 sheep originally brought onto Bradshaw Station in mid-1894, there were only 1553 left to be shorn in late 1896, producing 18 bales of wool. Nevertheless, Captain Joe was still optimistic and brought 17 rams to Bradshaw on the *Twins* in October 1896.[91] By July the following year, only 662 sheep were shorn for nine bales.[92] Then, in March 1899 a log book entry describes how:

> The wet season culminated in an exceptional flood which drowned nearly half the few surviving sheep although all hands were working up to their necks in water till midnight trying to save the sheep in boats. It might have been avoided if the sheep had been moved to the base of the mountain at the first indications of a high flood. The water was two feet deep in the dwelling house and three feet in the kitchen and outhouses.

---

88   HYL Brown, 'Northern Territory explorations', *South Australian Parliamentary Papers*, vol. 3, no. 82, 1895, p. 3.
89   NTA: 22nd September 1894, NTRS 2261.
90   SE Pearson to G Buchanan (senior), 31st March 1934. letter in possession of Buchanan family, South Australia. See also Dahl (p. 190), and 'Notes of the week', *Northern Territory Times*, 24th May 1895, p. 3.
91   ibid.
92   NTA: 15th October 1896, 16th October 1896, July 1897, NTRS 2261.

The station staff vacated the house and camped for ten days on a stony rise in the horse paddock.[93]

Probably largely as a result of this flood, in April 1899 Bradshaw reported that 'only 114 surviving sheep shorn today'. Sixteen bales of wool were shipped to Darwin the same month,[94] but some of these must have contained wool from an earlier shearing. By September 1899 there seem to have been only 62 sheep left.[95]

In spite of their dramatic decline, as late as 1902 Captain Joe imported 14 more sheep.[96] These 'declined' as fast as the others and in 1904 a visitor reported that, 'Fred Bradshaw had the six survivors ... kept in a wire-netted enclosure at the homestead, where they were fed and watered by the station gins. We used to jest with Fred, and call it his "sheep museum"'.[97]

This was the ignoble end of the 'Great Victoria River Sheep Saga' and dreams of vast sheep stations in the region, although some continued to think of the district as potential sheep country. In 1907 Surveyor LA Wells remarked that, 'A large tract of this country is well adapted for sheep, especially that lying latitudes south from Pigeon hole'.[98] In an interview he gave in 1908 he envisioned up to 2,000,000 sheep on the Victoria, Ord and Sturt Creek.[99] In 1913 the manager of Wave Hill thought that 'fully 65 per cent of the Wave Hill Station should be well adapted for sheep ... There were large areas of the Victoria River country suited for sheep, and he considered much of it would carry 120 sheep per square mile'.[100] On Argyle Station there was a thriving flock of sheep in the 1950s, apparently kept solely for meat,[101] but they were never again tried on a commercial basis in the Victoria River District.

Even though it's long been known that sheep have a more severe impact than cattle on vegetation, and the failure of the sheep experiment probably saved VRD from worse environmental degradation than has already

---

93   ibid., March 1899.
94   NTA: 5th April 1899, NTRS 2261.
95   ibid., 28th September 1899.
96   C Dashwood, 'Government Resident's Report on the Northern Territory, 1902', *South Australian Parliamentary Papers*, vol. 3, no. 45, 1903, p. 26.
97   Pearson to Buchanan.
98   LA Wells, *The Victoria River and the Adjacent Country*, Government Printer, Adelaide, 1907. p. 5.
99   NAA: Department of Territories, correspondence files NT series, CRS A1640, file 1908/43, 'Northern Territory. Interview with Mr LA Wells', pp. 3–4.
100   'The Railways Commission', *Northern Territory Times*, 7th August 1913, p. 2.
101   G Bolton, 'A survey of the Kimberley pastoral industry from 1885 to the present', MA thesis, University of Western Australia, 1953, p. 254.

occurred, the failure was still being lamented as recently as 1992. Jock Makin, a farmer and grazier from South Australia, discussed the attempt to establish sheep on VRD in his history of Victoria River Downs, *The Big Run*. His startling and hyperbolic conclusion was that 'For the Northern Territory, this was one of the greatest tragedies of all time. Had the sheep been kept on the Victoria there is every likelihood that stations now carrying cattle would also be counted as wool producers'.[102] Well might cattlemen today say, 'Baaa Humbug'!

---

102 Makin, p. 71.

Chapter 10

HARD-RIDING INDIVIDUALISTS

For 20 years after the first settlers arrived, the Victoria River country was the preserve of big stations, most of them being owned by wealthy companies and southern pastoralists. There never was a Northern Territory equivalent of the Robertson Land Acts which served to open up the big stations in New South Wales for closer settlement,[1] so once the big Victoria River runs were established in the 1880s the land within their leases couldn't be taken from them by 'selectors'. It was possible to gain a lease, or later a Pastoral Permit or Grazing Licence, on whatever land was left, but almost all the worthwhile pastoral land was locked up in these stations and only areas of rough ranges or arid country remained as Crown Land. Any later would-be landowner had to make do with these 'left-overs', and what was left was largely worthless for pastoralism.

When the journalist WM Burton described the makeup of Victoria River society in 1909 he included horse thieves and cattle duffers.[2] His account was accurate enough for the time, but a decade earlier he couldn't have written his story in quite the same way. Certainly horse stealing was a problem from the earliest times. During the gold rush to the Kimberley in 1886 and for some years afterwards, 'parties of horse-stealers and outlaws from Northern Queensland back stations' passed through the district.[3] Auvergne Station lost over 100 head and there were raids on other stations.[4] No doubt white travellers also killed the occasional beast for beef. During the Kimberley

---

1   *Crown Lands Acts 1861* [*NSW*]. This Act was passed in 1861 and enabled people to select an area from 40 to 320 acres anywhere on the large stations that existed at that time (S Roberts, *History of Australian Land Settlement (1788–1920)*, Macmillan and Co. Ltd, Melbourne, 1924, pp. 222–32).

2   'An irresponsible journalist'. *Northern Territory Times*, 30th April 1909, p. 2.

3   'News and notes', *Northern Territory Times*, 4th December 1886, p. 2 and 'Protection from blacks', *Northern Territory Times*, 11th March 1892, p. 2.

4   Noel Butlin Archives (NBA), Australian National University: Goldsbrough Mort and Co. Ltd: head office, Melbourne: letters received from HWH Stevens, Port Darwin, re. NT property and butchering business, 1889–92, 2/872, HWH Stevens to the manager of Goldsbrough Mort & Co, Ltd, 9th October 1891.

gold rush it was claimed that because of illegal cattle killing, most stations along the route were keeping their cattle 20 miles off the main road,[5] but until 1902 there wasn't a cattle duffer to be seen.

For two decades after the original leases were taken up, nobody bothered to gain title to, and stock, any of the left-over land. Then, almost overnight the country was overrun with 'small men' – 'battlers' who took up blocks here and there around the edges of the big stations. This influx began in 1902 and lasted a decade. So began the Golden Age of cattle duffing in the Victoria River District.

Quite often the people who figure in works of outback history are the 'big men' – the cattle barons, explorers, government officials and so forth. By contrast, the men who were the actors in this story are a microcosm of the types of ordinary workingmen who lived in the Territory in this early period. Their origins and lives are varied and colourful and the events involving them are complex. Their stories provide an insight into social attitudes and relations – between each other, between them and the big stations, between them and 'authority' and between them and the Aborigines – and so are worth telling in some detail.

Before addressing the rise and fall of the cattle duffers, the terms 'poddy-dodger' and 'cattle duffer' need to be explained. A poddy-dodger is one who places his brand on cleanskin cattle, more particularly on the unbranded calves of branded mothers. Poddy-dodging carries the risk of a cow bearing one brand being found with a calf bearing a different brand – clear evidence of 'dodgy' practices – though once the calf is weaned this risk disappears.

A cattle duffer is one who steals cattle, young or old, cleanskin or branded.[6] In terms of risk, branding cleanskin cattle in the early days was a relatively safe procedure. Because the runs were unfenced cattle regularly wandered from one station to another, so unless a man was actually caught branding cleanskins outside his own boundary, finding cattle bearing his brand on land which wasn't his own was not grounds for legal action.

Cross-branding cattle – that is, burning a new brand on top of an existing brand to change or obliterate it – was by far the riskiest business. For a variety of reasons a beast sometimes carried the original owner's brand on more than one part of its body. Double-branding was sufficiently rare that a

5   ibid.
6   Anon, *The Ringer's Book of Outback Terms & Phrases*, The Australian Stockman's Hall of Fame and Outback Heritage Centre, Longreach, 1988, pp. 10, 18.

cattle duffer wouldn't expect to encounter it, so when he cross-branded one original brand the other could be overlooked.[7] A second and much greater problem was that when a cross-branded hide was wet the original brand often could be detected under the new one.[8] Both situations have led to charges of cattle duffing being laid.[9]

In the early 1900s branding cleanskin cattle wasn't regarded as a crime by many people. The logic seemed to be that if the owner wasn't branding them he deserved to lose them; but cross-branding was not so readily condoned. In the Victoria River District and elsewhere the term 'cattle duffer' was often used rather loosely to include men who branded full-grown cleanskin cattle, those who cross-branded cattle and poddy-dodgers.

The second point of clarification concerns lease covenants. Once a person obtained land there were certain conditions that had to be met before they could become a cattleman. One was to stock the land with legitimately obtained cattle. No doubt some men bought cattle and moved them onto their land, but for those with limited cash or no desire to spend what money they had, there were other ways to become 'legal'. Ernestine Hill described how it was done on one of the Victoria River cattle duffer's blocks:

> The cattle that formed Illawarra were a mythical mob. Negotiations consisted of a cheque — never presented — and a receipt from a cattle-dealing friend that 'Jim Campbell has this day taken delivery of 500 mixed cattle of various breeds and colours' — the usual poddy-dodger legalities to stave off pertinent questions.[10]

The other legality – a formality – was to obtain a registered brand. This was supposed to be applied only to the progeny of the founding herd and officially this meant that no cattle could be turned off the property for 12 months. Any cleanskin cattle over 12 months old on Crown Land were regarded as

---

7   For example, in 1909, when the police were examining VRD cattle that had allegedly been stolen by Jim Campbell, they found a bull which bore both Campbell's diamond 40 brand and the VRD G10 brand (Timber Creek police journal, 3rd July 1909. Northern Territory Archives (NTA), F 302).

8   C Schultz and D Lewis, *Beyond the Big Run*, University of Queensland Press, Brisbane, 1995, p. 171.

9   An example of cattle theft being discovered occurred when a herd of cattle from Coolibah were dipped at Anthonys Lagoon in 1953. Once the brands were wet it was noticed that in some instances the 'Q' of the Coolibah brand 'MTQ' was superimposed on the VRD 'bulls head' brand (Keane, K. 'Justice rides the range', *A.M.*, 3rd November, 1953, pp 56–58).

10   E Hill, *The Territory*, Angus and Robertson, Sydney, 1951, p. 324.

the property of the Crown and were supposed to be sold at public auction.[11] However, this wasn't how things always happened.

It wasn't until the settlers had time to examine their leases that they began to redraw their boundaries to exclude much of the poorer country that lay between the best areas and, as a consequence, to make it available to others. However, for the first two decades, more or less, other factors discouraged the 'battlers' from entering the district. To make cattle duffing possible, two factors had to coincide. One was a plentiful supply of cleanskins and the other was a high market price for cattle. Without doubt the most important factor was the price of cattle. There wasn't much point in obtaining a block of country and branding cleanskins if there was little financial reward.

In the first few years after a station was stocked, the number of saleable cattle which could be turned off was low. Local demand for beef could absorb some surplus stock, but cattle numbers grew exponentially and soon far outstripped local needs. To make their stations profitable Victoria River station owners needed to access larger markets, but cattle prices had to be high enough to cover the costs of droving and still leave a worthwhile profit margin. Attempts were made in the 1880s to establish a live cattle trade to South-East Asian ports, but the prices achieved were too low. Then, in 1891, Australia entered a decade-long economic depression and cattle prices slumped.

Prices remained low throughout the 1890s and there were other problems peculiar to the Northern Territory which made it almost impossible to sell cattle. In 1892 Western Australia imposed a tax of 30 shillings per head on cattle entering the state. This tax was removed in 1896, but by this time all livestock from the northern areas of the Northern Territory had been banned from entering Western Australia, (and all the other colonies), to try and stop the spread of tick fever. These bans were dropped progressively by each jurisdiction, with South Australia the last to remove them in 1903, but while they were in place these bans effectively closed or restricted the outlets for many Territory cattle producers.[12]

The ban put in place to stop Territory cattle entering Queensland was completely ineffective because 'tick fever' had been present there since at least 1888. The disease only became a serious problem in 1893, but during the next seven years or so it spread rapidly and decimated the Queensland beef cattle

---

11   C Herbert, 'Government Resident's Report on the Northern Territory, 1905', *South Australian Parliamentary Papers*, vol. 2, no. 45, 1906, p. 9.
12   Duncan, pp. 58–59.

industry.[13] This calamity was overlapped by a series of dry years, beginning in 1895 and culminating in the 'Federation' drought of 1900–02.[14] The drought greatly reduced the cattle ticks, but also further reduced cattle numbers.

With little or no income from cattle sales during the 1890s, station owners couldn't afford the infrastructure and manpower needed to adequately look after their herds.[15] By the end of the 1890s there were about 50,000 cattle on Victoria River Downs[16] and probably more than 150,000 in the region as a whole. The cattle had spread out to the edges of the big stations and beyond, with untold thousands of cleanskin cattle roaming the district, but at this time they were not worth stealing.[17] However, the situation was about to change. When the Federation drought finally ended in 1903 there was a great demand for cattle to restock the Queensland stations and to supply meat to the eastern markets. As a result, the price of cattle increased significantly[18] and the scene was set for an influx of cattle duffers into the Victoria River District.

In the early 1900s any man who obtained a block of land on or near the boundary of one of the big stations had easy access to large numbers of unbranded cattle, a great incentive for cattle duffers to move in. For such men it was of no consequence that the available land was too poor or the area too small to form a viable cattle station. They could gain title over as little as 100 square miles, but because the station boundaries were unfenced until the 1960s, or even later, they could effectively use much more land. On the one hand, cleanskin cattle could wander onto their block from the neighbouring station, while on the other, these men could surreptitiously muster and brand cleanskin cattle on their neighbours' land. And, of course, any cattle branded on their own block could graze all over the good land of the neighbouring big station.

Even though there were almost unlimited cleanskin cattle available and the price of cattle was high, there was no immediate rush of cattle duffers into the Victoria River country. A couple of men took up leases early in 1902. At the same time another gained the use of a leasehold block that had been taken up by someone else in 1900, but in July 1902 the issuing of Pastoral

13   G Bolton, *A Thousand Miles Away: A History of North Queensland to 1920*, The Jacaranda Press in association with the Australian National University, Brisbane, 1963, pp. 219–21.
14   ibid., p. 221; Duncan , p. 131.
15   'The Victoria River and the meat works', *Northern Territory Times*, 20th June 1902, p. 3.
16   Herbert, p. 8.
17   R Duncan, *The Northern Territory Pastoral Industry 1863–1910*, Melbourne University Press, 1967, p. 60–65.
18   Duncan, pp. 163–65.

Leases was suspended while a new system of annual Pastoral Permits was introduced. This was done because plans were afoot to complete the Alice Springs to Darwin Railway under a land-grant system and land along the route had to be available for the system to work. The South Australian Government could resume both Pastoral Leases and Pastoral Permits, but permit holders could not claim compensation if their land was resumed while leaseholders could. In addition, the South Australian Government didn't want potential compensation claims to complicate negotiations with the Commonwealth Government for the transfer of the Northern Territory to Commonwealth control.[19]

It doesn't seem likely that the new permit system was an inducement to those considering taking up land for legitimate reasons. The annual Pastoral Permits were far less secure than Pastoral Leases which were issued for a period of 42 years, and for the first seven years the permits were dearer. From 1890 the annual rent on Pastoral Leases cost sixpence per square mile for the first seven years, one shilling for the next seven years, two shillings for the third seven years, with the charge for the remaining years of the lease to be determined by valuation.[20] Pastoral Permits were a flat one shilling per square mile per year.[21]

Nevertheless, during the time that Pastoral Permits were being issued, hundreds were taken up throughout the Northern Territory. Some were issued to existing large landholders but many permits were obtained by battlers who wanted a legal foothold on the edge of one of the big stations.[22] In the Victoria River District more than 20 permits were issued, of which eight or so formed the basis of about six small stations in the hands of perhaps a dozen men.[23] Together they represent a cross section of the types of bushmen on the North Australian frontier – colourful men whose backgrounds and personalities contributed to their individual experiences in the Victoria River country. They were industrious men. By 1905 one writer

---

19 NAA: A1640/1 1902/273, copy of wire addressed to the Government Resident Northern Territory, from FE Benda, secretary to the minister controlling the NT, 18th August 1902; C Herbert, p. 8; NAA: A1640 1905/552, 'Minutes forming enclosure to WJ, No. 552, 1905'; Private correspondence from Stuart Duncan, Secretary Place Names Committee for the Northern Territory, Department of Infrastructure, Planning and Environment, Land Information, Darwin, February 2010.
20 Duncan, p. 116.
21 NAA: A1640/1 1902/273, 18th August 1902.
22 Duncan (1967, p. 121) reports that by 1910, 49,150 square miles were held under permits.
23 At any one time there were about ten or a dozen men involved with these permits, but there were changing partnerships so the total number was more like 14 or 15.

declared that, 'The two principal industries on the East Kimberley side are cattle rearing and cattle "duffing" ... and cattle duffing is about the principal of the two industries'.[24]

The Victoria River cattle duffers settled in two widely separated localities, more or less on the eastern and western sides of the district. Although the two groups knew each other they aren't known to have interacted to any great degree, so their subsequent histories are significantly different. Because of this, they are dealt with as two distinct groups, the eastern duffers in this chapter and the western duffers in the next. The men who took up Pastoral Permits in the eastern Victoria River District were the brothers Jim and Mick Fleming, Jim Campbell and Ben Martin. Before describing their cattle duffing careers it's worth outlining what is known about them.

The Fleming brothers were both early Northern Territory pioneers. Jim is said to have been in charge of 50 Chinese who were brought to McArthur River Station in the 1880s to build yards, fences and huts.[25] For a period he was also proprietor of the Macarthur River Hotel at Borroloola.[26] Mick had been in the Kimberley gold rush of 1886[27] and in 1891 acted as a guide for the first sheep to be taken to VRD.[28] He was also one of the drovers who in the 1890s took VRD cattle to Darwin for live export.[29] In 1895 Mick, along with Tom Cahill, the manager of Wave Hill, was summonsed for failing to pay the rent on Pastoral Leases they jointly held in the Victoria River District.[30] In June 1899 Mick had a camp located 20 miles west of Wave Hill, so either he was working for the station or was living on the block he shared with Cahill.[31] In May 1902 he took 2000 cattle from Wave Hill to stock WF Buchanan's 'New Delamere' Station on Gregory Creek.[32] He built a homestead there and stayed on for some

24   H7H (Hely Hutchinson), 'How Cattle are Run in the East Kimberley', *The Pastoralists' Review*, February 1906, p. 1001.
25   CE Gaunt, 'Old time memories: The birth of Borroloola', *Northern Standard*, 16th October 1931, p. 4.
26   Untitled news item, *Northern Territory Times*, 15th September 1888, p. 2.
27   CE Gaunt, 'Old time memories: The lepers of Arnhem Land and sketches', *Northern Standard*, 10th July 1934, p. 6.
28   NBA: 2/872, report on NT stations, HWH Stevens to Goldsbrough Mort & Co. Ltd, 8th January 1891.
29   NBA: 2/872, T Meldrum to drover JA Davis, 6th July 1897.
30   NTA: Government Resident of the Northern Territory (South Australia) – inwards correspondence, 1870–1912, NTRS 790, item 6950, statement of charge, signed by plaintiff's attorney JK Stuart, 17th December 1895.
31   NTA: Timber Creek police journal, 27th June 1899, F 302.
32   ibid., 15th and 30th May 1902; WF Buchanan was the brother of Wave Hill pioneer, Nat Buchanan, and was the outright owner of Wave Hill from 1894 (B. Buchanan, *In*

time as manager.[33] With his extensive experience of the district, Mick clearly had ample opportunity to see the potential for a small station on the margins of VRD and Wave Hill.

Ben Martin originally came to the Victoria River District early in 1900, intending to take up a job offer made to him in Queensland many years before by Jim Ronan, now recently appointed manager of VRD.[34] Before Martin arrived he met Jim and Mick Fleming and decided to throw in his lot with them – to become 'another hard-riding individualist' on the eastern boundary of VRD.[35] Ben Martin certainly could ride. In 1887 he won tent-pegging and lemon-slicing contests at an athletics carnival in Darwin.[36] He could also shoot. While buffalo hunting in the 1890s he was credited with shooting 36 beasts from horseback with 36 shots. Incidentally, Paddy Cahill held the numerical record having shot 58 in one day.[37]

As for Jim Campbell, Ernestine Hill claims he came to the Territory with a mob of horses that had been stolen from the South Australian Commissioner of Police in 1893. She says that Campbell later worked as a sub-contract teamster for Tom Pearce, carting steel poles from Borroloola to the Overland Telegraph Line.[38] The final player in this cast of characters was 'Honest Tom' Pearce, hotelier and general businessman in Katherine. He was to play a major, but largely hidden role, in coming events.

Campbell was in the East Kimberley District as early as October 1898, working with Jack Beasley, Jack Frayne and others on the Durack's Argyle Station. According to MP Durack, Campbell and Beasley had a 'fighting partnership' and he claimed, 'There is nothing Campbell has not taught Beasley except for what Beasley already knew'.[39] Mounted Constable Jack Johns

the tracks of old Bluey, Central Queensland University Press, Rockhampton,1997, pp. 138–39).

33 Timber Creek police letter book, 27th June 1903. Photocopy held at the Berrimah Police Station, Darwin.

34 T Ronan, Deep of the Sky, Cassell & Company Ltd, Melbourne, 1962, p. 179; 'News and notes', Northern Territory Times, 22nd June 1900, p. 2.

35 Ronan, p. 179.

36 'Athletic sports', Northern Territory Times, 8th January 1887, p. 3; RS Summerhays' Encyclopaedia for Horsemen defines tent-pegging as 'A spectacular equestrian sport, which originated in India. A soft, white wooden peg, bound with wire, is placed in the ground at an angle ... and it has to be taken with a lance or a sword at full gallop' (Frederick Warne, London, 1975, pp. 332–33). Lemon-slicing is not defined in this book, but presumably it involves cutting a lemon with a sword at a full gallop.

37 'Big game hunt in Arnheim Land', Northern Standard, 27th January 1931, p. 4.

38 Hill, pp. 317–22; Hill's claim that Campbell worked as a sub-contractor is substantiated in 'News and notes', Northern Territory Times , 11th May 1900, p. 2.

39 M Durack, Sons in the Saddle, Corgi Books, Britain, 1985, pp. 69–70.

'Honest Tom' Pearce, 1909

Nott collection, Northern Territory Library

described Campbell in his prime as 'a splendid type of a man physically, standing well over six feet high ... a super horseman, a crack shot, a hard living man, master bushman, hard, defiant, cruel on occasion, and above all, apparently, a thief'.[40] Aborigines in the Victoria River country would add that he was a murderer.[41] Subsequent events were to reveal just how cruel Campbell could be.

---

40   D Lewis (ed.), *Patrolling the 'Big Up': The Adventures of Mounted Constable Johns in the Top End of the Northern Territory, 1910–1915*, Historical Society of the Northern Territory, Darwin, 1998, p. 41. Johns examined Campbell's body some weeks after he was killed but whether he actually met Campbell alive is unknown. However, he undoubtedly knew people who had met Campbell. When Campbell was being hunted by the police, a description of him was issued to all stations and interstate. This described Campbell as 'forty five feet nine about fourteen stone dark complection dark scraggly beard good moustache turning grey mark on forehead over one eye eyes weak' (State Records Office of Western Australia, Acc 741-9, Rough occurrence book [*Wyndham*] 1907–08, 10th May 1909).

41   Big Mick Kangkinang, pers. comm.

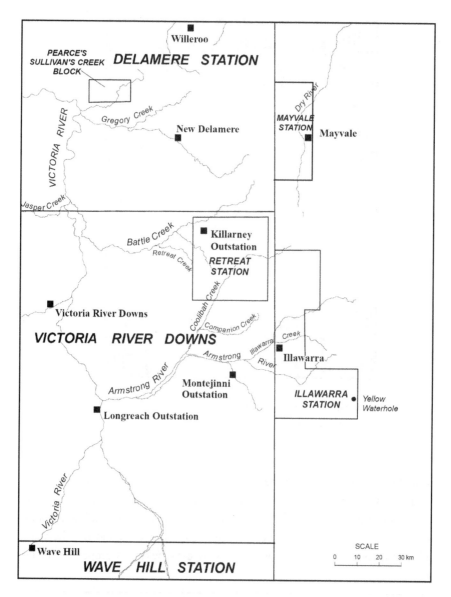

Map 11. The eastern Victoria River cattle duffer's blocks in relation to the big stations

The Fleming brothers obtained their first lease (PL 2198) on the eastern boundary of Victoria River Downs on 1st October 1901,[42] stocking it the following February or March with some cattle the police thought they'd

---

42   NTA: Department of Lands – Land Administration Branch, office copies of Pastoral
       Permits – 1902–22, F670 vol. 1, lease 2213.

Mr. W. F. Buchanan.

WF Buchanan, owner of Wave Hill, Killarney and
Delemere Stations

Pastoralist's Review, 15 January 1907, p. 936

obtained from Tom Pearce in Katherine.[43] The Flemings soon acquired
three other leases. Together, the four leases gave them a north-south strip
along the VRD boundary (Map 11).[44] They named their station Illawarra,
presumably a reference to their place of origin in New South Wales. From
November 1905 Mick also held Pastoral Permit 29 for a block further south,
near Camfield Creek on the western edge of Wave Hill. Although only
Mick's name appears on the lease documents for Illawarra,[45] various sources
state that he was in partnership with his brother Jim and probably at times
with Ben Martin and Jim Campbell.[46]

---

43   Timber Creek police letter book, 27th July 1903. Photocopy held at the Berrimah
     Police Station, Darwin.
44   They obtained leases 2212 and 2213 on 1st January 1902, and lease 2214 on 4th January
     1902 (information from the Office of the Placenames Committee, Lands Department,
     Darwin).
45   File at the Office of the Placenames Committee, Lands Department, Darwin.
46   An entry in the Timber Creek police letter book (12th March 1903) and others in the
     Timber Creek police journal (18th and 24th August 1902, 3rd November 1902, 12th
     March 1903 and 17th June 1903) (NTA: F 302) make it virtually certain that Campbell,
     Martin and Fleming were partners on Illawarra Station. Mounted Constable Edmond

Campbell was also in the district early in 1902, having obtained the right to use a 400 square mile Pastoral Lease that had been taken up in 1900 (but never used) by a New South Wales man named Kirby.[47] In one of the strange outcomes of the original system of land allocation, this block was actually inside the boundaries of VRD, in the north-east corner of the station (Map 11). It became Campbell's famous Retreat Station and lasted until 1904 when Kirby sold the lease to WF Buchanan, owner of Wave Hill.[48] Buchanan renamed the block Killarney after his home property of that name near Narrabri, in northern New South Wales.[49] Campbell also seems to have been in partnership with, or employed by, the Flemings. When Mick was setting up and managing New Delamere in 1902, he left Campbell in charge of Illawarra. Later Martin took on this role.[50]

Before he could begin work on Kirby's block Campbell had to have a brand. The one he devised shows that he intended to do more than brand cleanskins. At the Timber Creek Police Station some time in 1902 he registered a diamond-shaped brand ($\Diamond$).[51] This was to become the basis of one of the most famous and versatile brands in Australian cattle duffing history – the Diamond 88 ($\Diamond$88), along with the lesser known Diamond 40 and Diamond 30.[52] With these brands Campbell could cover the 62U brand used both on Delamere and Wave Hill,[53] the O55 on Ord River,[54] the O71 on Auvergne[55] and the

---

O'Keefe (cited in 'Government Resident's Report on the Northern Territory, 1905' (*South Australian Parliamentary Papers*, vol. 2, no. 45, 1906, p. 23), states that Fleming and Martin had dissolved their partnership.

47   Timber Creek police letter book, 12th March 1903. Photocopy held at the Berrimah Police Station, Darwin.
48   Vern O'Brien, 'A history of Killarney lease'. Unpublished manuscript, nd.
49   'Killarney', *The Pastoralists' Review*, 16th May 1910, pp. 272–75.
50   Timber Creek police letter book, 17th June 1903. Photocopy held at the Berrimah Police Station, Darwin.
51   The information about Campbell's diamond brand is on the inside of the front cover of the Timber Creek police journal (NTA: F 302). The journal begins on 31st March 1902, but whether the notes on the brand were written that day or some time later is unknown.
52   Timber Creek police letter book, 17th June 1903. Photocopy held at the Berrimah Police Station, Darwin; NTA: Timber Creek police journal, 3rd July 1909, F 302.
53   'Notice', *Northern Territory Times*, 19th June 1903, p. 3.
54   Since at least 1893 the Ord River brand was a circle with a dot in the centre followed by '55' (NAA: A3 NT 14/5459; G Bolton, 'A survey of the Kimberley pastoral industry from 1885 to the present', MA thesis, University of Western Australia, 1953, p. 169; Durack, p. 404.
55   F Burt, 'Report on the Victoria River District, 30th December 1905', cited in 'Government Resident's Report on the Northern Territory, 1905', *South Australian Parliamentary Papers*, vol. 2, no. 45, 1906, p. 24.

Boab believed marked by 'Diamond Jim' Campbell, near Timber creek

Lewis collection

G10 of VRD.[56] It was a 'brand of genius'[57] and led to Campbell's nickname of 'Diamond Jim', or more simply, 'The Diamond'. By contrast, Ben Martin's brand was M76[58] and the Flemings' brand was BMF,[59] neither of which was suitable for cross-branding other local brands.

---

56   NTA: Timber Creek police journal, 16th and 21st May 1904, F 302.
57   Hill, p. 324.
58   Timber Creek police letter book, 12th March 1903. Photocopy held at the Berrimah Police Station, Darwin.
59   'The Northern Territory. Huge pastoral holdings held at 1/– per square mile', *The Leader*, (Melbourne), 29th July 1922. It's probable that this brand incorporated the

Within months of Campbell and Martin beginning work in the eastern VRD area they were to face charges of 'unlawful possession of cattle on Armstrong Creek'. The case was heard at the Depot by Captain Joe Bradshaw, JP, on 3rd November, the day before race day. Jim Ronan and 'his man' Jack Frayne arrived on 2nd November, and Campbell, Martin and one of the Fleming brothers turned up together the next morning. At 5pm Captain Joe held court and asked the protagonists, Ronan and Martin, to 'come to some agreement and settle the case out of court'. This they were able to do, though no details of the settlement are known. This outcome probably annoyed Mounted Constable O'Keefe because 'previous to this [he] told Ronan he would have to go on with the case'.[60] In any event, from this time on the police began to pay special attention to the activities of Campbell, Martin and the Flemings.

Races were held on the day following the hearing, only the second race meeting ever held at the Depot and the first with sales of alcohol. This undoubtedly suited Frayne who'd been drinking rum for a day or two before he arrived at the Depot and who was drunk the whole time he was there. At one stage O'Keefe had to throw him out of the police station kitchen because he kept trying to entice Tracker Wombat to go with him. Then Campbell and Martin got into a fight and Campbell had to be restrained. No doubt a good time was had by all – except O'Keefe – and everyone – except O'Keefe – left the next day.[61]

Some station managers realised that the influx of small men around their boundaries could mean trouble for them. In December 1902, just four months after the permit system was introduced, Aeneas Gunn, then managing Elsey Station, wrote to the Government Resident protesting the allocation of Pastoral Permits and pointing out that:

> however honest the intentions of the lessees may be anyone who is acquainted with conditions of pastoral settlement & enterprise in this country is aware that it is almost impossible to profitably work a holding of 400 or 500 square miles on an honest basis unless such country is exceptionally good. A premium is given to illicit branding by the practise when as has been the case in most of the recent allotments, the country leased has been for years frequented

initials of Ben Martin and Mick Fleming.
60　NTA: Timber Creek police journal, 25th September 1902, 2nd and 3rd November 1902, F 302.
61　ibid., 2nd and 4th November 1902 5th November 1902.

by stragglers from the established stations' herds, the temptation to pick up any unconsidered trifles of clearskin cattle must be nigh irresistibly strong. [62]

Gunn argued that if permits couldn't be refused, the big stations should at least be given 'due notice that their cattle must be removed within a given time & that on the expiry of the term the right to the cattle running on the blocks will be sold by Public Auction'.

Other managers held a different view. According to Tom Ronan, his father Jim thought, 'Men like Ben Martin and Mick and Jim Fleming were good types' and 'The country could have done with more of them'.[63] He was of the opinion that, in general, the battlers:

> were actually the best friends Victoria River Downs had. For every cleanskin they picked up there were 50 cows and calves and young bullocks turned back into the herd. What's more, they kept the bush blacks out. Had it not been for them the G10 (V.R. Downs brand) cattle had nothing to stop them till they hit the Overland Telegraph Line, and the losses from spearing would have been much heavier than they were.[64]

A similar sentiment towards the battlers was voiced by MP Durack.[65] However, Ronan senior described Campbell as 'a bloody dingo' and Tom said that on one occasion when Campbell rode into his father's camp, Jim gave him food but refused to eat with him.[66] Jim Ronan reserved his anger towards Tom Pearce, who financed the battlers on his eastern boundary and bought their cattle:

> The poor devils would work like slaves and live like blackfellows, and when they got a few head of cattle he'd buy them at bedrock prices. He'd then poor rot-gut grog into them until they were so far in debt that all they could do was go out after another mob.[67]

In March 1903 Mounted Constable O'Keefe reported that Campbell had formed a camp at Coolibah Creek on Kirby's block, Retreat Station. He was of the opinion that Campbell and Martin were working for Tom Pearce and said

---

62 NAA: NTRS 790, item 11817, A Gunn, manager of Elsey Station, to the Government Resident, 9th December 1902.
63 Ronan, p. 180.
64 ibid, pp. 179–80.
65 Durack, p. 70.
66 ibid.
67 ibid.

that although Campbell had brought no cattle onto the block, in a few months' time there would be VRD cleanskins there and that Campbell and Martin intended 'to get all the clean skin Animals there is to be got in that country'. He also reported that Campbell and Martin had mustered a number of brumbies there the previous year, and said that either he or Mounted Constable Gordon would go 'to watch the movements and take particular notes of there work at Coolibah & Illawarra Downs'.[68] Finally, O'Keefe noted that he had heard that 'Mr Ronan and Martin has come to an understanding re the clean skins cattle'. On this subject, on 20th June 1903 he wrote to Ronan as follows:

> I am informed by good authority that you have offered the clean skin cattle east of Victoria river to Campbell and Martin also that you do not forget to notify Campbell and Martin when the police are in the neighbourhood.
>
> Yet you cry out about not being able to get justice, and have the audacity to write and say you have no relations with them whatever, and you supply Campbell with rations to enable him to prosecute his career amongst the clean skin herd at Vict River Stn.[69]

In April and May 1903 Gordon patrolled from Timber Creek to Illawarra Downs, Retreat Station and Delamere Station, interviewing Martin, Campbell and Fleming. His report paints a picture of volatile relationships and changing alliances between these men and possibly between them and Ronan. Martin told Gordon that he had bought Illawarra Downs, including the brands and stock. He also said that Ronan refused to cooperate in any way with him, but during a joint muster on Battle Creek, Ronan had said that if Campbell turned up he would give him (Campbell) a number of old cleanskin bulls they had in hand. Later Campbell told Gordon that Ronan had helped him repair his dray and lent him some rations to keep him going until his own rations arrived. Gordon then saw Mick Fleming at Delamere and Mick told him that the previous year he'd placed Campbell in charge of Illawarra, but that Ronan had 'bluffed him off all the good waters' and it was for that reason he then placed Ben Martin in charge.[70]

---

68   Timber Creek police letter book, 12th March 1903. Photocopy held at the Berrimah Police Station, Darwin. Many of the pages in this photocopy have the bottom line or two missing and in this case the signature is missing. However, by comparison with the handwriting on pages where O'Keefe's signature is present, it is clear that this report was written by O'Keefe.

69   ibid., 20th June 1903.

70   ibid., 17th June 1903.

It's difficult to reconcile these police reports with what Tom Ronan had to say about his father's relationship with Campbell, Martin and the Flemings. It may be that Ronan did make deals with the cattle duffers and was supportive of Campbell, but painted himself in a good light for his son's benefit. Or it may be that the cattle duffers lied to the police in order to make trouble for Ronan and perhaps for one or more of their fellow battlers.

Fleming also told Gordon that he 'had purchased the clean skin cattle running on the neighbourhood of Illawarra Station', presumably meaning those running on Crown Land east of Illawarra rather than those on VRD. This surprised O'Keefe because he hadn't heard that the government had sold the rights to any cleanskin cattle recently. However, he thought Fleming had bought the rights to cleanskin cattle on Armstrong Creek in 1898 and hadn't been able to muster them at the time because of the very bad season.[71]

In June 1903 the Timber Creek police reported that Campbell and Martin had been caught 'branding cleanskins 18 months old', but as no legal action seems to have been taken it may have been a reference to the 1902 case. In July O'Keefe reported that Martin intended to take some cattle in to the telegraph line for the butchers. He pointed out that 'Campbell Fleming & Martin are very little over 12 months at Illawarra station and if Martin can muster aged cattle fit for Butchers meat he must undoubtedly get them unlawfully'. Whether Martin did take cattle in to the line is unknown, but there's no record of any action being taken against him by the police. In August Fleming and Martin were fined £1 each and 15 shillings costs for possessing unregistered dogs, and at various times the police checked Campbell's horses to see if any were stolen.[72]

During 1905 Diamond Jim Campbell left his partnership with the Flemings and shifted his cattle to a block north of Illawarra, which he called Mayvale.[73] He also obtained Pastoral Permit 121 for a block between the western end of Delamere and the south-east corner of Bradshaw (Map 11).[74] This didn't please Fred Bradshaw who in October asked the police to check on Campbell's activities in the area.[75] Martin also dissolved his partnership

---

71   ibid., 27th June 1903.
72   NTA: Timber Creek police journal, 8th June 1903, 27th July 1903, 29th August 1903, 22nd May 1904, 1st August 1904, 10th October 1904. F 302,
73   Pastoral Permit 42, taken up on 21st February 1905.
74   Pastoral Permit 121, taken up on 21st February 1905.
75   NTA: Timber Creek police journal, 27th October 1905, F 302.

with the Flemings in 1905, and in September 1905 removed his share of the cattle, 950 head, to Scott Creek, between Willeroo and Katherine.[76] In 1909 the police ordered him and a partner, 'notorious duffers', to shift from this area.[77] Apparently he'd been squatting on Crown Land for four years and had never bothered to obtain a Pastoral Permit.

Martin got out of the Victoria River District in good time. In 1906 the surveyor LA Wells began the first official triangulation of the Victoria River District, which quickly led to substantial adjustments to the boundaries of some stations. The *Northern Territory Times* published a report on the early results of Wells' survey, and noted that:

> The readjustment of their boundaries — or what they have hitherto looked upon as their boundaries — has come as a great and a not too pleasant surprise to a few. It is found, for instance, that the Victoria River Downs boundary runs 25 miles further to the southward and 10 miles further to the eastward than was supposed by some of the settlers.[78]

This meant that for more than 20 years Wave Hill had been using something in the order of 2500 square miles of prime Mitchell grass downs country that really belonged to Victoria River Downs! Wells later claimed that because of this change, 'one station' (undoubtedly VRD) 'increased its carrying capacity by 20,000 head'.[79] This survey was bad luck for Wave Hill, but for the Fleming brothers and Jim Campbell it was a disaster. With a degree of sarcasm directed at the battlers the *Times* report continued that:

> the owner of the adjoining Illawarra Downs Station now discovers that all his principal sources of water supply are located on the rival territory [*VRD*]. As a consequence of this unpleasant discovery I hear that Mr. M. Fleming is now removing the whole of his herd to country on the Daly River. I fear that in that case he will not have so good a time as he has had on the Illawarra Downs country; the country on the Daly River is certainly not so good for cattle, and they will not thrive or breed so quickly there as on the rich pastoral lands around the Victoria Downs. I hear that Mr. Campbell is also beating a retreat from Maryvale [*Mayvale*]. He is said to be removing his cattle on to

76   Burt, p. 23.
77   NTA: Timber Creek police journal, 3rd July 1909, F 302.
78   'The Victoria River survey', *Northern Territory Times*, 23rd March 1906, p. 2.
79   W Steele and C Steele, *To the Great Gulf: The Surveys and Explorations of LA Wells*, Lynton Publications, Adelaide, 1978, p. 129.

Bradshaw's (Fred) Creek, situated between the Daly River and the head of the Fitzmaurice River.[80]

The Flemings were able to acquire Pastoral Permits for land in the Daly River country. Mick's block formed the basis of the future Douglas River Station and Jim's block became Ooloo Station. After this the brothers had no further connection with the Victoria River District.[81] Campbell was able to hang on, the last of the cattle duffers in the eastern part of the district. He retained the Mayvale block but may have shifted his base to Pastoral Permit (PP121) on Sullivan Creek.[82]

In 1907 Paddy Cahill, then manager of Delamere, made general complaints about Jim Campbell 'stealing calves and altering brands and earmarks'. There were suspicions that some stolen horses were at Campbell's camp, but no specific evidence could be found and no charges could be laid. Then, in 1909, all hell broke loose. On, or shortly before, 23rd April the police reported that Dick Townshend, who had replaced Ronan as VRD manager, and a VRD stockman named Harry Benning had:

> found James Campbell @ Muir, of Mah Vale, tailing 400 and odd mixed cattle on Dry River on the VR Downs station. The cattle had recently been branded ◊40 and earmarked ◁. The brands were deeply and widely burnt and no doubt covered the G10 which is the old VR Downs brand. The earmark would cut out ⊂, the VR Downs earmark.

This encounter was the end of Diamond Jim in the Victoria River country, but the beginning of one of the great cattle duffing stories of the Northern Territory. Townsend immediately took possession of the cattle and, as he began to shift them, Campbell called out, 'This would have been another Mount Cornish if I had got away with them'.[83] This was, of course, a reference to the famous cattle 'lift' by Harry 'Captain Starlight' Readford who in 1870 stole about 1000 head of cattle from Bowen Downs in western Queensland and drove them 1500 kilometres down Coopers Creek to South Australia. For much of the way their route was through unsettled and little-known

---

80   'The Victoria River survey'.
81   Files at the Office of the Placenames Committee, Darwin.
82   NTA: Department of Lands – Land Administration Branch, NTRS, F199, Box 3, PP 121/1907, office copies of Pastoral Permits – 1902–22; the Timber Creek police journal of 7th September 1907 states that Campbell was actually on country held by Willeroo (Permit 93). This appears to be wrong, but if it was correct it would once again highlight how close the relationship was between Pearce and the battlers (NTA: F302).
83   ibid. NTA: Timber Creek police journal, 7th September 1907, 20th May 1908, 14th June 1908, 25th April 1909, 3rd July 1909 F302.

desert country where only nine years earlier Burke and Wills had perished. Readford was eventually arrested, charged with the theft of a distinctive white bull and tried at Roma, but was acquitted, despite overwhelming evidence. As he left the court many people shook his hand and, because of his tremendous feat of daring and bushcraft, he was hailed a hero by many bushmen throughout the outback.[84]

Of the 428 cattle found in Campbell's possession, 23 bore the brands of Delamere, Ord River and Illawarra, or were old ◊88s. The remaining 405 were recently branded ◊88 or ◊40. In a remarkable echo of the Readford story, among the 405 was a white bull with a ◊40 brand and a VRD 'G' which had been overlooked. This bull was killed and the brand and earmark preserved as damning evidence against Campbell.

In a strange twist to the story, Tom Pearce, who had previously quietly supported (and allegedly exploited) Campbell and the other cattle duffers in their unlawful activities, was called upon in his capacity as Justice of the Peace to sign warrants for the arrest of Campbell and his accomplices. It seems quite possible that as Campbell fled the region he would have let Pearce know that he was in trouble, and to avoid any embarrassing connection being revealed Pearce would have helped him on his way. An intensive and sustained manhunt for Campbell and his known associates (Aboriginal and white) was carried out in the district, but no trace could be found. The police were convinced that 'all save Mr Townshend and the MC were actively working in his [*Campbell's*] interest'. The chances are that Campbell was out of the district before the police were even notified. Within three days of being caught with the cattle he'd arranged for a friend, Arthur Love, to sell his permit and stock. A drover named George Stevens, who was then in the Willeroo area, was the buyer and he installed Love as acting manager.[85] Meanwhile Campbell 'went into smoke' beyond the frontier in Arnhem Land[86] where he settled into a life of trepanging,[87] buffalo hunting and prospecting.[88]

Alf Brown, a trepanger who worked along the Arnhem Land coast, was a friend of Campbell's and would take his trepang and buffalo hides to Darwin

---

84   P McCarthy, *The Man who was Starlight*, Allen & Unwin, Sydney, 1987, pp. 43–44, 86–92.

85   NTA: Timber Creek police journal, 11th May 1909, 3rd July 1909, F 302.

86   E Mason, *An Untamed Territory: The Northern Territory of Australia*, Macmillan and Co. Limited, London, 1915, p. 162; Lewis, p. 41.

87   Trepang or *bêche-de-mer* is a sea slug that is used in Chinese cuisine (DJ Mulvaney and J Kamminga, *Prehistory of Australia*, Allen & Unwin, Sydney, 1999, pp. 412–13).

88   Lewis, p. 41.

Jim Cambell's grave on the Arnhem Land coast

Sydney Mail, 31 October 1917, p. 9

and bring rations and other goods out to him.[89] Eventually, the police found out where Campbell was and made several attempts to arrest him, but the 'bush telegraph' kept him informed of police movements. If the police came overland, Campbell would shift out to an offshore island, and if they came by sea he'd ride his horses inland for a while.[90]

Diamond Jim Campbell remained out of harm's way in the bush until 1913 when the charges against him were dropped and he was finally free to make a trip to Darwin.[91] In another parallel with the Readford story, according to an oral tradition Campbell was greeted in Darwin as a hero, carried shoulder-high down Smith Street and straight into the Victoria Hotel.[92] Unfortunately, he was unable to enjoy his hero status for long as he soon returned to Arnhem Land and within a few months was speared and killed while trepanging.[93]

---

89   J Rich, 'Emanuel Victor Brown' in D Carment, R. Maynard and A Powell (eds), *Northern Territory Dictionary of Biography: Volume. 1 to 1945*, Northern Territory University Press, Darwin, 1990, pp 38–39.

90   Lewis, p. 41.

91   'Murder by blacks', *Northern Territory Times*, 10th July 1913, p. 2.

92   Reg Wilson, pers. comm. Wilson was told the story by John Mott, a Territory surveyor in the period 1913–15.

93   'Murder by blacks'.

Campbell's murder caused the usual outrage amongst his friends and supporters who claimed he was 'one of the best', but at the trial of his alleged killers evidence was given that he had beaten a woman, forced an old man into a trepang boiler full of hot water until he was 'close up die', chained up a number of men who didn't want to work for him and shot dead the brother of one of the accused. Of nine Aborigines charged, four were acquitted and five sentenced to death, their penalties later commuted to life in prison.[94] After the trial the judge remarked that, 'The reputation of the deceased as regards the treatment of natives is of the worst.'[95] A man who had known Campbell echoed this assessment when he said, 'My friend Campbell, he very rough on blacks'.[96]

---

94   'Sentences Commuted', *Northern Star* (Lismore, NSW), 19 November 1913, p. 5.
95   NAA: CRS A3 Item 14/808. 'C.E. Campbell, Murder of'. Letter from Judge David J.D. Bevan to His Excellency the Administrator, 18th September 1913.
96   Mason, p. 162.

Chapter 11

THE NEST OF REPUTED THIEVES

At the time that the Flemings, Martin and Campbell were establishing themselves on the eastern side of the district, another group of battlers was doing the same further to the west. (Map 12) Of the ten or so men who between 1902 and 1912 were involved with small holdings in the western Victoria River District, WJJ 'Brigalow Bill' Ward, Jimmy Wickham, John Duggan, Jack Barry, Tom Hanlon and William Patterson appear out of the 'historical' blue. Fortunately, the backgrounds of Jack Beasley, Jack Frayne, Mat Wilson, James Kearney and 'Colorado' Jack Newton are less mysterious.

All that is known about Kearney is that, like many men in the outback, he was a man with a 'history'. In 1892 he and Sam Long had been charged with the murder of a Chinese miner on the Macarthur River. In spite of damning evidence against them, as soon as the Crown case was closed the jury acquitted them both, without even retiring to consider the matter.[1]

Somewhat more is known about Jack Newton, largely because a contemporary of his, Billy Linklater, compiled a short biography of him.[2] According to Linklater, Newton 'got left at Wyndham' by a cattle boat in about 1897. From there he went inland with a drover and received his nickname 'Colorado' on Argyle Station after he told a stockman there that he'd been in America. It seems likely that he had indeed been to America because he later built a Mexican-style pise homestead at Texas Downs, in the East Kimberley.[3] He was also a very good bush carpenter, building 'Government House' at Gordon Downs[4] and on one occasion in Jasper Gorge making a new wooden wheel for a Buick car to replace one that had

---

1   Untitled news item, *Northern Territory Times*, 15th July 1892, p. 2; 'The Northern Territory murder case', *The Adelaide Observer*, 1st October 1892, p. 36, and 15th October 1892, p. 31.
2   W Linklater, nd. Hand-written manuscript, in possession of Buchanan family, South Australia.
3   ibid; J Makin, *The Big Run*, Rigby Limited, Sydney, 1970, p. 124.
4   Linklater.

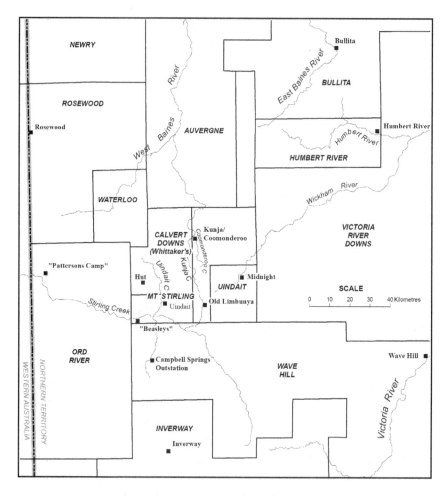

Map 12. The western Victoria River cattle duffer's blocks in relation to the big stations

been smashed.[5] Apparently he was a bit of a wild man, too, because he stood trial once for attempting to blow up the Wyndham Hotel.[6] Luckily for him the jury must have considered his actions as justifiable, or harmless fun, because it appears that he was acquitted.[7]

Matt Wilson had worked as a shearer in western Queensland and was an active member of the Queensland Bush Worker's Union, a forerunner to the Australian Workers' Union.[8] One source claims that he held Ticket No. 1

5   Makin, p. 104.
6   'Wyndham Explosion. A Man Arrested', *West Australian*, 5th August 1933, p15.
7   Linklater.
8   T. Ronan, *Deep of the Sky*, Cassell Australia Ltd, Melbourne 1962, p. 59.

The Victoria River Depot Store, c1912

Johns collection

with this union.[9] Another source says that he walked with a noticeable limp, the result of a bullet wound received during one of the big shearer's strikes of the 1890s,[10] but neither claim has been confirmed. Wilson was a long-time friend of Jim Ronan, and first came to the Victoria River country at Ronan's suggestion soon after Ronan became manager of VRD in 1900.[11] Initially he worked as a drover for Victoria River Downs, but in 1906 he took over the Depot store on the Victoria River. He remained there for 25 years and became something of an 'institution' in the region until his death by suicide in 1931.[12]

The South Australian census of 1891 lists Jack Frayne as having been born in Bendigo, Victoria, in about 1865.[13] In the late 1880s he held the licence for the Roper Bar Hotel[14] and in 1892 he was one of a party led by police

9   ibid.
10 CC Boulter, diary, 1914, p. 130. Boulter was assistant surveyor to Surveyor Scandrett who passed through Timber Creek in 1913.
11 Ronan, p. 174.
12 Northern Territory Archives (NTA): Timber Creek police journal, 31st March 1908, F 302; 'Death of M. B. Wilson', *Northern Standard*, 3 February 1931, p. 5..
13 Northern Territory 1891 census, compiled from the South Australian 1891 census by the Genealogical Society of the Northern Territory from original records held at the National Archives of Australia (Darwin), microfiche, 1986.
14 Untitled news item, *Northern Territory Times*, 15th September 1888, p. 2.

in hunting the Aborigines who murdered WS Scott at Willeroo.[15] Two years later he passed through the Victoria River country because Mounted Constable Willshire reported inspecting his horses there.[16] It's possible he was then on his way to the East Kimberley because in 1896 he was working as a drover for Connor, Doherty and Durack (CD&D),[17] and during 1898 and 1899 he was working as a stockman or drover on Auvergne, Newry and probably other Durack stations.[18]

Apparently Frayne was a highly competent all-round bush worker, an outstanding horseman and a great personality. Like many of his contemporaries he was fond of 'lifting his little finger', but Mary Durack states that he 'was too valuable a stockman to be dismissed for his drinking habits'. She adds that, 'It was obvious that [*her father*] MP had a considerable respect for Frayne, who would carry out a job he had undertaken where others might well give it up as impossible'.[19] Tom Ronan, author of several books on the Victoria River District, heard about Frayne's 'magnificent achievements' from his father Jim and others, and planned to write a full-length novel about him. Unfortunately he never did so. When Jim Ronan took over the management of Victoria River Downs in 1900, Frayne was one of the team of first-class stockmen he assembled. According to Tom Ronan, his father sent Frayne to establish Montejinni Outstation to prevent the Aborigines from killing cattle[20] and Frayne had a camp in that area by May 1902.[21]

Finally, there was Jack Beasley. Beasley was in the East Kimberley and Victoria River District from at least 1896.[22] He spent much of his life working on various stations in the region, including Auvergne, Ord River and VRD.[23] He must have also occasionally worked elsewhere because, according to Mat Savage, who was one of his contemporaries, it was Jack Beasley who formed Soudan Station on the Barkly Tableland. Savage says

15 'Another Murder in the Victoria River District', *Northern Territory Times*, 21st October 1892 p.3.
16 NTA: Timber Creek police journal, 8th July 1894, F 302.
17 State Records Office of Western Australia, Acc 741-3, Occurrence book [*Wyndham*] 1895–97, 10th January 1896 and 14th April 1896.
18 M Durack, *Sons in the Saddle*, Corgi Books, Sydney, 1985, pp. 69–70, 78–79, 104; State Records Office of Western Australia, Acc 741-4 Occurrence book [*Wyndham*] 1895–97, entry for 17th May 1899.
19 Durack, pp. 69–70.
20 Ronan, pp. 179, 195.
21 NTA: Timber Creek police journal, 11th May 1902, F 302.
22 N McLennan, *Ord River Station, WA 1895–1896, Yesterday and Today*, privately published, Stawell, Victoria, 1965, p. 7.
23 ibid., p. 7; Durack, p. 70; E Morey, 'Timber Creek patrols', pt. 2, *Northern Territory Newsletter*, Darwin, August issue, 1977, p. 18.

Jack Beasley, 1939

Lilly collection

Beasley couldn't write his own name but instead would sign with a conjoined JB, which was also his brand.[24]

Aborigines from one side of the Victoria River District to the other remember Beasley as a very hard man and one of the main culprits in early massacres.[25] He was certainly in the district early enough to have been

---

24 K Willey, *Boss Drover*, Rigby, Sydney, 1971, p. 40.
25 Albert Lalga and Old Jimmy Manngayarri, both deceased, told me about Beasley's involvement in the shooting of Aborigines. Lalga's country was Montejinni and Wave Hill and Manngayarri's country was southern VRD, Limbunya and Mistake Creek; See D Rose, *Hidden Histories* (Aboriginal Studies Press, Canberra, 1991, pp. 39–41, 67–68).

involved in such killings and Aboriginal oral traditions as widespread and consistent as the ones concerning Beasley should be taken seriously. However, there is only one written source which could support the oral traditions. When Doug Moore became bookkeeper on Ord River in 1900, Jack Beasley was the head stockman there. Years later Moore wrote a short memoir in which he remembered Beasley as 'a rough good natured chap who talked about gouging out blackfellows eyes with a blunt pocket knife'. At the time Moore thought it was 'only talk', but he was forced to reconsider when 'some built on it later'.[26] Old Jimmy Manngayarri, one of the oldest Aboriginal men I interviewed, had known Beasley. He claimed that on one occasion Beasley's Aboriginal wife ran away and, when Beasley caught her, he shot her.[27]

Billy Patterson and Jack Beasley were the first to take up a block in the western Victoria River country. In June 1903 they obtained Pastoral Permit 10 for an area extending north from Stirling Creek. This block abutted the eastern boundary of Ord River and the north-west boundary of Wave Hill. They built a small hut and a stockyard on the south bank of Stirling Creek and named the station Mount Stirling.[28] At the time they obtained their permit Beasley was working as head stockman on the neighbouring Ord River Station. He immediately commenced 'doing all he could to stock that country up for the partnership' by branding as many Ord River cleanskins as he could with the Mt Stirling brand.[29]

Jack Frayne came next. When he was sent to establish Montejinni Outstation on VRD, ostensibly to put a stop to cattle killing by bush blacks, he no doubt was also told to keep an eye on the local battlers. Apparently he liked what he saw. Not one to miss an opportunity himself, by August 1903 Frayne had left VRD and in September he moved onto Pastoral Permit 26, on the watershed between Stirling Creek, the West Baines River and Humbert River.[30] This location gave him access to Auvergne in the north, VRD to the east, Wave Hill to the south and Ord River to the west. Frayne built a hut on the banks of Kunja Rockhole on Kunja Creek, and applied this

---

26   Doug Moore, Memoirs, pt. 2, unpublished typescript, nd, Battye Library, Acc 3829A, MN 1237.
27   Manngayarri, taped interview with author, Midnight Station, 1989.
28   D Lewis, *In Western Wilds: A Survey of Historic Sites in the Western Victoria River District*, report prepared for the National Trust of Australia (Northern Territory), vol. 1, 1993, pp. 135–36 and vol. 2, pp. 108–09.
29   Moore.
30   National Archives of Australia (NAA): Pastoral Permit (PP) 26, CRS A1640, item 1903/553; NTA: Timber Creek police journal, 29th August 1903, F 302.

name to his station.[31] The Pastoral Permit records show that Frayne was in partnership with Matt Wilson,[32] though Wilson doesn't appear to have ever worked with Frayne on the station so he was probably a 'sleeping partner'.

After Frayne came Jimmy Wickham who, in July 1904, obtained Pastoral Permit 22 for an area on Uindait Creek, on the north side of the Stirling and east of Beasley and Patterson's block.[33] Later Wickham acquired Pastoral Permit 111, a long and very narrow strip of country adjoining the western end of the Humbert River block (Permit 56).[34] He called his place Uindait Station[35] and built a substantial homestead of local basalt rocks, bush timber and corrugated iron[36] – 'a little fortress of stone and ant-bed' as described by Ernestine Hill[37] – as well as two large basalt-walled yards and other stone structures.[38] Unlike the other battlers, Wickham was married to a white woman and had his wife and their children at Uindait.[39]

Finally, in May 1905, Newton and Kearney joined the other settlers when they took up Pastoral Permit 56, on the Humbert River.[40] In what was

---

31 In 1989 I was taken to the site of Kunja homestead by Old Jimmy Manngayarri, a senior Malngin-Bilinara elder, who told me the name of the rockhole. The name 'Kunja station' appears on various early maps.

32 NAA, CRS A1640, item 1903/553.

33 E O'Keefe, cited in 'Government Resident's Report on the Northern Territory, 1904', *South Australian Parliamentary Papers*, vol. 2, no. 45, 1905, p. 27; NTA: Department of Lands – Land Administration Branch, F 199, PP22/1910, office copies of Pastoral Permits – 1902–22.

34 NTA: F 199 PP111/1915. Wickham held this block from 10th June 1906 to 10th June 1912.

35 There are various spellings of this name, for example, 'Uyndoyte' (agreement signed by James Wickham, 14th June 1910, letter book, 1901–1912, inward and outward correspondence relating to Connor, Doherty & Durack, Rosewood records, Battye Library, Acc 2184A/1, MN485, p. 372); 'Uandyke' (Mounted Constable Dempsey to Sub-Inspector N Waters, 13th April 1908, re. Newton for unlawfully branding: and miscellaneous, NAA: CRS A1640, item 1906/223); 'Ewandyte' (Ernestine Hill, *The Territory*, Angus and Robertson, Sydney, 1951, p. 339); 'Nyerdoyle' (Durack, p. 331); 'Wyandotte' and 'Mindyit' (LA Wells to Mr Justice Herbert, Government Resident, Darwin, 8th November 1907, Department of Territories. Correspondence Dockets NT Series: Aborigines Reserve – Ord River District, NT – re proposal, NAA: CRS A1640, item 1906/223).

36 There is no corrugated iron at the site today, but Manngayarri who, as a child, visited the homestead with his parents – not long after the building was abandoned – remembered the upper part of the walls and the roof being clad with corrugated iron.

37 Hill, p. 339.

38 See Lewis, *In Western Wilds* (vol. 1, pp. 115–18 and vol. 2 pp. 93–98).

39 Hill, p. 399; In a letter written by MP Durack to Jimmy Wickham on 24th July 1910, Durack sends his regards to 'Mrs Wickham and child' (Battye Library, Acc 2184A/1, MN485).

40 NTA: F 199 PP 56/1908; NAA: WJJ Ward to Lands Department, 28 October 1906, 'Northern Territory Pastoral Permit No. 56 in name of J. Newton & P. Kearney, be

almost certainly a great joke on their part, both men described themselves on their Pastoral Permit as 'Halls Creek sheep farmers'.[41] In 1906 Kearney withdrew from his partnership with Newton and disappeared from the historical record. His place was taken by Brigalow Bill Ward, another self-proclaimed sheep farmer from Halls Creek.[42] On the south bank of the Humbert River near its junction with the Wickham, one or more of these men built a stockyard, and a hut with a bush timber frame clad with cane grass and roofed with thatch.

Apparently Colorado and Brigalow Bill couldn't get along because, by October 1906, Brigalow wanted to dissolve his partnership with Newton. He asked the Lands Department if he could pay half the rent for 'the portion next to the Victoria Station Boundary'[43] – the only part that wasn't spinifex-covered sandstone ranges! In May 1907 Newton tried to counteract Ward's move by sending in money for the entire rent and requesting the block to be transferred solely to his name.[44] There's no evidence that either man got what he wanted, but eventually only Brigalow Bill was living on the block.

Once the battlers obtained their permits, all was well for a while. Huts and yards were built and, no doubt, the men were quietly (and quickly) building up their herds. Then in 1907 surveyor LA Wells came along to 'readjust' all their boundaries, or more accurately, to place their boundaries in their proper positions. Wells' survey showed that the boundaries of most of the permits were further north and east than previously believed. As a result the homesteads built by Frayne, Wickham, and Beasley and Patterson, were not on their own land. As Wells explained to the Government Resident in November 1907:

> The Lessees of No 10 [*Beasley and Patterson's*] were settled on lease No 2227 [*Wave Hill's*] and lessees of [*Wickham's*] No 22 were on No 10 ... [*the southern boundary of*] Permit 10 is over 3 miles North of Stirling Creek and has but one creek, Wyandotte? ("Mindyit") of any

---

transferred to J. Newton and J Ward, requesting', A1640/1, item 1906/102. These records indicate that the Humbert River block was taken up in 1905, but other records suggest that it occurred in 1903. I have not yet been able to determine the facts of the matter (see 'Government Resident's Report on the Northern Territory, 1903', *South Australian Parliamentary Papers*, vol. 2, no. 45, 1904, p. 8).

41 NTA: F 199, box 2, PP 56/1908; NAA: A1640/1, item 1906/102.
42 ibid
43 NAA: WJJ Ward to Lands Department, 28th October 1906, A1640/1, item 1906/102.
44 NAA: J Newton to Lands Department, 1st May 1907, A1640/1, item 1906/102.

importance which trends South through the block from its North boundary where a permanent Spring exists.

Permit No 22 is a dry block except the East portion which is very rough and forms the source of the Wickham River. This block has never even been occupied by the Lessees. [45]

It's not clear if Beasley and Patterson moved at all. It may be that they stayed squatting on the south bank of Stirling Creek, on Wave Hill country. Jack Frayne built a new homestead further north at Coomanderoo Spring,[46] on the southern edge of the Boomondoo sandstone. In the early 1900s Boomondoo was a major refuge area for bush Aborigines and it appears that his move brought Frayne into conflict with them. Billy Linklater (alias Billy Miller), who worked for Frayne at 'Koonju' (Kunja), was 'warned to take no chances whatever with the blacks, for they were always ready to show a very practical belligerence towards the occupation of their country'. In spite of this warning Linklater was attacked and very nearly lost his life.[47] Old Jimmy Manngayarri told me that bush people had been shot near Coomanderoo, in one instance after they'd speared a number of milking cows near the homestead.[48]

The battler most seriously affected was Jimmy Wickham who had inadvertently built his homestead on Beasley and Patterson's block. There is no hard evidence that he abandoned the site, but this is likely because, in the middle of where Pastoral Permit 22 was shown to be – on the headwaters of the Wickham River – there are the remains of a hut made from basalt rocks and bush timber, constructed in a similar manner to the house at Uindait. Old Jimmy said that this site was named 'Midnight', probably a corruption of Uindait. This name appears in a few historical documents.[49]

---

45   NAA: L.A. Wells, 8th November 1907, CRS A1640, item 1906/223.
46   A White, Report of the Sub-Inspector of Stock, Victoria River District, cited in the 'Northern Territory. Report of the Government Resident for the Year 1910', *South Australian Parliamentary Papers*, vol. 3, no. 66, 1911, p. 25; this name is more accurately rendered 'Kumanturu'.
47   W Linklater and L Tapp, *Gather No Moss*, Hesperian Press, Perth, 1997 (1968), p. 122.
48   Manngayarri, 1989.
49   The name 'Midnight' first appears after Wickham sold his permits, in reference to a temporary police camp established there (Mounted Constable William Johns to Inspector N Waters, 8th January 1912, NAA: A3/1 NT 1914/6947; N Waters, police inspector's office, Darwin, 6th February, 1912, in 'Northern Territory. Report of the Acting Administrator for the Year 1911', *Commonwealth Parliamentary Papers*, vol. 3, no. 54, 1912, p. 29.

The remains of Jimmy Wickham's Yundait homestead, Limbunya Station
Lewis collection

The problems caused by this 'readjustment' of their boundaries were soon overtaken by a more serious threat. In April 1907 Mounted Constable Dempsey began a seven week patrol through the western district to report on, amongst other things, the suitability of various areas for an Aboriginal Reserve.[50] He recommended sections of Ord River Station along the Negri River, part of the north side of Stirling Creek and all of Patterson and Beasley's Permit 10 and Wickham's Permit 22.[51] Dempsey's report was forwarded to surveyor Wells who pointed out that Dempsey had made his suggestions in ignorance of the fact that·the supposed boundaries of the blocks had been corrected and, as a result, the areas that he recommended didn't in fact hold the abundant water and traditional foods that Dempsey believed they did. Wells instead suggested that Permit 56 (Ward's Humbert River Station) be declared an Aboriginal reserve.[52] Later he elaborated on his recommendation:

---

50   NTA: Timber Creek police journal, 11th June 1907, F 302.
51   NAA: Mounted Constable Dempsey to N Waters, Sub-Inspector of Police, Darwin, 13th June 1907, re. Aboriginal Reserve, vide GRO 14777/06 attached, CRS A1640, item 1906/223.
52   NAA: 8th November 1907, CRS A1640, item 1906/223.

Senior Constable Dempsey, 1911

Johns collection

Permit 56 has a few head of cattle, running on the Eastern end. It is of little value for depasturing, owing to its roughness, and is held by questionable characters, who are not likely to become good Crown tenants.

The latter block, having abundance of fish and game, I thought would be most suitable for a reserve.[53]

News of the plan to establish an Aboriginal reserve reached the battlers around the time that Mounted Constable Dempsey was on patrol in their district. Understandably they were outraged, and Dempsey later reported that,

---

53   NAA: LA Wells to Surveyor General's Office, Adelaide, 25th January 1908, CRS A1640, item 1906/223.

This they all bitterly resent and put it that it is because they are 'small settlers' that they are being driven off their country. To a man the workers of this district are in sympathy with them. All fail to recognize that these particular 'small settlers' are 'large thieves' It would appear that cattle raising blunts the moral principles and makes those working at it oblivious to the law of meum and tuum.[54]

Dempsey added that Wickham had gone to Adelaide to try to get the resumption notice revoked and Beasley had been to Wyndham to seek 'the aid of one Skinner there to prepare a long indictment against the squatters'. Beasley's 'long indictment' was in fact rather short:

please do utmost to prevent forfeiture lease represent matter as iniquitous harassment of small settler who Govt pretend desire no Aboriginal reserve required there even so why take small mans whole country after expensive improvements leaving untouched surrounding big stations Victoria Wave Hill Ord River proceedings appear monstrous please do best prevent such injustice.[55]

Beasley's partner, Patterson,[56] told Mounted Constable Dempsey that all the permit holders were planning to camp on the lease of Charlie Whittaker, north of the Mt Stirling block, and continue running their cattle on their old blocks. Dempsey convinced him that this plan wouldn't work and later summed up the situation as follows:

From such a nest as that on the Stirling may come a Kenif. It is politic that such people be dealt with promptly. I cannot but feel that the resumption was an excellent move and I would respectfully request you, Sir, to use your influence to see that it is not permitted to these people to sit down any longer on the country in question than is necessary in fairness to remove their stock.[57]

The 'Kenif' mentioned in this passage refers to brothers James and Paddy Kenniff, stock thieves-cum-bushrangers who were active in central

---

54   NAA: 13th April 1908, CRS A1640, item 1906/223.
55   NAA: W Skinner to Symes, solicitor, Darwin, 6th February 1908, A1640, item 1906/223.
56   Beasley had two partners named Patterson. The first was Billy Patterson who died at Mt Stirling on 24th February 1907 (Timber Creek police journal, 29th June 1907, NTA: F302). Another Patterson, possibly Billy's brother, is mentioned in records after that date (eg, Timber Creek police journal, 25th July 1908, NTA: F302; 13th April 1908, NAA: CRS A1640, item 1906/223).
57   NAA: 13th April 1908, CRS A1640, item 1906/223.

Queensland in the late 1800s–early 1900s.[58] Their exploits and final end were widely reported in newspapers of the time, including the *Northern Territory Times*.[59]

Brigalow Bill was the most strident in protesting the proposed resumptions. In April 1908 he wrote to the Lands Department saying:

> I have been informed that my country held by Newton & Ward Humbert River Block 53 has been canseled for Aboriginal reserve I should like to know the reason why after going to a lot of trouble of brining cattle from the Kimberley district in to the territory and stocking it and been put to a lot of truble time & money in settling the country to be Hunted of they were plenty of country before I came and are plenty now only fit for Black reserve without chising one of the only few that is there now it is a nice way of settling people on the land. I am put to a great deal loss I will have to give my cattle away.[60]

Brigalow went on to allege that the big stations were holding land that wasn't stocked and asked that he be allowed to keep the lower end of his country, or be given one of the blocks on VRD that he claimed was unstocked. He had good cause to be worried. Unbeknown to him, his block had already been singled out as the most suitable for an Aboriginal reserve. On top of that he had the bad luck to be linked to a man who was the subject of a police manhunt – Colorado Jack Newton.

During a joint muster on the boundary between Ord River Station and 'Whittaker's place' (near Waterloo) in September 1907, Ord River stockmen found a bullock and a cow, both branded with N93 on top of O55 – in other words, with Colorado Jack's brand superimposed on the Ord River brand. The earmarks had also been changed. The Timber Creek police were notified and began proceedings against Colorado. After sending Mounted Constable Artaud to Willeroo to get Tom Pearce, JP, to sign summonses for Newton and various witnesses, Dempsey then patrolled to the Stirling Creek country to serve these summonses.[61]

---

58   R Good, *Ketching the Kenniffs: The Origins and Exploits of the Kenniff Brothers – Patrick and James*, Booringah Shire Council & Booringah Action Group, Mitchell, Queensland, 1996, p. 121–28, 163–67, 190–96).

59   For example, see 'News and Notes' in the *Northern Territory Times*, 27th June 1902, p. 3.

60   NAA: WJJ Ward to Surveyor General's Department, 15th April 1908, CRS A1640, item 1906/223.

61   NTA: Timber Creek police journal, 13th December 1903, 17 October 1907, 21 October 1907, F 302.

However, the bush telegraph had been at work. Colorado Jack knew the police were onto him and the police later learnt that shortly after they'd been at Willeroo, he'd turned up there, asking if a summons had been issued against him.[62]

At Campbell Springs, an outstation of Wave Hill that was established close to the various battler's blocks by 1906,[63] Dempsey requested that the manager call a muster of the Campbell Springs country in the hope that they might find cross-branded cattle and that Newton would attend. Newton never appeared and nothing incriminating was found, so Dempsey had to return to Timber Creek empty-handed.[64] He came away feeling that 'the nest of reputed thieves on the Stirling should be broken up' and that Newton:

> must be driven from the district. He has no country in it and palpably is a thief. Only last year he put up a yard on Farquaharson's country [*Inverway*] and in it a 'crush'. This though his few head of cattle could have but calves that would not need 'crushing'. He was on the country too, without permission ... Newton may have left the country — he is in deadly fear of arrest — and if so the country will be rid of a nuisance.[65]

The police never did catch up with Colorado. In July 1908 they heard that he'd sold his cattle to Beasley and Patterson and gone to the Kimberley,[66] and furthermore, that the chief witness against him was no longer in the Territory.[67] A month or so later Newton applied to have his brand transferred to Beasley.[68] Referring to Newton and Ward, Dempsey declared:

> Both men are, as a matter of common notoriety, as are all the small settlers, cattle duffers if there be a chance to get clean skins from their neighbours, and they and their fellows with very few exceptions I regret to report, do not think that 'Thou shalt not steal' applies to clean skin cattle.[69]

62 NAA: 13th April 1908, CRS A1640, item 1906/223.
63 Timber Creek police letter book, 22nd August 1906.
64 NAA: 13th April, CRS A1640, item 1906/223.
65 ibid.
66 NAA: Mounted Constable Dempsey, Timber Creek Police Station, to Sub-Inspector N. Waters, Darwin, 15th August 1908, A1640/1, item 1906/223.
67 NTA: Timber Creek police journal, 25th July 1908, F 302.
68 NAA: Sub-Inspector N Waters to the Government Resident, 7th September 1908, A1640/1, item 1906/223.
69 NAA: 15th August 1908, A1640/1, item 1906/223.

Meanwhile, the government was moving inexorably towards declaring Newton and Ward's Humbert River block an Aboriginal reserve. In May 1908 the Government Resident expressed the opinion that a reserve should be declared 'before the country becomes more settled', adding that, 'If Newton is half as bad a character as MC Dempsey gives him, (and I have no reason to doubt the constables honesty of intention) he should be deprived of his Permit even were it not wanted for the purpose of a reserve'.[70] The Humbert River Permit expired 28th March 1909 and wasn't renewed.[71]

As well as being threatened with the loss of his Pastoral Permit, Brigalow Bill was being threatened by Aborigines. In March 1908 he wrote to the Lands Department asking once again to be given a separate permit for the lower half of the Humbert block and also complaining that 'after sivelizing the country and getting half my stock killed with Blacks' he might be forced off the place.[72] Three months later he wrote an urgent message to the Timber Creek police demanding 'your instant protection here at once the Blacks Killing Cattle & throwing spears at me. They are now hostile and defiant they forbid me to go out again I will expect you here in the course of a week'.[73] Afterwards he had cause to regret such precipitous action.

Mounted Constable Dempsey arrived a month later and heard both sides of the affair. The basic story was that while riding around his cattle Brigalow met a group of Aborigines, including a number of so-called 'outlaws'.[74] He accused them of killing his cattle. They told him they had indeed killed a beast, but it was a Victoria River Downs bullock they'd seen him muster from VRD to Humbert. As a result, it was agreed that if Brigalow didn't tell the police about their cattle killing, the Aborigines wouldn't tell the VRD manager about his cattle duffing. For some reason,

---

70   NAA: Government Resident Charles Herbert to the Minister Controlling the Northern Territory, Adelaide, 19th May 1908, CRS A1640, Item 1906/223.

71   NAA: 'Transfer of the Northern Territory to the Commonwealth: re terms of agreement of', A1640/1, item 1907/580.

72   NAA: WJJ Ward to Lands Department, 1st March 1908, CRS A1640, item 1906/223.

73   NAA: WJJ Ward to Mounted Constable Dempsey, Timber Creek Police Station, 28th June 1908 CRS A1640, item 1906/223.

74   NAA: 15th August 1908, A1640/1, item 1906/223; no Victoria River District Aborigines were officially outlawed. The term was applied to persistent, known troublemakers, who defied the whites in various ways – cattle spearing, stealing or threatening attack. In this instance, the 'outlaws' were Riley and his son, Malgat and his brother Picknarry, and Billy. Years later, Riley became a valued employee of Humbert River Station (C Schultz and D Lewis, *Beyond the Big Run*, University of Queensland Press, Brisbane, 1995, pp. 36, 43, 60).

when the Aborigines moved off into the hills Brigalow followed, so they threw spears at him. When all their spears were thrown there was a stalemate until one of the Aborigines said, 'you let us get our spears and we let you pass'. Brigalow let them get their spears and they let him pass. Mounted Constable Dempsey and Brigalow Bill made a search for the Aborigines involved, but Dempsey later remarked that, 'As the country is highly mountainous and affords splendid hiding places for the Natives, there appeared to be no chance of getting any of them and Ward was disinclined to prosecute if any were got'.[75]

In September 1908 Brigalow Bill again wrote to the Lands Department, this time asking for a Lease instead of a Permit, and once again asking to be given title to the lower half of the Permit area. He also complained about the rent, declaring 'I reckon the rent to high it aught to be sixpence insted of a shilling considering they are four watersheds on it country walls of mountains you cant get up and spinfix they call this a river the Humbert it is only a short creek'.[76]

Whatever letters Brigalow may have written after this time either have not survived or have not been found. The next mention of him is in March 1909 when Dempsey reported that Brigalow Bill was on the Murranji Track in pursuit of a man named Webb who had enticed away his (Brigalow's) Aboriginal wife and was headed for Borroloola. In pursuit of Brigalow was a man named Nye and 'a ruffian Known as "Rackarock"', Rackarock being the brand name of an explosive.[77] The police 'feared a tragedy might be the end of the affair', but Brigalow soon returned with the woman. A month later Webb wrote to the police reporting him for 'ill treating a lubra'.[78]

The Humbert River block was declared an Aboriginal Reserve in June 1909,[79] but Brigalow refused to leave and was still squatting there some months later when he was speared and killed at his homestead. Rumours

75 Mounted Constable Dempsey to Inspector Waters, 12th August 1908, Timber Creek police letter book, photocopy held at Berrimah Police Station, Darwin (location of original unknown).
76 NAA: WJJ Ward to the Lands Department, 20th September 1908, CRS A1640, item 1906/223.
77 NTA: Timber Creek police journal, 1st March 1909, F 302. 'Rackarock' Mahoney was 'a rough old bushman' and 'a famous bagman' whose nickname was the name of an explosive (G Broughton, *Turn Again Home*, The Jacaranda Press, Sydney, 1965, p. 102; Willey, p. 47; 'Rackarock', *The Adelaide Observer*, 27th December 1890, p. 48).
78 NTA: Timber Creek police journal, 15th March 1909, 21st April 1909, F 302.
79 *South Australian Government Gazette*, 17th June 1909, p. 15.

Mounted Constable Holland at Brigalow Bill's hut, 1910

Johns collection

of his death reached the police in February 1910.[80] They travelled to his hut and found it empty and ransacked, with bloodstains on the doorway. Later they learnt that Judy, almost certainly the woman that he had retrieved from Webb in 1908, had been a key player in his death. She had taken his pistol down to the river in a bucket and the bush Aborigines then attacked Brigalow and speared him. While he was dying they pulled out his beard[81] and then Judy and other women urinated on his face – a sign of contempt for his sexual demands.[82] Accounts vary as to what happened to his body. One says it was buried, another that it was thrown into the river and yet another that it was buried in the riverbed.[83] In any event, his final resting place today is unknown.[84]

According to the police account, during the hunt for Brigalow's murderers, an Aboriginal man named Gordon was shot dead.[85] However, Charlie

---

80   Mounted Constable Dempsey, 15th February 1910. Timber Creek police letter book, photocopy held at the Berrimah Police Station, Darwin.

81   NTA: Timber Creek police journal, 17th April 1910, F 302.

82   Schultz and Lewis, p. 45.

83   ibid., p. 43; NTA: Timber Creek police journal, 17th April 1910, F 302.; P Read and J Read, *Long Time, Olden Time: Aboriginal Accounts of Northern Territory History*, Institute for Aboriginal Development Publications, Alice Springs, 1991, p. 30.

84   NTA: Timber Creek police journal, 26th June 1910, F 302.

85   ibid.

Schultz, who owned Humbert River Station from 1928 to 1971, heard from old-time VRD locals that a great many Aborigines were shot.[86] Eventually Aborigines named Mudgela, Fishook, Longana and Walgarra were arrested and a number of witnesses detained, but Longana and one of the witnesses escaped before they could be taken to Darwin.[87] Of the others, only Mudgela and Fishook were convicted. Both were sentenced to death,[88] with the penalty later commuted to life.[89]

In 1914 it was reported that Mudgela had escaped,[90] but whether he was again captured or made it back to Humbert River and remained at large is unknown. Fishook must have eventually been released because in later years he worked for Charlie Schultz on Humbert River. Schultz didn't know his background, but said Fishook was always terribly afraid of the police.[91] Several other Aborigines implicated in the murder, including Maroun and Cockatoo, remained in the ranges as 'outlaws' for years.[92] Cockatoo was eventually arrested, but not for his involvement in Ward's murder. Instead, he was arrested for being one of three Aborigines who in 1924 'stuck up' the Mt Sanford cook with their spears, demanding flour from him.[93] The final irony of the Brigalow Bill saga is that although his block was declared an Aboriginal Reserve it was never used as such, and within five years of Brigalow's death Billy Butler was issued with a grazing license for the area.[94]

Brigalow Bill was murdered and Colorado Jack had 'gone into smoke', but what of the other battlers in 'the nest of thieves'? Beasley and his partners managed to avoid trouble with the law although through their association

86 Charlie Schultz, pers. comm.
87 NTA: Timber Creek police journal, 15th and 18th July 1910, F 302.
88 'Curcuit court', *Northern Territory Times*, 16th September 1910, p. 3. The September conviction of Fishook highlights problems the police sometimes had in identifying bush Aborigines or, at least, potential problems with the police accounts of events. The previous April, a man supposedly named 'Fishook' had been involved in an attack on Harry Condon, the manager of Bullita. He was later tracked by police and shot dead in the East Baines country (Timber Creek police journal, 4th April 1910, NTA: F 302).
89 Adelaide Register, 20th June 1907, p. 4.
90 NTA: Pine Creek police journal, 21st March 1914, F 294.
91 Schultz, pers. comm.
92 Schultz and Lewis, pp. 43, 60.
93 NAA: Department of Home and Territories, correspondence files, annual single number series, 1903–38: Victoria River "NT fight between police and natives". CRS A1, item 1926/2816, Mounted Constable Sheridan to Police Commissioner, 1926; 'VRD notes', *Northern Standard*, 16th March 1926, p. 1.
94 NTA: Lands Department to PR Allen and Co., agents for WH Butler, 21st November 1914, F28.

with Newton they were under suspicion of unlawful activities. They undoubtedly were among the East Kimberley duffers Hely Hutchinson wrote about in 1906 when he said that, 'Every cow they possess must have at least 20 calves per year, and many of the calves born with horns, and about two to three years of age at that'. Hutchinson quoted 'the managing partner of one of the largest cattle-buying firms the day he took delivery of a mob of 100 fats from a "small" man at £5 per head'. This man told Hutchinson, 'with a very bitter tone in his voice, "It is hard luck to be buying your own cattle back at £5 per head, especially when they have grown fat on your own country."'[95] The 'large cattle-buying firm' was probably CD&D which in the early 1900s was buying cattle from many stations in the region, including from Mt Stirling, Uindait and other small holdings.[96]

Billy Patterson died on 24th February 1907 and bequeathed all his property to Beasley.[97] It appears that Beasley then went into partnership with Jack Barry. In 1910 the police reported that, 'Messrs Barry and Beasley disposed of their Mount Stirling Station to Mrs Skuthorpe, of Waterloo',[98] but records in the Northern Territory Archives indicate that the block remained in Beasley's hands until 1911 when he sold it to WF and CH Buchanan of Wave Hill. On 16th December 1913 Wave Hill was sold to the Union Cold Storage Company (Vestey). Under Vestey's management the station was eventually divided to create two stations, with the Mt Stirling block becoming part of Limbunya.[99]

After the sale of Mt Stirling, Beasley went back to stock work and droving,[100] mostly in the Victoria River/East Kimberley districts. Apparently old habits died hard. In 1932 he was sacked from his position as head stockman at Moolooloo Outstation (VRD) because a number of Delamere-branded cattle were found with calves carrying the Moolooloo brand.[101]

---

95   H7H (Hely Hutchinson), 'How Cattle are Run in the East Kimberley', *The Pastoralists' Review*, February 1906, p. 1001.
96   Battye Library, Acc 2184A/1, MN485.
97   Timber Creek police letter book, 21st June 1907. Photocopy held at the Berrimah Police Station, Darwin.
98   White, pp. 24–25.
99   NTA: F 199, PP 279/1911.
100 'News and notes', *Northern Territory Times*, 10th February 1911, p. 3; 'Cattle shipment from Darwin', *Northern Territory Times*, 31st May 1912, p. 3.
101 Noel Butlin Archives (NBA), Australian National University: Bovril Australian Estates: correspondence between London and station manager 1927–32, 119/4/2, A Martin to the 'Chairman of Directors' (Lord Luke), 23rd March 1932.

Jack Barry also remained in the district for many years, working as a yard builder,[102] drover,[103] stockman,[104] station manager[105] and cattle duffer. In 1928 he stole a mob of cattle from Wave Hill and tried to take them south across the Tanami Desert, but the country was too dry and he turned them loose. Barry probably was lucky this had happened because the police were hot on his tracks, but when they found him at Hooker Creek they couldn't prove a connection between him and the cattle in the area, so he escaped arrest.[106] An oral tradition suggests that Barry could be cruel to the point of murder. According to Stan Jones – a former manager of Birrindudu and Gordon Downs who had met Jack Barry and heard stories about him – when Barry's Aboriginal wife ran away from Birrindudu to Turner Station he caught her there and 'flogged her back with the whip … on the horse back, and she died when she got back'.[107]

Jack Frayne never got into serious trouble with the law either, although the police were certainly suspicious of him, too, on one occasion declaring, 'He has not a halo'.[108] In 1908 after agreeing to sell 80 bullocks to CD&D Frayne instead sold them to Ord River, an action which MP Durack described as 'most dishonourable'.[109] He also sold cattle to the great friend of the battler, Tom Pearce.[110]

In 1911 Frayne agreed to sell Coomanderoo to Wave Hill,[111] but he must have retained ownership of his livestock and had time to muster them because

102 There is a 'Barry's yard' on the East Baines River, Gregory National Park, and nearby is a boab tree marked 'J Barry Feb 1907' (D Lewis, *The Boab Belt: A Survey of Historic Sites in the North-Central Victoria River District*, report prepared for the National Trust of Australia (NT), 1996, vol. 2, pp. 107–110).
103 'Victoria River notes', *Northern Territory Times*, 27th February 1918, p. 5 ; 'Cow Country: Editor's letterbox', *Hoofs & Horns*, June 1946, pp. 6–7.
104 Stan Jones, taped interview with the author, August 2000. Jones, who was manager of Gordon Downs from 1952 to 1964, met Barry when Barry was an old man. Jones said that Barry had once been head stockman at Birrindudu.
105 G Bolton, 'A survey of the Kimberley pastoral industry from 1885 to the present', MA thesis, University of Western Australia, 1953, p. 214; NTA: Wave Hill police journal, 27th September 23, F 292; M Terry, *Across Unknown Australia*, Herbert Jenkins, London, 1925, pp. 178–79.
106 V Hall, *Outback Policeman*, Rigby, Adelaide, 1970, pp. 181–85.
107 Jones. He was told this story by Jacky Burns, an old-timer who had worked at Birrindudu and Gordon Downs for many years, and who had known Barry in earlier decades.
108 NAA: 13th April 1908, CRS A1640, item 1906/223.
109 MP Durack, Diary 1st January 1908 to 31st December 1908, entry for 3rd July 1908, Battye Library, MN 71/3 4587A–28.
110 'Veterinary officer and inspector of stock', Mounted Constable WF Johns, 1st January 1912, cited in 'Northern Territory. Report of the Acting Administrator for the Year 1912', *Commonwealth Parliamentary Papers*, vol. 3, no. 54, 1913, p. 36.
111 ibid.

in June 1911 he was reported to be 'on his way in with all his stock, some 700 or 800 cattle' to a block on the Katherine River. In May the following year he started to bring another 500 head down the East Baines River, but this time he didn't get far – he died from fever on the headwaters of the East Baines in May 1912. Some time later his cattle were put up for auction by the administrator of his estate. Good old Honest Tom Pearce was the successful bidder and eventually mustered Frayne's cattle 'on the head of the Wickham River'.[112]

While based in the Victoria River country Wickham and his partners were never charged with any offence, nor were any specific allegations made against them. His partnership with Duggan was dissolved in August 1909[113] after which Duggan may have moved to a block immediately south of Katherine that he'd taken up in 1908.[114] Wickham soon acquired a new partner, a tall, solid man named Thomas Hanlon whose ancestry was reputedly Chinese, the name Hanlon coming from 'Han Loon'.[115] In March 1910 Hanlon tried to get the brand 'OIQ' transferred to his name, but the police were onto his game. His application was rejected on the grounds that it was 'too like other brands' – namely, the G10 of VRD and, to a lesser extent, the 055 of Ord River and the 071 of Auvergne.[116]

Jimmy Wickham, like Frayne before him, went back on his word to sell cattle to CD&D in 1908,[117] but this didn't stop them buying his cattle in subsequent years.[118] Wickham and Hanlon retained Permit 22 until July 1912 when they sold out to Wave Hill Station.[119] I suspect that Wickham, Beasley and Frayne had agreed to sell out to Wave Hill in 1911, but were given time to muster and dispose of their cattle. In 1911 Wickham and three companions took cattle down the Canning Stock Route, the second or third droving team to attempt the 1500 kilometre track. According to an old Canning drover, Ben Taylor, the drovers were Wickham, Beasley, Patterson and possibly Hanlon. On their way down the Canning, Wickham and his

112 'News and notes', *Northern Territory Times*, 30th June 1911, p. 3; 'News and notes', *Northern Territory Times*, 19th September 1912, p. 3; 'News and notes', *Northern Territory Times*, 6th February 1913, p. 3; 'Notice', *Northern Territory Times*, 13th February 1913, p. 4.
113 NTA: Timber Creek police journal, 3rd August 1909, F 302.
114 Information from files at the Office of the Placenames Committee, Darwin.
115 PA Scherer, *Sunset of an Era: The Heffernan's of Ti-Tree*, privately published, Alice Springs, 1993, p. 25.
116 (Mounted Constable?) John Needham to Sub-Inspector N Waters, Timber Creek police letter book, 14th March 1910. Photocopy held at the Berrimah Police Station, Darwin.
117 MP Durack, Diary, 3rd July 1908.
118 MP Durack to J Davis, 23rd July 1910, Battye Library, Acc 2184A/1, MN485.
119 NTA: F199, Box 1, PP 22/1910, Box 3, PP 111/1915.

companions found the murdered bodies of two drovers who had preceded them, Shoesmith and Thompson.[120]

After selling their stock, Wickham and Hanlon shifted to Pastoral Permits on the Frew River, south-east of Tennant Creek.[121] From there Wickham went on to other colourful exploits. In 1916 he lifted a mob of 600 cattle from Lake Nash and headed them back to Frew River, but was caught and spent five years in jail.[122] Later he spent years prospecting in the Tanami where some believed he found, and lost, a rich gold reef.[123] He was once reported murdered in the Tanami by bush blacks, but rose from the dead.[124] Eventually he acquired Willowra Station on the Lander River.[125]

Hanlon helped Wickham steal the Lake Nash cattle, but avoided conviction. One story has it that Wickham took the rap so that Hanlon could look after their Frew River block, but Hanlon sold the property and neglected to give Wickham's share of the money to Wickham's wife, Olive. As a result he spent years in fear of running into Wickham.[126] In the late 1920s Hanlon owned Huckitta Station, north-east of Alice Springs,[127] and in 1929 he was involved in the discovery there of a supposedly ancient Aboriginal skull.[128]

So why did Beasley, Wickham and Frayne all sell out at much the same time? Why didn't one or more of them continue on as landowners in the district for many years? There's no evidence that the government was going to resume

120 Bob Woods and Sandy Woods, pers. comm. The Woods have researched the Canning Stock Route for many years; M Terry, *Through a Land of Promise*, Herbert Jenkins Limited, London, 1927, p. 152; Hill, p. 298; another version has it that the bodies of the murdered men were found by Wickham and a man named Cole (A Lucanus, cited in C Clement and P Bridge (eds.), *Kimberley Scenes: Sagas of Australia's Last Frontier*, Hesperian Press, Perth, 1991, pp. 50–51).

121 Veterinary Officer and Inspector of Stock, Mounted Constable WF Johns, 1st January 1912.

122 'News & notes', *Northern Territory Times*, 14th December 1916, p3; 'News and notes', *Northern Territory Times*, 19th April 1917, p. 10 and p. 12; another version has it that Wickham and Hanlon only lifted about 200 cattle, but were blamed for the theft of another 400 that had been stolen by someone else (R Kimber, *Man from Arltunga: Walter Smith Australian Bushman*, Hesperian Press, Perth, 1986, endnote 12, pp. 111–12).

123 Terry, 1927, p. 154; M. Terry, *Hidden Wealth and Hiding People*, Putnam, London, 1931, pp. 167–69; Kimber, pp. 104–06.

124 NAA: Mounted Constable Dasmyth to Sergeant Stott, Alice Springs, 24th September 1923, A3/1, item 23/3646.

125 Scherer, p. 19.

126 Lester Caine, pers. comm. Caine worked with Hanlon for a time. Another version has it that Hanlon spent Wickham's share of the profit from a jointly owned Wolfram mine on a huge spree, and that when Wickham found out he accepted it as a *fait accompli* (Kimber, p. 107).

127 Scherer, p. 25.

128 T Griffiths, *Hunters and Collectors*, Cambridge University Press, Melbourne, 1996, pp. 65–66.

Walter Colley, Jimmy Wickham (centre) and Olive Wickham, early 1900s

Garling collection

their permits, or that the police placed them under severe pressure, or that Aborigines were killing all their cattle. The answer appears to be a reversal of one of the reasons that encouraged them to take up land in the first place – the price of cattle. In 1909 the price of cattle began to drop.[129] I'm not certain of the reason for this fall, but it may have been because the Queensland herds, depleted by the tick fever and drought in the period 1895–1902, had finally increased to the point where the eastern markets were well supplied.

The cattle duffers appeared in the Victoria River District, and elsewhere in the Northern Territory, because particular conditions had developed – relative peace between the whites and Aborigines, wide spaces where the chance of meeting a stockman was remote, plentiful cleanskin cattle and high cattle prices. They appeared in the district like crows to a carcass, and when cattle prices eventually dropped they 'flew' off to other vocations in other realms.

---

129 R Duncan, *The Northern Territory Pastoral Industry 1863–1910*, Melbourne University Press, 1967, p. 65.

Only Beasley, Wilson and Jack Barry remained in the region after selling out, and none of them ever married. Consequently, they didn't establish family dynasties in the Victoria River country which would remember them and the events they experienced. The only descendant of any of the Victoria River cattle duffers I ever met was a daughter of Jimmy Wickham, Patsy Garling, who lived in Darwin until her death in 2001.[130] She had photographs of her parents, but almost no knowledge of her father's station or his time in the region.

The Victoria River cattle duffers discussed here were typical outback bushmen of the time. In common with the majority of outback working people they engaged in various activities and regarded the law as a nuisance – something to be broken if circumstances required and opportunity permitted. They gave much greater loyalty to each other than they gave to the law or to law officers and were of the view that if the legitimate owners of cattle didn't brand them they deserved to lose them. The Timber Creek police highlighted this attitude when they wrote that all the workers in the district were in sympathy with the cattle duffers[131] and that few of them (the duffers) believed that 'Thou shalt not steal' applied to clean skin cattle.[132] A couple of the Victoria River duffers 'crossed the line' by cross-branding cattle, but even then they were protected from the police by their bush comrades.

Such attitudes were part of a long and honourable tradition. In 1873 Anthony Trollope wrote of stock theft in Australia that, 'It is like smuggling, or illicit distillation, or sedition, or the seduction of women. There is little or no shame attached to it among those with whom the cattle stealers live … A man may be a cattle-stealer, and yet in his way a decent fellow'.[133] Moore echoed these sentiments when he commented about Beasley and other duffers in the Ord River country in the early 1900s: 'What rogues these chaps were — all had something against them that they had done in the past but otherwise [were] very nice chaps to meet and converse with'.[134]

There were to be other 'hard-riding individualists' in the Victoria River country in the years to come and other instances of cattle theft, but never again were so many to be so active at the one time. Never again would there be a 'nest of reputed thieves' in the district, and when the last of the battlers left the country north of the Stirling the Golden Age of the cattle duffer in the Victoria River District came to an end.

---

130 'Duffer who pioneered outback', *Northern Territory News*, 24th July 2001, pp. 28–29.
131 NAA: 13th April 1908, CRS A1640, item 1906/223.
132 NAA: 15th August 1908, A1640/1 item 1906/223.
133 A Trollope, *Australia*, University of Queensland Press, Brisbane, 1967 (1873), p. 136.
134 Moore.

EPILOGUE

The people, places and events described in this book are only part of a cavalcade of wonderful stories that constitute Victoria River District history. Stories of paradise gained and paradise lost, of murder, massacre and manhunt, of wild and modest dreams, grand enterprises, successes and failures. Stories that were played out against the backdrop of great ranges and wide plains formed through a complex and ancient geological history.

When the Golden Age of cattle duffing ended in 1912, a social and economic situation was in place which remained little changed for more than 60 years. For all this time almost all the land in the district was cattle station land controlled by white men, and for most of this time the Aborigines were effectively slaves – unpaid, with few rights, and at the bottom of the station social hierarchy.[1] For whites in the region conditions were more congenial, but still hard. They, at least, were paid and had the option of leaving their situation any time that they desired.

While conflict with bush Aborigines diminished markedly once the homestead camps were established it wasn't the end of the frontier. There were still occasional, though localised, outbreaks of violence between Aborigines and whites, and most of the physical conditions of the first two decades of settlement continued for many more. There was change, but it came slowly until the 1960s. In the 1930s and 1940s Traeger two-way pedal radios were introduced. These enabled instant communications and, combined with the presence of aeroplanes based in Katherine and Darwin,[2] enabled the quick evacuation of serious medical cases. However, these radios and the two-way battery powered radios that superseded them were inefficient and couldn't always make a connection, especially during the wet season. Two-way radios remained the only means of electronic communication until the mid-1980s when telephones were installed throughout the region. Since then satellite and computer technology has linked the region directly to television and the internet – effectively, to the modern world.

Motor vehicles began appearing in the district in the 1920s and their use was firmly established by the 1930s. Trucks replaced the original packhorse

---

1   Their slave-like status was recognised by cattle station whites. During my conversations with long-time cattleman, Charlie Schultz. He actually referred to particular Aborigines as having been 'a good old slave'.
2   C Fenton, *Flying Doctor*, Georgian House, Melbourne, 1947; E Connellan, *Failure of Triumph*, Paradigm Investments, Alice Springs, 1992.

Mrs Fuller using a pedal radio at Newry Station, 1939
Millner collection

mail service in about 1939. Motor vehicles also replaced donkey teams, camel trains and pack horses in many areas, but for decades the main roads were little more than rough tracks. For months on end the country was too wet for motor travel or the roads were too badly damaged by water to be passable by them until repairs were made. On many stations there were few graded tracks until the 1950s and 1960s, and camels, donkeys, mules or horses were used to pull wagons or to carry packs into some areas until the 1960s, or later.[3] By the time I arrived in 1971 the main highway across the region had been sealed with a one-lane-wide strip of bitumen, but the Victoria River had still not been bridged and most rivers and creeks elsewhere had only culverts, low-level concrete crossings, or no improvements at all.

---

3   Stan Jones, who took over management of Gordon Downs in 1952, told me that he used
     pack camels on the station until he left in 1964.

Typical road conditions on VRD in the 1950s
Mahood collection

The open range system of cattle 'management' also remained in use until intensive fencing programs were implemented in the 1960s and 1970s. On VRD, hundreds of kilometres of fencing were erected in the 1960s,[4] but the paddocks were so large that in many instances it was still effectively open range mustering, with many beasts able to escape into rough or timbered areas. The same situation applied across the region. Wild bulls, brumbies and donkeys remained in plague proportions into the 1960s, and beyond. At times the stations employed full-time shooters, but they made little impression on the problem. For years on VRD wild bull numbers remained around 15,000 to 20,000.[5] Substantial inroads into the feral animal problem were made with the advent of the Brucellosis and Tuberculosis Eradication Program (BTEC) in the late 1970s and 1980s. Implementing this program required more intensive fencing and shooting from helicopters. This brought the numbers of the wild bulls under control during the 1980s, but not the

---

4   *The Territorian*, vol. 1, no 10, December 1967, p. 26.
5   Northern Territory Pastoral Lessees Investigation Committee Report, 1934; *Hoofs and Horns*, December 1947, p. 14; NBA: Hooker Pastoral Company Pty Ltd Records, station reports, 1959–68, 119/15, George Lewis, station report, 1960.

numbers of brumbies and donkeys. As recently as 1997 there was estimated to be 42,000 wild horses[6] and 103,000 donkeys in the district as a whole.[7] It's only with the introduction since then of the 'Judas collar' technique that the problem of feral horses and feral donkeys has been brought under control in most areas.[8]

The Golden Age of cattle duffing had passed by 1912, but there continued to be other episodes of cattle stealing over the years. In 1928 three men were jailed for stealing over 200 cattle from the VRD/Delamere boundary area and driving them across country to Dorisvale[9] and in 1953 the trial of well-known cattleman Wason Byers for stealing cattle from VRD caused a sensation both in the Territory and down South.[10] He got off in what a policeman involved said was 'a travesty of justice'.[11] Instances of alleged cattle stealing still occur and, although it's much more difficult to get away with now that there are aeroplanes, helicopters and modern communications, it's still difficult to obtain a conviction.

At the time of writing it's 128 years since the first settlers and cattle came to the Victoria. Their coming hasn't been kind to the land or to the Aborigines. A century of uncontrolled grazing by hard-hoofed animals has caused large-scale erosion and considerable damage to the ecosystems of the region. Some species of animals and plants are regionally extinct and others are rare. Although recently attempts have been made on some stations to alleviate the worst damage by fencing off riverbanks and shooting out the remaining feral donkeys, the problem is ongoing and may actually be increasing as land use in some areas is intensifying. Introduced weeds have also swept across the land. Prickly parkinsonia and rubber bush now inhabit the hills and plains, while castor oil bush and Noogoora burr choke long sections of the riverbanks. Devils claw, mesquite, neem trees and other weeds have appeared in recent years and are threatening to become major problems.[12]

6   Keith Sarfield, pers. comm. Sarfield is an invasive species management officer with the Northern Territory Parks and Wildlife Commission.
7   Darryl Hill, pers. comm. Hill has been a resident of the Victoria River District almost continuously since 1969, as station hand, station manager, soil conservation officer with the Conservation Commission of the Northern Territory, and project officer with the Victoria River District Conservation Association based in Katherine.
8   'Kimberley collars judas donkeys', *Savanna Links*, issue 9, March-April 1999.
9   'Supreme Court', *Northern Territory Times*, 20th July 1928, p. 1.
10   As well as being reported in the *Northern Territory News* (27th August 1953, 1st, 8th and 10th October 1953), the case received several pages of text and colour photographs in *AM* (Keane, K. 'Justice rides the range', 3rd November 1953, pp. 56–58).
11   John Gordon, pers. comm.
12   The scientific identification of these plants and more detailed information about them and other Victoria River weed problems, can be found in my book, *Slower than the Eye*

Vincent Lingiari and Gough Whitlam, 1975
Lewis collection

The Aborigines also suffered, first from shootings and poisonings, later from inadequate nutrition, housing and medical attention and sometimes from brutal treatment at the hands of whites. They were unpaid or poorly paid and effectively under the control of station whites until the mid-1960s. Before this time most Aborigines were denied access to the cash economy and when the wet season came their only means of travel was to walk, so the tradition of wet season walkabout continued until the late 1960s. Among the last Aborigines to go on walkabout were Old Tim Yilngayarri and his wife, Mary Rudungnali. In 1970 they set out with their dogs to walk from Daguragu to VRD. Along the way Old Tim became weak in the legs so he, Mary and their dogs camped at a bore until the following dry season, when they were found there by a bore-maintenance crew.[13]

Living and working conditions for Aborigines on most stations were extremely poor for decades after they came in from the bush. Infant mortality was extremely high and housing and sanitation ranged from

---

Can See (Tropical Savannas CRC, Darwin, 2002, pp. 41–42).
13   Tim Yilngayarri, pers. comm.

sub-standard to non-existent.[14] On Wave Hill the living conditions of the Aborigines and social relations between them and the whites had been so poor for so long that, in 1966, the local Gurindji people went on strike. Over the next six years other Victoria River Aborigines joined them and an initial demand for equal wages soon shifted to demands for the return of traditional lands.[15]

The strikes were a major turning point in the history of the district, spelling the end of the mustering and branding system that had been established in the founding years of settlement. Denied access to plentiful unpaid or low-paid Aboriginal labour the stations quickly turned to mechanisation, replacing horseback mustering with helicopter mustering,[16] and the labour-intensive bronco method of cattle branding with mechanical crushes.[17] The stations also ceased to provide rations to the station camps. In some instances they helped the Aborigines establish 'outstations', but in others they closed the camps down and forced the Aborigines to shift to the nearest town.[18]

The strikes focused attention on the plight of Aborigines nationwide, and legislation since the mid-1960s has brought equal pay, citizenship, education, health and legal services, and the passing of the *Aboriginal Land Rights Act (NT) 1976*. These legislative changes led to Victoria River Aborigines

---

14   See R Berndt and C Berndt, *End of an Era: Aboriginal Labour in the Northern Territory* (Australian Institute of Aboriginal Studies, Canberra, 1987, p. 57–83); D Rose, *Hidden Histories* (Aboriginal Studies Press, Canberra, 1991, p. pp. 149–157).

15   F Hardy, *The Unlucky Australians*, Thomas Nelson (Australia) Limited, 1972; see also Rose, pp. 225–35; L Riddett, 'The strike that became a land movement: a southern "do-gooder" reflects on Wattie Creek 1966–74', *Labour History*, no. 72, 1977, pp. 50–65; and M Hokari, 'From Wattie Creek to Wattie Creek: an oral history approach to the Gurindji walk-off', *Aboriginal History*, vol. 24, 2000, pp. 98–116; Doolan, J. 'Walk-off (and later return) of various Aboriginal groups from cattle stations: Victoria River District, Northern Territory', in R Berndt (ed.), *Aborigines and Change: Australia in the '70s*, Humanities Press Inc., New Jersey, 1977, pp. 106–13.

16   P Ogden, *Chasing Last Light: Aerial Mustering 1968–1978*, privately published, Darwin, 2000, p. 27.

17   Buck Buchester, pers. comm. Buchester lived and worked in the Victoria River country for over 50 years. In recent years the escalating cost of using helicopters and the stress they place on livestock has caused an increase in the use of horses during mustering (J Makin, *The Big Run: The Story of Victoria River Downs*, Weldon Publishing, Sydney, 1992, p. 172; *Outback*, December 1998 – January 1999, pp. 44–48).

18   For example, see 'Aborigines pondering their next move at Gordon Downs', *Canberra Times*, 31st January 1981; D Lewis, *A Shared History: Aborigines and White Australians in the Victoria River District, Northern Territory*, Timber Creek Community Government Council, Darwin, 1997, pp. 11–12.

regaining control of several cattle stations and other areas of land[19] and the breaking of a 90–year stranglehold on the land by white pastoralists. The first land title was handed over in 1973[20] and the Gurindji regained title to some of their land in 1975,[21] but it probably took at least another decade for the old whitefella mindset to begin to change. Once Aboriginal people became substantial landholders they had to be taken seriously by their white neighbours and government agencies, and they are now being incorporated into regional programs for the control of bushfires, weeds, stock diseases and feral animals.

The introduction of Aboriginal land rights wasn't the only change to land tenure in the region. First, in the 1980s portions of a number of cattle stations were bought or resumed by the Northern Territory Government to create the Keep River and Gregory National Parks. Second, in the late 1980s and mid-1990s the Federal Government purchased two areas of land for military purposes. The first was part of Delamere Station, designated for use as a bombing range.[22] The second was Bradshaw's Run, bought in 1995 for use as an army field-training area.[23]

Like other groups throughout the region, the Wardaman are now but a shadow of their former power. After they came in to Delamere, Willeroo and Manbuloo they became well-regarded station workers, but decades of sub-standard living and working conditions took their toll. However, the old warrior spirit remained strong. In 1944 on Delamere Station a dispute arose between head stockman, Jack Connors, and the Wardaman men. Several Aborigines confronted Connors with spears and boomerangs, and attempted redress of a perceived wrong, but the affair ended in tragedy when Connors

---

19 Aboriginal Freehold Title now exists on the Amanbidji (Kildurk), Mistake Creek, Fitzroy and Innesvale station leases, and a large section of Wave Hill Station. Other successful claims have been made over various areas of former Crown Land, including the Timber Creek Town Common, the Top Springs Travelling Stock Reserve, and long sections of stock routes.

20 This was Kildurk Station, purchased for the Aboriginal traditional owners by the Aboriginal Land Fund Commission, a Commonwealth Government-funded authority. It has since been renamed Amanbidji, and converted to Aboriginal Freehold Title through a successful land claim under the *Aboriginal Land Rights Act (NT) 1976* (B Higgins, *Historical Submission: Amanbidji Land Claim*, Northern Land Council, Darwin, August 1976; M Durack, *Sons in the Saddle*, Corgi Books, Sydney, 1985, p. 511).

21 I was privileged to have been present in 1975 to witness the hand-over of part of Wave Hill Station to the Gurindji when the Prime Minister, Gough Whitlam, poured a handful of sand into Vincent Lingiari's hand.

22 Part of Delamere Pastoral Lease No. 567 was purchased in 1989 (pers. comm., Vern O'Brien).

23 '$5m defence force cattle station sale', *NT News*, 25th December 1995, p. 5.

Confrontation between Land Council personnel (left) and
VRD employee at a locked gate on the Pigeon Hole road, 1989

Lewis collection

shot dead a Wardaman man named Tiger.[24] In common with Aboriginal
communities throughout Australia, in recent years the collective fortune of
the Wardaman has undergone a change for the better, but many problems
remain.

---

24 Northern Territory Archives (NTA): Commissioner of Police, correspondence files
    1935–1959, Constable Gordon Stott to Sergeant Smyth, 16th December 1944, F77,
    file 7/45.

So what, if anything, remains of the old frontier? Very little, it would seem. Even the original wild and ill-bred shorthorn cattle have been replaced with Brahman and Brahman-cross cattle. Technologies, cattle management and communications in the region have reached modern standards, but for some in a situation where frontier conditions were dominant until quite recently, the mentality of the frontier remains. One aspect of this is seen in the social relations between Aborigines and whites. While for many people these social relations have changed significantly since the tense days of the Aboriginal strikes, there are some who still hold to old attitudes, prejudices, fears and ignorance. The memories and experience of older residents extend back to the time before the Aboriginal strikes, when social relations between the Aborigines and the whites were still those of master and servant. Some have changed with the times, but others have not – they've passed their old attitudes on to their children and sometimes to newcomers to the district.

A sad demonstration of the old-time mindset of both whites and blacks occurred in September 1988 during fieldwork carried out for the Bilinara Land Claim on VRD. To proceed with this claim it was necessary to produce a map of Aboriginal and historic sites in and around the claim area. The land under claim was part of a stock route which passed through Victoria River Downs so access to the land was through the station, but the station owner was hostile towards land claims and Aborigines. In an attempt to thwart the land claim the owner had declared that Land Council employees were not to be allowed to access the claim area. Land Council lawyers were of the view that consultants were not Land Council employees, so were not subject to the ban imposed by the station owner. A consultant was hired and in company with senior Aboriginal traditional owner, Anzac Munnganyi, the mapping went ahead.

When only one more day was needed to complete the work, the presence of the consultant on the claim area became known to the staff of VRD. When Anzac realised the consultant had been 'sprung' and a confrontation with the station whites could be expected, he visibly panicked and couldn't get the consultant off the station quickly enough. This was surely a legacy of the 'old days' of complete domination by white people. Within hours of the consultant leaving Pigeon Hole the gates on every access track were padlocked.

The following September a group of Aborigines, their lawyers and other Northern Land Council employees set out to drive to Pigeon Hole Outstation on VRD. The lawyers advised the station manager of their intention, whereupon he contacted the station owner and received instructions to again lock the gates on all the access roads to Pigeon Hole. Several different access routes were tried, without success, so eventually several of the Land Council party climbed over a locked gate and attempted to walk the last ten kilometres to the site. On the way a station helicopter hovered overhead, engulfing the group in dust and gravel, and the station manager arrived to try and prevent them from continuing. This didn't stop them, but before they reached Pigeon Hole they were served with a court order denying them access.[25] The dispute was taken to court where, after hearing the evidence of an Aboriginal woman, the judge remarked that:

> The story this woman tells is a story of their being imprisoned there; the men are only allowed out to work, they can't get visitors and they can't visit other people. I find that extraordinary that people could behave so savagely in 1989 against fellow human beings. If it's true — it's an extraordinary thing.[26]

He ordered the gates unlocked on the same day as, by coincidence, a corporate takeover saw ownership of the station change hands. The new owner had a different attitude and the land claim proceeded unhindered.

A characteristic of frontier conditions is that both the population and the law are spread very thin. This is still the case in the Victoria River country and there have been some notable events in recent times that have taken advantage of this situation. In 1986 there was a court case in which some people were seen and photographed within their neighbours' lease, throwing and branding cleanskin cattle. Their defence was that, as there was no boundary fence between the two leases, cleanskin cattle could wander back and forth at will and it was therefore a moot point which side they were on when caught and branded. The judge agreed and the case was dismissed.

A more recent example concerns crocodile poaching. In 1994 I bushwalked through the remote Fitzmaurice River valley and saw very few saltwater crocodiles, yet the Northern Territory Conservation Commission rangers at Timber Creek later told me that the previous year crocodile numbers had been so high that, if you'd been stupid enough, 'you could have walked from back to back on them' in the waterholes. The rangers were of the opinion that someone must have gone into the valley during the previous wet season and shot the crocodiles for their skins.

---

25   *Land Rights News*, July 1989, p. 13.
26   Transcript of proceedings, Bilinara (*Coolibah–Wave Hill Stock Route*) Land Claim, 1989 pp. 11–13.

Another aspect of the frontier relates to the great size of the stations. Again, the memories of older residents extend back to a time when the stations were huge and unfenced and there was a corresponding social space in which individual personalities could reach their full potential. Although resumptions in the 1930s, 1950s and 1960s reduced the original size of some stations, many are still vast. For example, VRD is now a 'mere' 11,885 square kilometres, Bradshaw is 8710, Cattle Creek, formerly part of Wave Hill, is 7085 and many others are well over 4000 square kilometres.[27] These wide expanses still provide a social space within which human personalities are often more expansive and where there's still room for laws and social conventions to be 'bent'.

The Victoria River country has seen many changes since the coming of the white settlers. Yet in spite of the damage to the land and ecology, in spite of the spearings and massacres and brutalities, and the failed dreams of station owners and battlers alike, the aura of the land remains. The great ranges are still majestic, Jasper Gorge remains as beautiful and forbidding as ever and the great Mitchell grass downs are still a 'vision splendid' in the late afternoon sun. The mid-dry is still a delight, the lightning storms of the build-up are as spectacular and frightening as ever and the monsoons still bring tremendous floods as of old.

For 100 years the stories of the Victoria River country have been lost or only vaguely known to outsiders, and ultimately most were lost to local white station people as well. Aborigines retain the greatest knowledge of past events, but even among them the stories are slowly being forgotten. The aim of this book has been to begin the process of 'resurrecting' the history of the region and transforming various 'wild imaginings' into 'wild history'. The reader can judge whether this aim has been successful. Much more remains to be told, but that's a task for the future.

---

27 *Pastoral and General Tenure Map*, produced by the Mapping Branch, Northern Territory Department of Lands and Housing, Darwin, 1990.

BIBLIOGRAPHY

Books and Articles

Anon, *The Ringer's Book of Outback Terms & Phrases*, The Australian Stockman's Hall of Fame and Outback Heritage Centre, Longreach, 1988.

Arndt, W. 'The Dreaming of Kunukban', *Oceania*, vol. 35 (4), 1965.

Arthur, J. *Aboriginal English: A Cultural Study*, Oxford University Press, Melbourne, 1996.

Australian National Dictionary, Oxford University Press, Melbourne, 1988.

Baines, T. 'Additional Notes on the North Australian Expedition under Mr. A. C. Gregory'. *Proceedings of the Royal Geographical Society of London*, vol. 2, session 1857–8, 1858, pp. 3–16.

Baines, T. 'Journal of the detachment of the North Australian Expedition left by Mr Gregory at the Main Camp Victoria River 1856', Mitchell Library C408.

Baker, R. 'Coming in? The Yanyuwa as a case study in the Geography of Contact History', *Aboriginal History*, 1990, vol. 14, pt.1.

Basedow, H. 'Physical Geography and Geology of the Victoria River District, Northern Territory of Australia', *Proceedings of the Royal Geographical Society of Australasia, South Australian Branch*, vol. 16.

Bauer, F. *Historical geography of white settlement in part of the Northern Territory, part 2. The Katherine-Darwin region*, CSIRO Division of Land Research & Regional Survey, Divisional Report No. 64/1, Canberra, 1964.

Bauman, T. and Stead, J. *Fitzroy (Nungali/Ngaliwurru) Land Claim*, Northern Land Council, Darwin, 1992.

Beckett, B. *Lipstick, Swag and Sweatrag. Memoirs of a Patrol Padre's Wife'*, Central Queensland University Press, Rockhampton, 1998.

Berndt, R. (ed), *Aborigines and change: Australia in the '70s*, Humanities Press Inc., New Jersey, 1977.

Berndt, R. and Berndt, C. *End of an Era: Aboriginal Labour in the Northern Territory*, Australian Institute of Aboriginal Studies, Canberra, 1987.

Biltris, L. 'The Passing of the Pioneers', *Walkabout*, May 1st 1951: 44.

Birdsell, J. 'Some Environmental and Cultural Factors influencing the Structuring of Australian Aboriginal Populations.' *American Naturalist*, vol. 87, 1953.

Bolton, G. *Alexander Forrest – His Life and Times*, Melbourne University Press in association with the University of Western Australia Press, Perth, 1958.

Bolton, G. *A Thousand Miles Away: A History of North Queensland to 1920*, The Jacaranda Press in association with the Australian National University, Brisbane, 1963.

Braddon, R. *Thomas Baines and the North Australian Expedition*, Collins, Sydney, in association with the Royal Geographical Society, London, 1986.

Bradshaw, J. 'The Future of Northern Australia', *Transactions of the Royal Geographical Society of Australasia, Victorian Branch*, vol. 9, 1891.

Bradshaw, J. 'The Northern Territory', *Victorian Geographical Journal*, vol. 25, 1907.

Bradshaw, J. 'Notes on a recent trip to the Prince Regent's River', *Transactions of the Royal Geographical Society of South Australia*, vol. 9, pt 2, 1892.

Briggs, A. 'Joe Cooper', in D Carment, R Maynard and A Powell (eds.), *Northern Territory Dictionary of Biography: Volume 1 to 1945*. Northern Territory University Press, Darwin, 1990.

Broughton, G. *Turn Again Home,* The Jacaranda Press, Sydney, 1965.

Buchanan, B. *In the Tracks of Old Bluey: The Life Story of Nat Buchanan,* Central Queensland University Press, Rockhampton, 1997.

Buchanan, G. *Packhorse and Waterhole: With the first Overlanders to the Kimberleys,* Angus and Robertson, Sydney, 1934.

Butlin, N. *Our Original Aggression: Aboriginal populations of Southeastern Australia 1788– 1850.* George Allen & Unwin, Sydney, 1983.

Butlin, N. 'Macassans and Aboriginal Smallpox: the "1789" and "1829" epidemics.' *Historical Studies,* vol. 21, 1985.

Byrne, G. *Tom & Jack: A Frontier Story,* Fremantle Arts Centre Press, Fremantle, 2003.

Caley, N. *What Bird is That?: A Guide to the Birds of Australia.* Angus and Robertson, Sydney, third edition 1959 (originally published 1931).

Campbell, J. *Invisible Invaders: smallpox and other diseases in Aboriginal Australia, 1780– 1889.* Melbourne University Press, Melbourne, 2002.

Chimmo, W. 'Account of the Search for the North-Australian Exploring Expedition under Mr. A.C. Gregory'. *Proceedings of the Royal Geographical Society of London,* vol. 1, sessions 1855–6 and 1856–7.

Clement, C. *Pre-settlement Intrusion into the East Kimberley,* East Kimberley Working paper No. 24, Centre for Resource and Environmental Studies, Australian National University, Canberra, 1988.

Clement, C. and Bridge, P. (eds.) *Kimberley Scenes: Sagas of Australia's Last Frontier.* Hesperian Press, Perth, 1991.

Clinch, M. 'Paddy Cahill', in D Carment, R Maynard and A Powell (eds), *Northern Territory Dictionary of Biography: Volume 1 to 1945,* Northern Territory University, Darwin, 1990.

Clyne, R. *Colonial Blue: A History of the South Australian Police Force,* Wakefield Press, Netley, 1987.

Connellan, E. *Failure of Triumph,* Paradigm Investments, Alice Springs, 1992.

Costello, M. *Life of John Costello,* Hesperian Press, Perth, 2002 (originally published by Dymocks, Sydney, 1930).

Crauford [sic], L. cited by Edward Stirling in 'Victoria River Downs station, Northern Territory, South Australia', *Journal of the Royal Anthropological Institute of Great Britain and Ireland,* vol. 24, 1895, p. 180.

Crawford, I. *The Art of the Wandjina,* Oxford University Press, Melbourne, 1968.

Cumston, J. *Augustus Gregory and the Inland Sea,* Roebuck Society No. 9, Canberra, 1972.

Dahl, K. *In Savage Australia: an account of a hunting and collecting expedition to Arnhem Land and Dampier Land,* Phillip Allan & Co., Ltd. London, 1926.

Davidson, D. S. 'Archaeological Problems Of Northern Australia'. *Journal of the Royal Anthropological Institute,* vol. 65, 1935.

Davies, H. 'Hunt, Atlee Arthur (1864–1935)', *Australian Dictionary of Biography,* vol. 9, Melbourne University Press, 1983.

Debnam, L. *Men of the Northern Territory Police 1870–1914: Who They Were and Where They Were,* Elizabeth, South Australia, 1990.

De La Rue, K. *Evolution of Darwin, 1869–1911: A history of the Northern Territory's capital city during the years of South Australian administration.* Charles Darwin University Press, Darwin, 2004.

Donaldson, M. and Elliot, I. (eds), *Do Not Yield to Despair: Frank Hugh Hann's Exploration Diaries in the Arid Interior of Australia 1895–1908,* Hesperian Press, Perth, 1988.

Donovan, P.F. *A Land Full of Possibilities: A History of South Australia's Northern Territory,* University of Queensland Press, Brisbane, 1981.

Donovan, R. *The Northern Territory Pastoral Industry 1863–1910*, Melbourne University Press, 1967.

Doolan, J. 'Walk-off (and later return) of various Aboriginal groups from cattle stations: Victoria River district, Northern Territory', in R Berndt (ed.), *Aborigines and Change: Australia in the '70s*, Humanities Press Inc., New Jersey, 1977.

Duncan, R. *The Northern Territory Pastoral Industry 1863–1910*, Melbourne University Press, Melbourne, 1967.

Durack, M. *Sons in the Saddle*, Corgi Books, Sydney, 1985.

Durack, M. *Kings in Grass Castles*, Corgi, Sydney, 1986.

Durack, P.M. 'Pioneering in the East Kimberleys, *The Western Australian Historical Society, Journal and Proceedings*, vol. 2, pt. 14, 1933.

Elder, P. 'Charles Dashwood', in D Carment, R Maynard and A Powell (eds.), *Northern Territory Dictionary of Biography: Volume 1 to 1945*, Northern Territory University Press, Darwin, 1990.

Elsey, J.R. 'Report on the North Australian Expedition', *Journal of the Geographical Society of London*, 1858, vol. 28.

Favelle, H. 'Ralph Millner', in D Carment, R Maynard and A Powell (eds.), *Northern Territory Dictionary of Biography: Volume 1 to 1945*, Northern Territory University Press, Darwin, 1990.

Fenton, C. *Flying Doctor*. Georgian House, Melbourne, 1947.

Forrest, A. *Journal of Exploration from DeGrey to Port Darwin*. Government Printer, Perth, 1880.

Forrest, P. *Springvale's Story and Early Years at the Katherine*, Murranji Press, Darwin, 1985.

Fitzgerald, L. *Java La Grande: The Portuguese Discovery of Australia*. The Publishers Pty. Ltd., Hobart, 1984.

Gee, L.C.E. '*Journal and Detailed Description of Country Traversed*', Explorations Made by the Government Geologist and Staff during 1905'. Government Printer, Adelaide, 1906.

Gibbney, H., entry on J.A. Macartney in *Australian Dictionary of Biography*, vol. 5, 1966.

Giles, A. *Exploring in the 'Seventies and the Construction of the Overland Telegraph Line*, Friends of the State Library of South Australia, Adelaide, 1995 (originally published by W.K. Thomas & Co. Adelaide, 1926).

Giles, A. 'Early Drovers in the Northern Territory.– Leaves from the Diary of Alfred Giles', *The Pastoralists' Review*, 15 March 1906.

Good, R. *Ketching the Kenniffs: the origins and exploits of the Kenniff brothers – Patrick and James*, Booringah Shire Council & Booringah Action Group, Mitchell Queensland, 1996.

Gregory, A.C. 'North Australian Expedition', *Journal of the Legislative Council of New South Wales, Session 1856–7'*, vol. 1, 1857.

Gregory, A.C. 'Journal of the North Australian Exploring Expedition, under the command of *Augustus C. Gregory*, Esq. (Gold Medallist R.G.S. with report by *Mr. Elsey* on the Health of the Party.' *Journal of the Royal Geographical Society*, vol. 28, 1858.

Gregory, A.C. 'Report of the Progress of the North Australian Expedition'. *Proceedings of the Royal Geographical Society of London*, vol. 1, sessions 1855–6, 1857.

Gregory, A.C. and Gregory, F.T. *Journals of Australian Explorations*, Facsimile edition, Hesperian Press, Perth, 1981 (first published 1884).

Griffiths, T. *Hunters and Collectors*, Cambridge University Press, Melbourne, 1996.

Griffiths, T. 'How many trees make a forest?' *Australian Journal of Botany*, vol. 50, 2002.

Griffiths, T. and Robin, L. (eds), *Ecology and Empire: Environmental History of Settler Societies*, Keele University Press, Edinburgh, 1997.

Gunn, J. *'We of the Never-Never'*, Hutchinson, London, 1908.

Hall, V. *Outback Policeman*, Rigby, Adelaide, 1970.

Hardy, F. *The Unlucky Australians*, Thomas Nelson (Australia) Limited, 1972.

Harris, J. 'Contact Languages at the Northern Territory British Military Settlements 1824–1849', *Aboriginal History*, vol. 9, 1985, pt 2.

Hicks, A. 'The Kimberleys Explored: Forrest Expedition of 1879'. *Journal and Proceedings of the Western Australian Historical Society*, New Series, vol. 1, 1938.

Hilgendorf, M. *Northern Territory Days*, Historical Society of the Northern Territory, Darwin, 1994.

Hill, E. *The Territory*, Angus and Robertson, Sydney, 1951.

Hokari, M. 'From Wattie Creek to Wattie Creek: An Oral History Approach to the Gurindji Walk-Off', *Aboriginal History*, vol. 24, 2000.

Hordern, H. *King of the Australian Coast: The Work of Phillip Parker King in the Mermaid and Bathurst 1817–1822*, The Miegunyah Press (Melbourne University Press), Melbourne, 1997.

Hordern, M. 'John Lort Stokes', in D Carment, R Maynard and A Powell (eds), *The Northern Territory Dictionary of Biography: Volume 1 to 1945*, Northern Territory University Press, Darwin, 1990.

Jones, R. 'The neolithic, palaeolithic and the hunting gardeners: man and land in the antipodes', in R Suggate and M Cresswell (eds), *Quaternary Studies*, The Royal Society of New Zealand, 1975.

Jones, T. *Pegging the Territory: A history of mining in the Northern Territory of Australia, 1873–1946*, Northern Territory Government Printer, Darwin, 1987.

Keane, K. 'Justice rides the range', *A.M.*, 3 November, 1953.

Kelly, C. archivist at the Royal Geographical Society, letter to NB Nairn, general editor of the Australian Dictionary of Biography, 28 January 1982. File on Joseph Bradshaw at the Australian Dictionary of Biography Centre, Australian National University, Canberra.

Kelly, K. *Hard Country Hard Men: In the Footsteps of Gregory*, Hale and Iremonger, Sydney, 2000.

Kimber, R. *Man from Arltunga: Walter Smith Australian Bushman*, Hesperian Press, Perth, 1986.

Kimber, R. 'Smallpox in Central Australia: Evidence for Epidemics and Postulations about the Impact', *Australian Archaeology*, vol. 27, 1988.

Kimber, R. 'WH Willshire', in D Carment, R Maynard, and A Powell (eds), *Northern Territory Dictionary of Biography: Volume 1 to 1945*, Northern Territory University Press, Darwin, 1990.

Kintore, Earl 'Despatch from the Earl of Kintore, GCMG, governor of South Australia, reporting upon his visit to Port Darwin, and upon the affairs of the Northern Territory of South Australia'. Presented to both Houses of Parliament by Command of Her Majesty, London, July 1891.

Kyle-Little, S. ('Culkah'). 'In North Australia', pt. 1, *The Pastoral Review*, 15th September 1928.

Lee, D.H.K. 'Variability in Human Response to Arid Environments', in W.G. McGinnies and B.J. Goodman (eds), *Arid Lands in Perspective*, University of Arizona Press, Tuscon. 1969.

Leichhardt, L. *Journal of an Overland Expedition from Moreton Bay to Port Essington*, T. & W. Boone, London, 1847.

Lewis, D. *The Rock Paintings of Arnhem Land, Australia: Social, Ecological and Material Culture Change in the Post-Glacial Period*. British Archaeological Reports International Series 415, Oxford, 1988.

Lewis, D. *A Shared History: Aborigines and White Australians in the Victoria River District, Northern Territory*. Timber Creek Community Government Council, Darwin, 1997.

Lewis, D. (ed), *Patrolling the 'Big Up': The Adventures of Mounted Constable Johns in the Top End of the Northern Territory, 1910–15*. Historical Society of the Northern Territory, Darwin, 1998.

Lewis, D. *A Brief History of Racing in the Victoria River District*, Timber Creek Race Club Incorporated, NT, 1995.

Lewis, D. *Slower that the Eye Can See: Environmental change in northern Australia's cattle lands*, Tropical Savannas CRC, Darwin, 2002.

Lewis, D. 'Invaders of a peaceful country': Aborigines and explorers on the lower Victoria River, Northern Territory, *Aboriginal History*, vol. 29: 2005.

Lewis, D. 'The Fate of Leichhardt', *Historical Records of Australian Science*, vol. 17 (1), 2006.

Lewis, D. *The Murranji Track: Ghost road of the Drovers*, Central Queensland University Press, Rockhampton, 2007.

Lewis, D. *Roping in the History of Broncoing*, Central Queensland University Press, Rockhampton, 2007.

Lewis, D. 'Samuel Croker', in D Carment and H Wilson, (eds.), *Northern Territory Dictionary of Biography: Volume 3*, Northern Territory University Press, Darwin, 1996.

Lewis, D. and Rose, D. *The Shape of the Dreaming: The Cultural Significance of Victoria River Rock Art*, Aboriginal Studies Press, Canberra, 1988.

Lewis, D. and Simmons, L. *Kajirri, the Bush Missus*, Central Queensland University Press, Rockhampton, 2005.

Lewis, J.C. 'Veterinary and Stock Report', *NT Bulletin No. 8*, South Australian Government Printer, 1913.

Linklater, W. and Tapp, L. *Gather No Moss*, Hesperian Press, Perth, 1997 (first published by Macmillan of Australia, Sydney, 1968).

Long, J. 'Leaving the Desert: Actors and Sufferers in the Aboriginal Exodus from the Western Desert', *Aboriginal History*, 1989, vol. 13, pt. 1.

Macknight, C. *The Voyage to Marege: Macassan Trepangers in Northern Australia*, Melbourne University Press, 1976,

McCarthy, P. *The Man who was Starlight*, Allen & Unwin, Sydney, 1987.

McConvell, P. and Palmer, A. *Yingawunarri Mudburra Land Claim*, Northern Land Council, Darwin, 1979.

McCool, C. et al, *Feral Donkeys in the Northern Territory*, Technical Bulletin no. 81/39, Conservation Commission of the Northern Territory, Darwin, 1981.

McGrath, A. *'Born in the Cattle': Aborigines in Cattle Country*, Allen & Unwin, Sydney, 1987.

McLennan, N. *Ord River Station, W.A. 1895–1896, Yesterday and Today*, privately published in Stawell, Victoria 1965.

Magoffin, D. *From Ringer to Radio*, privately published, Brisbane, nd.

Makin, J. *The Big Run: The Story of Victoria River Downs Station*, Weldon Publishing, 1992 (first published by Rigby, 1970).

Martin, F. *Three Families Outback in Australia's Tropic North*, privately published, Geralton, 1980.

Mason, E. *An Untamed Territory: The Northern Territory of Australia*, Macmillan and Co. Limited, London, 1915.

Mathews, R.H. 'Ethnological Notes on the Aboriginal Tribes of the Northern Territory'. *Queensland Geographical Journal*, vol. 16, 1901.

Maynard, R. 'Joseph Bradshaw', in D Carment, R Maynard and A Powell (eds), *Northern Territory Dictionary of Biography: Volume 1 to 1945*, Northern Territory University Press, Darwin, 1990.

Maze, W.H. 'Settlement in the East Kimberleys, Western Australia', *The Australian Geographer*, vol. 5, no. 1, 1945.

Merlan F. *A Grammar of Wardaman: A Language of the Northern Territory of Australia*, Mouton de Gruyter, New York, 1994.

Milton, S. 'The Transvaal beef frontier: environments, markets and the ideology of development, 1902–1942', in T Griffiths and L Robin (eds), *Ecology and Empire: Environmental History of Settler Societies*, Keele University Press, Edinburgh, 1997.

Moffatt, L. *Luck and Tragedy in the New Country*, privately published, Melbourne, 1990.

Moore, WD. 'Bush ingenuity: on a Kimberley cattle station in the early days', *North Australian Monthly*, December 1959.

Morey, E. 'The Donkey Man', *Northern Territory Newsletter*, February issue, 1977.

Morey, E. 'Timber Creek Patrols', pt. 1, *Northern Territory Newsletter*, Darwin, July issue, 1977.

Morey, E. 'Timber Creek Patrols', pt. 2 *Northern Territory Newsletter*, Darwin, August issue, 1977.

Mulvaney, DJ. '"The chain of connection": the material evidence', in N Peterson (ed.), *Tribes And Boundaries In Australia*, Social Anthropology Series no. 10, Australian Institute of Aboriginal Studies, Canberra, 1976.

Mulvaney, D.J. *Encounters in Place*, chapter titled 'Central Australia: Land of the Dawning', University of Queensland Press, Brisbane, 1989.

Mulvaney, D.J. *Paddy Cahill of Oenpelli*, Aboriginal Studies Press, Canberra, 2004.

Mulvaney, D.J. and Kamminga, J. *Prehistory of Australia*, Allen & Unwin, Sydney, 1999.

Mulvaney, D.J. and Peter White, J. (eds.), *Australians to 1788*, Fairfax, Syme & Weldon Associates, Sydney, 1987.

Nesdale, I. (ed). Kelsey, D. *The Shackle: A Story of the Far North Australian Bush*, Lynton Publications, Adelaide, 1975.

Ogden, P. *Chasing Last Light: Aerial Mustering 1968–1978*, privately published, Darwin, 2000.

Pearson, SE. 'The Passing of Mudburra', *Frank Clune's Adventure Magazine*, 1948.

Pedersen, H. and B. Woorunmurra, *Jandamarra and the Bunuba Resistance*, Magabala Books Aboriginal Corporation, Broome, 1995.

Peterson, N. (ed.) *Tribes and Boundaries in Australia*, Social Anthropology Series No. 10, Australian Institute Of Aboriginal Studies, Canberra, 1976.

Pollard, J. *The Horse Tamer: The Story of Lance Skuthorpe*, Pollard Publishing Company, Woolstoncraft (N.S.W).

Pyne, S. *Burning Bush*, University of Washington Press, Seattle, 1991.

Radford, E. and Radford, M.A. *Encyclopaedia of Superstitions*, Hutchinson & Co., London, 1961.

Read, P. and Engineer Jack Japaljarri, 'The Price of Tobacco: The Journey of the Warlmala to Wave Hill, 1928', *Aboriginal History*, vol. 2, pt. 2, 1978.

Read, P. and Read, J. *Long Time, Olden Time*, Institute for Aboriginal Development Publications, Alice Springs, 1991.

Reece, B. 'George Windsor Earl', in D Carment, R Maynard and A Powell (eds.), *Northern Territory Dictionary of Biography: Volume 1 to 1945*. Northern Territory University Press, Darwin, 1990.

Reece, B. 'Boyle Travers Finniss', in D Carment, R Maynard and A Powell (eds), *Northern Territory Dictionary of Biography: Volume 1 to 1945*, Northern Territory University Press, Darwin, 1990.

Rees, W. *Walkabout*, June issue, 1950 p. 8.

Reynolds, H. 'Before the Instant of Contact: Some Evidence from Nineteenth-Century Queensland, *Aboriginal History*, vol. 2, 1978.

Reynolds, H. *The Other Side of the Frontier*, History Department, James Cook University, Townsville, 1981.

Reynolds, R. 'Recalling the Past. The Brothers Farquharson', *The Pastoral Review*, 19th April 1965.

Rich, J. 'Emanuel Victor Brown', in D Carment, R Maynard, and A Powell (eds), *Northern Territory Dictionary of Biography: Volume 1 to 1945*, Northern Territory University Press, Darwin, 1990.

Richards, M. 'Aborigines in the Victoria River Region: 1883–1928'. *Australian Institute of Aboriginal Studies Newsletter*, New Series 17, 1980.

Richardson, A. *The Story of a Remarkable Ride*, Dunlop Pneumatic Tyre Company of Australasia, Ltd., Perth, 1900.

Richardson, W. *Was Australia Charted Before 1606: The Java la Grande inscriptions*. National Library of Australia, Canberra, 2006,

Riddett, L. 'The Strike that Became a Land Movement: A Southern "Do-Gooder" Reflects on Wattie Creek 1966–74', *Labour History*, No. 72, 1977.

Riddett, L. *Kin, Kine and Country: The Victoria River District of the Northern Territory 1911–1966*, Australian National University North Australia Research Unit Monograph, Darwin 1990.

Roberts, S. *History of Australian Land Settlement (1788–1920)*, Macmillan and Co. Ltd., Melbourne, 1924.

Roberts, T. *Frontier Justice: A History of the Gulf Country to 1900*. University of Queensland Press, Brisbane, 2005.

Rolls, E. *A Million Wild Acres,* Penguin Books Australia, Melbourne, 1984.

Ronan, T. *Deep of the Sky: An Essay in Ancestor Worship*, Cassell & Co. Ltd., Melbourne, 1962.

Rose, AL *et al*, 'Field and Experimental Investigation of "Walkabout" disease of horses (Kimberley horse disease) in northern Australia: Crotallaria Poisoning in horses. Part 1', *The Australian Veterinary Journal*, February 1957, pp. 25–33.

Rose, AL *et al*, 'Field and Experimental Investigation of "Walkabout" disease of horses (Kimberley horse disease) in northern Australia: Crotallaria Poisoning in horses. Part 2', *Australian Veterinary Journal*, March 1957, pp. 49–62.

Rose, D. *Hidden Histories: Black Stories from Victoria River Downs, Humbert River and Wave Hill Stations*, Aboriginal Studies Press, Canberra, 1991.

Rose, D. *Dingo Makes Us Human*, Cambridge University Press, Melbourne, 1992.

Rose, D. and Lewis, D. *Kidman Springs/Jasper Gorge Land Claim*, Northern Land Council, Darwin, 1986.

Rose, D. and Lewis, D. 'A Pinch and a Bridge'. *Public History*, vol. 1, no. 1, 1994.

Scherer, P.A. *Sunset of an Era: The Heffernan's of Ti-Tree*, Privately published, Alice Springs, 1993.

Schultz, C. and Lewis, D. *Beyond the Big Run: Station Life in Australia's Last Frontier*. University of Queensland Press, Brisbane, 1995.

Searcy, A. *In Northern Seas*, W.K. Thomas, Adelaide, 1905.

Searcy, A. *In Australian Tropics*, George Robinson & Co., London, 1909.

Searcy, A. *By Flood and Field*, Keagan Paul, Trench and Trubner, London, 1912.

Sergison, A.W. *The Northern Territory and its pastoral capabilities, with notes, extracts, and map*, Sands and McDougall, Printers, Melbourne, 1878.

Sharp, A. *The Voyage of Abel Janzoon Tasman*, Oxford at the Clarendon Press, London, 1968.

South, Mounted Constable W to Inspector B Besley, in R Clyne, *Colonial Blue: A History of the South Australian Police Force*, Wakefield Press, Netley, 1987.

Spillett, P. *Forsaken Settlement: An illustrated history of the settlement of Victoria, Port Essington north Australia 1838–1849*. Lansdowne Press, Sydney, 1972.

Stanner, W.E.H. *White Man Got No Dreaming*, Australian National University Press, Canberra, 1979.

Steele, W. and Steele, C. *To the Great Gulf: The Surveys and Explorations of L.A. Wells*, Lynton Publications, Adelaide, 1978.

Stokes, J.L. *Discoveries in Australia...During the Voyage of H.M.S. Beagle in the years 1837–43*, T. and W. Boone, London, vol. 2, 1846.

Suggate, R. and M. Cresswell, M. (eds), *Quaternary Studies*, The Royal Society of New Zealand, 1975.

Sullivan, P. *All free man now: culture, community and politics in the Kimberley region, north-western Australia*, Aboriginal Studies Press, Canberra, 1996.

Sullivan, J. and Shaw, B. *Banggaiyerri: The Story of Jack Sullivan as told to Bruce Shaw*, Australian Institute of Aboriginal Studies Press, Canberra, 1983.

Summerhays, R.S. *Encyclopaedia for Horsemen*, Frederick Warne, London, 1975.

Sutton, P., Coultheart, L. and McGrath, A. *The Murranji Land Claim*, Northern Land Council, Darwin, 1983.

Swan, D., cited in C Clement and P Bridge (eds), *Kimberley Scenes: Sagas of Australia's Last Frontier*, Hesperian Press, Perth, 1991.

Sweet, I., et al, *The Geology of the Northern Victoria River Region, Northern Territory*, Department of Minerals and Energy, Bureau of Mineral Resources, Geology and Geophysics, Report no. 166, Australian Government Publishing Service, Canberra, 1974.

Sweet, I., et al, *The Geology of the Southern Victoria River Region, Northern Territory*, Department of Minerals and Energy, Bureau of Mineral Resources, Geology and Geophysics, Report no. 167, Australian Government Publishing Service, Canberra, 1974.

Terry, M. *Across Unknown Australia*, Herbert Jenkins, London, 1925.

Terry, M. *Through a Land of Promise*, Herbert Jenkins Limited, London, 1927.

Terry, M. *Hidden Wealth and Hiding People*, Putnam, London, 1931.

Tindale, N. *Aboriginal Tribes of Australia*. Australian National University Press, Canberra, 1974.

Trollope, A. *Australia*, University of Queensland Press, Brisbane, 1967 (first published as *Australia and New Zealand*, Chapman and Hall, London, 2 vols., 1873).

'Vanguard', 'North Australia: The Real Backblocks', *Cummins & Campbell Monthly Magazine*, February issue, 1934, p.81–83.

Walsh, B. 'Feral Animals', *Northern Grassy Landscapes Conference 29–31 August 2000 Katherine NT: Conference Proceedings*, Tropical Savannas CRC, Darwin, 2000.

Walsh, M. 'Northern Australia', in S Wurm and S Hattori (eds), *Language Atlas. Pacific Area*, The Australian Academy of the Humanities, Canberra, 1983.

Ward, R. *The Australian Legend*. Oxford University Press, Melbourne, 1958.

Wells, L.A. *The Victoria River and the Adjacent Country*, Government Printer, Adelaide, 1907.

White, I. 'The Birth and Death of a Ceremony', *Aboriginal History*, vol. 4 (1–2), 1980.

White, J.P. and DJ Mulvaney, 'How many people?', in DJ Mulvaney and J Peter White (eds), *Australians to 1788*, Fairfax, Syme & Weldon Associates, Sydney, 1987.

Whyte, W.F. '"Never Never" People. Their Strange Fate,' *Sydney Morning Herald*, 21 February 1942.

Wildey, W.B. *Australia and the Oceanic Region*, George Robinson, Sydney, 1876.

Willey, K. *Eaters of the Lotus*, The Jacaranda Press, Brisbane, 1964.

Willey, K. *Boss Drover*, Rigby, Sydney, 1971.

Willing, T. and Kenneally, K. *Under a Regent Moon: A historical account of pioneer pastoralists Joseph Bradshaw and Aeneas Gunn at Marigui Settlement, Prince Regent River, Kimberley, Western Australia*, Department of Conservation and Land Management, Western Australia, 2002.

Willshire, W.H. *Land of the Dawning: Being Facts Gleaned from Cannibals in the Australian Stone Age*, W.K. Thomas and Co., Adelaide, 1896.

Wilson, J. 'Extracts from Notes on the North Australian Expedition'. *Proceedings of the Royal Geographical Society of London*, vol, 1, sessions 1855–6, 1856.

Wilson, J. Notes on the Physical Geography of North-West Australia. *Journal of the Geographical Society of London*, vol. 28, 1858.

Wozitsky, J. *Born Under The Paperbark Tree: A Man's Life*, ABC Books, Sydney, 1996.

Newspapers and Periodicals

A.M. magazine, 3 November, 1953.

Hoofs and Horns, 1946–1947, 1959.

Land Rights News, July 1989.

Outback, December 1998–January 1999.

Savanna Links, issue 9, March–April 1999.

Savanna Links, issue 29, July–September, 2004.

The Advertiser (Adelaide), 1893, 1900, 1905–1906, 1909, 1922, 1934.

The Adelaide Observer, 1880, 1890–1892, 1895–1896, 1901, 1905.

The Register (Adelaide; formerly *The South Australian Register*), 1892, 1900, 1905–1907.

The Age, 1883, 1921.

The Argus, 1884.

The Australasian, 1906.

The Bulletin, 1881.

The Canberra Times, 1981.

The Graziers' Review, 1926, 1929.

The Leader, (Melbourne), 1922.

The Mackay Daily Mercury, 1927.

The Morning Bulletin (Rockhampton), 1905–1906.

The North Australian, 1885–1886, 1889–1890.

The North Australian Monthly, December, 1959.

The North Queensland Herald, 1906, 1911.

The Northern Standard, 1926, 1931, 1934, 1936.

The Northern Star (Lismore, NSW), November, 1913.

The Northern Territory News, 1953, 1995, 2001.

The Northern Territory Times, 1873, 1876, 1878–1881, 1883–1889, 1891–1896, 1898–1903, 1905–1918, 1920–1921, 1925, 1928.

The Pastoralists' Review, 1899, 1906, 1910, 1912, 1914, 1916, 1928–1929, 1947, 1953, 1961, 1965 (Note: At various times this journal was known as *The Pastoral Review, The Pastoralists' Review and Graziers' Record, and The Australasian Pastoralists' Review*).
The Prahran Telegraph, 1899.
The Queenslander, 1879.
The South Australian Chronicle, 1873.
The Sydney Morning Herald, 1880–1881, 1887, 1906, 1921, 1942.
The Territorian, vol. 1, No. 10, December 1967.

Other Documentary Sources

Archival Material

National Archives of Australia
6000 square miles of country north of Victoria River be Offered at auction, Asking that, CRS A1640, Item 93/302.
Aborigines Reserve – Ord River District, N.T. – re proposed, A1640/1, item 1906/223.
Country 25 miles on either side of Overland Telegraph Line to be withdrawn as open for application for lease, CRS A1640/1, Item 1902/273.
Northern Territory Pastoral Permit No. 56 in name of J. Newton & P. Kearney, be transferred to J. Newton and J Ward, requesting, CRS A1640/1, Item 1906/102.
Copley Brothers and Paterson. Transfer of Pastoral Leases & Permit to Vestey Brothers. A3 NT, Item 14/5459.
Cumbit, Donah and Charley, Aboriginals sentenced to imprisonment for life, Petition for Release, CRS A3 NT, Item 1918/2640.
Department of Home and Territories, Correspondence Files, Annual Single Number Series, 1903–38: Victoria River "N.T. Fight between police and Natives". CRS A1, Item 1926/2816.
F.J.S. Wise, agricultural adviser to Sir Charles Nathan, Perth, 15th August 1929, A494/1, Item 902/1/82.
J. Wickham & T. Murray Alleged Murder of, CRS A3/1, Item NT 1923/3646.
New Police Buildings at Horseshoe Creek, Anthony's Lagoon & Midnight Creek, A3/1, Item NT 1914/6947.
Northern Territory Pastoral Permit No. 56 in name of J. Newton & P. Kearney, be transferred to J. Newton and W. Ward, requesting. CRS A1640/1, Item 1906/102.
Pastoral Permit, Part Block No. 11: J. Frayne applies for protection of, CRS A1640, Item 1903/553.
Re Aboriginal Reserve, vide G.R.O. 14777/06 attached, CRS A1640, Item 1906/223.
Report on Bradshaw station, Northern Territory Pastoral Leases Investigation Committee, CRS F658, Item 25.
Transfer of the Northern Territory to the Commonwealth: re terms of Agreement of, A1640/1, Item 1907/580.
Victoria River Country: Some particulars of, CRS A1640, file 1908/43.
Department of Territories, correspondence files NT series, 'Northern Territory. Interview with Mr LA Wells', CRS A1640, file 1908/43.
W.F. Buchanan. Application for Pastoral Block, CRS A1640, Item 1901/46.
Minutes forming enclosure to WJ, No. 552, 1905, A1640, Item 1905/552.

Noel Butlin Archives, Australian National University

Goldsbrough Mort and Co. Ltd: HWH Stevens report on NT stations, 23rd October 1891, 2/871.

Goldsbrough Mort and Co. Ltd., Head Office, Melbourne: Letters received from HWH Stevens, Port 'Darwin, re NT property and butchering business, 1889–1892, 2/872.

Goldsbrough Mort and Co. Ltd: Sundry papers re CB Fisher and the Northern Australia Territory Co., 1886–1892, 2/876.

Goldsbrough Mort and Co. Ltd: Board Papers, 1893–1927, 2/124.

Goldsbrough Mort and Co. Ltd: "General Letters", Papers of Head Office, Melbourne, 1874–1901, 2/176.

Goldsbrough Mort and Co. Ltd: Reports on station properties, 1890–1897, 2/306.

Goldsbrough Mort and Co. Ltd: Reports on properties, 1898–1901. Reports on station properties, Oct 1898–Dec 1901, 2/307.

Goldsbrough Mort and Co. Ltd: Victoria River Downs Ledgers, 1909–1944. Noel Butlin Archives, Australian National University, 42/15, Ledger 4.

Goldsbrough Mort and Co. Ltd., Gregory's map, Goldsbrough Mort Collections, F246, 2/859/379.

Bovril Australian Estates Pty. Ltd. Correspondence between Perth Office of Bovril, and Alfred Martin, manager/Attorney of VRD, 1933–37, 87/8.

Bovril Australian Estates Pty. Ltd. Bovril Australian Estates, Correspondence between London and station manager 1927–1932, 119/4.

Bovril Australian Estates: Correspondence between Australian Mercantile Land & Finance Co. Ltd. (AML&F) Sydney, and BAE Ltd., London, and Station manager, 1939–1955, 119/6.

Bovril Australian Estates: Correspondence between AML&F Co. Ltd, Sydney, and station manager 1953–1955, 119/7.

Hooker Pastoral Company Pty. Ltd. Records: Station Reports, 1959–1968, 119/15.

Northern Territory Archives

Commissioner of Police, correspondence files, 1935–1959, F77.

Department of Lands – Land Administration Branch. Correspondence files, 'GL' series (grazing licences) NTRS F28.

Department of Lands – Land Administration Branch, office copies of pastoral permits – 1902–1922, NTRS F199.

Department of Lands – Registers of Northern Territory pastoral leases – 1890–1928, NTRS, F670, vol. 1.

Government Resident of the Northern Territory (South Australia) – Inwards Correspondence, 1870–1912. NTRS 790.

Joyce Falconbridge's diary, NTRS 853.

Log Book of Bradshaw's Run, NTRS 2261.

Pine Creek police journal, F294.

Police Station, Katherine, NTRS 2732, Register of reported felonies, 1887–1930.

Timber Creek police journal, 1894 to 1910, F 302 (The journals from the Gordon Creek police station, which existed from May 1894 to September 1898 and preceded the Timber Creek station, are listed in the Northern Territory Archives under the heading 'Timber Creek police journals').

Timber Creek police letter book, 1911–1925, NTRS 2223.

Timber Creek police station, copy book, 1895–1940, NTRS 2224.

Wave Hill police journal, F292.

State Records of South Australia
Minister Controlling the Northern Territory – Inwards Correspondence, 1868–1910. GRS 1, 581/1905.
Correspondence files from the police commissioner's office, GRG5/2, 1872/941.
Northern Territory "Department" Incoming Correspondence (Outgoing Correspondence), 87/1878.
Giles, A. *The First Pastoral Settlement in the Northern Territory*. GRG154/3 Overland Telegraph survey Expedition – Diaries kept by Alfred Giles.

Western Australian State Records Office
Occurrence Book [Wyndham police station], 1886–1888. Acc 741-1.
Occurrence Book [Wyndham police station], 1895–1897. Acc 741-3.
Occurrence Book [Wyndham police station], 1895–1897. Acc 741-4.
Occurrence Book [Wyndham police station], 1899–1902, Acc 741-5.
Rough Occurrence Book [Wyndham police station] 1907–1908. Acc 741-9.
Letter Book, 1901–1912. Inward and outward correspondence relating to Connor, Doherty & Durack. Acc 2184A/1, MN485.
Letter Book [Wyndham police station], 1901–1902. Acc 741-13.
Letterbook, 1901–1912. Inward and outward correspondence relating to Connor, Doherty & Durack. Acc 2184A/1, MN485.

Government Publications and Documents

Commonwealth Government
Aboriginal Land Rights Act (NT) 1976.
'Northern Territory. Report of the Acting Administrator for the Years 1911', *Commonwealth Parliamentary Papers*, vol. 3, no. 54, 1912.
'Report of the Acting Administrator for the Year 1912', *Commonwealth Parliamentary Papers*, vol. 3, no. 54, 1913.
'Report of the Administrator of the Northern Territory for the Year ended 30th June 1933'. *Commonwealth Parliamentary Papers*, vol. 3, session 1932–33.
Commonwealth Gazette, No. 55.

Northern Territory Government
Northern Territory Government Gazette, No. G38, 21 September 1979.
Northern Territory Government Gazette, No. G8, 22 February 1995.

South Australian Government
'Dispatches From Northern Territory'. *South Australian Parliamentary Papers*, vol. 2, no. 83, 1866.
'Exploration Northern Territory', 7th January 1868. *South Australian Parliamentary Paper*, vol. 2, no. 24, 1869.
'Quarterly Report on the Northern Territory', 7th August 1883. *South Australian Parliamentary Papers*, vol. 4, no. 53A, 1884.
'Quarterly Report on Northern Territory', 1st January 1885, *South Australian Parliamentary Papers*, vol. 3, no. 53, 1885.
'Quarterly Report on Northern Territory, June 30th, 1885', *South Australian Parliamentary Papers*, vol. 3, no. 54, 1885.
'Quarterly Report on Northern Territory', 11th November 1884, *South Australian Parliamentary Papers*, vol. 3, no. 53B, 1885.

'Half-Yearly Report on Northern Territory to June 30th, 1886.' *South Australian Parliamentary Papers*, vol. 3, no. 53, 1886.

'Half-Yearly Report on Northern Territory to June 30th, 1886.' *South Australian Parliamentary Papers*, vol. 3, no. 54, 1886.

'Half-Yearly Report on Northern Territory to December 31st, 1886', *South Australian Parliamentary Papers*, vol. 3, no. 53, 1887.

'Report on the Northern Territory for the Year 1889', *South Australian Parliamentary Papers*, vol. 2, no. 28, 1890.

'Government Resident's Report on Northern Territory for the Year ended June 30th, 1891', *South Australian Parliamentary Papers*, vol. 2, no. 28, 1891.

'Government Resident's Report on the Northern Territory', 13th December 1893. *South Australian Parliamentary Papers*, vol. 3, no. 158, 1893.

'Government Resident's Report on the Northern Territory', 24th July 1894. *South Australian Parliamentary Papers*, vol. 2, no. 53, 1894.

'Government Geologist's Report on Explorations in the Northern Territory. Fountain Head to Victoria Downs Station'. *South Australian Parliamentary Papers*, vol. 3, no. 82, 1895.

'Report of the Northern Territory Commission together with Minutes of Proceedings, Evidence, and Appendices', *South Australian Parliamentary Papers*, vol. 2, no. 19, 1895.

'Government Resident's Report for the Northern Territory for 1896', *South Australian Parliamentary Papers*, vol. 2, no. 45, 1897.

'Government Resident's Report for the Northern Territory, 1898', *South Australian Parliamentary Papers*, vol. 2, no. 45, 1899.

'Select Committee of the Legislative Council on the Aborigines Bill, 1899: Minutes of Evidence and Appendices', *South Australian Parliamentary Papers*, vol. 2, no. 77, 1899.

'Government Resident's Report for the Northern Territory, 1899'. *South Australian Parliamentary Papers*, vol. 3, no. 45, 1900.

'Justice in the Northern Territory', *South Australian Parliamentary Papers*, vol. 3, no. 60, 1900.

'Government Resident's Report on the Northern Territory, 1901', *South Australian Parliamentary Papers*, vol. 2, no. 45, 1901.

'Government Resident's Report on the Northern Territory, 1902', *South Australian Parliamentary Papers*, vol. 3, no. 45, 1903.

'Government Resident's Report on the Northern Territory, 1903', *South Australian Parliamentary Papers*, vol. 2, no. 45, 1904.

'Report by His Excellency the Governor on his visit to the Northern Territory,' *South Australian Parliamentary Papers*. vol. 2, no. 49, 1905.

'Government Resident's Report on the Northern Territory, 1904', *South Australian Parliamentary Papers*, vol. 2, no. 45, 1905.

'Report by his Excellency the Governor of South Australia', 1905, *South Australian Parliamentary Papers*, vol. 2, no. 49, 1906.'

'Government Resident's Report on the Northern Territory, December 1905', *South Australian Parliamentary Papers*, vol. 2, no. 45, 1906.

'Report of the Government Resident for the Year 1910'. *South Australian Parliamentary Papers*, vol. 3, no. 66, 1911.

South Australian Government Gazette, June 17th, 1909.

Western Australian Government
Western Australian Parliamentary Debates, sessions 1893, vol. 4, 1894.

Libraries

Battye Library
Doug Moore's Memoirs, nd. Unpublished typescript, Acc 3829A, MN 1237.
Diary of M.P. Durack, 1st January 1908 – 31 December 1908. MN 71/3 4587A-28.
Lucanus, Constable A, to Sub-Inspector Drewry, 7th October 1893, Occurrence Book
[Wyndham police station], ACC 741/1.
Letter book, 1901–1912, inward and outward correspondence relating to Connor,
Doherty & Durack, Rosewood records, Acc 2184A/1, MN485.

National Library of Australia
Elsey, J.R. *Diary of Dr Joseph Ravencroft Elsey esq. Surgeon & Naturalist to Gregory's
Australian Expedition, from March 1855 to January 1856*, MS 25.
Elsey, J.R. to 'Dear John', dated 13th April 1856, MS 25.
Elsey, J.R. to his 'beloved parents', undated, written over an extended period at Victoria
River Depot, MS 25.

Northern Territory Library
Manuscript Collection, Bradshaw Family 1840–1940, 'Bradshaw Letters', 1/5a-c.

Queensland State Library
'KH Wills diary extracts', Henry Brandon Collection, OM 75–75.

South Australian State Library
A. Giles, *The First Pastoral Settlement in the Northern Territory*, State Library of South
Australia, V 10082.

State Library of New South Wales
Baines, T. *Journal of the Detachment of the North Australian Expedition left by Mr. Gregory
at the Main Camp Victoria River 1856*, C408.
Bradshaw, J. *Journal, 31st Jan – 6th June 1891, on an expedition from Wyndham, W.A. to the
Prince Regent River district, W.A.* B967, CY reel 1515.
Creaghe, EC. Diary, MSS 2982.
Stockdale, H. 'Exploration in the far north west of Australia 1884–5', unpublished
manuscript, MSS A1580.
Linklater, W. Untitled, undated article about Raparee Johnson, in miscellaneous papers
of W Linklater, MSS 198 (microfilm copy CY 3506), p. 5.
Pearce, T. to Linklater, W., 9th October 1948, A1 10/3–37.
Pearce, T. to Linklater, W., 27th May 1950, MSS 955 8–195B.
Ricketson, J.H. nd. *Journal of an Expedition to Cambridge Gulf, the North-west of Western
Australia, and a ride through the Northern Territory of South Australia, 1884–1885.*
MSS 1783, item 2.
Stockdale, H. nd. *Exploration in the far north-west of Australia, 1884–85.* ML1580.
Wickham, J.S. *Description of the River Victoria on the N.W. coast of New Holland with
directions for approaching it*, A 308.
Wilson, J.S. *Journal by J.S. Wilson, 31st January-28th May 1856*, ZC 411–2.
Wilson, J.S. and J.R. Elsey, *Journal Kept at the Main Camp, Victoria River By J.S. Wilson -
Geologist and J.R. Elsey Surgeon, to the North Australian Expedition,1856*, [1st January-
9th May 1856], Z C 411–1.

Royal Geographical Society of South Australia

Bradshaw, J. to the President of the Royal Geographical Society, South Australian
Branch, 20 April 1900. Royal Geographical Society of South Australia, Ms 14c.
Gee, L.C.E. to W. P. Auld, 24th May 1910. Correspondence file 1885–1915 of the Royal
Geographical Society of Australasia (South Australian Branch).

South Australian Museum

W.H. Willshire to Professor E. Stirling, 4th December 1896, AD43.
M. Terry, Notebook 14. 'No. 1, Port Hedland-Melbourne, 1928, C62.

Unpublished and Miscellaneous Sources

Maps

Ikymbon 1:100,000 topographic map, sheet 5067 (edition 1, co-ordinates 949 327, Royal
Australian Survey Corps, 1992).
Millik Monmir 1:100,000 topographic map (sheet 4965, edition 1, Royal Australian
Survey Corps, 1992).
Pastoral and General Tenure Map, produced by the Mapping Branch, Northern
Territory Department of Lands and Housing, Darwin, 1990.

Taped Interviews

Jimmy Manngayarri, Midnight station homestead, 1989 (deceased).
Stan Jones, Katherine, August 2000 (deceased).

Unpublished Documents

Bilinara (*Coolibah-Wave Hill Stock Route*) Land Claim, Transcript of proceedings, 1989.
Biography of Jim Randall, compiled by and in possession of the Randall family.
Bolton, G. *A Survey of the Kimberley Pastoral Industry from 1885 to the Present*,
unpublished Masters thesis, University of Western Australia, 1953.
Boulter, C.C., assistant to Surveyor Scandrett in 1914 (Original given to the Historical
Society of the Northern Territory by Boulters' daughter, in 1970, and apparently lost
in Cyclone Tracy).
Buchanan, G. 'Old Bluey', 1942. Unpublished manuscript in possession of Buchanan
family.
Cahill, T to J.W. Durack (letter, unprovenanced), 25th April 1926.
Census, 1891, details on microfiche compiled by the Genealogical Society of the
Northern Territory from original records held at the Australian Archives, Darwin,
1986.
Flinders, C. *45 years in the great nor-west of Western Australia*, unpublished typescript,
1933, North Australia Research Unit, Darwin.
Hallam, D. 'The Leichhardt nameplate – a report on authenticity testing'. Unpublished
report to the National Museum of Australia, 2006.
Higgins, B. *Historical Submission: Amanbidji Land Claim*, Northern Land Council,
Darwin, August 1976.
Kelly, C. Archivist at the Royal Geographical Society to N.B. Nairn, General Editor of
the Australian Dictionary of Biography, 28th January 1982. File on Joseph Bradshaw
at the Australian Dictionary of Biography Centre, Australian National University,
Canberra.

Lewis, D. *Report on Field Work for the Jasper Gorge – Kidman Springs Land Claim*, prepared for the Northern Land Council, Darwin, 1977.

Lewis, D. *"They Meet Up At Bilinara": Rock Art in the Victoria River Valley*. Unpublished Masters thesis, Australian National University, 1990.

Lewis, D. *In Western Wilds: A Survey of Historic Sites in the Western Victoria River District*, 1993. Report prepared for the Australian National Trust (N.T.).

Lewis, D. *The Boab Belt: A Survey of Historic Sites in the North-Central Victoria River District*. Report prepared for the Australian National Trust (N.T.), 1996, vol. 2.

Lewis, D. *The Final Muster: A Survey of Previously Undocumented Sites throughout the Victoria River District*, 2000. Report prepared for the Australian National Trust (N.T.).

Low, W.A., Strong, B. and Roeger, L. *Wave Hill Station Pastoral Lease 911*. Report prepared for the Conservation Commission of the Northern Territory, Alice Springs, by W.A. Low Ecological Services, Alice Springs. 1986.

Low, W.A., Dobbie, W.R. and L. Roeger, *Resource Appraisal of Victoria River Downs Station Pastoral Lease 680*, prepared for the Conservation Commission of the Northern Territory, Alice Springs, by W.A. Low Ecological Services, Alice Springs. 1988.

Linklater, W. Hand-written manuscript in possession of Buchanan family, nd.

Martin, Flo. Notes compiled for a reading at a writer's club in Western Australia (in possession of Martin family, nd).

Northern Territory 1891 census, compiled from the South Australian 1891 census by the Genealogical Society of the Northern Territory from original records held at the National Archives of Australia (Darwin), microfiche, 1986.

Notes of interview with W. Rees, by Helen West (nee Healy) in 1950. Originals in possession of author.

Department of Lands — Land Administration Branch, office copies of pastoral permits — 1902–22. NTRS, F199, Box 3.

Pearson, S.E. to Buchanan, G. (senior), 31ˢᵗ March 1934. Buchanan family papers.

Rees, W.A. to Martin, A. 12ᵗʰ July 1945. Unprovenanced. Copy in possession of author.

Rosewood station rainfall book, held at the station.

'Summary of deaths in the Timber Creek/Bradshaw police district', Compiled by the Genealogical Society of the Northern Territory, Darwin. Covers the period 1856–1975.

Timber Creek police letter book, 1911–1918. Photocopy held at Berrimah police station, Darwin.

Watson family papers.

Woodley, P. [ed.], *"Young Bill's Happy Days": Reminiscences of Rural Australia, 1910–1915*, by W. Lavender. Unpublished Masters thesis, Australian National University, 1981.

INDEX

Note: Page numbers in bold indicate photographs or maps.

INDEX